THE MORNING CHRONICLE
SURVEY OF LABOUR AND THE POOR:
THE METROPOLITAN DISTRICTS

VOLUME 2

THE MORNING CHRONICLE
SURVEY OF LABOUR AND THE POOR:
THE METROPOLITAN DISTRICTS

Volume 2

HENRY MAYHEW

CALIBAN BOOKS

This edition first published 1981
by Caliban Books
c/o Biblios, Glenside Industrial Estate,
Star Road, Partridge Green, Horsham,
Sussex

ISBN 0 904573 214

Typesetting by
Eager Typesetting Company, 22a Westbourne Place, Hove, East Sussex

Printed and bound in Great Britain by
REDWOOD BURN LIMITED
Trowbridge, Wiltshire

CONTENTS

LETTER XIII
Friday, November 30, 1849

The *Hucksters,* or street tradesmen, are divisible into five classes, viz., the hucksters of provisions — the hucksters of articles of household use — the hucksters of hardwear — the hucksters of stationery, songs, and literature — the hucksters of live birds, live gold fish, dogs, and flowers.

The hucksters of provisions are chiefly costermongers, or itinerant dealers in vegetables, fruit, and fish — the vendors of oranges and nuts — of shellfish — of sweetmeats — baked potatoes — ham sandwiches — meat and fruit pies — puddings — hot coffee and tea — game, rabbits, and poultry — fried fish — ginger beer — elder wine — cakes and gingerbread nuts — cough drops — and dogs' meat.

Of this class the costermongers, or street vendors of vegetables, fruit, and fish, constitute by far the largest number. They are the parties principally through which the working classes and the poor obtain the greater portion of their food. Hence, in an inquiry like the present, it becomes most important to investigate the gains of the street vendors of provisions, not only as forming a large proportion of the poor themselves, but as being the parties through whom the poor obtain their vegetables, fish, etc. The hucksters of provisions, therefore, require consideration in a double point of view. The class must be regarded as purveyors to the poor, and their earnings taken as the rate of profit that the working classes have generally to pay upon whatever they consume. The trade may also be regarded as an outlet or means of living for the surplus labour of the metropolis, for we shall find that, with the exception of the costermongers, who appear to be "born and bred" to the business, the other classes of street provision merchants are mostly artisans and labourers who have been unable to obtain work at their calling.

In my last letter I pointed out that the pound weight of the costermonger is mostly deficient four ounces, and frequently eight or ten ounces; that the pint measure is at least one-third short; that the fish supplied to them is generally what is called "rough," or, in other words, two or three days old before it is bought, and frequently putrid when sold by them to the poor; and, moreover, that they almost invariably horrow the capital with which they purchase their goods, and pay interest at the rate of nearly 1,000 per cent. for the money. All this information, be it remembered, I had direct, not from one, but several of the class, by whom I was shown the weights and measures ordinarily used by the people, as well as the quantity that they were deficient. When we consider, therefore, that this enormous interest must be paid out of the profits of the articles sold, and when we think of the short weights and measures, and the quality of the articles supplied, we shall readily perceive how cruelly the poor are defrauded, and that if they are underpaid for what they do, they are at the same time fearfully overcharged for all they buy.

As a body, the costermongers rank high amongst the criminals of the country. This will be seen by the following list: — Of carpenters, there is one criminal in every 810 individuals; of masons, one in every 480; of boot and shoe makers, one in every 462; of blacksmiths, one in every 400; of sawyers, one in 290; of bakers, one in 270; of butchers, one in 247; of seamsters and seamstresses, one in 100; whereas, of hawkers, hucksters, and pedlars, there is one criminal in every 86 individuals. The above facts are deduced from the Government Returns of the occupations of the inmates of the gaols throughout Great Britain in the year 1841.

I now proceed to deal with the rest of the street provision vendors. The earnings of the class will be seen to be in some cases superior to those of the most skilful artisans; indeed, they are generally such as to yield a competence to such of the working classes as resort to them. We must, however, make an exception of the sale of watercresses. This calling, as will be shown hereafter, is followed only by the very old and the very young, the gains being insufficient for any other persons than those whose labour is of the very lowest value.

And first, of the *Coffee-stall Keepers* — or vendors of saloup, as they are frequently called. From these the poor man mostly obtains his breakfast. They have a stall generally at the corner of a street, and this is very often pitched in front of a tea-dealer's shop. The cause of this is, that the coffee-stall keeper usually purchases his goods there, and so obtains leave of the shopkeeper to stand at the kerb. In the centre of the fruit and meat markets there are generally two or three coffee-stalls, and one or two in the streets leading to them. In Covent-garden market there are no less than four coffee-stalls, and one or two in Billingsgate market, and one also in the Haymarket. In the street leading to Farringdon market there is one, and one also in the streets leading to Hungerford market, Newgate market, the Borough market, and the Whitechapel market. The principal station, or pitches, throughout London, are at the corner of Duke-street, Marylebone-lane; at the Cumberland-gate, Hyde-park (this stall is kept by a celebrated character called "Old Jack"); at the Regent-circus, Oxford-street (kept by an elderly female); at the Elephant and Castle; at the end of the New-cut, Lambeth; in the Blackfriars-road; at the Surrey side of London bridge; at Aldgate church; at the railway station, Shoreditch; at each end of Euston-square; at the top of High-street, Camden-town; at the Blind Asylum, Westminster-road; at the corner of the Wandsworth-road; at the top of Sloane-street, Knightsbridge; and at the end of the City-road, opposite St. Luke's. There are some half-dozen in the Edgware-road, and about a dozen in the New-road; indeed, wherever there is a public thoroughfare frequented by working people, on their way to their day's labour, there the coffee-stall keeper is sure to be seen. The best "pitch" in London is supposed to be at the corner of Duke-street, Oxford-street. The proprietor of that stall is said to take full 30s. of a morning in halfpence; and when "upon the drink" — to use the words of my informant — he thinks nothing of spending his £10 or £15 per week. A party assured me that once, when the stall-keeper was away "on the spree," he took up his stand there, and got from four to five shillings in the course of ten minutes at the busy time of the morning.

The coffee-stall usually consists of a spring barrow with two, and occasionally four, wheels. Some are made up of tables, and some have a trestle and board. On the top of this stand two or three, and sometimes four, large tin cans, holding upon an average five gallons each. Beneath each of these cans is a small iron firepot, perforated like a rushlight shade, and in this charcoal is continually burning, so as to keep the coffee or tea with which they are filled hot throughout the early part of the morning. The board of the stall has mostly a compartment for bread and butter, cake, and ham sandwiches, and another for the coffee mugs. There is generally a small tub under each of the stalls, in which the mugs and saucers are washed. The grandest stall in this line is the one before mentioned as standing at the corner of Duke-street, Oxford-street. It is a large truck on four wheels, and painted a bright green. The cans are four in number, and of bright polished tin mounted with brass plates. There are handsome compartments for bread and butter, sandwiches, and cake. It is lighted by three large oil lamps, with bright brass mountings, and covered in with an oil-cloth roof. The coffee-stalls generally are lighted by candle-lamps, and some have tarpauling screens run up round them, to shelter the proprietor and customers from the bleak morning air. Some of them make their appearance at twelve at night, and some not till three or four in the morning. Those that come out at midnight are for the accommodation of the "night-walkers" — fast gentlemen and loose girls; and those that come out in the morning are for the accommodation of the working men. They usually sell coffee and tea, and some of them cocoa. They keep hot milk in one of the large cans, and coffee, tea, or cocoa in the others. They supply bread and butter, or currant cake, in slices — ham sandwiches, water-cresses, and boiled eggs. The price they charge is 1d. per mug, or ½d. per half-mug, for the coffee, tea, or cocoa; and ½d. a slice the bread and butter or cake. The ham sandwiches are 2d. each, the boiled eggs 1d., and the water-cresses a halfpenny a bunch. The coffee, tea, cocoa, and sugar they generally purchase by the single pound, at the grocer's nearest to their stands. Those who do a very extensive trade purchase their articles in larger quantities. The coffee is usually bought in the berry, and ground by themselves at home. Many purchase chicory to mix with it. For the coffee they pay about 1s.; for the tea about 3s.; for the cocoa, 6d. per lb.; and for the sugar, 3½d. to 4d. For the chicory the price is 6d., and it is mixed with the coffee at the rate of 3 oz. to the pound; many use as much as 6 oz. The coffee is made of a dark colour by means of what are called "finings," which consist of burnt sugar — such, indeed, as is used for browning soups. Coffee is the article mostly sold at the stalls; indeed, there is scarcely one stall in a hundred that is supplied with tea, and not more than a dozen in all London that furnish cocoa. They usually make the cake themselves. A 4 lb. cake generally consists of a half a pound of currants, half a pound of sugar, six ounces of beef dripping, and a quartern of flour. The ham for ham sandwiches costs about 7½d. per lb.; and this, when boiled, produces in sandwiches about 2s. 6d. per lb. It is usually cut up in slices about as thick as paper. The bread they pay for at the rate of 5d. a quartern. This is usually "second bread." The butter is usually salt, and purchased at about 8d. the pound. Some of them borrow their barrows; and pay 1s. a week for the hire of them. Many borrow the capital upon which they trade. They borrow this probably of their landlord. Some get credit for their grocery — some for their bread.

If they borrow they pay about 20 per cent. per week for the loan. I was told of one man that makes a practice of lending money to the coffee-stall keepers and other hucksters, at the rate of at least 20 per cent. a week. If the party wishing to borrow a pound or two is unknown to the money lender, he requires security, and the interest to be paid him weekly. He has been transported once for receiving stolen property, and would now purchase any amount of plate that might be taken to him. To commence as a coffee-stall keeper in a moderate manner would require about £5 capital. The truck would cost £2, and the other utensils £3. The expense of the cans is near upon 16s. each. The class of persons usually belonging to the business have been either cabmen, policemen, labourers, or artisans. Many have been bred to dealing in the streets, and brought up to no other employment, but many have taken to the business owing to the difficulty of obtaining work at their own trade. The generality of them are opposed to one another. It is believed by one who has been several years in the business, and who asserts that he knows pretty well every coffee-stall in it, that there are nearly 200 coffee-stall keepers throughout the metropolis, I asked one in a small way of business what was the average amount of his profits; and his answer was, "I usually buy 10 ounces of coffee per night. That costs me 1s. 0½d. With this I should make five gallons of coffee, such as I sell in the street. This would require three quarts of milk at 3d. per quart, and 1½ lb. of sugar at 3½d. per lb. This would come to 2s. 2¾d.; and, allowing 1¼d. for a quarter of a peck of charcoal to keep the coffee hot, would give 2s. 4d. for the cost of five gallons of coffee. This I should sell out at about 1½d. per pint; so that the five gallons would produce me 5s., or 2s. 8d. clear. I generally get rid of one quartern loaf and 6 oz. of butter with this quantity of coffee, and for this I pay 5d. the loaf and 3d. the butter, making 8d.; and these I make into 28 slices at ½d. per slice; consequently the whole brings me in 1s. 2d., or about 6d. clear. Added to this, I sell a 4 lb. cake, which costs me 3½d. per lb. — 1s. 2d. the entire cake; and this in 28 slices, at 1d. per slice, would yield 2s. 4d., or 1s. 2d. clear; so that altogether my clear gains would be 4s. 4d. upon an expenditure of 2s. 2d. — say 200 per cent. This is said to be about the usual profit of the trade. Sometimes they give credit. One person assured me he trusted as much as 9½d. that morning, and out of that he was satisfied there was 4d. at least that he should never see. Many of the stalls are stationary, and many locomotive. Some cans are carried about with yokes, like milk cans, the mugs being kept in a basket. The best district for the night trade is the City. There are more men and women walking along Cheapside, Aldersgate-street, Bishopsgate-street, and Fleet-street. In the latter place a good trade is frequently done between twelve at night and two in the morning. For the morning trade the best districts are the Strand, Oxford-street, City-road, the New-road (from one end to the other), the markets, especially Covent-garden, Billingsgate, Newgate, and the Borough. No coffee-stalls are allowed in Smithfield. The reason of this is, the drovers on arriving at the market are generally tired and cold, and prefer sitting down to their coffee in a warm shop rather than standing to drink it in the open street. The best days for coffee-stalls are on market mornings, *i.e.,* Tuesday, Thursday, and Saturday. On these days the receipts are generally half as much again as those of the other mornings. The best time of the year for the business is in the summer season. This is because there is more doing, and the workpeople and costermongers have more money to spend. Some save sufficient to take a shop, but these are only such as have a "pitch" in the best thoroughfares. But the coffee-stall keeper at the corner of Duke-street, in Oxford-street, does a better trade than any coffee-shop keeper in Marylebone. One who did a little business informed me that he cleared, including Sunday, 14s. last week, and the week before his gains were 15s.; the week before that he could not remember. He is very frequently out all night, and does not earn sixpence. This is on wet and cold nights, when there are few people about. His is generally the night trade. The average weekly earnings of the trade throughout the year are said to be £1. The trade, I am assured by all, is overstocked. They are half too many, they say. "Two of us" — to use their own words — "are eating one man's bread." "When coffee in the streets first came up, a man could go and earn," I am told, "his 8s. a night at the very lowest; but now the same class of men cannot earn more than 3s." Some men may earn a great sum, as much as 38s. or £2, but the generality of the trade cannot make more than £1 per week. The following is the statment of one of the class: — "I was a mason's labourer, a smith's labourer, a plasterer's labourer, or a bricklayer's labourer. I was indeed a labouring man. I could not get employment. I was for six months without any employment. I did not know which way to support my wife and family (I have only one child). Being so long out of employment, I saw no other means of getting a living but out of the streets. I was almost starving before I took to it — that I certainly was. I'm not ashamed of telling anybody that, because it's true, and I sought for a livelihood wherever I could. Many said they wouldn't do such a thing as keep a coffee-stall, but I said I'd do anything to get a bit of bread

honestly. Years ago, when I was a boy, I used to go out selling
water-cresses, and apples, oranges, and radishes, with a barrow,
for my landlord; so I thought when I was thrown out of employment I would take to selling coffee in the streets. I went to a tinman and paid him 10s. 6d. (the last of my savings, after I'd been
four or five months out of work) for a new can, and I bought at
the same time a few ginger-beer bottles. I got my living anyhow.
I didn't care how, so long as I could turn an honest penny. Well,
I went on and knocked about, and couldn't get a pitch anywhere;
but at last I heard that an old man, who had been in the habit of
standing for many years at the entrance of one of the markets,
had fell ill; so what did I do, but I goes and pops into his pitch,
and there I've done better than ever I did afore. I get 20s. now
where I got 10s. before; and if I only had such a thing as £5 or
£10, I might get a good living for life. I'd pay it back at the rate of
10s. a week; but as it is, my turn-out is so short that I cannot do
half as much as the man that was there before me. He used to
make his coffee down there, and had a can for hot water as well;
but I have but one can to keep coffee and all in; and I have to
borrow my barrow, and pay 1s. a week for it. If I sell my can
out, I can't do any more. The struggle to get a living is so great,
that what with one and another in the coffee trade, it's only those
as can get good 'pitches' that can get a crust at it."

The *Irish Fruit-stall Keeper* is another distinct class of street
provision vendors. They are mostly females, and make but a scanty
living. They deal in oranges, lemons, chestnuts, walnuts, etc.,
which is quite a different trade from that of the general dealer.
They purchase their nuts of each kind in Covent-garden market.
They pay for Brazil nuts and chestnuts 3s. a peck. They trade upon
their own capital generally. In order to commence fairly in this
line it would "make a hole in a sovereign." The class generally are
very poor. They get about 9d. clear profit upon a peck of chestnuts
and Brazil nuts too. They get their oranges and lemons at Duke's-
place, Whitechapel. They pay for lemons 3s. 6d., and for oranges
4s. 6d. a long hundred. They sell them two a penny, both oranges
and lemons. They sell upon the average, Brazil nuts and chestnuts,
about one peck of each weekly, and oranges and lemons about one
hundred of each, the long hundred; so that their weekly gross
returns are 17s. 6d.; but after taking the cost price of the Brazil
nuts, chestnuts, oranges, and lemons, which is 13s. 6d., their clear
profits will be about 4s. weekly. There is no fear of nuts spoiling,
and oranges and lemons will keep long enough to get rid of them.
The best days for the sale of their goods are Saturdays and Mon-

days. On a Saturday they take from 3s. 9d. to 5s.; on Mondays from 2s. to 4s. It all depends on the stock: if they have a good stock, they get a better sale. There are very few who have any education among the class, as the greater portion of them are Irish. One of this class, whom I spoke to, informed me: — She is a widow with three children. Her husband died about three years since. She had then five children, and was near her confinement with another. Since the death of her husband she has lost three of her children; a boy about twelve years died of stoppage on his lungs, brought on through being in the streets, and shouting so loud to get sale for the fruit. She has stood in Clare-street, Clare-market, seven years with a fruit stall. In the summer she sells green fruit, which she purchases at Covent-garden. When the nuts come in season, and oranges, etc., she furnishes her stall with that kind of fruit, and continues to sell until the spring salad comes in: she thus strives to get a living for herself and family. During the spring and summer her weekly average income is about 5s., but the remaining portion of the year her income is not more than 3s. 6d. average weekly; so that, taking the year through, her average weekly income is about 4s. 3d., out of which she pays 1s. 6d. a week rent, leaving only 2s. 9d. a week to find necessary comforts for herself and family. For fuel they go up to the market and gather up the waste walnuts, and bring them home and dry them; and these, with a pennyworth of coal and coke, serve to warm their chilled feet and hands. They have no bedspread, but a flock bed in one corner of a room, upon the floor, with only an old sheet, blanket, and quilt to cover them at this inclement season. No chair nor table: a stool serves for the chair, two pieces of board upon some baskets serve for a table, and an old penny tea-canister for a candlestick. She has parted with every article of furniture to get food for her little family. She receives not a farthing from the parish, but is entirely dependent upon the sale of her fruit for a living for herself and three children.

The *Baked Potato* trade is more profitable than the trade in fruit, but continues only for six months in the course of the year.

The potatoes are bought at the greengrocers' shops, at the rate of 5s. 6d. the cwt. They are usually a large-sized potato, running about two or three to the pound. The kind generally bought is what are called the "French Regents." They are mostly French potatoes that are used now. The reason of this is, the French are cheaper than the English. The potatoes are picked, and those of a large size, and with a rough skin, selected from the others, because they are always the mealiest. A waxy potato shrivels in the baking. There are usually from 280 to 300 potatoes in the cwt.; these are cleaned by the huckster, and, when dried, taken in baskets, about a quarter cwt. at a time, to the baker's, to be cooked. They are baked in large tins, and require an hour-and-a-half to do well. The price paid for baking is 9d. the cwt., the baker usually finding the tins. They are taken home from the bakehouse in a basket, with a yard-and-a-half of green baize in which they are covered up, and so prevented from going cold. The huckster then places them in his can. This can consists of a tin with a half-lid, and standing on four legs. It has a large handle to it, and an iron fire-pot is suspended immediately beneath the vessel which is used for holding the potatoes. Directly over the fire-pot is a boiler for hot water. This is concealed within the vessel, and serves to keep the potatoes always hot. Outside the vessel where the potatoes are kept is, at one end, a small compartment for butter and salt, and at the other end another compartment for fresh charcoal. Above the boiler, and beside the lid, is a small pipe for carrying off the steam. These potato-cans are sometimes brightly polished and sometimes painted red, and occasionally brass-mounted. Some of the handsomest of the cans are all brass, and some are highly ornamented with brass mountings. Great pride is taken in the cans. The baked-potato man usually devotes half an hour to polishing them up, and they are mostly kept as bright as silver. The grandest potato-can that I have seen was in the New-cut. It was made entirely of copper, and kept brightly polished. It was lighted by a couple of oil lamps, mounted with brass, that cost 30s. the two. The cost of the can itself was £5. The expense of an ordinary can, tin and brass mounted, is about 50s. They are mostly made by a tinman in the Ratcliff-highway. The usual places for these cans to stand are the principal thoroughfares and street-markets. There are three at the bottom of Farringdon-street, two in Smithfield, and three in Tottenham-court-road (the two places last named are said to be the best 'pitches' in all London), two in Leather-lane, one on Holborn-hill, one at King's-cross, three at the Brill, Somers-town, three in the New-cut, three in Covent-garden (this is considered to be on market-days the second-best pitch), two at the Elephant and Castle, one at Westminster bridge, two at the top of Edgware-road, one in St. Martin's lane, one in Newport-market, two at the upper end of Oxford-street, one in Clare market, two in Regent-street, one in Newgate market, two at the Angel, Islington, three at Shoreditch church, four about Rosemary-lane, two at Whitechapel, two near Spitalfields market, and more than double the above number wandering about London. It is considered by one who has been many years at the business that there are, taking those who have regular stands and those who are travelling with their cans on their arm, at least 150 individuals engaged in the trade in London. The business continues only during the winter months. It begins about the middle of August and continues to the latter end of April. As soon as the potatoes get to any size, the baked-potato season generally commences, and it lasts till the potatoes get bad. The season upon an average continues about half the year. The business is found to depend much upon the weather. If it is cold and frosty the trade is generally much brisker than in wet weather; indeed then very little is doing. The best times for the business in the course of the day are from half-past ten in the morning till two in the afternoon, and from five in the evening till about eleven or twelve at night. The night trade is considered the better trade. In cold weather they are frequently bought to warm the hands, and in the morning some buy them for lunch, and some housekeepers send out to the stand for them for their dinner. At night, about nine o'clock, which is found to be the best time in the night, they are purchased for supper. The customers consist of all classes. Many gentlefolks buy them in the street, and take them home for supper in their pockets. The working classes, however, constitute the greater part of the purchasers. Many boys and girls lay out a halfpenny in a baked potato. Irishmen are particularly fond of them, but they are the worst customers; they want the largest potatoes in the can. Women buy a great number of those sold. Some take them home, and some eat them in the street. Three baked potatoes are as much as will satisfy the stoutest appetite. One potato dealer in Smithfield is said to sell about 2½ cwt. of potatoes on a market-day; or, in other words, from 900 to 1,000 potatoes, and to take upwards of £2. My informant tells me that he himself has often sold 1½ cwt. of a day, and taken £1 in halfpence. I am informed that upon an average, taking the good stands with the bad ones, throughout London, there are about 1 cwt. of potatoes sold by each baked-potato man — and there are 159 of these throughout the metropolis — making the total quantity of baked potatoes consumed every day upwards of seven tons. The money spent upon these comes to within a few shillings of £100 (calculating 300 potatoes to the cwt., and each of those potatoes to be sold at a halfpenny). Hence, there are forty-two tons of baked potatoes eaten in London, and £600 spent upon them, every week during the season. Saturdays and Mondays are found to be the best days for the sale of baked potatoes in those parts of London that are not near the markets; but in those in the vicinity of Clare, Newport, Covent-garden, Newgate, Smithfield, and other markets, the trade is the briskest on the days when the market is held. The hucksters of baked potatoes are many of them broken-down tradesmen. Many of them are labourers who find a difficulty of obtaining employment in the winter time, some of them are costermongers; some have been artisans; indeed, there are some of all classes among them. After the baked potato season is over, the generality of the hucksters take to selling strawberries, raspberries, or anything as it comes in season. Some go to labouring work. My informant, who had been a bricklayer's labourer, said that after the season he always looked out for work among the bricklayers, and this kept him employed until the baked potato season came round again. "When I first took to it I was very badly off. My master had no employment for me, and my brother was ill, and so was my wife's sister, and I had no way of keeping 'em, or my-self either. The labouring men are mostly out of work in the winter time, so I spoke to a friend of mine, and he told me how he man-aged every winter, and advised me to do the same. I took to it, and have stuck to it ever since. The trade was much better then. I could buy a hundred-weight of potatoes for 1s. 9d. to 2s. 3d., and there were fewer to sell them. But now I have to pay 5s. 6d. for the very same quantity, and can't sell half as many as I did then. We generally use to a cwt. of potatoes three-quarters of a pound of butter — tenpenny salt butter is what we buy — a pennyworth of salt, a pennyworth of pepper, and five pennyworth of charcoal. This, with the baking, 9d., brings the expenses to just upon 7s. 6d. per cwt., and for this our receipts will be 12s. 6d., thus leaving about 5s. per cwt. profit. Hence the average profits of the trade are about 30s. a week — and more to some," said my informant. The man in Smithfield-market, I am credibly informed, clears at the least £3 a week. On the Friday he has a fresh basket of hot potatoes brought to him from the baker's every quarter of an hour. Such is his custom that he has not even time to take money, and his wife stands by his side to do so.

Among the street vendors of fish there is one class who get a living by the sale of fried fish. They purchase their fish at Billingsgate — a species termed dabs. Some are called plaice dabs, and others are called sole dabs. They buy by the pot, which con-tains from 70 to 80 fish, for which they pay from 1s. to 1s. 6d. per pot. This is the average price the year through. Some have barrows, others pots, and some get porters. They pay for barrows 3d. a day; the pot is given in with the fish, and for porters they pay from 4d. to 6d., according to the load. Some trade upon their own capital, and others borrow enough to purchase stock, for which they pay 1s. in the pound. Those who generally lend stock-money are persons who keep coal-sheds, or shopkeepers. In commencing this business it would require about twenty shillings to start fairly. Sometimes they use linseed oil, sometimes fish oil; but the Jews use salad oil; and in order to give the fish a rich colour they use turmeric, which gives it a yellow cast. Linseed oil averages 8d. per quart, fish oil the same, but salad oil runs from 1s. 6d. to 1s. 8d. per quart. The class generally live in a low neighbourhood, because people object to the bad smell in frying the fish. Boys and girls, as well as men and women, are engaged in selling the fish. They give upon the average 1s. 3d. a pot, which generally contains seventy-five fish, for which they generally get, in selling out at ½d. and 1d. a slice, about 3s. 5d. gross profit. Then out of that they have to pay for oil, flour, and fuel to fry them with, about 2s. 6d. to the pot, which leaves a clear profit of 11d. the pot. A pot will take, when they have a good sale, two days in selling. In the summer time their fish will not keep more than a day, but in the winter two or three days. If there are a few left, they generally eat them; but if a great many, they take them out again the next evening about six o'clock. The reason is, because they won't sell in the daytime. Mondays and Saturdays are their best days. In taking the average of these two days throughout the year, they take 2s. 6d. a night on Mondays and Saturdays; on the other nights they take about 1s. 6d. a night average throughout the year. Their chief custom lies among mechanics and labourers in the public-houses, and in the streets various persons buy them. The summer season is their best time; they then average about 5s. a week clear profit; but in the winter, only at the rate of 2s. 6d. a week clear profit. They are out in all kinds of weather. The fried fish vendor whom I saw informed me he had been brought up to the trade of a fishmonger, and had worked at one fishmonger's between seventeen and eighteen years. Since then he has taken to the selling of fried fish. He has a wife and six children "dependent on him for victuals." The Jews fry in salad oil, and eat fish on Friday and Saturday. The reason of their being fried in oil is because dripping takes away the flavour of the fish. Oil makes them superior in flavour. The Jews also use eggs in frying them instead of the turmeric.

Another peculiar class among the street provision merchants are the *Vendors of Cough Drops.* In preparing the articles which they sell, they purchase their ingredients at different places. Their herbs they purchase at Covent-garden, and their sugar at the grocer's. The sugar they procure is, and must be, the raw material, as other sugar will not cand. They make up, upon the average, 6 lbs. of sugar per day, for which they pay 4½d. per lb., and to every 6 lbs. of sugar it takes about four pennyworth of herbs. When they sell at home they charge a halfpenny the ounce, but when they sell in the street it is dearer, about a penny an ounce; so that their gross income is about the average of 6s. a day. After deducting expenses, their gross earnings average about 2s. 7d. each day. They trade upon their own capital. In order to commence in the line it will take about £3. The still itself costs as much as a sovereign. There are very few in the same line of business. The goods they sell are composed of sugar, which is boiled in the liquor distilled from the herbs. When caught in the rain, their articles lose about three ounces in the pound; and they are unfit for sale till boiled up again. They go out about eleven o'clock in the morning, and return about half-past ten o'clock at night. Holborn is considered to be the best district for the sale of their goods. Monday, Tuesday, and Saturday are the best days of sale. On these days they average about 5s. a day, but on the other days in the week they average only about 2s. per day; and on Sunday mornings they take about 2s. 6d.; making, upon the average, 23s. 6d. gross earnings per week. It costs per week for sugar, coal, charcoal, herbs, and truck, 16s. 6d.; leaving clear profit just 7s. a week. Their tongues, they say, are continually going, from the time they commence selling till they leave off at night, so that when they return they are so hoarse that they can scarcely speak. It is almost impossible to know the various speeches they make to the public upon the excellence and efficacy of their articles for coughs, colds, asthma, and hooping-cough. It is the universal cure-all, they declare, of all diseases of the chest, etc. My informant was brought up as a professional singer, and was in the habit of attending concerts and private parties; he followed his calling till he broke his voice; after which he commenced in the old clothes line, but having no capital, he was obliged to relinquish it, and take to vending fruit; from that he turned to dealing in artificial flowers, and finally he entered into the cough-drop line, which he has followed ever since. When he first began the cough-drop business, he worked with a man at half profit, but finding it not sufficient for the wants of his family, he "fished out the way" to make his own articles. From the sale of them he manages to get along, he says, through rough and smooth. Within these last three weeks he has contrived to open a little shop for the sale of spice, sweetmeats, etc. The way he went to work, he told me, was "by taking up a tally-bill," and then, by pawning the goods purchased, he got enough money to open and stock the little shop; so that while the husband is out with his barrow the wife is at her little shop, which has, since they first opened it, brought them in as much as 5s. a week clear. Their earnings together now amount to 12s. a week upon the average. The house where they live, and the shop they have lately taken, stand them in 4s. a week rent, leaving for their subsistence 8s. a week to keep seven — that is, the man and his wife and five children. Sunday being the only day they are all together, they always make a shift to get a hot dinner on that day.

The *Dealers in Watercresses* are generally very old or very young people. The cause of this is, that the children are sent out by their parents "to get a loaf of bread somehow" (to use the words of an old man in the trade), and the very old take to it because they are unable to do hard labour, and they strive to keep away from the workhouse. ("I'd do anything before I'd go there — sweep the crossings or anything; but I should have had to have gone to the house before, if it hadn't been for my wife. I'm sixty-two," said one who had been sixteen years at the trade.) The old people are both men and women. The men have been sometimes one thing, and sometimes another. "I've been a porter myself, jobbing about in the markets, or wherever I could get a job to do. Then there's one old man goes about selling watercresses, who's been a seafaring man; he's very old, he is — older than what I am, sir. Many a one has been a good mechanic in his younger days, only he's got too old for labour. The old women have, many of them, been laundresses, only they can't now do the work, you see, and so they're glad to pick up a crust anyhow. Nelly, I know, has lost her husband, and she hasn't nothing else but her few cresses to keep her. She's as good, honest, hard-working a creature as ever were, for what she can do — poor old soul! The young people are most of them girls. There are some boys, but girls are generally put to it by the poor people. There's Mary Macdonald, she's about fourteen. Her father is a bricklayer's labourer. He's an Englishman, and he sends little Mary out to get a halfpenny or two. He gets sometimes a couple of days' work in the week. He don't get more now, I'm sure, and he's got three children to keep out of that; so all on 'em that can work are obligated to do something. The other two children are so small they can't do nothing yet. Then there's Louisa, she's about twelve, and she goes about with cresses, like I do. I don't think she's got ne'er a father. I know she's a mother alive, and *she* sells cresses like her daughter. The mother's about fifty odd, I dare say. The sellers generally go about with an arm-basket, like a greengrocer's, at their side, or a 'shallow' in front of them; and plenty of them carry a small tin tray before them, slung round their neck. Ah! it would make your heart ache if you was to go to Farringdon market early, this cold weather, and see the poor little things there without shoes and stockings, and their feet quite blue with the cold — oh, that they are; and many on 'em don't know how to set one foot before the t'other, poor things! You would say they wanted something give to 'em." The small tin tray is generally carried by the young children. The cresses are generally bought in Farringdon-market. "If we was to go to Covent-garden to buy 'em, we couldn't do nothing with 'em; they are all tied up in market bunches there; but at Farringdon-market they are sold loose, out of big hampers, so they give you a large handful for a penny. The usual time to go to the market is between five and six in the morning, and from that to seven. Myself, I'm generally down in the market by five o'clock. I was there this morning at five, and bitter cold it was, I give you my word. We poor old people feel it dreadful. Years ago I didn't mind cold, but I feel it now cruel bad, to be sure. Sometimes, when I'm turning up my things, I don't hardly know whether I've got 'em in my hands or not — can't even pick off a dead leaf. But that's nothing to the poor little things without shoes. Why, bless you, I've seen 'em stand and cry, two and three together, with the cold. Ah! my heart has ached for 'em over and over again. I've said to 'em, 'I wonder why your mother sends you out, that I have; and they said they were obligated to try and get a penny for a loaf for breakfast. We buy the watercresses by what is called the 'hand.' One hand will make about five halfpenny bundles; at least they will do so now, for there is not the same sale for them just now as there is in the spring. They give a little more now than they do then for the money." The cresses are sent up by the growers in the country. "A great many come out of Hertfordshire to the salesmen in the market that they are assigned to, and they retails them out. The salesmen are obligated to get a certain price for the hamper, and if they can make any more on it, it goes for themselves. Besides this, they has 1s. a hamper into the bargain, for the trouble of selling it. A hamper will fetch about 25s. in the spring of the year, and not much above 10s. in the winter. You see, there's more call for 'em in the spring of the year than what there is in the winter. Why, they're reckoned good for sweetening the blood in the spring; but for my own eating, I'd sooner have the cress in the winter than I would have it in the spring of the year. There's an old woman sits in Farringdon market, of the name of Burrows, that's sat there 24 years, and she's been selling out cresses to us all that time. The sellers usually goes to market with a few pence. I myself goes down there and lays out sometimes my 4d.; that's what I laid out this morning. Sometimes I lay out only 2d. or 3d., according as how I has the halfpence in my pocket. Many a one goes down to the market with only three halfpence, and glad to have that to get a halfpenny on anything so as to earn a mouthful of bread — a bellyful, that they can't get no how. Ah, many a time I walked through the streets, and picked a piece of bread that the servants chucked out of the door — maybe to the birds. I've gone and picked it up when I've been right hungry. Thinks I, I can eat that as well as the birds. None of the sellers ever goes down to the market with less than a penny. They won't make less than a pennorth, that's one 'hand;' and if the little thing sells that, she won't earn more than three halfpence out of it. After they have bought the cresses, they generally take them to the pump to wet them. I generally pump upon mine in Hatton-garden. This is done to make them look nice and fresh all the morning, so that the wind shouldn't make them flag. You see, they've been packed all night in the hamper, and they get very dry. Some ties them up in ha'porths as they walks along. Many of them sit down on the steps of St. Andrew's Church, and make them up into bunches. You'll see plenty of them there of a morning between five and six." "Plenty poor little dear souls sitting there," said the old man to me. There the hand of cresses (for which a penny has been given) is parcelled out into five halfpenny bunches. In the summer the dealers often go to market and lay out as much as 1s. "On Saturday morning, this time of year, I buys as many as nine hands; there's more call for 'em on Saturday and Sunday morning than on any other days; and we always has to buy on Saturdays what we want for Sundays — there ain't no market on that day, sir. At the market sufficient cresses are bought by the sellers for the morning and afternoon as well. In the morning some begin crying their cresses through the streets at half-past six, and others about seven. They go to different parts, but there is scarcely a place but what some goes to — there are so many of us now — there's twenty to one to what there used to be. Why, they're so thick down at the market in the summer time, that you might bowl balls along their heads, and all a-fighting for the cresses. There's a regular scramble, I can assure you, to get at 'em, so as to make a halfpenny out of them. I should think in the spring mornings there's 400 or 500 on 'em down at Farringdon market all at one time — between four and five in the morning — if not more than that, and as fast as they keep going out, others keep coming in. I think there is more than a thousand, young and old, about the streets in the trade. The working classes are the principal of the customers. The bricklayers and carpenters, and smiths, and plumbers, leaving work and going home to breakfast at eight o'clock, purchase the chief part of them. A great many are sold down the courts and mews, and bye streets, and very few are got rid of in the squares and the neighbourhood of the more respectable houses. Many are sold in the principal thoroughfares; a large number in the City. There is a man who stands close to the Post-office, at the top of Newgate-street, winter and summer, who sells a great quantity of bunches every morning. This man frequently takes between 4s. and 5s. of a winter's morning, and about 10s. a day in the summer." "Sixteen years ago," said the old man who gave me the principal part of this information, "I could come out and take my 18s. of a Saturday morning, and 8s. on a Sunday morning as well; but now I think myself very lucky if I can take my 1s. 3d., and it's only on two mornings in the week that I can get that." 10s. a day is the largest sum that can possibly be got now in the best time of the year, and where there is the best traffic. But the average amount taken by the hawkers of water-cresses on Saturday and Sunday mornings, is now about 1s. each day for the winter, and 2s. per day in the spring. And for the rest of the week, they take, one with the other, about 9d. each day — that is, including the morning and afternoon trade — and 1s. each day in the spring. In winter they clear about 5d. a day, and in the spring 6d. On Saturday and Sunday, however, they clear 1s. per day in the spring, and 6d. a day in the winter; so that their earnings are about 3s. 1d. per week in the winter, and 4s. 6d. a week in the summer. This would make the gross sum spent in watercresses about £400 per week, out of which £200 goes to the support of 1,000 old and young people. The hucksters of watercresses are generally an honest, industrious, striving class of persons. The young girls are said to be well-behaved, and to be the daughters of poor struggling people. The old men and women are persons striving to save themselves from the workhouse. The old and young people generally travel nine and ten miles in the course of the day. They start off to market at four and five, and are out on their morning rounds from seven till nine, and on their afternoon rounds from half-past two to five in the evening. They travel at the rate of two miles an hour. "If it wasn't for my wife, I must go to the workhouse outright," said the old watercress man. "Ah, I don't know what I should do without her, I can assure you. She earns about 1s. 3d. a day. She takes in a little washing, and keeps a mangle. When I'm at home I turn the mangle for her. The mangle is my own. When my wife's mother was alive she lent us the money to buy it, and as we earnt the money we paid her back so much a week. It is *that* what has kept us together, or else we shouldn't have been as we are. The mangle we gave 50s. for, and it brings us in now 1s. 3d. a day with the washing. My wife is younger than I am. She is about 35 years old. We have got two children. One is 13 and the other 15. They've both got learning, and both in situations. I always sent 'em to school. Though I can't neither read nor write myself, I wished to make them some little scholars. I paid a penny a week for 'em at the school. Lady M——— has always given me my Christmas dinner for the last five years, and God bless her for it! — that I *do* say indeed."

The *Sheep's-Trotter Vendors* purchase the trotters at the fell-mongers', Bermondsey. They pay 1s. for twelve hands (a hand is a set of four trotters): the price is the same throughout the year. It takes about 10s. to commence in this line of business. "The class who compose this body are mostly a very drunken set; there are some who are different." These are the poorest wretches upon the face of the earth. In the winter the trotters are of good quality; but in the summer they find many of them almost rotten, which they fling away to the dogs, as the people won't buy them. There are some of the class who go to the public-houses. These care not about the quality of their articles, as they sell them to the men when they are half-drunk. The parties who belong to the sheep's-trotter class live in the cheapest rooms they can get; and it is often the case that several of them live in one room together. The parties who sell them generally are the low Irish, but the English sellers generally sell cats' meat with their trotters; so that they can get on better than those who deal in trotters only. If the whole of the trotters were saleable, their profits would be about 7d. or 8d. in the shilling; but upon the average their profits do not amount to above 4d. or 5d. in the shilling. The best day for the sale of their articles is Saturday. They do not average above 6d. a day clear, taking one day with another. Their customers generally consist of errand-boys, prostitutes, and carters. One man, earning his living in this way, told me he and his wife had been in the line six years. Before they engaged in it they lived at Southampton. The husband was a captain's clerk on board a man-of-war. He was discharged in time of peace, without a pension. He was then in the police force, in Ireland and in Southampton, nearly seventeen years. Previously to his entering the police force he was sergeant in the 49th regiment of foot. He enlisted on limited service, so that he was not entitled to a pension. The dealers buy the trotters already boiled, and freed from the wool. It takes them the whole morning

to get them ready for sale. Some nights they go out till eleven or
twelve at night, and don't take 4d.; at other times about 9d. They
never sell a shilling's worth of a night. They don't average 6d. a
night, through the week, clear. They often return and have only
taken about 2d. or 3d., and have come home dripping with rain.
Their average income a week is about 3s. throughout the year.
Out of this they pay 1s. 6d. a week rent; so that all they have to
subsist upon is 1s. 6d. a week. One party has sometimes received
a trifle from one of his daughters, who was in service, but she is
now out of a situation. He has another daughter, 25 years of age.
She has been paralysed all over ever since she was teething, and
some parochial relief is allowed for her, but not for the parents.
While they are out selling their trotters they are obliged to lock
their poor paralysed child in, "without any one but the Lord to
take care of her." The wife suffered very much from an attack of
cholera, from which she has not entirely recovered. They have very
little bedding. The father lies upon a kind of bed made of rags,
with a sheet and blanket to cover him; and the mother lies with the
afflicted daughter. The father has an abscess formed in the ear, and
is blind with one eye.

The *Cat and Dogs' Meat Dealers,* or "carriers," as they call themselves, generally purchase the meat at the horse-slaughterers' yards.
There are nearly twenty of these in and around London. There
are three or four in Whitechapel, one in Wandsworth, two in Cow-
cross — one of these is the largest establishment in London — two
in Maiden-lane, and two over the water, about Bermondsey. The
proprietors of these yards purchase live and dead horses. They contract for these with most large firms — such as brewers, coal-
merchants, and large cab and 'bus yards — giving so much per
head for their old live and dead horses through the year. The price
they pay is from £2 to 50s. the carcase. The horse-slaughterers also
have contractors in the country (harness-makers and others), who
bring or send up to town for them the live and dead stock of those
parts. The dead horses are brought to the yard, two or three upon
one cart, and sometimes five. The live ones are tied to the tail of
these carts, and behind the tail of each other. Occasionally, a string
of fourteen or fifteen are brought up, head to tail, at one time.
The live horses are purchased merely for slaughtering. If among
the lot purchased there should chance to be one that is young, but
in bad condition, this is placed in the stable, and fed up, and then
put into their carts, or sold by them, or let on hire. Occasionally
a fine horse has been rescued from death in this manner. One person is known to have bought an animal for 15s. for which he after-

wards got £150. Frequently young horses that will not work in cabs — such as jibs — are sold to the horse-slaughterers as useless. These are kept in the yard, and after being well fed, often turn out good horses, and are let for hire. The live horses are slaughtered by a class of persons called knackers. These men get upon an average 4s. a day. They begin work at twelve o'clock at night. The reason of this is, that some of the flesh is required to be boiled before six in the morning; indeed, a great part of it is delivered by the carriers before that hour. The horse to be slaughtered has his mane clipped as short as possible (on account of the hair, which is valuable). It is then blinded with a piece of old apron smothered in blood, so that it may not see the slaughterman when about to strike. A pole-axe is used, and a cane, to put an immediate end to their sufferings. After the animal is slaughtered, the hide is taken off, and the flesh cut from the bones in large pieces. These pieces are termed, according to the part from which they are cut, hind-quarters, fore-quarters, crambones, throats, necks, briskets, backs, ribs, kidney pieces, hearts, tongues, liver or lights. The bones (they are called the "racks" by the knackers) are chopped up and boiled, in order to extract the fat from them. This is used for greasing harness, and the wheels of carts and drags, etc. The bones are afterwards sold for manure. The pieces of flesh are thrown into large coppers or pans, about nine feet in diameter, and about four feet deep. Each of these pans will hold about three good-sized horses. Sometimes two large brewers' horses will fill them, and sometimes as many as four "poor" cab horses may be put into them. The flesh is boiled about an hour and twenty minutes for a "killed" horse, and from two hours to two hours and twenty minutes for a dead horse. The flesh when boiled is taken from the coppers, laid on the stones, and sprinkled with water to cool it. It is then weighed out in pieces of a hundred, half a hundred, twenty-eight, twenty-one, fourteen, seven, and three pounds and a half weight. These are either taken round in a cart to the "carriers," or else at about five o'clock the carriers begin to call at the yard to purchase it themselves, and continue doing so till twelve o'clock in the day. The price is 14s. per cwt. in the winter, and 16s. in the summer time. The tripe is served out at 12 lbs. for 6d. All this is sold for cats and dogs. The carriers then take the meat round town, wherever their walk might lie. They sell it out to the public at the rate of 2½d. per lb., and in small pieces, on skewers, at a farthing, a halfpenny, and a penny each. Some carriers will sell as much as a hundred-weight in a day, and about half a hundred-weight is about the average quantity disposed of by the carriers in London. Some sell much cheaper than others. They will frequently knock at the doors of persons whom they have seen served by another on the previous day, and show them that they can let them have a larger quantity of meat for the same money. The class of persons belonging to the business are mostly those who have been unable to obtain employment at their trade. Occasionally a person is bred to it, having been engaged as a lad by some carrier to go round with the barrow and assist him in his business. These boys will, after a time, find a "walk" for themselves, beginning first with a basket, and ultimately rising to a barrow. The barrow and basket, weights and scales, knife and steel, or blackstone, will cost about £2 when new, and from 15s to 4s. second-hand. Many of them give light weight to the extent of 2 oz. and 4 oz. in the pound. It is supposed there are about 300 cats'-meat carriers in and about London. At one yard alone near upon a hundred carriers purchase the meat, and there are, upon an average, 150 horses slaughtered there every week. Each slaughter-house may be said to do, one with another, sixty horses per week throughout the year, and there are from fifteen to twenty of these slaughter-houses. It is believed by one who has been engaged at the business for twenty-five years, that there are from 900 to 1,000 horses, averaging 2 cwt. of meat each, little and big, boiled down every week; so that the quantity of cats' and dogs' meat used throughout London is about 200,000 lbs. per week, and this, sold at the rate of 2½d. per lb., gives £2,000 a week for the money spent in cats' meat. The slaughtermen are said to reap large fortunes very rapidly — indeed, the carriers say they coin the money. Many of them retire after a few years, and take large farms. One, after 12 years' business, retired with several thousand pounds, and has now three large farms. The carriers are men, women, and boys. Very few women do as well as the men at it. The carriers are generally sad drunkards. Of the three hundred, it is said two hundred at least spend £1 per head a week in drink. One party in the trade told me that he knew a carrier who would often spend 10s. in liquor at one sitting. The profit they make upon the meat is at present only a penny per pound. In the summer time the profit per pound is reduced to a halfpenny, owing to the meat being dearer on account of its scarcity. The carriers give a great deal of credit — indeed, they take but little ready money. Some days they do not come home with more than 2s. One with a middling walk pays for his meat 7s. 6d. per day. For this he has half a hundred-weight. This he will sell out in pounds, half-pounds, pennyworths, halfpennyworths, and farthingworths, and get as much as 11. 6d. by it, so that his profit will be 4s. This is about a fair average of the earnings of the trade. One carrier in the trade is said to have amassed £1,000 at the business. He usually sold from 1½ to 2 cwt. per day, so that his profits were generally from 16s. to £1 per day. But the trade is much worse now. There are so many at it, that there is barely a living for any. One carrier assured me that he seldom went less than thirty miles, and frequently forty miles, through the streets every day. The best districts are among the houses of tradesmen, mechanics, and labourers. The coachmen in the mews at the back of the squares are very good customers. "The work lays thicker there," said my informant. Old maids are bad, though very plentiful, customers. They cheapen the carriers down so, that they can scarcely live at the business. They will pay one halfpenny and owe another, and forget that after a day or two. The cats' meat dealers generally complain of their losses from bad debts. Their customers require credit frequently to the extent of £1. "One party owes me 15s. now," said a carrier to me, "and many 10s.; in fact, very few people pay ready money for the meat." The carriers frequently serve as much as ten pennyworths to one person in a day. One gentleman has as much as 4 lbs. of meat per day for two Newfoundland dogs; and there was one woman — a black — who used to have as much as 16 pennyworth every day. This person used to get out on the roof of the house and throw it to the cats on the tiles. By this she brought so many stray cats round about the neighbourhood, that the parties in the vicinity complained; it was quite a nuisance. She *would* have the meat always brought to her before ten in the morning, or else she would send to a shop for it, and between ten and eleven in the morning the noise and cries of the hundreds of stray cats attracted to the spot was "terrible to hear;" and when the meat was thrown to them on the roof, the riot, and confusion, and fighting, was beyond description. "A beer-shop man," says he, "was obliged to keep five or six dogs to drive the cats from his walls." There was also a mad woman in Islington, who used to have 14 lbs. of meat a day. The party who supplied her had his money often at £2 and £3 at a time. She had as many as thirty cats at times in the house. Every stray one that used to come she used to take in and support. The stench was so great that she was obliged to be moved. The best days for the cats' meat business are Mondays, Tuesdays, and Saturdays. A double quantity of meat is sold on the Saturday, and on that day and Monday and Tuesday the weekly customers generally pay. "My father was a baker by trade," said a carrier to me, "but through an enlargement of the heart he was obliged to give up working at the trade; leaning over the trough used to increase his complaint so severely, that he used to fall down, and be obliged to be brought home. This induced him to take to the cats' and dogs' meat trade, and he brought me up to it. I do pretty comfortably at it. I have a very good business, having been all my life at it. If it wasn't for the bad debts I should do much better; but some of the people I trust leave the houses, and actually take in a double quantity of meat the day before. I suppose there is at the present moment as much as £20 owing to me that I never expect to see a farthing of." The generality of the dealers wear a shiny hat, black plush waistcoat and sleeves, a blue apron, and corduroy trousers, and a blue and white spotted handkerchief round their necks. Some, indeed, will wear two and three handkerchiefs round their necks, this being considered fashionable among them. A great many meet every Friday afternoon in the donkey market, Smithfield, and retire to a public-house adjoining, to spend the evening.

The "cats' meat carrier" that supplied me with the above information was more comfortably situated than any of the lower classes that I had yet seen. He lived in the front room of a second floor, in an open and respectable quarter of the town, and his lodgings were the perfection of comfort and cleanliness in an humble sphere. It was late in the evening when I reached the house, and I found the "carrier" and his family preparing for supper. In a large morocco leather easy chair sat the cats' meat carrier himself; his "blue apron and black shiny hat" had disappeared, and he wore a blue "dress" coat and a black satin waistcoat instead. His wife, who was a remarkably pretty woman, and of very attractive manners, wore a "Dolly Varden" cap, placed jauntily at the back of her head, and a drab merino dress. The room was cosily carpeted, and in one corner stood a mahogany crib with cane-work sides, in which one of the children was asleep. On the table was a clean white table-cloth, and the room was savoury with the steaks, and mashed potatoes that were cooking on the fire. Indeed, I have never yet, since I started on my travels, seen such comfort in the abodes of the poor. The cleanliness and wholesomeness of the apartment were doubtless the more striking from the unpleasant associations connected with the calling.

LETTER XIV
Tuesday, December 4, 1849

Of the hucksters of provisions but one class remains to be described, and even that is seldom to be met with now-a-days. The penny-pie trade has passed from the streets into the shops. The following statement may be taken as a fair average of the condition of the class at present: —

The itinerant meat and fruit pieman is another class of street provision merchant. The meat pies consist of mutton and beef; the fruit, of apple, and, occasionally, mince-meat. These are sold in the streets at 1d. each. A few years ago the meat and fruit pies used to sell very well, but lately too many of the people are out of work, and they have not any money to spend. Fairs and races are generally the best places for the sale of pies in the summer. In London the best times for the sale of pies are during any grand sight or holiday-making — a review in Hyde Park, the Lord Mayor's show, the opening of Parliament, Greenwich fair, Whitsun Monday — and, indeed, whenever anything is going on that brings the people together in large crowds. The piemen in the streets of London are seldom stationary; they go along with their pie-can on their arm, crying "Pies all hot! meat and fruit, pies all hot! " This can is somewhat similar to a potato-can, but it has no boiler inside it. The pies are kept hot by means of a charcoal fire beneath, and there is a partition in the body of the can, to separate the hot from the cold pies. There are two tin drawers — one at the bottom where the hot pies are kept, and above these are the cold ones. As fast as the hot pies are sold, the cold ones above are placed on the drawers below. There is a pieman who goes about Billingsgate market, who has a pony and "shay cart." He does the best business in the pie line in town. It is believed he sells £1 worth every day; but the generality of piemen throughout London do nothing like this. "I was out myself, last night," said one to me, "from four in the afternoon till half-past twelve, and went from Somers-town down to the Horse Guards, and looked in at all the public-houses

on the way, and I didn't take above 1s. 6d. I have been out sometimes all those hours, and haven't taken more than 4d.; and out
of that I have had to pay a penny for charcoal." The piemen usually
make the pies themselves. The meat is mostly bought as "pieces,"
and paid for at the rate of 3d. a pound. "People, when I go into
houses, often begin at me, crying 'Molrow!' and 'Bow-wow!' at
me; but there's nothing of that kind. Meat, you see, is so cheap
now." The pieman usually makes about five dozen of pies at a time.
To do this, he takes one quartern of flour, at 6d.; two pounds of
suet, at 6d.; one pound and a half of meat, at 3d., amounting, in all,
to about 2s.; to this must be added 3d. for the expense of baking,
1d. for the cost of keeping hot, and 2d. for pepper, salt, and eggs
with which to wash them over. Hence the cost of the five dozen
would be 2s. 6d., and the profit the same. The usual quantity of
meat in each pie is about half an ounce. There are not more than
a dozen hot-piemen now in London. There are some who carry
pies about on a tray slung before them; these are mostly boys, and,
including these, the number may amount to 25 in the winter time,
and to double that number in the summer. In the summer time the
most business is done; the trade then is nearly double as brisk as
in the winter. This is owing to the markets being better attended;
the people generally have more money to spend. The penny-pie
shops have done the street trade a great deal of harm. They have
got mostly all the custom. They make them much larger than those
sold in the streets. The pies in Tottenham-court-road are very
highly seasoned. "I bought one there the other day, and it nearly
took the skin off my mouth; it was full of pepper," said a pieman
to me. The reason why they put in so large a quantity of pepper is
because persons can't exactly tell the flavour of the meat with it.
Piemen generally are not very particular about the flavour of the
meat they buy, for they know that they can season it up into anything. The usual part of beef used, is what are called "the stick-
ings." This is what is mostly used for sausages, and costs about 3d.
per pound. In the summer time, a pieman about the street thinks
he is doing a good business if he takes 5s. per day, and in the winter
if he gets half that. On a Saturday night, however, he generally
takes 5s. in the winter, and about 8s. in the summer. At Greenwich
fair he will take about 14s. At a review in Hyde-park, if it is a
good one, he will sell about 10s. worth. The generality of the
customers are the boys of London. The women seldom, if ever,
buy them in the streets. At the public-houses a few are sold, and
the pieman makes a practice of looking in at all the public-houses
on his way. Here his customers are found principally in the tap-

room. "Here's all hot!" they cry, as they look into the tap-room. "Toss or buy; up and win 'em!" This is the only way that the pies can be got rid of. "If it wasn't for tossing we shouldn't sell one." The pieman never tosses himself, but always calls head or tail to the customer. At the week's end it comes to the same thing, whether they toss or not. "I've taken as much as 2s. 6d. at tossing, which I shouldn't have had if I hadn't done so. Very few people buy without tossing, and the boys in particular. Gentlemen 'out on the spree' at the late public-houses will frequently toss when they don't want the pies, and when they have won they will amuse themselves by throwing the pies at one another, or at me. The boys have the greatest love of gambling, and they seldom, if ever, buy without tossing. Sometimes I have taken as much as half-a-crown, and the people has never eaten a pie." For street mince-meat pies the pieman usually makes about 5 lb. of mince-meat at a time; and for this he will put in two dozen of apples, 1 lb. of sugar, 1 lb. of currants, 2 lb. of "critlings" (critlings being the refuse left after boiling down the lard), a good bit of spice to give the critlings a flavour, and plenty of treacle to make the mince-meat look rich. The "gravy" which used to be given with the meat pies consisted of a little salt and water poured out of an oil-can. A hole was made with the little finger in the top of the meat pie, and the "gravy" poured in until the crust rose. With this gravy a person in the line assured me that he has known pies four days old to go off very freely, and be pronounced excellent. The street piemen are mostly bakers, who are unable to obtain employment at their trade. "I myself," said one, "was a bread and biscuit baker. I have been at it now about two years and a half, and I can't get a living at it. Last week my earnings were not more than 7s. all the week through, and I was out till three o'clock in the morning to get that." The piemen seldom begin business till six o'clock, and some remain out all night. The best time for the sale of pies is generally from ten at night to one in the morning.

I now pass to the hucksters of articles of domestic use. These include principally the street dealers in blacking, boot-laces, hareskins, crockeryware, old clothes, hearthstones, lucifers, and cotton, tapes, and thread. These are the principal varieties of the class. It is true, there are others, such as the street vendors of brooms, of door-mats, of umbrellas, of fire-guards, of bonnet-boxes, and other household articles; but these do not strictly belong to the species, for they generally make the goods which they sell in the street, and so come more properly under the head of artisans than hucksters.

Of the hucksters of the articles of domestic use, I shall deal first with the itinerant vendors of crockeryware: —

The *hucksters of crockeryware* are a considerable class. One who has great experience in the business thinks there must be some hundreds employed in it throughout London. He says he meets many at the warehouses on the evenings that he goes there. He is often half an hour before he can be served. There are seven or eight warehouses frequented by the hucksters; and at the busy time my informant has often seen as many as twenty-five at each house, and he is satisfied that there must be two or three hundred hucksters of china and glass throughout the metropolis. The china and glass in which they deal are usually purchased at the east-end of the town, upon the understanding that if the huckster is unable to dispose of them in the course of the day the articles will be taken back in the morning, if uninjured, and the money returned. The hucksters usually take out their goods in the morning. Their baskets are commonly deposited at the warehouse, and each ware-house has from thirty to forty baskets left there over-night, when the unsold articles are returned. The baskets are usually filled with china and glass and ornaments, to the amount of from 5s. to 15s., according to the stock-money of the huckster. A basket filled with 15s. worth of china is considered, I am told, "a very tidy stock." In the same neighbourhood where they get the crockery, are made the baskets in which it is carried. For these baskets they pay from 1s. 6d. to 3s., and they are made expressly for the hucksters; indeed, on one side of a well-known street at the east-end, the baskets made in the cellars may be seen piled outside the houses up to the second-floor windows. The class of persons engaged in hawking china through the metropolis are either broken-down tradesmen or clerks out of place, or Jews, or they may be Staffordshire men who have been regularly bred to the business. They carry different kinds of articles. The Staffordshire man may generally be known by the heavy load of china that he carries with him. He has few light or fancy articles in his basket; it is filled chiefly with plates and dishes and earthenware pans. The broken-down tradesman carries a lighter load. He prefers tea services and vases, and "rummers" and cruet-stands, as they are generally of a more delicate make than the articles carried by the Staffordshire men. The Jew, however, will carry nothing of any considerable weight. He takes with him mostly light, showy, Bohemian goods — which are difficult "to be prized" by his customers, and do not require much labour to carry about. The hucksters usually start on their rounds about nine. They mostly live in the neighbourhood of

Bethnal-green-road. There are very few who take money; indeed, they profess to take none at all. "But that is all flam," said my informant. "If anyone was to ask me the price of an article in an artful way like, I shouldn't give him a straightforward answer. To such parties we always say, 'Have you got any old clothes?'" The hucksters *do* take money when they can get it, and they adopt the principle of exchanging their goods for old clothes merely as a means of evading the licence. Still they are compelled to do a great deal in the old clothes line. When they take money they usually reckon to get 4d. in the shilling, but at least three-fourths of their transactions consist of exchanges for old clothes. "A good tea service we generally give," said my informant, "for a left-off suit of clothes, hat, and boots — they must all be in a decent condition to fetch as much as that. We give a sugar-basin for an old coat, and a rummer for a pair of old Wellington boots. For a glass milk-jug I should expect a waistcoat and trousers; and they must be tidy ones, too. But there's nothing so saleable as a pair of old boots to us. There is always a market for old boots, when there is not for old clothes. You can always get a dinner out of old Wellingtons; but coats and waistcoats — there's a fashion about them, and what pleases one don't another. I can sell a pair of old boots going along the streets, if I carry them in my hand. The snobs will run after us to get those — the backs are so valuable. Old beaver hats and waistcoats are worth little or nothing. Old silk hats, however, there's a tidy market for. They are bought for the shops, and are made up into new hats for the country. The shape is what is principally wanted. We won't give a farden for the polka hats with the low crowns. If we can double an old hat up and put it in our pockets, it's more valuable to us than a stiff one. We know that the shape must be good to stand that. As soon as a hatter touches a hat, he knows by the touch or the stiffness of it whether it's been 'through' the fire or not; and if so, they'll give it you back in a minute. There is one man who stands in Devonshire-street, Bishopsgate-street, waiting to buy the hats of us as we go into the market, and who purchases at least thirty dozen of us a week. There will be three or four there besides him, looking out for us as we return from our rounds, and they'll either outbid one another, according as the demand is, or they'll all hold together to give one price. The same will be done by other parties wanting the old umbrellas that we bring back with us. These are valuable principally for the whalebone. Cane-ribbed ones are worth only from 1d. to 2d. and that's merely the value of the stick and the supporters. Iron skewers are made principally out of the old supporters of umbrellas. The china and crockery bought by the hucksters at the warehouses are always second-rate articles. They are most of them a little damaged, and the glass won't stand hot water. Every huckster, when he starts, has a bag, and most of them two — the one for the inferior, and the other for the better kind of old clothes he buys. We purchase gentlemen's left-off wearing apparel. This is mostly sold to us by women. They are either the wives of tradesmen or mechanics who sell them to us; or else it is the servant of a lodging-house, who has had the things given to her, and with her we can deal much easier than the others. She's come to 'em light, and of course she parts with 'em light," said the man, "and she'll take a pair of sugar-basins worth about 6d., you know, for a thing that'll fetch two or three shillings sometimes. But the mistresses of the houses are she-dragons. They wants a whole dinner *chany* service for their husband's rags. As for plates and dishes, they think they can be had for picking up. Many a time they sells their husband's things unbeknown to 'em, and often the gentleman of the house, coming up to the door, and seeing us making a deal — for his trousers maybe — puts a stop to the whole transaction. Often and often I've known a woman to sell the best part of her husband's stock of clothes for *chany* ornaments for her mantel-piece. And I'm sure the other day a lady stripped the whole of her passage, and gave me almost a new great coat, that was hanging up in the hall, for a few trumpery tea-things. But the greatest 'screws' we have to deal with are some of the ladies in the squares. They stops you on the sly in the streets, and tells you to call at their house at sitch a hour of the day, and when you goes there they smuggles you quietly into some room by yourselves, and then sets to work Jewing away as hard as they can, prizing up their own things, and downcrying yourn. Why, the other day I was told to call at a fashionable part of Pimlico; so I gave a woman 3d to mind the child, and me and my good woman started off at eight in the morning with a double load. But, bless you, when we got there, the lady took us both into a private room unbeknown to the servants, and wanted me to go and buy expressly for her a green-and-white chamber service all complete, with soap trays and brush trays, together with four breakfast cups — and all this here grand set-out she wanted for a couple of old washed-out light waistcoats, and a pair of light trousers! She tried hard to make me believe that the buttons alone on the waistcoats was worth 6d. a piece, but I knowed the value of buttons afore she were born; at first start-off I'm sure they wouldn't have cost 1d. each; so I couldn't make a deal of it no how, and I had to take all my things back for my trouble. I asked her even for a pint of beer, but she wouldn't listen to such a thing. We generally cry as we go, 'Any old clothes to sell or exchange?' and I look down the area, and sometimes knock at the door. If I go out with a 15s. basket of crockery, may be after a tidy day's work I shall come home with one shilling in my pocket (perhaps I shall have *sold* a couple of tumblers, or half a dozen plates), and a bundle of old clothes, consisting of two or three old shirts, a coat or two, a suit of left-off livery, a woman's gown may be, or a pair of old stays, a couple of pair of Wellingtons, and a waistcoat or so. These I should have at my back, and the remainder of my *chany* and glass on my head, and werry probably a humberella or two under my arm, and five or six old hats in my hand. This load altogether will weigh about three-quarters of a hundredweight, and I shall have travelled fifteen miles with that at least; for as fast as I gets rid on the weight of the crockery, I takes up the weight of the old clothes. The clothes I hardly know the value on till I gets to the Clothes Exchange, in Houndsditch. The usual time for the hucksters arriving there is between three and four at this time of year, or between five and six in the summer. In fact, we must be at the Exchange at them hours, because there all our buyers is, and we can't go out the next day until we've sold our lot. We can't have our baskets stocked again until we've got the money for our old clothes." The Exchange is a large square plot of damp ground, about an acre in extent, enclosed by a hoarding about eight feet high, on the top of which is a narrow sloping roof, projecting sufficiently forward to shelter one person from the rain. Across this ground are placed four rows of double seats, ranged back to back. Here meet all the Jew clothes-men, hucksters, dealers in second-hand shoes, left-off wardrobe keepers, hare-skin dealers, umbrella dealers and menders, and indeed buyers and sellers of left-off clothes and worn-out commodities of every description. The purchasers are of all nations and in all costumes. Some are Greeks, others Swiss, and others Germans; some have come there to buy up old rough charity clothing and army coats for the Irish market, others have come to purchase the hare-skins and old furs, or else to pick up cheap old teapots and tea-urns. That man with the long flowing beard and greasy tattered gaberdine is worth thousands, and he has come to make another sixpence out of the rags and tatters that are strewn about the ground in heaps for sale. At a little before three o'clock the stream of rag-sellers sets in in a flood towards this spot. At the gate stands "Barney Aaron," to take the halfpenny admission of everyone entering the ground. By his side stands his

son, with a leather pouch of halfpence to give change for any
silver that may be tendered. The stench of the old clothes is positively overpowering. Everyone there is dressed in his *worst*. If he
has any good clothes he does not put them on to go there. Almost
each one that enters has a bag at his back, and scarcely has he
passed the gate before he is surrounded by some half-dozen eager
Jews: one feels the contents of the bundle on the huckster's back —
another clamours for the first sight — a third cries, "I'm sure you
have something that'll suit me." "You know me," says a fourth,
"I'm a buyer, and give a good price." "Have you got any breaking?" asked this Jew, who wants an old coat or two to cut up into
cloth caps — "Have you got any fustian, any old cords, or old
boots?" And such is the anxiety and greediness of the buyers,
that it is as much as the seller can do to keep his bundle on his
back. At length he forces his way to a seat, and as he empties the
contents of his sack on the ground, each different article is snapped
up and eagerly overhaued by the different Jews that have followed
him to his seat. Then they all ask what sum is wanted for the
several things, and they, one and all, bid one quarter of the price
demanded. I am assured that it requires the greatest vigilance to
prevent the things being carried off unpaid in the confusion. While
this scene is going on, a Jew, perched upon a high stage in the
centre of the ground, shouts aloud to the multitude, "Hot wine,
a halfpen'y a glass here!" Beside him stands another, with smok-
ing cans of hot eels; and next to this one is a sweetmeat stall, with
a crowd of Jew boys gathered round the keeper of it, gambling
with marbles for Albert rock and hardbake. Up and down between
the seats push women with baskets of sheep's trotters on their
arms, and screaming, "Legs of mutton, two for a penny; who'll
give me a handsel — who'll give me a handsel?" After them comes
a man with a large tin can under his arm, and roaring, "Hot pea,
oh! Hot pea, oh!" In one corner is a coffee and beer shop. Inside
this are Jews playing at draughts, or settling and wrangling about
the goods they have bought of one another. In fact, in no other
place is such a scene of riot, rags, and filth to be witnessed. The
cause of this excitement is the great demand, on the part of the
poor, and the cheap clothiers as well, for those articles which are
considered as worthless by the rich. The old shoes are to be cobbled
up, and the cracks heelballed over, and sold out to the working
classes as strong durable articles. The Wellingtons are to be new
fronted, and disposed of to clerks who are expected to appear respectable upon the smallest salaries. The old coats and trousers
are wanted for the slop-shops; they are to be "turned," and made

up into new garments. The best black suits are to "clobbered" up;
and those which are more worn in parts are to be cut up and made
into new cloth caps or gaiters; whilst others are to be transformed
into the "best boys' tunics." Such as are *too* far gone are bought
to be torn to pieces by the "devil," and made up into new cloth,
or "shoddy," as it is termed; while such as have already done this
duty are sold for manure for the ground. The old shirts, if they
are past mending, are bought as "rubbish" by the marine-store
dealers, and sold as rags to the paper-mills, to be changed either
into the bank-note, the newspaper, or the best satin note-paper.
The average earnings of the hucksters who exchange crockery,
china, and glass for the above articles, are from 8s. to 10s. a week.
Some days, I am told, they will make 3s., and on others they will
get only 6d. However, taking the good with the bad, it is thought
that 10s. a week is about a fair average of the earnings of the
whole class. The best times for this trade are at the turn of the
winter, and at the summer season, because then people usually
purchase new clothes, and are throwing off the old ones. The
price of an old hat varies from 1d. to 8d.; for an old pair of shoes,
from 1d. to 4d.; an old pair of Wellingtons fetch from 3d. to 1s. 6d.
(those of French leather are of scarcely any value). An old coat is
worth from 4d. to 1s.; waistcoats are valued from 1d. to 3d.;
trousers are worth from 4d. to 8d.; cotton gowns are of the same
value; bonnets are of no value whatever; shirts fetch from 2d.
to 6d.; stockings are 1d. per pair; a silk handkerchief varies in
value from 3d. to 1s. The party supplying me with the above
information was originally in the coal and greengrocery business,
but, owing to a succession of calamities, he has been unable to
carry it on. Since then he has taken to the vending of crockery in
the streets, but owing to an insufficiency of capital he is incapable
of making a living at it. He says if he could get £5, it would be
the making of him in his present business. He seems to be a man
far above the average of the class to which he at present belongs.

The regular itinerant old-clothes dealers are generally Jews;
there are a few Christians among them, but these are exceptions.
A Jew tells me that the Gentiles are not so speculative as they are,
and the people do not like to deal with them. My informant, who
is an Israelite, speaking and writing some dozen languages, and
who has been fifty years in the business, says, "He is no bigot;
indeed, he does not care where he buys his meat, so long as he
can get it. He often goes into the Minories and buys some, without
looking to how it has been killed, or whether it has a seal on it
or not." The Christians, he says, are not near so speculative as we

are. "Now, our people will be out all day in the wet, and begrudge themselves a bit of anything to eat till they go home, and then maybe they'll gamble away their crown just for the love of speculation." He is confident there must be at least from 800 to 1,000 persons in the business. This he knows by the multitude of people about Petticoat-lane and Middlesex-street, and also by the number that pay to go into the Clothes Exchange every day. Part of the people that enter this place are Christians; these are chiefly the hucksters of crockeryware. Of these there are about 150 to 200, and not above six of these are Jews. The itinerant Jew clothesman is generally the son of a former old-clothesman, but many are cigar makers, and some pencil makers, who take to the business whenever their trade is slack; but nineteen out of twenty have been born to it. If the parents of the Jew are poor, and the son is a sharp lad, he generally commences business at ten years of age, by selling lemons or oranges in the street. The Jew boys are in general good boys to their fathers and mothers, and bring home every sixpence they earn. With his lemons the Jew boy will "get a round," or street connection, by becoming known to the neighbourhoods he visits. If he sees a servant, he will, when selling his lemons, ask if she has any old shoes or old clothes, and, if so, say he'll be a purchaser of them. If the clothes should come to more money than the Jew boy has in his pocket, he'll leave what silver he has as "an earnest upon them," and then go seek some regular old Jew clothesman, who will advance the purchase-money. This the old Jew agrees to do upon the understanding that he is to have "half Rybeck," that is, a moiety of the profit, and he will accompany the boy to the house to pass his judgment on the goods, and to see that the lad is not giving too much for them. After this he goes with the lad to Petticoat-lane, and there they will share together whatever money the clothes may bring over and above what has been paid for them. By such means the Jew boy gets his knowledge of the old clothes business; and so quick are these lads generally, that in the course of two months they will acquire sufficient experience in connection with the trade to begin dealing on their own account. There are plenty of them, I am told, at the age of fourteen, as sharp as a man of fifty. They are mostly in Petticoat-lane, Middlesex-street, and Cutler-street, where the business is principally carried on. The itinerant Jew clothesman lives at the east-end of the town. The greater number of them reside in Portsoken ward, Houndsditch; and their favourite localities in this district are either Cobb's-yard or Roper's-buildings, or Wentworth-street. Here they mostly occupy small houses, about

4s. 6d. a week rent, and live with their families. They are generally sober, though not particularly honest, people. It is seldom, however, that a Jew leaves his house and owes his landlord any money; and if his goods should be seized, the rest of his tribe will go round and collect what is owing. As a body of persons, they are particularly charitable one to the other, and never allow any of their own people to be in want or distress, if it is possible to prevent it. It is very seldom that an itinerant Jew clothesman takes away any of the property of the house that he may be called into. "I expect there's a good many of 'em," said my informant, "is fond of cheating — that is, they won't mind giving only 2s. for a thing that's worth five." They are remarkably fond of money, and will do almost anything to get it. They are perhaps the most money-loving people in all England. There are certainly some old-clothesmen, I am told, who will buy articles at such a price that they must know them to have been stolen. Their rule, however, is to ask no questions, and to get as cheap an article as possible. Jews are sober people in general, and the Jew clothesman is seldom or ever seen in liquor. They are particularly fond of "plays;" indeed, on a Friday night the Standard Theatre is above half filled with old-clothesmen. They love gambling for money, and at this they are mostly engaged, either at their own homes or at the public-houses in the neighbourhood. Their favourite games are tossing, dominoes, and cards. I am credibly informed by one of the people, that he has seen as much as £30 in silver and gold lying upon the ground when two parties have been playing at throwing three halfpence in the air. On a Saturday they gamble the whole of the morning and the greater part of the afternoon. They meet in some secret back place, about ten, and begin playing for what they call "one a time" — that is, tossing up three halfpence, and staking a shilling on the result. Other Jews, and occasionally a few Christians, will then gather round the gamblers, and bet upon them. Sometimes the bets laid by the Jew bystanders will be as high as £2 each; and I am assured that on more than one occasion he has seen the old-clothesmen wager as much as £50. But this is only done after great gains at gambling. If they *can* they will cheat, and this is frequently done by means of a halfpenny with a head or a tail on both sides, commonly called "a gray." The play lasts till the Jewish Sabbath is nearly over, and after this they retire either to their business or the theatre. They seldom or never say a word while they are losing, but merely stamp their foot on the ground; but it is dangerous to interfere with them when luck is against them. The rule is, when a man is losing, to let him alone.

My informant has seen them often play for three hours together, and nothing be said all that time but head or tail. They seldom go to synagogue, and on a Sunday evening have generally card parties at their own houses. They seldom or never eat anything while on their rounds. The reason of this is, not because they object to eat meat killed by a Christian, but because they are afraid of losing "a deal," or, in other words, the chance of buying a lot of old clothes by so doing. They are generally too lazy to light their own fire before they start of a morning, and consequently nineteen out of twenty obtain their breakfasts at the coffee-shops in the neighbourhood of Houndsditch. When they return from their day's work, they have mostly some stew ready, prepared by their parents or wife, or, if they are not family men, they betake themselves to an eating-house. This is sometimes a Jewish house, but occasionally, if no one is looking, the Jew will steal into a Christian "cook-shop" — for they are not particular about eating "tryfer" — that is, meat that has been killed by a Christian. Those that are single will generally go to a neighbour, and agree with him to be found in food during the Sabbath; and for this the charge is generally about 2s. 6d. On a Saturday they always have cold fish for breakfast and supper; indeed, my informant assures me that a Jew would pawn the shirt off his back sooner than go without it; and in holiday-time he *will* have it, if he has to get it out of the stones. It is not reckoned a holiday among them unless they have fish. At Billingsgate the fish salesmen are so well acquainted with this fact, that the price of fish is always double on a Jews' holiday. The Jew clothesmen are generally far more cleanly in their habits than the lower orders of English people. Their hands they always wash before their meals; and this is done whether the party is a strict Jew or "Meshumet." Again, he will never use the same knife to cut his meat that he previously used to spread his butter, and he will not even put his meat on a plate that has had butter in it. Nor will he use for his soup the spoon that has had melted butter in it. This objection to mix butter with meat is carried so far, that, after partaking of the one, Jews will not eat of the other for the space of two hours. They are generally, when married, most exemplary family men. There are few fonder fathers than they are, and they will starve themselves sooner than their wives and children should want. Whatever their vices may be, at least they are good fathers, husbands, and sons. Their principal characteristic is their extreme love of money; and though the strict Jew will seldom trade himself on his Sabbath, he does not object to employ either one of his tribe, as well as a Gentile, to do so for him. The capital required for commencing in the old clothes line is generally about one pound. This the Jew frequently borrows, especially after holiday-time, for then he has generally spent all his earnings, excepting when he is a provident and saving man. When his stock-money is exhausted, he goes either to a neighbour or to a publican in the vicinity, and borrows £1 on the Monday morning, "to strike a light with," as he calls it, and agrees to return it on the Friday evening, with 1s. interest for the loan of it. This he always pays back. If he was to sell the coat off his back, he would do this, I am told, because to fail in so doing would be to prevent his obtaining any stock-money for the future. With this capital he starts on his rounds about eight in the morning; and I am assured he will frequently begin his work without tasting food, rather than break into the borrowed stock-money. Each man has his particular walk and never interferes with that of his neighbour; indeed, while upon another's beat he will seldom cry for clothes. Sometimes they go half "Kybeck" together — that is, they will share the profits of the day's business; and when they agree to do this, the one will take one street, and the other another. The lower the neighbourhood the more old clothes are there for sale. At the east-end of the town they like the neighbourhoods frequented by sailors, and there they purchase of the girls and the women the sailors' jackets and trousers. But they buy the most of the marine-store dealers; for as the Jew clothesman never travels the streets by night-time, the parties who have old clothes to dispose of in the evening usually sell them to the marine-store dealers. The first thing that the Jew does in the morning is to seek out these shops, and see what he can pick up there. At the west-end the itinerant clothesmen prefer the mews at the back of gentlemen's houses to all other places, or else the streets where the little tradesmen and small genteel families reside. But he does the most of his business at the marine-store shops at the west as well as at the east end of London. What they purchase overnight, the Jew buys in the morning. He mostly looks out for old hats that are not worn at the tip (that is round the crown). Let them be crushed flat, it is no matter to him; they can be made as good as new if the tip is unworn. For these he generally gives 6d, never more, and often 2d. or 1d., "if people knows no better," says my informant; and he will sell them for 1s. or 1s. 3d. each. Dress coats are of no great value to the Jew; for these are chiefly cut up for the cap-makers. He never gives more than 1s. for these, and they fetch him but 1s. 6d. The cause of these coats being of so little value arises from the little demand there is for them among poor or working men. But old frock coats are always saleable, summer and winter; and if they are wanted for cutting up, there is a good skirt, they say, hanging to them, that will make plenty of caps; whereas dress coats, if the body is bad, will not cut up into even one cap. The caps made out of the skirts of the oldest frock coat will fetch as much as 4s. 6d. each. All the cap shops at the east and west part of London are supplied by the Polish Jews with cloth caps that are made out of the skirts of the left-off frock coats. This article is the Jew's greatest gain. The parties who sell them to him are generally unacquainted with the difference in value between the frock and dress coat. The frock coat, even if the sleeves and collar be an inch thick in grease, is worth about 4s. 6d. to the Jew, whereas the dress coat is only one-third of the value to him. The thicker the grease, the fresher is the wool beneath, and the "clobberer" can clean up the dirtiest coat in a few minutes. The Jew, in buying a frock coat, first overhauls it, as he terms it, and regulates his price according to the wear of the sleeve. If the coat is good throughout, with the exception of the "under sleeve," this can be put in new, and matched so perfectly that the buyer cannot tell the new from the old cloth, nor the seller either, after a few weeks' wear; and by this means a very serviceable coat for the mechanic or clerk is produced out of a gentleman's left-off surtout. The coats are generally renovated, that is, recoloured in the parts where they have gone white at the seams. The dye used for recolouring old "seedy" coats is gall and logwood, with a small portion of copperas. The crockcoat, when renovated and new undersleeved, will be sold for 10s., in case they can get no more. "The Jew salesman will often ask 25s. — and take it, too," says my candid Israelite, "if the buyer is flat enough to give it." — The conversation that generally goes on at such times, he tells me, is the following: — "How much is this here?" says the man who comes to buy it. "One pound five," replies the Jew seller. "I won't give you above half the money." "Half the money!" cries the Jew, "I can't take that money. What above the 16s. that you offer now will you give for it? Will you give me eighteen?" asks the Jew. "Well, come, give us your money, I've got ma rent to pay." But the man says, "I only bid you 12s. 6d., and I shan't give no more." And if the Jew finds he can't get him to "spring," or advance any further, he says, "I suppose I must take your money, even if I lose by it. You'll be a better customer another time." This is the usual "deal," I am assured by one who began the business at thirteen years old, and is now upwards of sixty years of age. The Jew will always ask at least twice as much as he means to take. With trousers, the itinerant Jew clothesman does very well — indeed, better than with coats. The trousers, if broken at the knee are almost useless, and only fit for cutting up; but if broken at the seat they are easily repaired, and this is so well done that it makes little or no difference to the wearer. For trousers the old-clothesman will give from 1s. to 4s. For doing up an old pair of trousers with new waistband linings, cleaning, and reseating them complete, the Jew clothesman pays 1s., and he sells them from 4s. to 8s. each. Boots are the most difficult things to buy in the whole of the old-clothes business. If they are not sound behind, the regular height, and the straps perfect at the top, they are scarcely worth carrying home, being fit only for cutting. The price usually given for boots with unsound backs is about 3d., and with sound backs they are of the value of 1s. 6d., no matter what may be the state of the soles or upper leathers. The boots sold by the Jew clothesmen are generally purchased by bootmakers who are in connection with some working man's "boot club;" they are new footed, and then sold at 14s. the pair. There are two exchanges for the sale of the old clothes that the itinerant Jew purchases on his rounds. One of these is called "Isaac's Exchange," and is situate at Phil's-buildings, Houndsditch; the other is in Cutler-street, and is known by the name of "Simmons's Exchange." To either of these places the Jew clothesman makes his way in the afternoon. Wherever his round may be in London, to one of those quarters he will come in the evening. The business in these places begins at one, and ends at four in the winter and eight in the summer. These are the great marts where all the left-off wearing apparel is disposed of. "Forty years ago, I have made as much as £5 in a week by the purchase of old clothes in the streets," says my Jew informant. Upon an average then, I could earn weekly about £2. But now things are different. People are more wide awake. Every one knows the value of an old coat now. The women knows more than the men. The general average, I think, take the good weeks with the bad, throughout the year, is about £1 a week; some weeks they get £2, and some they gets scarcely none."

According to the above statement of the weekly gains of the Jew clothesmen, and the number of the itinerant purchasers of left-off wearing apparel, frequenting the streets of London, it follows that the value of the old clothes of the metropolis amounts to about £52,000 per annum.

The street *Lucifer-Match Trade* is in the hands of persons who are unable to earn a penny by any other means, or who resort to it through roguery, or through sheer idleness, as a pretext for begging. It is mentioned by the poor as the *very last shift*. The persons who sell lucifer matches are of every age. In the New Cut, Lambeth, for instance, on a Saturday night especially, are many hale, strong, Irish labourers, some of whom beg vociferously, telling the most pitiful stories, and following the passers-by with provoking pertinacity. A man who has a long time had "a pitch" in the New Cut — a decent, intelligent man, who through accident had been crippled in his business of a glass-blower, and so was driven to his present occupation sells sometimes two dozen boxes a day — very rarely more — and seldom less than one dozen. He unites with the lucifer trade the sale of envelopes, writing paper, and other articles. He can leave his stock in the street, merely covered over, not even locked up — it is comprised in a sort of desk — because it says "it's hardly worth robbing; and who would rob a poor man?" The lucifer boxes cost him 3d. a dozen; he sells them for a halfpenny each, his customers being servant-maids and the wives of working men. He sometimes clears 15d. a day — averaging, perhaps, something less than 1s. — and considers that he is the most prosperous of any of his class in that populous neighbourhood, though he is always outsold on a Saturday night by a big Irishman, who sings "Mary Blane," and dances, and capers, and performs many antics, as a means of attracting a crowd about him, and so obtaining a great sale for his boxes or other wares. The really poverty-stricken vendors of lucifers are persons who have been discharged from the hospitals, friendless and penniless, and women, who have been in the House of Correction for petty offences, and have regained their liberty. Children are frequently sent out, their raggedness being rendered as conspicuous as possible, by parents who do not mind exposing them to any inclemency for a few pence. Within the recollection of my informant the sellers of lucifer-boxes have greatly increased. Within these three months he has recognised between thirty and forty new faces in and about the Cut; many of them he considers rather well-educated women. Among those driven to lucifer-match selling, I may instance the case of a soldier's widow. She lived in comfort with her husband, who had a pension of 6d. a day, while she carried on the business of a laundress, sometimes employing six women to wash, and as many to iron for her. Her husband's long illness enforced her constant attendance upon him; she had in consequence to neglect her business, and lost her connection, and at her husband's death was in the greatest distress. She sells lucifer matches, not having any other resource, the parish refusing her relief; she never sells more than two dozen, which leaves her a profit of 5d., as she gives 3½d. a dozen for them.

In bad weather she sells hardly any, and has sometimes to walk the streets all night, for want of a shelter. She knows very many in the same condition as herself. Some of the dealers in lucifers let out boxes by the dozen or half-dozen, on trust, to girls, for sale or return, exacting daily payment with a per-centage. The lucifer-match sellers are a *fluctuating* class, and are comprised of every description of the wretched, the feeble, the imbecile and the cheating. I did not hear of any who purchased their wares at the manu-facturer's, but always at the oilman's. Among the little girls who sell lucifers, and say that they clear 1d. or 2d. a day, some are quick and intelligent as regards their account of their way and means of living; indeed, they are painfully quick, I may say. They are untaught, barefooted, half-clad, shivering with cold, and their parents sick, or starving, or roguish. Their probable fate may be conjectured.

The *Sellers of Boot and Stay Laces* are of the same character as the sellers of lucifers. Either calling can be started by any one with a few pence. In the sale of laces, persons of both sexes are engaged; but the most successful, and those who make themselves known in a neighbourhood, are generally men who loudly announce their wares. One man, a baker by trade, who had come from Shrop-shire to London in search of employment, through sickness and inability to get work, sells boot and stay laces. He might, on *fine days* — for all these poor people represent the weather as of great importance in the successful pursuit of their avocations — sell a dozen of boot laces, and another dozen of stay laces; these cost him 3d. or 4d. a dozen at any draper's, according to the quality, and are sold at a halfpenny a-piece. Children are not so much employed in vending these wares, as it has been long the custom of the dealers to cry them, and not unfrequently with the tag of a rhyme — "Long and strong, a penny a pair!" "Two a penny, the best of any!" and such like. With the sale of these laces the man we have mentioned combined that of *hearthstones* — pursuing one in the morning, the other in the after-part of the day — which is a common arrangement with these articles. His great sale, as he called it, was on Fridays and Saturdays, when he would sell eighteen hearthstones, which brought him 9d., and cost him 6d. On other days he would sell eight, or six, or four, or none. Those who take up this business from destitution and necessity find it their interest to search out new neighbourhoods, often going great distances from their lodging-houses, because in the more frequented localities some old woman, or infirm man, inheriting somewhat the privileges of "the long-remembered beggar," has a sort of monoply

in the business, having been long known to the inhabitants. The
man from whom I derived my information, which was confirmed
on all hands as to the state of this trade generally, was a sickly-
looking, well-spoken man, living in a Westminster lodging-house —
"for travellers," as the shutters announced — a place unventilated,
dirty, foul in air, and crowded beyond decency. What all these
poor creatures seem to esteem a luxury is *warmth* — no matter
with what unhealthy accompaniments.

The *street vendors of Blacking* purchase it at the blacking
manufactories. They buy it by the half-gross, for which they pay
1s. 6d. The class who vend it are the poorest of the poor. It takes
from 2s. to 2s. 6d. to commence blacking vendor. The quality
is very good generally; sometimes it is not quite so good as at
other times. They are obliged to live in low-rented rooms, and
those who have no home live in lodging-houses. There are some
hundreds who sell blacking in London, but it is generally confined
to boys and girls. They get 6d. a dozen profit, or 1s. 6d. a half-
gross. They can sell half a gross from Saturday night at six o'clock
till Sunday morning at eleven o'clock. On the Saturday night they
stop out till twelve o'clock. They only sell on the Saturday nights
and Sunday mornings, as no one will buy on the other nights in
the week. Sometimes the poor are their customers, and sometimes
the rich, but mostly the poor. Some of their customers want three
skins a penny, but they won't let them have them. Sometimes they
suffer from the wet and cold, as they are always out of a Saturday
night and Sunday morning, let the weather be ever so wet and
cold. Their meals sometimes consist of bread and butter, and
sometimes of bread and dripping, and often dry bread. "It's only
them that's got a father or mother as can get a bit of meat. There
are many as ain't got no father nor mother, and they sleeps under
the arches, or else in some of them 'ere houses that nobody lives
in." These destitute boys, beside earning a small sum by selling
blacking, get some halfpence by holding gentlemen's horses, carrying small parcels, and sweeping the crossings; and some of them
go and pick up coals that fall off the barges. These coals
they sell to poor people about 2d. a quarter of a cwt. They will
often earn as much as 4d., and sometimes 6d. a day. "They often
play at pitch in the hole and toss with the money they get. If
they lose all, they are forced to lie all night under the arches.
These often turn out thieves and pick-pockets, and everything
else that is bad."

The next class that I sought out were the hucksters of tape and
cotton. These are usually elderly females; and I was directed to

one who had been getting her living by such means for nine years. I was given to understand that the woman was in deep distress, and that she had long been supporting a sick husband by her little trade; but I was wholly unprepared for a scene of such startling misery, sublimed by untiring affection and pious resignation, as I there discovered.

I wish the reader to understand that I do not cite this case as a type of the sufferings of this particular class, but rather as an illustration of the afflictions which frequently befall those who are solely dependent on their labour, or their little trade, for their subsistence, and who, from the smallness of their earnings, are unable to lay by even the least trifle as a fund against any physical calamity.

The poor creatures lived in one of the close alleys at the east-end of London. On inquiring at the house to which I had been directed, I was told I should find them in the "the two-pair back." I mounted the stairs, and on opening the door of the apartment I was terrified with the misery before me. There, on a wretched bed, lay an aged man in almost the last extremity of weakness. At first I thought the poor old creature was really dead, but a tremble of the eyelids as I closed the door, as noiselessly as I could, told me that he breathed. His face was as yellow as clay, and it had more the cold damp look of a corpse than that of a living man. His cheeks were hollowed in with evident want, his temples sunk, and his nostrils pinched close. On the edge of the bed sat his heroic wife, giving him drink with a spoon from a tea-cup. In one corner of the room stood the basket of tapes, cottons, combs, braces, nutmeg-graters and shaving-glasses, with which she strove to keep her poor old dying husband from the workhouse. I asked her how long her husband had been ill, and she told me he had been confined to his bed five weeks last Wednesday, and that it was ten weeks since he had eaten the bulk of a nut of solid food. Nothing but a little beef-tea had passed his lips for months past. "We have lived like children together," said the old woman, as her eyes flooded with tears; "never had no dispute. He hated drink, and there was no cause for us to quarrel. One of my legs, you see, is shorter than the other," said she, rising from the bedside, and showing me that her right foot was several inches from the ground as she stood, "You see my hip is out. I used to go out washing, and walking in my pattens I fell down. My hip is out of the socket three-quarters of an inch, and the sinews is drawn up. I am obliged to walk with a stick." Here the man groaned, and coughed so that I feared the exertion must

end his life. "Ah, the heart of a stone would pity that poor fellow!"
said the fond wife. "After I put my hip out, I couldn't get my
living as I'd been used to do. I couldn't stand a day if I got five
hundred pounds for it. I must sit down. So I got a little stall,
and sat at the end of the alley here, with a few laces and tapes
and things. I've done so for this nine year past, and seen many
a landlord come in and go out of the house that I sat at. My
husband used to sell small ware in the streets — black lead, and
furniture paste, and blacking. We got a sort of a living, you see,
by this, the two of us together. It's very seldom we had a bit of
meat. We had 1s. 9d. rent to pay. Come, my child, will you have
another little drop to wet your mouth?" said the woman, breaking
off. "Come, my dearest, let me give you this," said she, as the
man let his jaw fall, and she poured some warm sugar and water,
flavoured with cinnamon (it was all she had to give him) into his
mouth. He's been an ailing man these many years. He used to
go on errands for me, buy my little things for me, on account
of my being lame. We assisted one another, you see. He wasn't
able to go about; so he used to go about and buy what I sold
for me. I am sure he never earned above 1s. 6d. in the week. He
used to attend me, and many a time I've sat for ten and fourteen
hours in the cold and wet, and didn't take a sixpence. Some days
I'd make a shilling, and some days less; but whatever I got, I
used to have to put a good part into the basket to keep my little
stock. [A knock here came to the door; it was a halfpenny-worth
of darning cotton.] You know a shilling goes further with a poor
couple that's sober than two shillings does with a drunkard. We
lived poor, you see, never had nothing but tea, or we could not
have done anyhow. If I'd take 18d. in the day, I'd think I was
grandly off, and then if there was 6d. profit got out of that, it
would be almost as much as it would. You see these cotton braces
here (said the old woman, going to her tray). Well, I gives 2s. 9d.
a dozen for these, and I sells 'em for 4½d., and oftentimes 4d. a
pair. Now this piece of tape would cost me seven farthings in
the shop, and I sells it at six yards a penny. It has the name of
being eighteen yards. The profit out of it is five farthings. It's
beyond the power of man to wonder how there's a bit of bread
got out of such a small way! Now the times is bad, too — I
think I could say I could get 8d. a day profit if I got any sort
of custom, but I couldn't exceed that at the best of times. I've
often sat at the end of the alley and taken only 6d., and that's
not much more than 2d. clear — it ain't 3d., I'm sure. I think I
could safely say that for the last nine years me and my husband

has earned together 5s. a week, and out of that the two of us had to live and pay rent — 1s. 9d. a week. Clothes I could buy none, for the best garment is on me; but I thank the Lord still! I've paid my rent all but three weeks, and that isn't due till to-morrow. We have often reckoned it up here at the fire. Some weeks we have got 5s. 3d., and some weeks less, so that I judge we have had about 3s. to 3s. 6d. a week to live upon, the two of us, for this nine years past. Half-a-hundred of coals would fit me the week in the depths of winter. My husband would have the kettle always boiling for me against I'd come in. He used to sit here, reading his book; he never was fit for work, at the best; and I used to be out minding the basket. He was also so sober and quiet. His neighbours will tell that of him. Within the last ten weeks he's been very ill indeed, but still I could be out with the basket. Since then he's never earnt me a penny: poor old soul, he wasn't able! All that time I still attended to my basket. He wasn't so ill then but what he could do a little here in the room for himself; but he wanted little. God knows! He couldn't eat. After he fell ill, I had to go all my errands myself. I had no one to help, for I'd nothing to pay them; and I'd have to walk from here down to Sun-street with my stick, till my bad leg pained me so that I could hardly stand. You see, the hip being put out has drawn all the sinews of my hip up into my groin, and it leaves me incapable of walking or standing constantly; but I thank God that I've got the use of it anyhow! Our lot's hard enough, goodness knows; but we are content. We never complain, but bless the Lord for the little he pleases to give us. When I was away on my errands, in course I could'nt be minding my basket; so I lost a good bit of money that way. Well, five weeks on Wednesday he has been totally confined to his bed, excepting when I lift him up to make it some nights; but he can't bear *that* now. Still, the first fortnight he was bad I did manage to leave him, and earn a few pence; but latterly, for this last three, I haven't been able to go out at all, to do anything." "She's been stopping by me, minding me here night and day all that time," mumbled the old man, who now for the first time opened his grey glassy eyes, and turned towards me, to bear, as it were, a last tribute to his wife's incessant affection. "She has been most kind to me. Her tenderness and care has been such that man never knew from woman before, ever since I lay upon this sick bed. We've been married five-and-twenty years. We have always lived happily — happily, indeed — together. Until sickness and weakness overcome me, I always strove to help myself a bit, as well as I could; but since then she has done all in her power for me — worked for me — aye, she has worked for me, surely, and watched over me. My creed through life has been repentance towards God, faith in Jesus Christ, and love to all my brethren. I've made up my mind that I must soon change this tabernacle; and my last wish is that the good people of this world will increase her little stock for her. She cannot get her living out of the little stock she has, and since I lay here it's lessened so, that neither she nor no one else can live upon it. If the kind hearts would give her but a little stock more, it would keep her old age from want, as she has kept mine. Indeed, indeed, she does deserve it. But the Lord, I know, will reward her for all she has done to me." The old man's eyelids dropped exhausted. "I've had a shilling and a loaf twice from the parish," continued the woman. "The overseer came to see if he was fit to be removed to the workhouse. The doctor gave me a certificate that he was not; and then the relieving officer gave me a shilling and a loaf of bread, and out of that shilling I bought my poor old man a sup of port wine. I bought a quartern of wine, which was 4d., and I gave 5d. for a bit of tea and sugar, and I gave 2d. for coals; a halfpenny rush-light I bought, and a short candle; that made a penny — and that's the way I laid out that shilling. If God takes him, I know he'll sleep in Heaven. I know the life he's spent, and am not afraid; but no one else shall him from me — nothing shall part us but death in this world. Poor old soul, he can't be long with me. He's a perfect skeleton. His bones are starting through his skin. But he's clean, thank goodness, I can say — not a speck upon his body." I asked what could be done for her; and the old man thrust forth his skinny arm, and laying hold the bed-post, he raised himself slightly in his bed, as he murmured, "If she could be got into a little parlour, and away from sitting in the streets, it would be the saving of her." And so saying, he fell back, overcome with the exertion, and breathed heavily. The woman sat down beside me and went on: "What shocked him most was that I was obligated in his old age to go and ask for relief at the parish. You see, he was always a spiritful man, and it hurted him sorely that he should come to this at last, and for the first time in his lifetime. The only parish money that ever we had was this, and it does hurt him every day to think that he must be buried by the parish after all: he was always proud, you see."

I told the kind-hearted old dame that some benevolent people had placed certain funds at my disposal for the relief of such distress as hers; and I assured her that neither she nor her husband should want for anything that might ease their sufferings.

LETTER XV
Friday, December 7, 1849

I shall in this letter conclude my remarks on the hucksters or
street-dealers of the metropolis. The classes of whom I have still
to treat include the hucksters of street literature and arts — such
as the "flying stationers" or dealers in last dying speeches and
three yards of new and popular songs, the umbrella printsellers,
the wall-song men, the play-bill sellers, and the vendors of four
sheets of note-paper for a penny. All these are included under the
term "street paper-sellers," and they constitute a large body of
individuals. Those that remain are difficult to classify. They may
be enumerated under the titles of dog-dealers, flower-girls, vendors
of corn salve and compositions for removing grease spots from
cloth, sellers of small coins and jewellery, purchasers of hareskins,
hawkers of hearthstones, sand, and gravel; and lastly, the most
degraded of all, viz., the street pickers-up, or "bone-grubbers," and
"mud-larks." These, with a few exceptions, exhaust the class of
hucksters. It is true there are varieties that are still undescribed —
such as the donkey-boys (but these belong to the suburbs of
London itself); then there are the street vendors of gold fish, of
cutlery, of hardware, of tea-trays, of slippers, of wash-leathers and
sponges, of sheeting and table-covers, and of pretended smuggled
goods; but these varieties of the order are far too limited in numbers to be worthy of special description.

When first treating of the class, I gave a statement as to the
criminality of the calling, as compared with other occupations.
According to deductions made from the last census, in 1841, one
in every 86 hawkers, hucksters, and pedlars was a prisoner in some
gaol, and one in every 100 seamstresses; the average number of
prisoners being, for the entire population, one in 718 individuals.
Resorting to this mode of estimating the *poverty* of the class,
I find that in the same year one in 179 hawkers, hucksters, and
pedlars were paupers or inmates of some parish union; whereas
one in every 36 seamsters and seamstresses were in the same

condition; the average number of paupers for the entire population being one in every 159. Hence it is evident that the class of hucksters, compared with the people generally, are considerably above the average in crime, and below it in poverty; whereas the seamstresses are comparatively but little above the average in crime, and greatly above it in poverty. It may therefore be said of the hucksters generally, that while they are highly criminal, they are not particularly poor; and of the seamstresses, that while they are very poor, they are not near so criminal as their poverty would lead us to expect. These calculations I have found fully borne out during my investigation into the conditions and habits of the two classes. The one are toiling day and night to earn 2s. 10½d. a week (these were the average earnings of the 1,200 individuals who were present at the British school-room in Shadwell on last Monday evening), while the others are clearing their 15s. to £1 weekly. The hucksters, we have seen, are habitually dishonest, whereas we have found the seamstresses working day and night in the summer to repay the inevitable debts of the winter. From all I have witnessed, the criminality of the one seems to be a natural result of "the roving disposition" which the hucksters themselves say is the characteristic of the class; whereas the errors of the others appear to me to be the necessary consequence of the wretched price paid for their labour. The wages of the needlewomen generally are so far below subsistence point, that, in order to support life, it is almost a physical necessity that they must either steal, pawn, or prostitute themselves. The amount of goods in pawn among the needlewomen present at the meeting on Monday night last was stated at £1,200; and this I am assured is far below the truth, many having mistaken the question, and believed it to refer to the work given out to them, instead of to their own property.

The *Flying Stationers* are divisible into four classes — the running and the standing patterers, the long-song sellers, the song-book dealers, and the ballad-singers. Besides these, there are others who can turn their hands to any one of the different branches of the calling, and are termed general paper-sellers. The whole class are called "paper" workers. There are several printers at the east and west end of London who are generally engaged in supplying the paper workers. The principal of these printers and publishers are Mrs. Ryall (late Jemmy Catnach), Miss Hodges (late Tommy Pitt, of the toy and marble warehouse), G. Birt, Little Jack Powell (formerly of Lloyd's), Jim Paul (from Catnach's), and Good, of Clerkenwell. The leading man in the "paper" trade was the late

"Jemmy Catnach," who is said to have amassed upwards of £10,000 in the business. He is reported to have made the greater part of this sum during the trial of Queen Caroline, by the sale of whole-sheet "papers," descriptive of the trial, and embellished with "splendid illustrations." The next to Catnach stood Pitt, of the noted toy and marble warehouse. These two parties were the Colburn and Bentley of the "paper" trade. In connection with these printers and publishers are a certain number of flying stationers, ready to publish by word of mouth anything that they may produce. These parties are technically called "the school," and are "at the Dials" altogether from 80 to 100 in number. The running patterers" are those that describe the contents of their papers as they go. They seldom or ever stand still, and generally visit a neighbourhood in bands of two or three at a time. The more noise they make, they say, the better the "papers" sell. They usually deal in murders, seductions, crim. cons., explosions, alarming accidents, assassinations, deaths of public characters, duels, and love-letters. The standing patterers are men who remain in one place — until removed by the police — and who endeavour to attract attention to their papers, either by means of a board with pictures daubed upon it, descriptive of the contents of what they sell, or else by gathering a crowd round about them, and giving a lively or horrible description of the papers or books they are "working." Some of this class give street recitations or dialogues. The long-song sellers, who form another class, are those who parade the streets with three yards of new and popular songs for a penny. The songs are generally fixed to the top of a long pole, and the party cries the different titles as he goes. This part of "the profession" is confined solely to the summer; the hands in winter usually take to the sale of song-books instead, it being impossible to exhibit "the three yards" in wet weather. The last class are ballad singers, who perambulate the streets, singing the songs they sell. Included in these classes are several well-known London characters. These parties are chiefly what are called "death-hunters," from whom you may always expect a "full, true, and particular account" of the last "diabolical murder." These full, true, and particular accounts are either real or fictitious tragedies. The fictitious ones are called "cocks," and usually kept stereotyped. The most popular of these are the murder at Chigwell-row — "that's a trump," says my informant, "to this present day. Why, I'd go out now, sir, with a dozen of Chigwell-rows, and earn my supper in half an hour off of 'em. The murder of Sarah Holmes at Lincoln is good, too — that there has been worked for the last five year successively every winter," said my informant. "Poor Sarah Holmes! Bless her, she has saved me from walking the streets all night many a time! Some of the best of these have been in work twenty years — the Scarborough murder has full twenty years. It's called, 'THE SCARBOROUGH TRAGEDY.' I've worked it myself. It's about a noble and rich young naval officer seducing a poor clergyman's daughter. She is confined in a ditch, and destroys the child. She is taken up for it, tried, and executed. This has had a great run. It sells all round the country places, and would sell now if they had it out. Mostly all our customers is females. They are the chief dependence we have. The Scarborough Tragedy is very attractive. It draws tears to the women's eyes, to think that a poor clergyman's daughter, who is remarkably beautiful, should murder her own child; it's very touching to every feeling heart. There's a copy of verses with it too. Then there's the Liverpool Tragedy — that's very attractive. It's a mother murdering her own son, through gold. He had come from the East Indies, and married a rich planter's daughter. He came back to England to see his parents after an absence of thirty years. They kept a lodging-house in Liverpool for sailors; the son went there to lodge, and meant to tell his parents who he was in the morning. His mother saw the gold he had got in his boxes, and cut his throat — severed his head from his body; the old man, upwards of seventy years of age, holding the candle. They had put a washing-tub under the bed to catch his blood. The morning after the murder the old man's daughter calls and inquires for a young man. The old man denies that they have had any such person in the house. She says he had a mole on his arm in the shape of a strawberry. The old couple go upstairs to examine the corpse, and find they have murdered their own son, and then they both put an end to their existence. This is a deeper tragedy than the Scarborough Murder. That suits young people better; they like to hear about the young woman being seduced by the naval officer; but the mothers take more to the Liverpool Tragedy — it suits them better. Some of the 'cocks' were in existence," he says, "before ever I was born or thought of." The "Great and important battle between the two young ladies of fortune" is what he calls a ripper. "I should like to have that there put down correct," he says, "'cause I've taken a tidy lot of money out of it." My informant, who had been upwards of twenty years in the running patter line, tells me that he commenced his career with the "Last Dying Speech and Full Confession of William Corder." He was sixteen years of age, and had run away from his parents. "I worked that there," he says, "down in the very town (at Bury) where he was executed. I got a whole hatful of halfpence at that. Why, I wouldn't even give 'em seven for sixpence — no, that I wouldn't. A gentleman's servant come out, and wanted half a dozen for his master, and one for himself in, and I wouldn't let him have no such thing. We often sells more than that at once. Why, I sold six at one go to the railway clerks at Norwich, about the Manning affair, only a fortnight back. But Steinburgh's little job — you know, he murdered his wife and family, and committed suicide after — that sold as well as any 'die.' Pegsworth was an out-an-out lot. I did tremendous with him, because it happened in London, down Ratcliff-highway — that's a splendid quarter for working — there's plenty of feelings; but, bless you, some places you go to you can't move no how — they've hearts like paving-stones. They wouldn't have 'the papers' if you'd give them to 'em — especially when they knows you. Greenacre didn't sell so well as might have been expected, for such a diabolical out-and-out crime as he committed; but you see, he came close after Pegsworth, and that took the beauty off him. Two murderers together is never no good to nobody. Why, there was Wilson Gleeson, as great a villain as ever lived — went and murdered a whole family at noon-day; but Rush coopered him — and likewise that girl at Bristol — made it no draw to anyone. Dan'el Good, though, was a firstrater; and would have been much better if it hadn't been for that there Madame Toosow. You see, she went down to Roehampton, and guv £2 for the werry clogs as he used to wash his master's carriage in; so, in course, when the harrystocracy could go and see the real things — the werry identical clogs — in the Chamber of Orrors, why, the people wouldn't look at our authentic portraits of the fiend in human form. Hocker wasn't any particular great shakes. There was a deal expected from him, but he didn't turn out well. Courvoisier was much better — he sold werry well; but nothing to Blakesley. Why, I worked him for six weeks. The life of the murdered man kept the King's Head that he was landlord on open on the morning of the execution, and the place was like a fair. I even went and sold papers outside the door myself. I thought if she war'nt ashamed, why should I be? After that we had a fine 'fake' — that was the fire of the Tower of London — it sold rattling. Why, we had about forty apprehended for that — first we said two soldiers was taken up that couldn't obtain their discharge; and then we declared it was a well-known sporting nobleman who did it for a spree. The boy Jones in the Palace wasn't much more of an affair for the running patterer; the ballad-singers — or street screamers, as we calls 'em — had the pull out of that. The patter wouldn't take; they had read it all in the newspapers before. Oxford, and Francis, and Bean were a little better, but nothing to crack about. The people doesn't care about such things as them. There's nothing beats a stunning good murder after all. Why, there was Rush — I lived on him for a month or more. When I commenced with Rush I was 14s. in debt for rent, and in less than ten days I astonished the wise men in the East by paying my landlord all I owed him. Since Dan'el Good there had been little or nothing doing in the murder line — no one could cap him — till Rush turned up a regular trump for us. Why, I went down to Norwich expressly to work the execution. I worked my way down there with *'a sorrowful lamentation'* of his own composing, which I'd got written by the blind man, expressly for the occasion. On the morning of the execution we beat all the regular newspapers out of the field; for we had the full, true, and particular account down, you see, by our own express, and that can beat anything that ever they can publish; for we gets it printed several days afore it comes off, and goes and stands with it right under the drop; and many's the penny I've turned away when I've been asked for an account of the whole business before it happened. So you see, for herly and correct hinformation, we can beat the *Sun* — aye, or the Moon either, for the matter of that. Irish Jem, the Ambassador, never goes to bed but he blesses Rush, the farmer; and many's the time he's told me we should never have such another windfall as that. But I told him not to despair; 'there's a good time coming, boys,' says I; and sure enough, up comes the Bermondsey tragedy. We might have done very well, indeed, out of the Mannings, but there was too many examinations for it to be any great account to us. I've been away with the Mannings in the country ever since. I've been through Hertfordshire, Cambridgeshire, and Suffolk, along with George Frederick Manning and his wife — travelled from 800 to 1,000 miles with 'em; but I could have done much better if I had stopped in London. Every day I was anxiously looking for a confession from Mrs. Manning. All I wanted was for her to clear her conscience afore she left this here whale of tears (that's what I always calls it in the patter); and when I read in the papers (mind, they was none of my own) that her last words on the brink of eternity was, 'I've nothing to say to you, Mr. Rowe, but to thank you for your kindness,' I guv her up entirely — had completely done with her. In course the public looks to us for the last words of all monsters in human form; and as for Mrs. Manning's, they were not worth the printing. The papers are paid for," continued the man, "according to their size." The quarter-sheets are 3d. a quire of twenty-six, half-sheets are 6d., whole sheets 1s. Those that are illustrated are 2d. more per quire than those that are plain. The books — which never exceed eight pages (unless ordered) — are 4s. a gross. The long-songs are 1s. per quire, and they are so arranged that a single sheet may be cut into three. The song-books are all prices, from 3d. a dozen up to 8d. a dozen, and the latter price alone is demanded for Henry Russell's pieces. The papers and books are sold at ½d. or 1d. each, according to the locality. The average earnings of the class are, taking dull and brisk, about 10s. The best hand can make 12s. a week through the whole year, but to do this he must be a "general man," ready to turn his hands to the whole of the branches. If a murder is up, he must work either a "cock" or a conundrum book, or almanacs, according to the season; and when the time for these is past, he must take either to "Sarah Simple" ("she that lived upon the raw potato peelings," says my informant), or the highly amusing legend of the "Fish and the Ring at Stepney;" or else he must work "Anselmo; or the Accursed Hand."

I then sought out a *Standing Patterer,* and found one in a low threepenny lodging-house in Mint-street, in the Borough. Some standing patterers are brought up to the business from childhood. Some take to it through loss of character, or through their inability to obtain a situation from intemperate habits. "It was distress that first drove me to it," said my informant. "I had learnt to make willow bonnets, and that branch of trade went entirely out. So, having a wife and children, I was drove to write out a paper that I called 'The People's Address to the King on the Present State of the Nation.' I got it printed, and took it into the streets and sold it. I did very well with this, and made about 5s. a day at it while it lasted. I never was brought up to any mechanical trade. My father was a clergyman [here the man burst out crying]. It breaks my heart when I think of it. I have as good a wife as ever lived, and I would give the world to get out of my present life. It would be Heaven to get away from the place where I am. I am obliged to cheer up my spirits. If I was to give way to it, I shouldn't live long. It's like a little hell to be in the place where we live [crying], associated with the ruffians that we are. If I had a friend to help me out of my present situation, I should be a new man, and lead a new life. My distress of mind is awful, but it won't do to show it at my lodgings; they'd only laugh to see me down-hearted; so I keep my trouble all to myself. Oh, I am heartily sick of this street work — the insults I have to put up with — the drunken men swearing at me. Yes, indeed, I am heartily sick of it."

The standing patterers are generally a very drunken and disorderly set. Their earnings are quite uncertain. It depends all upon their gift, I am told: to attract attention is half the business. "The more lies they tell, the more cheek they have got, the better they do." A good day's work is about 1s. "I have taken my 5s. (said my informant); but 'paper' selling now isn't half so good as it used to be. People haven't got the money to lay out; for it all depends with the working man. The least we make in a day is upon an average sixpence; but taking the good and bad together, I should say we take about 2s. a day, or 10s. a week. I know there's some get more than that, but then there's many take less. Lately, I know, I haven't taken 9s. a week myself, and people reckon me one of the best patterers in the trade. I'm reckoned to have the gift — that is, the gift of the gab. I never works a last dying speech on any other than the day of the execution — all the edge is taken off of it after that. The last dying speeches and executions are all printed the day before. They're always done on the Sunday, if the murderers are to be hung on the Monday. I've been and got them myself on the Sunday night, over and over again. The flying stationers goes with the papers in their pockets, and stand under the drop, and as soon as ever it falls, and long before the breath is out of the body, they begin bawling out, 'Here is printed and published the last dying speech and confession of George Frederick Manning, who was executed this morning at Horsemonger-lane Gaol, for the murder of Mr. Patrick O'Connor, at Minver-place, Bermondsey,' and they dress it up just as they think will tell best — tell the biggest lies," says my informant, "that they think of — say the man made a full confession, when may be he never said a word; and there is not a syllable in the paper. 'Here you have also an exact likeness,' they say, 'of the murderer, taken at the bar of the Old Bailey!' when all the time it is an old wood-cut that's been used for every criminal for the last forty years. I know the likeness that was given of Hocker was the one that was given for Fauntleroy; and the wood-cut of Tawell was one that was given for the Quaker that had been hanged for forgery twenty years before. Thurtell's likeness was done expressly for the 'papers;' and the Mannings' and Rush's likeness too. The murders are bought by men, women, and children. Many of the tradespeople bought a great many of this last affair of the Mannings. I went down to Deptford with mine, and did uncommonly well with 'em. I sold all off. Gentlefolks won't

have anything to do with murders sold in the street; they've got
other ways of seeing all about it. We lay on the horrors, and
picture them in the highest colours we can. We don't care what's
in the 'papers' in our hands. All we want to do is to sell 'em;
and the more horrible we make the affairs, the more sale we have.
We do very well with 'love-letters.' They are 'cocks;' that is, they
are all fictitious. We give it out that they are from a tradesman
in the neighbourhood, not a hundred yards from where we are
a-standing. Sometimes we say it's a well-known sporting butcher;
sometimes it's a highly respectable publican — just as it will suit
the tastes of the neighbourhood. I got my living round Cornwall
for one twelvemonth with nothing else than a love-letter. It was
headed, 'A curious and laughable love-letter and puzzle, sent by a
sporting gentleman to Miss H—s—m, in *this* neighbourhood;' that
suits any place that I may chance to be in; but I always patter the
name of the street or village where I may be. This letter, I say, is
so worded, that had it fallen into the hands of her mamma or
papa, they could not have told what it meant; but the young lady,
having so much wit, found out its true meaning, and sent him an
answer in the same manner. You have here, we say, the number
of the house, the name of the place where she lives (there is nothing of the kind, of course), and the initials of all the parties concerned. We dare not give the real names in full, we tell them;
indeed, we do all we can to get up the people's curiosity. I did very
well with the 'Burning of the House of Commons.' I happened
by accident to put my pipe into my pocket amongst some of my
papers, and burnt them. Then, not knowing how to get rid of them,
I got a few straws. I told the people that my burnt papers were
parliamentary documents that had been rescued from the flames,
and that, as I dare not sell them, I would let them have a straw
for a penny, and give them one of the papers. By this trick I got
rid of my stock twice as fast, and got double the price that I
should have done. The papers had nothing at all to do with the
House of Commons. Some was 'Death and the Lady,' and 'Death
and the Gentleman,' and others were the 'Political Catechism,'
and 365 lies, Scotch, English, and Irish, and each lie as big round
as St. Paul's. We don't care what there is in the papers, so long
as we can sell them. I remember a party named Jack Straw, who
laid a wager, for half a gallon of beer, that he'd bring home the
money for two dozen blank papers in one hour's time. He went out
into the Old-street-road, and began a patter about the political
affairs of the nation, and Sir Robert Peel, and the Duke of
Wellington, telling the public that he dared not sell his papers,

they were treasonable; so he gave them with a straw — that he
sold for one penny. In less than the hour he was sold clean out,
and returned and drank the beer. The chief things that I work are
quarter-sheets of recitations and dialogues. One is 'Good Advice
to Young Men on Choosing their Wives.' I have done exceedingly
well with that — it's a good moral thing. Another is the
'Drunkard's Catechism;' another is 'The Rent-day, or the Landlord gathering his Rents.' This is a dialogue between the landlord
and his tenant, beginning with 'Good morning, Mrs. Longface;
have you got my rent ready ma'am?' The next one is 'The Adven-
tures of Larry O'Flinn.' This is a comic story, and a very good
got-up thing. Another is 'A Hint to Husbands and Wives;' and
'a pack of cards turned into a Bible, a Prayer-book, and an
almanac.' These cards belonged to Richard Middleton, of the 60th
regiment of foot, who was taken a prisoner for playing at cards
in church during divine service. But the best I do is 'the remarkable dream of a young man of loose character, who had made an
agreement to break into a gentleman's house at twelve at night on
Whitsun Monday, but, owing to a little drink that he took, he had
a remarkable dream, and dreamt he was in hell. The dream had
such influence on his mind that he refused to meet his comrade.
His comrade was taken up for the burglary, found guilty, and
executed for it. This made such an impression on the young man's
mind that he became a reformed character.' There is a very
beautiful description of hell in this paper," said my informant,
"that makes it sell very well among the old women and the apprentice lads, for the young man was an apprentice himself. It's all
in very pretty poetry, and a regular 'cock.' The papers that I
work chiefly are what are called 'the standing patters;' they're all
of 'em stereotype, and some of them a hundred years old. We consider the 'death hunters' are the lowest grade in the trade. We can
make most money of the murders while they last, but they don't
last, and they merely want a good pair of lungs to get them off.
But it's not everyone can work the standing patters. I believe
there's only another man in London can do 'em beside me. It's too
much for the common sort of flying stationers — it requires the
gift of the gab. Many persons I've seen try at it and fail. One old
man I knew tried the 'Drunkard's Catechism' and the 'Soldier's
Prayer-book and Bible.' He could manage to patter these because
they'll almost work themselves; but 'Old Mother Clifton' he broke
down in. I heard him do it in Sun-street and in the Blackfriars-
road; but it was such a dreadful failure — he couldn't humour it
a bit — that, thinks I to myself, you'll soon have to give up, and

sure enough he's never been to the printer's since. He'd a very poor audience, chiefly boys and girls, and they were laughing at him because he made so many blunders in it. A man that's never been to school an hour can go and patter a dying speech or a battle between two ladies of fortune — they're what we call running-patters — you're obliged to keep moving on with them. They require no scholarship at all. All you want is to stick a picture on your hat to attract attention, and to make all the noise you can. It's all the same when they does an 'Assassination of Louis Philippe' or a 'Diabolical Attempt on the Life of the Queen' — a good stout pair of lungs and plenty of impudence is all that is required. But to patter 'Bounce, the workhouse beadle, and the examination of the paupers before the Poor-law Commissioners,' takes a good head-piece and great gift of the gab, let me tell you. It's just the same as a play-actor. I can assure you I often feel very nervous. I begin it, and walk miles before I can get confidence in myself to make the attempt. Without confidence, you know, you can't do anything. We buy the papers at 3d. a quire of 26 the quarter-sheets, and 6d. a quire the half-sheets. Those we sell in the streets at 1d. the half-sheets and ½d. the quarter-ones. I got rid of two quire last night. I was up among the gentlemen's servants in Crawford-street, Baker-street, and I had a very good haul out of the grown-up people. Boys won't buy anything but 'Mother Clifton,' and all comical things. But the 'Good Advice to Young Men and Young Women in Choosing Husbands and Wives' tickles the grown-up folks. I cleared 1s. 8d. altogether. I did that from seven o'clock till nine in the evening. It's all chance-work. If it's fine, and I can get a crowd of grown-up people round me, I can do very well, but I can't do anything amongst the boys. There's very little to be done in the daytime. I begin at ten in the day, and stop out till one. After that I starts off again at five, and leaves off about ten at night. Marylebone, Paddington, and Westminster I find the best places. The West-end is very good the early part of the week for anything that's genteel, such as the 'Rich Man and his Wife quarrelling because they have no family.' Our customers there are principally the footmen, the grooms, and the maid-servants. The east end of the town is the best on Friday and Saturday evenings. I very often go to Limehouse on Friday evening. Most part of the dock-men are paid then, and anything comic goes off well among them. On Saturdays I go to the New-cut, Ratcliff-highway, the Brill, and such places. I make mostly 2s. clear on a Saturday night. After nineteen years' experience of the patter and paper line in the streets, I find that a foolish nonsensical thing will sell twice as fast as a good moral sentimental one; and, while it lasts, a good exciting murder will cut out the whole of them. It's the best selling thing of any. I used at one time to patter religious tracts in the street, but I found no encouragement. I did the 'Infidel Blacksmith' — that would not sell. 'What is Happiness? a Dialogue between Ellen and Mary' — that was no go. No more was the 'Sorrows of Seduction.' So I was driven into the comic standing patters."

The *Sellers of Play-bills* require a few more words in the way of description than might be thought necessary. The sellers of play-bills purchase their stock of the wholesale dealers, at 3s. 4d. the hundred. They are the poorest of the poor: after they have had one meal, they do not know how to get another. They reside in the lowest localities. There are as many as 400 engaged in this calling on this side of the water alone. They consist of boys, girls, men, and women. Taking the average of this class, they are the most abandoned and profligate in character. They get, upon the average, cent. per cent. They reckon it a good night to earn 1s. clear. They can earn, upon an average, 3s. per week. They lose sometimes by not selling out their nightly stock. What they have left, they sell for waste paper at 2d. per pound. Christmas, Easter, and Whitsuntide are generally their best times — they will then make 9d. per night clear. Their customers are the pit and box gentry. The printer of the play-bills prints but a certain number, the demand being pretty closely ascertained week by week. These are all sold (by the printer or some person appointed) to the regular customers. If, however, by any contrivance, any "new hand" venture upon the sale of play-bills, he is scouted by the fraternity as an intruder; he is not "free of the company." A lame woman of sixty-eight, who for twelve years has sold play-bills, gave me the following information: —

She commenced selling play-bills at Astley's, and then realised a profit of 4s. per week. When the old Amphitheatre was burnt down, she went to the Victoria, but "business was not what it was." The Victoria is considered one of the most profitable stations for the play-bill seller, the box-keeper there seldom selling any bill in the theatre. "The boxes" more frequently buy them outside. Another reason why "business" is better at the Victoria than elsewhere was represented to me, by a person familiar with the theatres, to be this: Many go to the Victoria who cannot read, or who can read but imperfectly, and they love to parade the consulting of a play-bill! The bills cost the vendors 6d. for 13, the general decline in prices having affected them, for they used to be but 12 for 6d. The profits of play-bill selling, according to concurrent testimony, are 3s. a week now that the theatres are open generally. When some are closed, these dealers are driven to other theatres, and as the demand is necessarily limited, a super-flux of sellers affects the profits, and 2s. 6d. is then considered a good week's work. At the Victoria, the sellers are two old women (each a widow for many years), two young men, and from two to four and sometimes six children. The old women "fell into the business" — to use the words of one of them — as successors by virtue of their predecessors' leave, who had to relinquish their post from sickness. The children are generally connected with the older dealers. The young men had been in this business from boyhood; some sticking to the practice of their childhood unto manhood, or towards old age. The number at the Victoria is about the average at the other theatres. The youths who have been in the trade from childhood are generally those who run recklessly by the side of cabs and carriages. One of these youths said to me, when I spoke of the danger incurred, "The cabman knows how to do it, sir, when I runs and patters; and so does his hoss." I did not bear of *one* person who had been in any way connected with the stage, even as a supernumerary,, resorting to play-bill selling when he did not earn a shilling a week within the walls of a theatre. These bill sellers confine themselves, as far as I could ascertain, to that particular trade. The youths say that they sometimes get a job in errand-going in the daytime, and the old men and women generally say they can do nothing else. As a body, these people know and care little or nothing of the contents of the bill they sell. Not one of all I talked to was familiar with the names of actors or authors, and many could not read. I have spoken hitherto of the dealers on the Surrey side of the water. I found their statements, however, fully confirmed by the Middlesex play-bill sellers, but they com-plained more of encroachments by people "who had no business there." Sometimes even, if the demand seemed to justify it, an unauthorised bill has been printed, and sold by newcomers; but this happens rarely.

The *Wall Song-sellers* (displaying their stock against any dead wall, but attached to boards, and sometimes on a sort of stall) so far form a class that they are not migratory. Some continue many years on the same spot, and as they are diminishing — for the alterations in the streets sweep away many of the old stands, and new ones are rarely allowed — these people may be classed among the disappearing street-aborigines. I should rank the average earnings of those at the best stands, who unite the sale of a few

old books, etc., with their ballads, at 10s. weekly; some inferior
stations earn no more than 5s. Among the best-accustomed stands
are some in Tottenham-court-road, the New-road, the City-road,
near the Vinegar-works, Oxford-street, the Westminster-road,
Shoreditch, near the Eastern Counties station, and other places.
I give the information as closely as possible, which was supplied
to me by one of the most communicative I met with: — "I'm 49.
I've no children, thank God, but a daughter, who is 18, and no
incumbrance to me, as she is in a 'house of business;' and as she
has been there nine years, her character can't be so very bad.
(This was said heartily.) I worked 22 years with a great sculptor
as a marble polisher, and besides that I used to run errands for
him, and was a sort of porter, like, to him. I couldn't get any more
work, because he hadn't no more marble work to do, so I went
in this line. It cost me £2 10s. to stock my stall, and get all together
comfortable. I got leave to stand here (against the wall) from the
landlord. The policemen can't touch *us* if we don't hawk things
about the streets. I sell ballads and manuscript music (beautifully
done these music sheets were), which is 'transposed' (so he worded
it) from the nigger songs. There's two does them for me. They're
transposed for the violin. One that does them is a musicianer, who
plays outside public-houses, and makes half his living by this;
but I think his daughter does most of it. I don't know what she
is, nor what she can make a week by it. I buy my ballads for 2d.
a dozen; but them that buys them by the dozen quires gets 'em
for 1½d. — and, yes, as low as 1d. a dozen; that's 2d. a quire.
I don't buy 'em all of one man. I has to go sometimes of a morning from Clerkenwell to Hoxton, and from Hoxton to Holywell-
street. Then to 'The Dials.' Most of the printers live there. Business
is not good. I don't make sometimes 9d. or 10d. all day. The most
I have ever taken of a day was 5s.; of this, perhaps, half was
profit. I sell my ballads at a halfpenny, and, when I can get it, a
penny a piece. But then I sell books when I pick 'em up cheap,
and prints — not in an umbrella, to be sure not. The best time for
my trade is a month before and a month after Christmas. I sometimes get a job in my own line — that's the marble polishing — but
that's very seldom. But I've got a good *karacter*, thank God; and
if there was work to do I should get employment; but there ain't
no marble work done now. Do I yarn a pound a week? Lor' bless
you, no. Nor 15s. nor 12s. I don't yarn, one week with another,
nor 10s. My wife don't yarn nothing. She used to go out charring,
but she can't now. I am at my stall at nine in the morning, and
sometimes I have walked five or six miles to buy my 'pubs' before

it. I stop till ten at night. But the wet days is the ruin of us. Such a day as yesterday I didn't take (not make) as much as would pay for a pint of beer and a mouthful of bread and cheese. My rent's 2s. 3d. a week for one room, and I've got my own bits of sticks there. I've always kept them, thank God!" "Do you know anything about those who sing their songs as well as sell them?" I asked. "No, sir, not I. I ain't got nothing to do with that lot. They're travellers, or anythink. Those are the ones that cry the murders about, and sing the flash songs in the 'publics.' They're all travellers. You may see a many of 'em in the Dials a-selling onions, and some goes in Tottenham-court-road on a Saturday night — but they're all travellers." For "travellers" he seemed to entertain a thorough scorn. Generally, they know nothing of the character of the songs they sell, taking the printer's word, when they lay in a new stock, as to "what was going." These wall song-sellers consider that they have a property in their stands, to be sold or bequeathed. A few have sold ballads all their lives. Some, like my informant, have adopted the business on the failure of others. None could tell me of any especial ballad having had a very great and continued sale. The most popular comic songs are not sold so abundantly as some others, because, as I was told, boys soon picked them up by heart, hearing them so often; and so don't buy them. Neither was the best demand for nigger songs, nor for what they called "flash ditties," but for ballads, such as "A Life on the Ocean Wave," "I'm Afloat," "There's a Good Time Coming," "Farewell to the Mountain," etc., etc. Three-fourths of the customers of the man whose statements I have given were, he told me, boys, who cut them out, stick them with paste into books, and sing them at sing-songs. As a rule, the ballads are wretchedly printed, and some of them are adorned with head or tail pieces, which are, with the rarest exception, singularly inappropriate. One old man calculated that there were not fifty of those street stores of songs now in London. He could remember three times as many.

The *Hare and Rabbit Skin Buyers* are the class who go round purchasing the skins of those animals from the servants of the wealthy, and — but to a small extent — from the wives of little tradesmen or artisans. With some of these tradesmen or artisans, rabbits, I am told, have become a more frequent fare than they were; but they are generally bought skinned, or, if bought whole, the shopkeeper will skin the animal, receiving the skin for his trouble. These tradesmen of course dispose of the skins wholesale, and were described to me by a very old man, who hobbles about buying hare-skins, as "spoiling business — it was different in his time." I will now give the narrative of a woman upwards of fifty, who has been from her childhood in this trade, as was her mother. Her husband — who seemed uncertain about his age, except that he was rather older than his wife — had been all his life a *street seller of hearthstones,* and a *field catcher of birds.* They have been married thirty-one years, and reside in the garret of a house in a street off Drury-lane — a small room, not by any means to be called filthy, but with a close smell about it. The room cannot be described as unfurnished — it is, in fact, crowded. There are bird-cages, with and without birds (the birds looked brisk and healthy), over what *was* a bed; but the bed had been sold to pay the rent, and a month's rent was again in arrear; and there were bird-cages on the wall by the door, and bird-cages over the mantelshelf. There was furniture, too, and crockery; and a vile oil painting of "still life;" but an eye used to the furniture in the rooms of the poor could at once perceive that there was not *one* article which could be sold to a broker or marine-store dealer, or pledged at a pawnshop. I will, in her own words, give the account I received from the wife: — "I've sold hare-skins all my life, sir, and was born in London; but when hare-skins isn't in, I *sells flowers.* I goes about now for my skins every day, wet or dry, and all day long — that is, till it's dark. Today (Wednesday) I've not laid out a penny, but then it's such a day for rain. I reckon that if I gets hold of eighteen hare and rabbit skins in a day, that is my greatest day's work. I gives 2d. for good hare's, what's not riddled much, and sells them all for 2½d. I sells them to a Jew, sir. Oh, yes, Jews gives us better prices than Christians, and buys readier. Last week I sold all I bought for 3s. 6d. I have taken some weeks as much as 8s. for what I picked up, and if I could get that every week I should think myself a lady. The profit left me a clear half-crown. There's no difference in any perticler year — only that things gets worse. The game laws hasn't made no difference in my trade. Indeed, I can't say I know anything about the game laws, or hears anything consarning 'em. I goes along the squares and streets. I buys most at gentlemen's houses. We never calls at hotels. The servants, and the women that chars, and washes, and jobs, manages it there. Hare-skins is in — leastways I c'lects them — from September to the end of March, when hares, they says, goes mad. I can't say what I makes one week with another — perhaps eighteen-pence may be clear. In the summer I sells flowers. My customers knows good flowers, and so I doesn't buy them at Common-garden, but goes and gets them fresh from the gardens they're grown in. On my best days I takes 12s. I have taken 15s.; that (15s.) leaves a profit of 5s. I sells them in the squares; goes only two days a week, and has a connection. The summer helps the winter. The flowers is made up in 6d. and 1s. posies. I dares say they're taken to the theatre by the ladies. I've heard so; but I never was in the theatre in my life myself. My flowers is wiolets — no, sir, not primroses, them's reckoned wulgar — helli-trops, carnations, pinks, and roses. After flowers, I goes a-hopping; can then earn 1s. or 1s. 6d. a day, according to crops and times; but that only for a short time; and there's goings and comings back to pay. Thank God, I've no children — only a nephew what strives as we strives."

The *Flower Girls* are not a very numerous class. It is supposed that they do not exceed 200. They are generally young girls from 14 to 20 years old. Some of them are orphans, and some are the children of poor parents, who send them out into the streets to earn a few pence by the sale of flowers. The flower season is prin-cipally in the spring and summer time. It commences mostly with wall-flowers, and ends with lavender. Some few of the street vendors continue the business through the winter, when they sell violets and dry flowers. The flowers are purchased principally at Covent-garden market. The girls visit the market about six o'clock, and buy generally from 6d. to 1s. worth of whatever may be in season. On Saturday they frequently lay out 2s. 6d. if they have so much. Sometimes the "stock-money" is given to them by their parents; and those who cannot obtain it in this way borrow "a trifle" of some friend. One girl whom I saw told me that when-ever her father was unable to give her any money to buy her flowers with, she got her stock-money of a washerwoman, who lived next door to her parents; but the woman never expected anything for the loan of the sum, which was generally either nine-pence or a shilling. This money she used to return when she came home from her day's work, and if the woman had as much still in her possession she used to re-lend it to her the next morning. The fathers of the flower girls are mostly labouring men, frequently porters in the market, and the mothers take in needle-work. They are in general persons of large families. The parents of my informant, who was a young girl 18 years of age, had as many as seven children, five being younger than herself. The flowers are bought in large bunches, or else (as in the case of dry flowers) by the ounce. For wall-flowers, heartsease, and violets they usually pay 1d. the bunch; for sweet peas, 1½d.; for forget-me-nots the cost price is from 1½d. to 2½d. the bunch; dahlias are

2d. and 2½d.; pinks are 3d.; China roses from 1d. to 2d.; and moss roses from 2½d. to 4d.; while lavender costs 3d. and 4d. Dry flowers are 2d. the ounce. The bunches, after they are bought by the girls, are by some taken home, and, being untied, are made up into smaller lots. One market bunch they usually convert into six of such a size as they sell in the streets at 1d. or ½d. each. They generally regulate the size of the bunches so that they can clear about 9d. out of every shilling they take. Many girls sit on the step of a door, and tie up their bunches in the street. They generally go towards the West-end to sell them. A few go to the City, but not many. Their customers are mostly ladies and gentlemen passing by in the street. The working classes seldom or never buy of them; nor do the girls frequently dispose of their flowers to the inmates of houses. The best places for the sale of flowers are the public fashionable thoroughfares, such as Regent-street, Portland-place, Oxford-street, Piccadilly, Bond-street, and Pall-mall. A few are sold in the Strand, and some through the other parts of London. The flower girl commences business about ten o'clock in the morning. The bunches having been tied up, and occasionally done round with paper, are placed in an arm-basket, and carried into some public thoroughfare, the girl crying as she goes, "Handsome flowers, a penny a paper!" or "Two bunches a penny, sweet wall-flowers!" or "Four bunches a penny, blooming lavender!" or "Handsome moss roses, ½d. each!" according to the description of flower in season. They return home about three in the afternoon. If the girls have any of their stock remaining, they go out again in the evening about six, and come back at ten, and occasionally as late as twelve o'clock at night. The best business days are Tuesdays, Thursdays, and Saturdays, these being market-days. On these occasions the flower girls will earn sometimes as much as 2s. and 2s. 6d. clear, and sometimes only 9d. On a wet day, I am told, they seldom earn more than 6d. On the Mondays, Wednesdays, and Fridays they take scarcely any money at all. Occasionally they clear from 7d. to 8d., and sometimes only 3d. or 4d. But Saturday, they say, is the best day of all; then they frequently gain from 3s. to 4s., and sometimes their profit is as much as 5s. But they get thus much only in the summer-time. In the winter they can earn scarcely anything by the sale of the dry flowers. They do a little better, I am told, with their violets, but even these will not afford them a subsistence. Most of the flower girls take to selling other articles after the summer. Some deal in apples and oranges, and others in combs, or stay-laces, or cedar pencils. Upon an average the earnings of the girls appear to be about 5s. a week in the summer and 2s. 6d. a week in the winter time from the sale of flowers.

The girls are generally of an immoral character. Several of them are sent out by their parents to make out a livelihood by prostitution: indeed from all I can learn, the sale of flowers in the streets is frequently, if not generally, resorted to merely as a cover for purposes of the vilest kind. One of this class, whom I saw, had lately come out of prison. She is not nineteen years old, and was sentenced about a twelvemonth ago to three months' imprisonment with hard labour, "for heaving her shoe," as she says, "at the Lord Mayor." This she did, she tells me, to get a comfortable lodging, for she was tired of being about the streets. After this she was locked up for breaking the lamps in the street. Her motive for this was a belief that by committing some such act she might be able to get into an asylum for females. She was sent out into the streets by her father and mother, at the age of nine, to sell flowers. Her father used to supply her with the money to buy the flowers, and she used to take the proceeds of the day's work home to her parents. She used to be out in the streets frequently till past midnight, and seldom or never got home before nine at night. She used to associate only with flower-girls of loose character. The result may be imagined. At length she made a regular habit of always remaining from home till twelve at night, and giving the money that she got by prostitution to her mother, and occasionally to her father. She cannot state positively that her parents were aware of the manner in which she got the money that she took home to them. She supposes that they must have imagined what her practices were, because the sums she used to give them every night were much larger than she could possibly have got by the sale of flowers. "When I was thirteen years of age," she says, "a young girl that used to keep company with me told my father what I was in the habit of doing. He scolded me for it a little, but he did not take me away from the streets. He sent me out the next day as usual, and didn't say anything to me about coming home early." A few months after this he used to tell her to go into the streets at night and meet with gentlemen, and sent her out regularly every evening at dusk to do so. He used to give her no supper if she didn't bring home a good bit of money. Her father and mother used to do little or no work all this while. They lived on what she brought home. At 13 years old she was sent to prison for selling combs in the street (it was winter, and there were no flowers to be had). She was incarcerated fourteen days, and when liberated she returned to her former practices. The very night that she came home from gaol her father sent her out in the streets again. She continued in this state, her father and mother living upon her prostitution, until about nine months ago, when her father turned her out of his house because she couldn't bring home money enough to him. She then went into Kent, hop-picking, and there she fell in with a beggar, who accosted her while she was sitting under a tree. He said, "You have got a very bad pair of shoes on; come with me, and you shall have some better ones." She consented, and walked with him into the village close by, where they stood out in the middle of the streets, and the man began addressing the people, saying, "My kind good Christians, me and my poor wife here is ashamed to appear before you in the state we are." She remained with this person all the winter, and travelled with him through the country, begging their way. He was a regular beggar by trade. In the spring she returned to the flower-selling, but scarcely got any money either by that or other means. At last she grew desperate, and wanted to get back to prison. She broke the lamps outside the Mansion-house, and was sentenced to fourteen days' imprisonment. She has been out of prison nearly three weeks, and is now in training to go into an asylum. She is sick and tired, she says, of her life.

The *Rag-Gatherers* and *Bone-Pickers,* and *"Pure" Collectors,* are different names for one and the same class. Of bone-pickers, rag-gatherers, and pure collectors, it is considered that there are 800 to 1,000 resident in London. My informant judges, he says, from the number he sees about the streets every morning. One-half of the above number he thinks are to be found in the low lodging-houses of London, and the rest dwell in wretched, half-furnished rooms. In no case has a bone-grubber ever been known to rent even the smallest house for himself. Upon an average, he thinks there must be at least two of the class living at each of the low lodging-houses. This would give 442 as the number there located (the Government returns estimate the number of mendicants' lodging-houses in London at 221); so that, doubling this, we have 884 as the gross number of individuals engaged in this calling — a conclusion which agrees closely with my informant's previous statement. The "pure" collectors have generally been country labourers that have come up to London in the winter time to avail themselves of the shelter of the night asylums or refuges for the destitute (these places are usually called "straw-yards" by the poor). They walk up to London, not to look for work, but because they hear that they can have a nightly lodging, and bread night and morning, for nothing, during the winter months; and they know that if they remain in the country they must go from one union to another; and so travel from ten to fifteen miles per day, for they cannot sleep in the casual wards *more* than one night at a time. There is scarcely any work to be obtained in the country during the winter by the labourers who have gone there to get employment in the summer; so that as soon as the harvest and potato-getting is over, the country labourers make their way back to the metropolis. The country labourers here alluded to belong especially to the class called "trampers." They have no fixed place of residence, and are wandering about the whole of the summer, in small bands of two or three, through the country. They start off, I am told, as soon as the "straw-yards" close, which is generally at the beginning of April, and either beg or work their way through the villages, sleeping in the casual wards of the unions on their way. The bone-pickers belong mostly to this class. The "pure" pickers, however (or those who make a living by collecting dogs' dung in the streets), are generally to be found in London all the year round, with the exception of the hay season, the corn harvest, and hop-picking time, when a very large portion leave London. The bone-pickers who do not belong to the class of country labourers have been either navvies, or men that have not been able to obtain employment, and have been driven to it by necessity, like myself (said my informant), merely as a means of obtaining a little bread for the time being, without any intention of pursuing the calling regularly. When they once begin it they cannot leave it, for at least they can make certain of getting a few halfpence by it, and they cannot afford the time to look after other employment. There is no class of men getting their living in the streets that work half so hard as the bone-pickers. They walk from twenty to thirty miles each day, with a quarter to a half hundred-weight on their backs. A few of the bone-pickers and rag-gatherers are old men and women, or very young children, who have no other means of living. In the summer time the bone-pickers rise at two in the morning, and sometimes earlier. It is not quite light at this hour, but bones and rags they can discover before daybreak. They go to different parts of London. In the neighbourhood of Petticoat-lane and Rag-fair they are more numerous than elsewhere, the Jews having so many rags to throw out. But they abound in every part of London and the suburbs. The bone-picker, immediately on quitting the lodging-house, starts off to his particular district. This will sometimes be from four to five miles distant. Some districts will lie as far as Peckham, Clapham, Hammersmith, Hampstead, Bow, Stratford, and indeed all parts within about five miles of London. The bone-grubber strives to reach his district, wherever it may lie, before any others of the same class can go over the ground. It is important that he should be *first* of all on the spot. Here he generally seeks out the narrow back streets, where dust and refuse are thrown, or where any dustbins are accessible. The bone-picker has generally a bag on his back, and a stick in his hand. With this stick he turns over the different heaps of ashes or dust that are thrown out of the houses, and rakes among the dustbins to see if they contain anything that is saleable to the rag and bone shop, or marine-store dealer. The articles for which he chiefly searches are rags and bones — rags he prefers of the two; but waste metal, such as bits of lead, pewter, copper, brass, or old iron, he prizes above all. Whatever he meets with that he knows to be any way saleable, he puts into the bag at his back. He often finds large lumps of bread, which have been thrown out as waste by the servants. These constitute the morning meal of most of the class. Occasionally the housekeepers on their way will give them a few bones, upon which there is a little meat remaining. My informant a few days ago had a large rump-of-beef bone given to him, upon which there was not less than one pound of good meat. Sometimes they will pick up a stray sixpence or a shilling that has been dropped in the street. "The handkerchief I have round my neck," said my informant, "I picked up, with a shilling in the corner. The greatest prize I ever picked up was the brass cap of the nave of a coach-wheel, and I *did* once find a quarter of a pound of tobacco in Sun-street, Bishopsgate. The best bit of luck of all that I ever had was finding a cheque for £12 15s., lying in the gateway of the mourning-coachyard in Titchborne-street, Haymarket. I was going to light my pipe with it; indeed I picked it up for that purpose, and then saw it was a cheque. It was on the London and County Bank, 21 Lombard-street. I took it there, and got 10s. for finding it. I went there in my rags, as I am now, and the cashier stared a bit at me. The cheque was drawn by a Mr. Knill, and payable to a Mr. Cox. I *did* think I should have got the odd 15s." It generally takes the bone-picker from seven to nine hours to go over his rounds. In the summer he gets home about eleven in the day, and in the winter about one or two. On his return home he proceeds to sort the contents of his bag. He separates the rags from the bones, and these again from the old metal (if he is lucky enough to have found any). He divides the rags into various lots, according as they are white or coloured; and if he has picked up any pieces of canvas or sacking, this he makes up into a separate parcel. When he has done this, he takes them all to the marine-store shop, and realises upon them whatever they may be worth. For the white rags he gets from 2d. to 3d. per pound, according as they are clean or soiled. The white rags are very difficult to be found; they are mostly very dirty, and are sold with the coloured ones, at the rate of about five pounds for 2d. The bones are usually sold with the coloured rags at one and the same price. For fragments of canvas or sacking he gets about ¾d. a pound, and old brass, copper, and pewter about 4d., and old iron ¾d. per pound. The bone-grubber thinks he has done an excellent day's work if he can earn 8d., and some of them, especially the very old and very young, do not get more than 2d. to 4d. a day. To get 10d. in the day, at the present price of rags and bones, he must be remarkably active — and lucky too — adds my informant. He must be out two hours at least before broad daylight, and not return till two in the afternoon. The average amount of earnings, I am told, varies from about 4d. to 6d. per day, or from 2s. 6d. to 3s. a week. The highest price that a man, the most active and persevering at the business, can earn in one week is about 5s. But this could only be done with great good fortune and industry, and the usual amount is about half that sum. In bad weather they cannot do so well, because the rags are wet, and then they can't sell them. Some take them home and wash and dry them, but the generality pick up only bones in wet weather. The state of the shoes of the rag and bone-picker is most important to the pursuit of his calling. If he is well shod, he can get quickly over the ground; but he is frequently lamed and unable to make any progress from the blisters or gashes on his feet, occasioned by the want of proper shoes.

Some of the class above described collect only bones and rags, but others pick up bones, rags, and what is called "pure" — or dogs' dung — as well. Their habits and mode of proceeding are nearly similar to the rag and bone-pickers proper, with the exception that the latter is a regular trade. The parties following it pick up but few rags or bones, and only such as are of the best quality. What they look for most is the "pure." Some of the regular collectors of this article have been mechanics, and others small tradesmen. They are a superior class of persons to the mere rag and bone-pickers, and those who have a good connection and the right of cleansing certain kennels obtain a very fair living at it, earning from 10s. to 15s. a week. These, however, are very few. The majority have to seek the article solely in the streets, and by such means they can obtain only from 6s. to 10s. a week. The average weekly earnings of this class are thought to be between 7s. and 8s.

The "pure" gatherer, after he has been his rounds, makes the best of his way to some tanner in Bermondsey, to whom he is in the habit of selling the article. He sells it to the tanner by the stable bucketful, and gets from 8d. to 10d. per bucket for it. It is used for the purpose of cleansing sheep and calf skins after they are taken out of the "lime-pits." A man generally picks up about a bucketful in the course of the day. My informant earned last week 5s. 2d., and the week before about 6s.; and these he believes to be a fair sample of the earnings of the class. He has been at the calling about four years. He was originally in the Manchester cotton trade, and held a lucrative situation in a large country establishment. His salary one year exceeded £250, and his regular income was £150. This, he says, he lost through drink and neglect. His master was exceedingly kind to him, and has even assisted him since he left his employ. He bore with him patiently for many years; but the love of drink was so strong upon him that it was impossible for his master to keep him any longer. He has often been drunk for three months together, and he is now so reduced that he is ashamed to be seen. When at his master's, he tells me that it was his duty to carve and help the other assistants belonging to the establishment, and that his hand used to shake so violently that he has been ashamed to lift the gravy spoon. At breakfast he has frequently waited till all the young men had left the table, before he ventured to taste his tea; and immediately, when he was alone, he has bent his head down to his cup to drink, being utterly incapable of raising it to his lips. He says he is a living example of the degrading influence of drink. All his friends have deserted him. He has suffered enough, he tells me, to make him give it up.

Mudlarks are boys who roam about the sides of the river at low tide, to pick up coals, bits of iron, rope, bones, and copper nails that fall while a ship is being repaired. They are at work sometimes early in the morning, and sometimes late in the afternoon, according to tide. They usually work from six to seven hours per day. My informant, a quick intelligent little fellow, who has been at the business three years, tells me the reason they take to mudlarking, is that their clothes are too bad to look for anything better, and that they are nearly all fatherless, and their mothers are too poor to keep them; so they take to it because they have nothing else to do. This boy works with about twenty to thirty mudlarks every day, and they may be seen, he tell me, at daybreak, very often, with their trousers tucked up, groping about, and picking out the pieces of coal from the mud. They go into the river up to their knees, and in searching the mud they very often run pieces of glass and long nails into their feet. When this is the case, they go home and dress the wounds, and return directly, for, should the tide come up without their finding anything, they must starve that day. At first it is a difficult matter to stand in the mud, and he has known many young beginners fall in. The coals the mudlark finds he sells to the poor people in the neighbourhood at a penny the "pot," the weight of which is 14 lb. The iron, bones, rope, and copper nails he sells to the rag shops. They sell the iron 5 lb. for a penny, the bones 3 lb. for one penny, rope a halfpenny per pound wet, and three farthings dry. The copper nails fetch four-pence per pound, but they are very difficult to find, for the mudlark is not allowed to go near a vessel that is being coppered (for fear of their stealing the copper), and it is only when a ship has left the docks that the nails are to be had. They often pick up tools — such as saws, hammers, etc. — in the mud; these they either give to the seamen for biscuits and beef, or sell to the shops for a few half-pence. They earn from 2½d. to 8d. per day, but 8d. they consider a very good day's work, and they seldom make it; their average earnings are three-pence a day. After they leave the river they go home and scrape their trousers, and make themselves as tidy as possible; they then go into the streets and make a little by holding gentlemen's horses, or opening cab-doors. In the evening they mostly go to the ragged schools. My informant and his sister keep their mother — the boy by mudlarking, the girl by selling fish. The poor little fellow owes 5s. rent; he has a suit of clothes and a pair of boots in pawn for 4s.; if he could get them out he would be enabled to find something better to do.

THE OPERATIVE TAILORS
LETTER XVI
Tuesday, December 11, 1849

Having given a full account of the earnings and condition of the various classes of hucksters in London, I now return to consider the state and income of the artisans.

If we wish to obtain a knowledge of the history and progress of the slop-trade, we must first inquire into the nature and characteristics of that art of which it is an inferior variety; and it is with this view that, before investigating the condition of the male slop-worker, I have made it my business to examine into the state of the Operative Tailors of London.

The Tailors, as a body, form a very large proportion of the population of London. Arranging the occupations of the people of the metropolis in the order of the number of individuals belonging to them, we shall find that the tailors stand fourth upon the list. First come the Domestic Servants of London, numbering as many as 168,000 individuals, and constituting about one-twelfth of the whole population of the metropolis. The second in the order of their numbers are the Labourers, who are 50,000 strong. Third in numerical rank stand the Boot and Shoe Makers, mustering upwards of 28,000; and fourth, the Tailors, amounting to 23,517. After them come the Milliners and Dressmakers; and then follow the Commercial Clerks — both of which classes comprised, at the time of taking the last census for London, upwards of 20,000 individuals.

Of the above 23,517 tailors, there are, according to the Post-office Directory, 2,748 in business for themselves. This leaves a total of 20,769 operatives. But several of those whose names are entered in the Directory are also, I am told, working men; that is to say, they act as journeymen as well as work upon their own account. We may therefore fairly estimate the number of operative tailors in the metropolis at not less than 21,000 individuals.

Taking the number of persons in the parish unions as a test of the poverty or competence of the class, I find that tailoring is far from being a pauperising occupation. Of tailors there is, according to the last Government returns, one pauper in every 241 individuals; whereas of hook-and-eye makers, though the whole class consists of only 144 persons, no less than 142 were, at the time of taking the last census, inmates of some parish union. The framework knitters, according to the same report, were in equally indigent circumstances, two out of three being paupers. In the class of merchants, however, there was only one pauper in every 12,000 persons. I subjoin a statement of the number of paupers in each of the classes of which I have already treated; so that the reader may compare them with the tailors, and, by referring to the account I have given of the habits and earnings of the people, be enabled to say how much of the pauperism arises from deficient wages, and how much from those habits of improvidence which are the necessary consequence of uncertainty of employment.

Persons engaged as —   *One Pauper in every*

ABOVE THE AVERAGE

Seamstresses and seamsters	36.1 individuals
Labourers	140.8 ,,
Weavers	141.0 ,,
Stay and corset makers	143.9 ,,
Average of England and Wales	159.5 ,,

BELOW THE AVERAGE

Hawkers, hucksters, and pedlars	179.3 ,,
Tailors and breeches makers	241.2 ,,
Bonnet makers	294.5 ,,
Furriers	363.6 ,,
Milliners and dressmakers	582.4 ,,

Adopting the same means to arrive at an estimate of the moral character of a particular class of persons, I find that at the time of taking the last census there was one in every 340 tailors confined in gaol; whereas, in the class of knitters (the most criminal of all), one in every five individuals was an inmate of a prison; while among stuff manufacturers (which appears to be the least criminal class), there was but one prisoner in every 6,590 persons. I subjoin a comparative table of the criminality of the classes that I have already investigated, together with that of the tailors: —

Persons engaged as —   *One Prisoner in every*
ABOVE THE AVERAGE
Hawkers, hucksters, and pedlars	71.0	individuals
Labourers	120.0	,,
Seamstresses and seamsters	260.0	,,
Weavers	323.8	,,
Tailors and breeches makers	340.4	,,
Stay and corset makers	383.8	,,
Average of England and Wales	718.1	,,

BELOW THE AVERAGE
Bonnet makers	1,001.4	,,
Milliners and dressmakers	1,109.0	,,
Furriers	1,818.0	,,

By the above tables we shall find that, as regards the number of paupers in the trade, the tailors are 81 *below* the average for England and Wales, while, as regards the number of criminals, they are as many as 377 *above* the average. The cause of this excessive criminality I leave the more intelligent of the operatives to discover. What connection it has with the acknowledged intemperance of the class, the defective state of the Government returns unfortunately prevents me from calculating. The causes of crime and poverty are so little studied amongst us, that, with the exception of the trite and useless division of criminals into those who can and those who cannot read and write, we have no means of arriving at any conclusion on the subject.

The tailoring trade is divided by the workmen into "honourable" and "dishonourable." The honourable trade consists of that class who have the garments made on their own premises, at the supposed rate of 6d. per hour; the dishonourable, of those who give the work out to "sweaters," to be done at less than the standard price. The dishonourable part of the trade is again subdivided into the classes belonging to show-shops — that is, such as do a cheap bespoke business — and those belonging to slop-shops, or, in plainer terms, to such as do a cheap ready-made business.

Of the 21,000 working tailors above specified, as resident in London, I should add that there are not above 3,000 belonging to what is called the honourable portion of the trade. The remaining 18,000 are those who are engaged in the cheap, slop, or dishonourable trade; and from the condition of the operatives working at what are called the standard prices, I am satisfied that but little of the crime above enumerated is connected with that class.

The journeymen tailors working for the "honourable" part of the trade are in "union." This "union" consists of six distinct societies, which meet at certain taverns or public-houses at the west end of the town. The number of journeymen at present in union is 3,000. In the year 1821 there were between 5,000 and 6,000. It is supposed that from two to three thousand have left the "honourable" trade and become "sweaters."

Besides the above-mentioned six societies there are four "outstanding houses," as they are termed, which, though not acting in union with the six others, still are regulated by the same laws and conducted upon the same principles. Two of these are foreign societies, and two supply Stultz only with workmen. The number in connection with the four outstanding houses is 400.

The different societies are likewise used as houses of call for the masters. The men belonging to a particular society, who are out of employ, attend the house at the appointed call-times (there are three in the day). A master requiring extra hands directs the captain of the workshop to engage the requisite number. He generally sends to the society of which he is a member, and there the workmen who stand next upon the books are taken on.

The date and purport of the various enactments in connection with the trade I find stated as follows, in a memorial of the operative tailors of London, to the "Right Hon. the Lords of the Privy Council for Trade," in the year 1845: —

"So far back as the 33rd Edward I, the 6th Henry VI, and the 2nd and 3rd Edward VI, the law directed that master tailors residing within the weekly bills of mortality should, under severe penalty, provide on their own premises healthful and commodious apartments wherein to execute to completion the materials entrusted to their skill and honour. From the 7th George I to the 8th George III, chief magistrates were empowered to regulate the place of work, the hours, and wages of journeymen tailors, within the weekly bills of mortality."

"Within these last twelve or fifteen years, however," says a subsequent memorial from the same parties, "the corrupt middle-man system has sprung up amongst us, which is the cause of leaving so many first-rate operatives unemployed the greater part of the year; for when two home workers, by working over-hours and Sabbath-days, perform the work of three men employed on the premises of the master tailor, as intended by the Legislature, it must prove a great grievance to the numerous unemployed, who are compelled in hundreds of instances to make application for parochial relief as well as the other private charities, for themselves and numerous families; a circumstance unknown until the corrupt middle-man system crept amongst us."

"Many of our unemployed," continues the memorial, "are compelled by necessity to make application to this class of middlemen for employment, who practise the most grievous impositions upon the persons employed by them, by reducing their wages and enforcing the truck system, by compelling the men to take their diet with them at whatever price they think proper to charge, though many of those men have large families of their own to support; and frequently by obliging their men to lodge with them."

Up to the year 1834, the 8th of George III ("which," I am told, "regulated the time of labour for tailors at twelve hours per day, with the intent of compelling the masters to get their work done on their premises, as well as of equalising employment, and giving to each operative tailor the opportunity of earning a decent maintenance for himself and his family") was tolerably well adhered to; but at that period the masters gradually infringed the provisions of the act. Sweaters became numerous, and a general strike was the consequence. The strike acted antagonistically to the views of the journeymen tailors; and from that time up to the present, sweaters and underpaid workmen have increased, until the state of trade, as regards the operative tailors, appears to be approaching desperation.

Before entering upon my investigations, I consulted several of the most experienced and intelligent workmen, as to the best means of arriving at a correct opinion respecting the state of the trade. It was agreed among us that, first, with regard to an estimate as to the amount of wages, I should see a hand employed at each of the different branches of the trade. After this I was to be taken to a person who was the captain or leading man of a shop; then to one who, in the technicality of the trade, had a "good chance" of work; and, finally, to one who was only casually employed. It was considered that these classes, taken in connection with the others, would give the public a correct view of the condition, earnings, and opinions of the trade. To prevent the chance of error, however, I begged to be favoured with such accounts of earnings as could be procured from the operatives. This I thought would place me in a fair condition to judge of the incomings and physical condition of the class; but still I was anxious to arrive at something like a criterion of the intellectual, political, and moral character of the people, and I asked to be allowed an interview with such persons as the parties whom I consulted might consider would fairly represent these peculiar features of their class to the world. The results of my inquiry I shall now proceed to lay before the public. Let me, however, first acknowledge the courtesy and consideration with which I was everywhere received; indeed, the operatives generally seemed especially grateful that their "cause" had at length been espoused by the press, and wherever I went I found all ready to give or obtain for me any information I might desire.

The first I saw was a trousers hand.

There are three classes of workmen, said my informant — coat, waistcoat, and trousers hands. The trousers hands are a class by themselves. Occasionally the persons who make the trousers make waistcoats also, and these are called "small workers." But in some shops there are different hands for each different garment. For all garments there is what is termed a "log" — that log is the standard of prices in the trade. Formerly the rate of payment was by the day — 6s. for twelve hours' work; but at the time of the general strike (about 16 or 18 years ago) the masters made out another scale of prices, and changed the mode of payment from day work to piece work. The prices of each garment, as determined by them, were regulated according to the quantity of work in it, and the time that such work would take to do. The workman by this log is still paid at the rate of 6d. per hour, but the time required to make each garment is estimated, and the workmen are paid by the garment rather than by the time. An ordinary pair of gentlemen's trousers, without pockets (such as are known in the trade as plain trousers), are estimated at ten hours' work, and consequently are paid 5s. for. The pockets are calculated at one hour extra, and the price paid for making trousers with them is 6d. more. Straps are reckoned to occupy the workman two hours more, and he therefore receives an extra shilling for the making of such garments as have them. If "faced bottoms" (that is, if lined inside at the bottom with a piece of cloth to make them set well) they are 6d. extra. If the trousers are "fork-lined" it is considered to be a half-hour's work, and is paid for accordingly. If the trousers have "lipe seams" (that is, if they are made with stripes down the side seam), they are paid 9d., and sometimes 1s. extra, according to the work. Regimental trousers, with gold lace or scarlet stripe down the side seams, are paid 2s. as four hours' extra work. If they are for riding trousers, and "strapped" — that is, made with an extra piece of cloth laid over the leg seam, and double-stitched all round — then this additional work is reckoned to occupy the workman six hours more than a plain pair of trousers, and then the price for making such garments is 3s. more than that given for an ordinary pair. This scale of prices is in some establishments written out upon a sheet of paper, and hung up in the workshop, to prevent disputes; or, if not, it is so generally understood, both by the masters and the workmen, that it is seldom or never questioned. If any deviation be made from "the log," it is always agreed upon before the garment is made; but if no such agreement is entered into, the workman charges according to the regular scale. Such garments as are not included in the log are paid for according to the time they take making, and at the rate of 6d. per hour. Trousers are generally very good jobs, because I am told the time they take in doing is reckoned "pretty fairly." By the change from day work to piece work the regular trousers hands suffered scarcely any loss upon the prices of the garment. The time of making was justly reckoned, and the price paid in the regular and "honourable" trade remains about the same. The trousers hands have not suffered so much by the change of payment from day work to piece work as by the prevalence of the system of sweating, which has increased considerably since the alteration in the rate of payment.

Next I visited a coat hand. He lived in a comfortable first-floor, and had invited several fellow-workmen to meet me. He had also obtained for me an account of the earnings of one journeyman for two years. There are generally three hands, he told me, engaged upon a coat. One makes the collar and sleeves, and the two others are engaged each upon one of the fore parts, or right or left side of the coat. The prices paid for making each of these parts of the coat depend upon the quantity of work. These prices are regulated by the log of the shop. There is no general log for the West-end, but each particular house fixes its own price for the different garments to be made; or rather each particular house estimates the time required for making each garment as it thinks fit, and pays at the rate of 6d. an hour for the work. The estimate of the time for making is frequently under, and never over, the hours necessary for doing the work. "In the shop at which I work," said my informant, "a plain dress coat or frock coat is reckoned at two days eight hours' labour. If with silk sides, and stitched with nine rows of stitches, it is calculated at two hours' extra work; if with edging cord along the edges, it is estimated at two hours more; if with cut sides 'rantered' (that is, fine drawn in a peculiar manner, so that the seam may be rendered invisible), one hour extra; if 'unrantered,' half an hour. This estimate as to the time is paid for at the rate of 6d. per hour; that is to say, we receive 16s. for making a plain dress or frock coat. There are other houses, however, in the trade, who are considered equally 'honourable' by the public, but who pay considerably less than the above price." A person who was present at the house of my informant, assured me that the shop for which he worked paid only 15s. 3d. for precisely the same quantity of work as that for which my informant's shop paid 16s.; the amount of work in the coat being estimated by the one master at two days six-and-a-half hours, and at two days eight hours by the other. All agreed that there are many houses in the "honourable" trade who estimate the time even much lower than the above; so that the log, instead of being a general standard, appears to be merely an arbitrary measure as to time. It is generally understood among the workmen who "belong to society" that they are not to work for less than sixpence per hour. The masters are well aware of this, and consequently never offer to pay less, but avail themselves of their privilege of reducing the estimate as to the time of making. If they wish to have a coat at a lower price than is usually paid, they declare that it takes so many hours less to make. The workmen often object to this, and the consequence is, the master seeks out other hands, who are willing to accept the work at the time stated. In the year 1834 the system of payment was changed from day work to piece work. Before that time, each man employed received 6d. per hour for every hour that he was upon the establishment: it mattered not whether the master found him in work or not; he was paid all the same. Since the piece work system, however, men are kept for days upon the establishment without receiving a penny. It is a general rule now throughout the trade for masters to keep more hands than they have employment for, especially in the slack or "vacation," as it is called. The effect of the piece work system has been this, I am told — that the work-man has to work now a day-and-a-half for a day's wages; and that system alone has been instrumental to the reduction of prices. Men have more work to do now to get the same amount of money; and the consequence is, fewer hands are employed, and the surplus workmen offer their labour at a lower price. Again, under the piece work system, work is given out to be done. Hence, the journeyman who takes it home, and gets other hands to do it for him at a lower price than he himself receives, thus becomes changed into a sweater, or middle-man, trading upon the labour of others. Finding that he can get the work done as low as he pleases, by employing women and children upon it, he goes to the master and offers to do it at a lower price than is usually paid for it. Again, the price paid to each particular person is unknown to the other; so that the master, finding that the sweaters can get work done at almost any price, keeps continually cutting down the sum paid for making up the different garments, and then tries to force the regular hands to take the same price. Indeed, this is so frequently the case now in the shops, that I am told that it is the common practice to take off the price paid for some "extra" upon a garment, and to threaten the workmen, if they refuse, to give it out to the sweaters. One master whom I have been told of offered a journeyman certain work to do at a certain price. This the journeyman objected to do, whereupon the master stated "that women did it at a much lower figure." The workman replied, "That to do it and live they were obliged to make up their subsistence-money by prostitution." The answer of the master was, "That he cared nothing how they did it; he had to compete with others." The master, I am informed, bears the character of being a highly religious man.

After this I visited a waistcoat hand. The male waistcoat hands, he told me, are very few, and they are growing fewer every year. In the workshop they are paid by "the log." "The log reckons nine hours for making a single-breasted roll-collar waistcoat, but we cannot do the work that is in them now in less than twelve hours, there are so many extras introduced — such as wadding to pad the breast, back straps, edging, and 'V' cuts, which were all paid for over and above the regular charge till within the last five years, but which are now all included in the price stated by the log. Hence the waistcoats which were originally reckoned at nine hours' work take us now twelve hours to make, and are paid for only at the stated price, viz., 4s. 6d. According to the standard of 6d. per hour, we should get 6s. for the same garment as we now make for 4s. 6d. The extras were gradually reduced." "My master," says my informant, "first objected to pay anything additional for putting on the edging. Then he refused to allow us anything for inserting the wadding in the breast. After this he cut off the extra pay for back straps, telling us that, if we did not consent to this, he would put them all out to be made; and saying that he could get them done much cheaper out of doors. When I first began waistcoat-making I could earn 36s. every week, during the season, with ease; and, indeed, I did as much up to six years ago. But now I must work hard to get 24s. Since the years 1843 and 1844 the prices have been gradually declining, and the waistcoat business getting worse every year for the male hands employed in the workshop; and so I believe it has for everybody outside the shop, excepting the sweaters. What they get, I'm sure I don't know. We never can find out their prices. We only know they get the work done much cheaper than we can do it, for if we murmur in the least at the price paid us, we are told by the master that he can have it made much cheaper out. The reason why they can do this is, because of late years women have been generally employed at the trade. When I first began working at this branch there were but very few females employed in it: a few white waistcoats were given out to them, under the idea that women would make them cleaner than men; and so indeed they can. But since the last five years the sweaters have employed females upon cloth, silk, and satin waistcoats as well, and before that time the idea of a woman making a cloth waistcoat would have been scouted. But since the increase of the puffing and the sweating system, masters and sweaters have sought everywhere for such hands as would do the work below the regular ones. Hence the wife has been made to compete with the husband, and the daughter with the wife: they all learn the waistcoat business, and must all get a living. If the man will not reduce the price of his labour to that of the female, why he must remain unemployed; and if the full-grown woman will not take the work at the same price as the young girl, why she must remain without any. The female hands, I can confidently state, have been sought out and introduced to the business by the sweaters, from a desire on their part continually to ferret out hands who will do the work cheaper than others. The effect that this continual reduction has had upon me is this: Before the year 1844 I could live comfortably, and keep my wife and children (I had five in family) by my own labour. My wife then attended to her domestic and family duties; but since that time, owing to the reduction in prices, she has been compelled to resort to her needle, as well as myself, for her living." (On the table was a bundle of crape and bombazine ready to be made up into a dress.) "I cannot afford now to let her remain idle; that is, if I wish to live, and keep my children out of the streets, and pay my way. My wife's earnings are, upon an average, 8s. per week. She makes dresses. I never would teach her to make waistcoats, because I knew the introduction of female hands had been the ruin of my trade. With the labour of myself and wife now I can only earn 32s. a week, and six years ago I could make my 36s. If I had a daughter I should be obliged to make her work as well, and then probably, with the labour of the three of us, we could make up at the week's end as much money as, up to 1844, I could get by my own single hands. My wife, since she took to dressmaking, has become sickly from over-exertion. Her work, and her domestic and family duties altogether, are too much for her. Last night I was up all night with her, and was compelled to call in a female to attend her as well. The over-exertion now necessary for us to maintain a decent

appearance has so ruined her constitution that she is not the same
woman as she was. In fact, ill as she is, she has been compelled
to rise from her bed to finish a mourning dress against time, and
I myself have been obliged to give her a helping hand, and turn
to at woman's work, in the same manner as the women are turning to at mine. My opinion is that the waistcoat-makers generally
are now unable to support themselves and families by their un-
assisted labour. A number of female hands have been forced into
the trade who otherwise would have been attending to their duties
at home."

I shall now lay before the reader certain accounts of the earnings
of workmen that have been furnished to me, and of which I have
calculated the weekly averages at different periods: —

	1848				1849		
January	£2	5	6		£5	16	6
February	2	15	6		4	6	9
March	3	17	0		6	13	3
April	6	18	6		5	11	9
May	7	6	6		5	12	0
June	7	2	6		6	16	0
July	4	6	0		4	1	4
August	2	15	6		2	7	6
September	4	18	9		2	15	6
October	6	15	0			sick	
November	7	7	6		5	10	9
December	4	16	6			—	

By the above account it will be seen that the gross earnings for
the year 1848 were £61 4s. 9d.; hence the average weekly earnings
were £1 3s. 6d. It will likewise be found that the average weekly
earnings from the beginning of April to the end of June were
£1 12s. 10½d., and that the average weekly earnings from the beginning of Agust to the end of September were 17s. 1½d.

The average weekly earnings from the beginning of April to
the end of June, 1849, were £1 7s. 8d., or 5s. 2½d. per week less
than those of 1848; and the average weekly earnings from the
beginning of August to the end of September, 1849, were 11s. 5¼d.,
or 5s. 8¼d. less than those of 1848.

"The above average may be considered high," says the party
forwarding me the account; "but I think it is a fair estimate of
the wages that may be earned by a steady man in the highest-paid
shops at the west-end of London, when regularly employed. One
great drawback is the extreme irregularity and fluctuation of the
trade, which prevents a working man, in a great measure, from
regulating his expenditure to his income, and is, I firmly believe,

the great cause of much of the dissipation which occurs amongst the trade, it being literally either a 'hunger or a burst' with them."

Another account, extending over a period of 46 weeks, and which consists of the gross earnings of the men in the honourable part of the trade, gives an average of £1 1s. 5½d. received weekly by each workman throughout the whole of that period. The gross earnings were £474 10s. 3d., and the total number of hands employed during the 46 weeks were 442.

By another account I find the weekly earnings to have been £1 6s. 5½d. during the whole of 1848.

I am assured by those who are, and have long been, intimately acquainted with the trade, that the above are far beyond the average earnings of the class. I can only say that I have not selected the cases. The accounts have been forwarded to me, and I give the bare truth.

I was desirous of seeing certain hands whose earnings might be taken as the type of the different classes of workmen in the trade. These, I had been informed, consisted of three distinct varieties: —first, those who are in constant employment at a particular shop as captains; secondly, those who are tolerably well employed during the year, and have the preference for work as leading men in particular shops; thirdly, those who are only casually employed, either in the brisk season, or when there is an extra amount of work to be done. The captains have continual employment, and receive from three shillings to six shillings per week, over and above their own earnings, for the superintendence of the workmen. The leading men are generally employed. They are always connected with the shop, and remain there whether there is work to be done or not. The casual men are such as are taken on from the house of call when there is an extra amount of work to be done. The casual hand is engaged sometimes for two or three days, and sometimes for only two or three hours—to the great accommodation of masters, who are certain of having their work not only done to time, but paid for by the society to which the hands belong, if damaged or spoiled by the workmen.

I consulted several gentlemen connected with the trade as to a person who might be taken as a fair type of the first class, and was directed to one who gave me the following information: —

"I am a captain at an old-established house; indeed, one of the first and best at the West-end. I receive £1 19s. per week—that is, £1 16s. for my week, and 3s. extra for my duties as captain. My wages never amount to less. I have been twenty years employed at the same house in the same capacity, and for the whole of those twenty years my earnings have remained the same. I have brought up a large family, and am landlord of the house in which I live. I pay £55 a year for it, and let off nearly sufficient to pay the rent. Four or five of my shopmates are housekeepers, and they have been in our establishment as many years as myself. It is one of the few honourable houses remaining in the trade, and may be cited as an instance of what the trade formerly was. The workmen in our establishment are all, without any exception, honest, sober, industrious, moral men; the majority of them are married, and maintain their wives and families in decency and comfort. The workmen there employed may be taken as a fair average of the condition, habits, and principles of the journeyman tailor throughout the trade before the puffing and sweating system became general. Ever since the alteration from day work to piece work the condition of the working tailor has materially declined. Under the day-working system a master, taking on a man from a house of call, was obliged to find him work or pay him his wages during the time he remained in his workshop; but now, under the piece-working system, a master will often keep and send for more men than he requires, knowing that he has only to pay for the quantity of work done, and being desirous to make as great a display of 'hands' as possible. Further than this, under the piece-working system, the workman has the opportunity of taking garments home to be made; and the consequence is, being out of the master's sight, he puts on inexperienced hands to the different parts of the garment; and then, finding that by the assistance of women and girls he can get through a greater amount of work than he possibly could by his own unaided labour, he seeks employment from other masters at a lower price than the regular standard, and so subsides into a sweater, and underbids the regular workman. The masters have now learned that tailoring work, under the sweating system, can be done at almost any price; and hence those who are anxious to force their trade by underselling their more honourable neighbours advertise cheap garments, and give the articles out to sweaters to be made by women and girls. By such means the regular tailor is being destroyed; indeed, a man's own children are being brought into competition against himself, and the price of his labour is being gradually reduced to theirs. These evils, I am convinced, do not arise from over-population, but rather from over-competition. Women and children, who before were unemployed in the tailoring trade, now form a large proportion of the operative part of it. I know myself that, owing to the reduction of prices, many wives, who formerly attended solely to their domestic duties and their family, are now obliged to labour with the husband, and still the earnings of the two are less than he alone formerly obtained. The captains of shops in the honourable trade generally make as much as I do. By the sweating system I am satisfied the public are no gainers; the price of the workmen is reduced, but still the garment is no cheaper. The only parties profiting are the sweater and the dishonourable tradesman. In fact, another profit has now to be paid; so that, though the party doing the work is paid less, still the sweater's profit, which has to be added, makes little or no difference in the price of the garment to the public. I know myself that it is so."

The next person I sought out was one who might be taken as a fair average of the industrious and fortunate workmen. I was anxious to meet with a person whose earnings might be considered as a type, not of the *highest* wages received by the operatives, but of the earnings of those who are fully employed, in a shop where the best prices are paid, and where the customers are of the highest rank. I consulted with a number of workmen as to a person of such a character, and I was sent to an individual who gave me the following statement: —"I have been fifteen years employed in the same house. It is one of the first-rate houses at the West-end. My master pays the best prices, and I consider him a very fair man. He gives the same price for the better class of garments as he did fifteen years ago. The only articles for which he pays less than at the rate of 6d. per hour are the new-fashioned wrappers or paletots, and these he is obliged to reduce, much against his will, by the competition of other houses. Gentlemen want a cheap over-coat, and tell him that they can get it at such houses for such a price; and my master is compelled to make it at the same price as the cheap West-end slop-houses, or he would surely lose his customers. It is now about five years ago since my master began to make any reduction upon the price paid for making any garment whatsoever. Before that every article was paid for at the rate of 6d. per hour; but between the years 1844 and 1845—I cannot call to mind the exact date—my master had a consultation with his captain as to making up the new cheap tweed wrappers, which were coming into general fashion at that time; and he decided upon paying for them at a rate which, considering the time they took to make, was less than the regular sixpence per hour. He said that the show-shops at the East-end were daily advertising tweed wrappers at such a low figure that his customers, seeing the prices in the news-papers, were continually telling him that if he could not do them they must go elsewhere. Since then cheap over-coats, or wrappers, have been generally made in our shop, and I believe that my master would willingly give over making them, if it were not for the extreme competition which has been going on in the tailoring trade since their introduction. Amongst all the best and oldest houses in the trade at the West-end they are gradually introducing the making of the cheap paletots, Oxonians, Brighton coats, Chester-fields, &c. &c.; and even the first-rate houses are gradually sub-siding into the cheap advertising slop tailors. If the principle goes on at the rate that it has been progressing for the last five years, the journeymen tailors must ultimately be reduced to the position of the lowest of the needlewomen. I have kept an account of my wages for the last sixteen years; but I have destroyed several of the books, thinking them of no value. My wages have not declined since that period, because I am regularly employed, and my master's house has not yet become one of the cheap advertising shops—and I don't think it will in *his* time. In the year 1833, being the first I was in London, I remember well that my wages throughout the year averaged £1 6s. per week. I can say so positively, for I have long been in the habit of estimating them. I never did so before that time (because I was not out of my apprenticeship till then), and I recollect the first year particnularly. Indeed, as it happens, I have the account here. I thought I had burnt it." He then showed me an account of his earnings for the year above mentioned. It began April 6, 1833, and ended 29th March, 1834. The gross earnings was £69 3s. 6d., which gave an avearage of £1 6s. 7½d. per week. The lowest sum received in any one week during that year was 4s. 6d., and the next week he had no employment what-soever. This occurred in the month of September. The highest sum earned was £1 16s., and this occurred for seven weeks in succession during the months of May and June. At the latter period the business, I am told, is always brisk, and lasts generally three months. The slack usually begins in August and lasts till the middle of October, or two months and a half. The average weekly earnings for three months during "the brisk" of the year 1833 year £1 14s. 8½d. The average weekly earnings for ten weeks during the slack of the same year were 17s. 1d. He has no account-books from the years 1833 to 1844 at present with him. In the year 1844 his gross earnings were £76 15s. 9d., which gives an average of £1 9s. 5¾d. The average weekly earnings during "the brisk" season were £1 13s. 3½d., and the average earnings per week during the slack were £1 9s. 9½d. He tells me that the cause of the difference between these two years was, that in the year 1844 he had got the best chance of work in his shop; and this is shown by the difference between his earnings during the slacks of those two years. In 1844 he made 12s. 8d. per week *more* than he did in 1833; whereas, during the brisk season, he made 1s. 4½d. *less* per week in 1844 than he did in 1833. He tells me that the cause of this last difference is, that the men are now paid by the piece instead of by the day, and their masters' shops are consequently not opened so early in the morning as they were formerly. During 1843 his gross earnings were £76 17s. 3d., which gives an average per week of £1 9s. 6¾d. During the brisk of last year he made £1 10s. 0¼d. The cause of the difference between the brisk of this year and that of 1844 was that my informant was partially engaged for six weeks of the time upon a jury at Westminster. In the slack of the year the average weekly earnings were 19s. 9d. During the brisk months of the present year he has earned £1 3s. 8½d.; so that the decline in the earnings of this person since 1844 has been 1s. 0¾d. during the brisk, and 6s. 1d. per week during the slack. The gross earnings during the present year have been £82 4s., which gives an average per week of £1 12s. 4¼d. per week more than he did in 1844, and 2s. 9¼d. per week more than he did in 1848.

The cause of his wages not having declined is, he tells me, that he has the first chance of work at his shop; but his earnings constitute no average of the earnings of the workmen generally. He estimates the weekly income of those who have the second-best chance of work, and are employed in the same shop all the year round, at £1 2s. During the slack he considers their average weekly earnings to be about 10s., and during the brisk about £1 5s. He tells me that of those that are casually employed (and such appear to constitute about one-tenth of the trade) the average earnings are about 12s. a week all the year round. During the brisk (which with them lasts but two months of the year) he thinks they make £1 1s. per week, and during the slack (which with them lasts full three months) they are *wholly* unemployed, and make nothing whatsoever. They then generally pass their time in the tap-room or the club-room of some society's tavern. The number of journeymen employed in the regular and honourable trade has decreased, he tells me, nearly one-half since the year 1834, and this, he says, is owing to the increase of the principle of sweating, which he asserts to be mainly owing to the system of giving out the work to be done. Before the introduction of piece work the men were employed generally in the shop, and paid at the rate of 6d. per hour; then the great majority of the workmen were contented and happy; but since then, owing to the work being taken home to be done, those who before were journeymen tailors have passed into sweaters, and live upon their fellow-workmen's labour. These sweaters will take work at any price, and they are the principal cause of the decline of the trade; and my informant says his opinion is, that if the masters were prohibited from giving their work *out* to be done, and compelled to find comfortable workshops for all the hands engaged upon their work, the people employed in the trade would be as comfortable as before.

The statement of the casual hand is far different from either of the above. He says: "I am not 'in the command of a shop'— that is, I have no regular work, but am employed principally at the brisk season of the year. The brisk season lasts for three months in the shop, and for two months outside of it, or, in other words, the work at the commencement and end of the brisk season is only sufficient to keep the hands, regularly employed in the shop, fully engaged, and between these two periods extra hands are taken on to do the work, which then becomes more than the regular hands can accomplish. I am one of those extra hands, and May and June are the two months I am principally employed. During those months I earn £1 5s. per week, and I must be fully employed to get as much as that. The reason of this is, because the time required for making the garments is not fairly estimated. After the brisk season the casual hands are mostly off trade, and have little or no work at the honourable part of the business. From the month of July to the end of the month of April, the journeymen tailors who have not the command of a shop are principally dependent upon what is termed 'sank work.' This consists of soldiers', police, Custom-house, post, and mail clothing. At this work I could earn about 6s. per week if I could get as much as I could do, but there is not enough to keep all the men in full employment. Some weeks I do make my 6s.; others I make only 4s.; then again I occasionally make only 6s. in a fortnight. I think I can safely say my weekly earnings at 'sank work' average about 4s.; but during the time I am engaged at 'sank work' I have the chance of the calls at my society. I attend at the house twice a day regularly. Since the brisk season I have not been employed at the honourable part of the trade more than one day per month, and I never missed attending a single call. Hence I make upon an average about £10 by my work at the honourable part of the trade during the two months of the brisk season; then I get about £8 16s. by 'sank work,' at 4s. per week, for the rest of the year; and besides this I earn by casual employment at the honourable part of the trade about £3; this altogether brings my yearly income to £21 16s., which gives an average of 8s. 4½d. per week. This I really believe to be exactly what I *do* get. Those casual hands that do not take to 'sank work' work under the sweaters, at whatever the sweater may be pleased to give them. At the sweaters they make more than at the 'sank work,' but then they have to work much longer hours. Such is the difference of prices in my trade, that during the months of May and June I make trousers at 5s. per pair, and after that I make them at 6½d. per pair. The garments, of course, have not the same amount of work in them, but at those which are better paid I can earn in a day 5s., whilst I can only earn 1s. at the others in the same time. I believe the hands that cannot command a shop are similarly situated to myself. There are from 600 to 700 persons off work for ten months in the course of the year. I know this from having heard a gentleman who has paid great attention to the trade affirm that the unemployed were from 20 to 25 per cent. of the whole number of the operative 'in union.'"

The next party whom I saw was one to whom I had been referred as a type of the intemperate and improvident, but skilful tailor. I was anxious, as intemperance is said to be one of the distinguishing characteristics of the working tailors, to hear from one who was notorious for his indulgence in this vice what were the main causes that indunced the habit, so that by making them public the more intelligent workmen might be induced to take some steps to remedy the evil. As I before said, the necessary consequence of all uncertain labour is to produce intemperate habits among the labourers; and tailoring, it has been shown, has its periods of slack and brisk, as well as dock-labour. But it will be seen that there are other causes as well at work to demoralize, and occasionally to change, the operative tailor from the sober, industrious, and intelligent artisan, into the intemperate, erratic, and fatuous workman. I would not, however, have it inferred from the above remarks that the intemperance is a vice for which the whole or even the majority of the class are distinguished. On the contrary, from all that I have lately seen and heard, it is my duty to state that I believe intemperance to be an exception rather than a rule with the body. I have found the operative tailors—and especially those who have regular employment—enlightened, provident, and sober to a degree that I certainly did not anticipate. Indeed, the change from the squalor, fœtor, and wretchedness of the homes of the poor people that I had lately visited, to the comfort, cleanliness, and cheerfulness of the dwellings of the operative tailors, has been as refreshing to my feelings as the general sagacity of the workmen has been instrumental to the lightening of my labours. The person to whom I was referred gave me the following extraordinary statement: —"I work at coats generally, and for one of the best houses. I am reckoned one of the most skilful hands in the trade. I might be always in work if it were not for my love of drink. Most of the foremen know me, and object to give me work on account of my unsteadiness. If it were not for my skill I should be out of work altogether, for I never would consent to work under a sweater. I would rather starve than be instrumental to the reduction of the price of my labour. As an instance of my skill, I may mention that I recently made a waistcoat of my own invention, which was highly esteemed by my fellow-workmen. I do not wish to particularize the waistcoat more fully, lest it should be known who it is that supplies you with this information. I am not a leading hand in any shop, but one who is casually employed. I might be a leading man if it were not for my love of drink, but, owing to that, I am only taken on when the brisk season commences. It is to the casual hands that the intemperance of the tailors as a class is mostly limited; those who have regular employment are in general steady, decent, and intelligent people. The intemperance for which the casual hands are distinguished arises chiefly from their being 'called on' at public-houses. A master who wants an extra number of workmen to complete his work, sends to a certain house of call in the neighbourhood; this house of call is invariably a public-house, and there the men who are out of work assemble as early as a quarter before nine in the morning, to hear whether any call will be made. There are three of these calls in the course of the day; one at a quarter before nine (as before mentioned), a second at a quarter before one, and a third at a quarter before nine at night. Then men off trade, and seeking for employment, are kept knocking about at the public-house all the day through. The consequence of this is, that the day is passed in drinking, and habits of intemperance are produced which it is almost impossible to withstand. Those who have got money treat those who have none; and indeed, such are the inducements to drink, that it is almost impossible for the tailor who is not regularly and constantly employed to remain sober. During the slack season or vacation, there are from 50 to 100 hanging about each of the houses of call; and there are five of these houses 'in society.' and four foreign houses, or nine in all. In the vacation there must be from 500 to 1,000 people out of employ, who pass their days continually at the public-house. It astonishes me how some of them live. They cannot go home to their garrets, for they have no fire there, and if they absent themselves from the public-house they lose their chance of work. Some of those who are 'off trade' go into the country during the vacation, and others join the sweaters. But the majority remain about the public-house. They can't spend much, because they have it not to spend, but every penny they can get goes in drink, and many of the number pawn their coats and waistcoats in order to get liquor. I myself have duplicates enough to make a small pack of cards, for things that I have converted into gin. Ah! I like gin; you can see through it. Beer is like a fish-pond. What I hang on to is 'Old Tom;' a glass of that neat is my weakness; to mix it spoils it, to my fancy—that's true. I drink a tremendous lot. I can drink twenty glasses in the course of the day easy. I drank more than that yesterday, I am sure; I know that by 'the shakes' I have got to-day. I have them 'rattling bad' this morning. When I get another glass—or two, or three—I shall be all right. If I was to try to lift a glass to my mouth now, I should spill the half of it before I could get it there. One barman, who knows me, always puts my gin into a large tumbler for me, when I go to him the first thing in the morning. I have tried to give it up, but I never shall be able. The scars on my face do not arise from the small-pox, but solely from drink. When I take a great deal it flies to my nose and breaks out, and about five years ago my face was one mass of sores, of which these 'pits' are the scars. When I can get it, I will drink as much as three pints of gin in the course of the day. Upon an average, I think I drink about half-a-pint of raw gin every day, and if I could get the money I should drink double that quantity. I am sure it costs me 5s. a week in gin. I used to be a very lucky chap at the 'DERBY-SWEEPS' that used to be held at the public-houses. I have won as much as £8, £6, £5, and £4 twice; and whenever I got a prize I never did a stitch of work until I had drunk all the money away, and then I was sure to get the sack from my employer. The £8 did not last me above two or three days; I was 'roaring drunk' all that time, and afterwards I was ill for a week. I made all my companions in the same state. I am not very greedy over my half-pence, and always share what I get. The public-house got all I won. Another cause of the intemperance of the tailors is, that the operatives are usually paid at a tavern or beer-shop. There are generally three hands employed in making one coat, and these go partners—that is, they share among them the sum of money paid for making the entire garment. It is necessary, therefore, that change should be got in order to divide the proceeds into 'thirds.' This change the publican always undertakes to provide, and the consequence is, the men meet at his house to receive their weekly earnings. I have known the publican often keep the men an hour waiting for their change. The consequence of this system of paying at public-houses is, that the most intemperate and improvident of the workmen spend a large portion of their wages in drink. I myself generally spend half (unless my Missus comes and catches me); and on several occasions I have squandered away in liquor all I had earned in the week. My Missus knows my infirmity, and watches me of a Saturday night regularly. She was waiting outside the public-house where you picked me up, and there were three or four more wives of journeymen tailors watching outside of the tavern, besides my old woman. These were mostly the wives of the men who are casually employed. The intemperate operative tailors seldom take half of their earnings home to their wives and families. Those who are employed by the sweaters are as intemperate as the casual hands in the honourable part of the trade. The cause of the drunkenness of the men working under sweaters is, that the workmen employed by them are the refuse hands of the regular trade. They mostly consist of the men who have been scratched off the books of the societies through spoiling or neglecting the work of their employers from intemperate habits. I know the misery and evil of this love of drink; it is the curse of my life, but I cannot keep from it. I have taken the pledge four or five times, and broken it just as often. I kept it six weeks once, and was quite a little king at that time. I had always money in my pocket, and my wife got me a watch out of my earnings as well. Doctor Wormwald told me, when my face was bad, I should lose my nose if I continued drinking, and I said I would have my drop of gin if I had no nose at all. Any person who could prevail upon me to take the pledge, and make me keep it, would be the saviour of me. My wife is a hard-working body, and is obliged to keep me half the year round. I am a civil and well-disposed person when I am sober, but when I get a drop of drink I am a madman. I break open the doors and smash the teapot and tea-things, and indeed break or disfigure everything I can lay my hands on."

The man has given me his solemn promise that, "for the honour of his craft" and "the sake of his wife," he will keep from all intoxicating drink for the future.

I now give the views of an intelligent Chartist, in the same calling, and in his own words: —"I am a Chartist, and did belong to the Chartist Association. My views as to way in which politics and Government influence the condition of journeymen tailors are these—Government, by the system now adopted with regard to army and police clothing, forces the honest labouring man, struggling for a fair remuneration for his labour, into a false position, and makes him pay extra taxes to those paid by other branches of the community; they force him into this false position by disposing of Government work at such contract prices that no man can make a decent livelihood at it. One of the best workmen, employed the whole week, cannot earn more than 12s. weekly on soldiers' or policemen's clothing, out of which he must pay for all the sewing trimmings, except twist; and having to make the articles at his own place, of course he must find his own fire, candles, &c. Tailors in prison are put to work by the Government at clothes that come into the market to compete with the regular trader employing the regular artisan. The public pays the taxes from which prisons are supported, and the smallest amount, even a penny a pair, is regarded by the authorities as a saving on the cost of prisons; and, indeed, they keep the prisoner at work, if he earns nothing, as the public pays all the expense of the prison. The working tailor pays *his* quota of the taxes out of which the tailor put to work in prison is maintained, and the prisoner so maintained is made to undersell the very tax-payer who contributes to his support. My opinion is, that if tailors in gaol were not employed by Government, it would leave the market more open to the honourable portion of the trade, and there would be no discreditable employing of a felon—for felons *are* so employed—to diminish the small earnings of an honest man. At Millbank, they teach men to be tailors, who are always employed, while the honest operative is frequently subjected to three months' compulsory idleness; six weeks, towards the close of the year, is a very common period of the tailor's non-employment. I think that if the Charter became law, it would tend to improve our (the journeymen tailors') condition, by giving us a voice in the choice of our representatives, who might be so selected as thoroughly to understand the wants of the working man, and to sympathise with his endeavours for a better education and a better lot altogether."

To the gentleman who furnished me with the subjoined account of the causes of the decline of the honourable part of the trade, I was referred to as one of the most intelligent and experienced of the class. I was informed that he had made the trade his peculiar study for years, and was one of the representatives of the societies "in union," and consequently a member of the general committee, and one of the arbitrators between workman and workman, or between workman and master. I found him a person of superior understanding, and a man who had evidently thought long upon the subject. He placed in my hands a variety of statistical papers connected with the trade, and several documents of his own drawing up. He had evidently the interest of his class deeply at heart, and was altogether a fine specimen of the better kind of English artisan. He said, "I have been connected with the honourable part of the tailoring trade 24 years. I have paid considerable attention to the circumstances affecting the interests of the operative tailors. When I first joined the trade there were about 5,000 men in union. The number of men in full employment at that time was, as well as my memory serves me, about four-fifths of the whole, or 4,000. The average earnings of these were £1 16s. per week, making a total of £374,400 per annum. Besides this, the casual men averaged about half the amount, which gave a gross total of £46,800 per annum; and this sum added to the other makes the gross annual earnings of the operative tailors in union at that time amount to £421,200, or say, in round numbers, £42,000. The average number of men in union is, in round numbers, 3,000. Of these there are 1,000 earning weekly upon an average 25s., and 1,000 earning 18s., and the remaining 1,000 earning 8s. At this rate the gross annual income of the working tailors at present would be £132,000. Now, if we compare the present earnings of the class with the past, it will be seen that the gross annual income of the operative tailors in union has fallen off no less than £288,600, or upwards of a quarter of a million pounds sterling, in twenty-four years, while the number of workmen has declined nearly one-half. The cause of this serious decrease is the employment given to workmen at their own homes, or, in other words, to the 'sweaters.' The sweater is the greatest evil in the trade, as the sweating system increases the number of hands to an almost incredible extent—wives, sons, daughters, and extra women, all working 'long days'—that is, labouring from sixteen to eighteen hours per day, and Sundays as well. By this system two men obtain as much work as would give employment to three or four men working regular hours in the shop. Consequently, the sweater, being enabled to get the work done by women and children at a lower price than the regular workman, obtains the greater part of the garments to be made, while men who depend upon the shop for their living are obliged to walk about idle. A greater quantity of work is done under the sweating system at a lower price. I consider that the decline of my trade dates from the change of day work into piece work. According to the old system, the journeyman was paid by the day, and consequently must have done his work under the eye of his employer. It is true that work was given out by the master before the change from day work to piece work was regularly acknowledged in the trade; but still it was morally impossible for work to be given out and not paid by the piece. Hence I date the decrease in the wages of the workman from the introduction of piece work, and giving out garments to be made off the premises of the master. The effect of this was, that the workman making the garment, knowing that the master could not tell whom he got to do his work for him, employed women and children to help him, and paid them little or nothing for their labour. This was the beginning of the sweating system. The workmen gradually became transformed from journeymen into 'middlemen,' living by the labour of others. Employers soon began to find that they could get garments made at a less sum than the regular price, and those tradesmen who were anxious to force their trade, by underselling their more honourable neighbours, readily availed themselves of this means of obtaining cheap labour. The consequence was that the sweater sought out where he could get the work done the cheapest, and so introduced a fresh stock of hands into the trade. Female labour, of course, could be had cheaper than male, and the sweater readily availed himself of the services of women on that account. Hence the males who had formerly been employed upon the garments were thrown out of work by the females, and obliged to remain unemployed, unless they would reduce the price of their work to that of the women. It cannot, therefore, be said that the reduction of prices originally arose from there having been more workmen than there was work for them to do. There was no superabundance of hands until female labour was generally introduced; and even if the workmen had increased twenty-five per cent. more than what they were twenty years back, still that extra number of hands would be required now to make the same number of garments, owing to the work put into each article being at least one-fourth more than formerly. It is the principle of the workmen generally to uphold the price of their labour, and of the master continually to reduce it, which the sweating system has afforded him the means of doing. So far from the trade being over-stocked with male hands, if the work were confined to the men or the masters' premises, there would not be sufficient hands to do the whole."

LETTER *XVII*
Friday, December 14, 1849

I now proceed in due order to give an account of the cheap clothes trade in the East-end of London. I deal with the Eastern slop tailors first, because I am informed that the slop-trade of the West is of more recent date.

I believe that the facts which I publish in my present communication will lay bare a system unheard of and unparalleled in the history of any country; indeed, there appears to be so deep laid a scheme for the introduction and supply of underpaid labour to the market, that it is impossible for the working man not to sink and be degraded by it to the lowest depths of wretchedness and infamy. If we wish to see the effect of this system upon the physical, intellectual, and moral character of the workpeople, we should spend a week in visiting the homes of the operative tailors connected with the honourable part of the trade, and those working for the slop-trade. The very dwellings of the people are sufficient to tell you the wide difference between the two classes. In the one you occasionally find small statues of Shakespeare beneath glass shades; in the other all is dirt and fœtor. The working tailor's comfortable first-floor at the West-end is redolent with the perfume of the small bunch of violets that stands in a tumbler over the mantelpiece; the sweater's wretched garret is rank with the stench of filth and herrings. The honourable part of the trade are really intelligent artisans, while the slopworkers are generally almost brutified with their incessant toil, wretched pay, miserable food, and filthy homes.

Nor are the shops of the two classes of tradesmen less distinct one from the other. The quiet house of the honourable tailor, with the name inscribed on the window blinds, or on the brass plate on the door, tells you that the proprietor has no wish to compete with or undersell his neighbour. But at the show and slop shops every art and trick that scheming can devise, or avarice suggest, is displayed to attract the notice of the passer-by and filch the customer from another. The quiet, unobtrusive place of business of the old-fashioned tailor is transformed into the flashy palace of the grasping tradesman. Every article in the window is ticketed—the price cut down *to the quick*—books of crude, bald verses are thrust in your hands, or thrown into your carriage window—the panels of every omnibus are plastered with showy placards, telling you how Messrs. ——— defy competition.

The principal show and slop shop at the East-end is termed the ———, and now occupies the ground of several houses. The windows are of rich plate glass—one window, indeed, is nearly thirty feet high—and it is said, that at the time of the attack upon the house by the mob, the damage done by breaking two of the windows amounted to £150. The business is not confined to tailor's work. The proprietors are furriers, hatters, and bootmakers, hosiers, cutlers, trunk-sellers, and milliners. They keep six horses and carts constantly employed in their business, and, I am told, pay above £1,000 a year for gas. The show-rooms are lighted by large ormolu chandeliers, having thirty-six burners each.

In pursuance of the system I have adopted, in order to arrive at a correct estimate as to the earnings of the labouring class whose condition I may be investigating, I invited the working tailors of the East-end to meet me on Tuesday evening last, at the British and Foreign School, Shakespeare's-walk, Shadwell. A reporter was sent from the office of this journal to give an account of the meeting, and the following is his report of the statement made on the occasion: —

The METROPOLITAN CORRESPONDENT of *The Morning Chronicle* informed the meeting that he was now directing his attention to the operative tailors of the metropolis, in connection both with the honourable and the dishonourable part of the trade; and that consequently, he was anxious to arrive at certain facts in relation to their earnings and their condition, in order to lay them before the public. The objects of the meeting were the following: —1. To learn whether, and how, the slop trade influences the regular and honourable tailoring trade. 2. To ascertain the amount of the average weekly earnings of the hands engaged in the slop and regular trade. 3. To hear an account of the sufferings and privations endured by the workpeople through the low price paid for their labour. 4. To discover, if possible, whether the low prices arise from competition among the masters, or from competition among the workpeople. 5. To find out whether there is any practical remedy for the evil. It was only facts that were required. Perhaps the most important of these objects was the fourth; and he had called together those who were present for the purpose of ascertaining their opinions upon the question. Did the existing depression arise from the struggle of the trading classes to live, or from the struggle of the labour classes to live? Were masters continually underselling one another, or were workmen continually underbidding one another? This was what he wanted to learn from individuals practically acquainted with the subject. He wished to know further, whether it was acknowledged that the commencement of the system of piece work in 1834, instead of the system of day work, was the commencement of the declension in the price of their labour?

Several men exclaimed that it was. One man added that the decline began to be more rapid after that time; but piece work as well as day work was carried on to a small extent in some shops at the West-end. He was one who joined in the strike at that period, and he remembered working in a shop where piece work was carried on at the same time with day work, but at good and fair prices. Another man said he remembered no piece work in the best shops; but there was extra work, which was paid for at the rate of sixpence the hour.

The meeting then expressed its conviction, by a show of hands, that the cause of the declension of wages had been the change from day work to piece work; that this change had led to great competition among workmen, and to the introduction of female labour in the craft. Before this period, the meeting further signified, a journeyman tailor could support a wife and family by his own labour; and a respectable-looking elderly man declared that it could be done much better in those times, for the wages of a man then were twenty-five per cent. more than the wages now of the man and his wife put together. The depression had not arisen from an excess in the number of tailors, but from females and children, who originally did not work, being brought into the trade, as well as from the introduction of "sweaters." The depression was further promoted by a certain amount of competition from the prisons and the workhouses.

These principles having been distinctly enunciated by the meeting, they were earnestly desired to mention nothing but facts in the statements they might make, and to abstain from all personal or offensive remarks.

A journeyman tailor then came forward, and spoke at some length. He said the present system of labour wasted the physical and mental energies of the class to which he belonged. Their grievances were not imaginary, and he complained that the cause of the labouring poor had been hitherto neglected. He had himself just made a Wellington surtout, which took him twenty-six hours' hard work. He was paid 5s. for it, but out of this small amount he had 1s. 6d. for trimmings, thread, candles, and fire, so that there was just 3s. 6d. left. His wife was ill, being in a consumption. A physician who had seen her told him that if he did not apply for relief to the parochial officers he would be guilty of manslaughter. But he would not so degrade himself. He further complained of the misery caused by the sweating system, and mentioned some establishments at the East-end where men were apparently employed upon the premises. They were, however, merely for a deception, being only finishers. In one large shop the middle-man and sweater received 7s. 6d. for making a coat, but he only paid to the poor tailor 5s., who had to provide out of it thread, trimmings, and other materials. How, he asked, was it possible for men with families to live upon such wages?

Another tailor here stepped forward, and said that although a great deal of distress and privation had been laid bare by the exertions of *The Morning Chronicle,* not one-half or one-quarter had yet been discovered. So it was with the wages of the poor. Much was known in relation to them, but not all. He attributed a large amount of distress among the London tailors to certain large establishments conduting their business through "sweaters." They were sweaters upon a large scale. These places did not work for the poor, but for the aristocracy. He was himself employed in making coats which were advertised at from five to twenty guineas. The aristocracy, not the poor, bought these coats, though the labour in making them was not half-paid. Indeed, he knew that customers belonging to the aristocracy, though they were ashamed of being seen in certain large establishments at the East-end, sent written orders for the foremen to wait upon them. The great financial economist of the age, ————, was also such a customer. Such, further, were some of the principal inhabitants of ————, whose names could be furnished; and even clergymen of the Church of England. A tailor who had a family needed the aid of his wife to assist him in making a living. The woman, in some cases, was absolutely needed to make three-fourths of the garments; and he knew a man who worked for one of the cheap establishments, now in almost the last stage of a consumption, who had paid to the establishment out of his miserable earnings 30s. in less than three months, in the shape of fines. Another journeyman tailor, who was known to most present, had a wife and five children, several of whom were ill with fever. He had, further, to support an aged father. This man made a coat for 8s. for the house in question; but he was half an hour behind time in taking it in. He therefore got nothing for making it, though he had found thread, candle, and fire. This was a positive fact.

"And there are many others besides that! " exclaimed a voice.

A person inquired whether it was meant that the man got nothing for making the coat?

"Not a farthing," replied the narrator.

"He was fined the 8s. for being behind time," observed a person in the crowd.

An inquiry was here made whether such a custom as this was likely to become general?

The TAILOR who made the statement said that would depend upon others. He was speaking, however, of the establishment to which he belonged, and in which he was for the present permitted to be a "captain." The same establishment sometimes put out bills, "A thousand tailors wanted," and he had been caught by them. He had been working for a very good shop at the West-end, but happened to be idle for a few weeks, consequently he was "hard up." A friend advised him to apply where the 1,000 tailors were wanted, and he got work. This was his first introduction to the slop system; and his earnings had been so small, with the assistance of a female — though he would not acknowledge himself a "sweater"— that, if he were fined as some had been, he should have to give the employer more money than he received himself. Distress among the operative tailors had been brought on to a greater extent than in other classes by female competition. He hoped public opinion would be elicited in their favour, and then he was sure the splendid palaces of beauty, erected out of the toils of the poor, would fade away.

A PALETOT MAKER said the party for whom he worked—and he made the best coats in the establishment—had two shops, and that there was a difference in the prices paid at the two places. Coats made neat, with capes, were charged 1s. more than a dress coat at one shop; and at the other 1s. less; and the prices were so calculated, that the man who obtained it had to calculate upon his wife helping him. Drab coats with capes, stitched all round, were paid for at 12s., the man finding his own trimmings [hear, hear]. He knew it for a fact, for he had done the work and received the money himself. At the commencement of winter, a Witney coat was sent out to be made, with double seams, but because the cloth was softer, he could only obtain 8s., although the work in it was the same as in the last. First one man refused it, and then another, and then a complaint went to the employer, who was told by the men that, as they had to pay 1s. for trimmings, they could not, at such a price, get a living by it. The price was raised to 10s., and at 10s. it now remained; but for the same description of coat, which he had made, not in the house, but in the shop, he had received 24s. There would be no difference made in the price upon account of the softness of the cloth. At the same shop 8s. was paid for extra paletots to a Jew who contracted for the whole, and 7s. 6d. for others. For exactly the same garments he had received from a regular shop 16s. Another "novelty," as it was called, had just been introduced in a coat with eight or nine rows of stitching inside and out and round the cape, for making which 18s. was paid. The ordinary price for making such a coat was 36s.; consequently, the employer paid just one-half the money he ought to do, solely from expecting women to take part in the work. In this case the workmen had to find their own trimmings and silk, which he estimated would cost 1s. 9d. He could scarcely make half of such a coat in two days, even by working extra hours.

"You must work hard to do that," said a middle-aged man.

One of the previous speakers said the selling price of this kind of coat was four guineas. It was made of Tweed cloth at 6s. 6d. a yard, and it would take 2½ yards. He went into the shop in question, and asked what had been paid for the labour upon it, but they refused to tell him. But he should say that, taking twelve hours to be a fair day's labour, it could not be made under eight or nine days.

An OPERATIVE TAILOR declared that the great middleman in the establishment referred to got half-a-crown out of the making of every paletot.

"What is your opinion," it was asked, "as to the cause of the depreciation in prices?"

The answer, prompt and ready, was—"Men of capital underselling each other."

"Do you know," it was further inquired, "of any place where sweaters seek out for female labourers" [hear]?

"Yes," was the reply, "a man in Windmill-street sought out for females and boys; and he gave 2s. 6d. a day to a man who could finish very well. This person worked for a tailor who in his turn worked for the —— of ——. A coat was made for the —— with thick beaver coat flaps, and stitched, and richly lined through with silk—containing nine pockets, four upon one side, five on the other, and two with flaps. For this he received only nine shillings, and found his own trimmings. The regular price would, at least, be 24s."

"Aye, 28s. would be nearer the mark."

The same operative tailor proceeded to state that shooting coats, single breasted, with pockets, creased, &c., were only paid, in the establishment to which he referred, 22s.; whilst in the first-rate shops in St. James's-street, at least, 35s. 6d. would be given for the same work [hear, hear].

At this stage a young man came forward and said he lived in the neighbourhood of New-buildings, Gravel-lane, Houndsditch. There was a place, he said, kept by a well-known sweater in that vicinity, where each woman paid 3d. to have her name put down on a slate for work. The name being on the slate any foreign tailor could apply to see it, and the proprietor was thus enabled to supply either girls or women. In short, the house to which he referred was a house of call for women who were seeking for labour to compete with men. He worked for ——, at what was called the up-stairs trade. Last week he made a coat, double-stitched and braided, for 8s., out of which he had to find his own trimmings; but the coat was thrown back on his hands because the double stitches were not all sewn with silk. The making of the coat cost him three-and-a-half days' labour; but he might possibly have made it in three days by working sixteen or eighteen hours [hear, hear]. He had made a coat of bear-skin, which took him four days' hard work, at about eighteen hours each day, for 8s. The creasing alone was a day's work for any man. He had also made shooting-coats with eight pockets, laps, and seamed, for 7s., finding his own trimmings [hear]. But further, if work was not delivered at the exact time, there was a fine of 3d. for the first hour, and 6d. for every hour afterwards. These rules were written up in the place where the work was given out. Besides, if the garment was not in till four o'clock on Friday, they would not take it in, and you were obliged to wait till the next week for your money. He wished it to be known that only five months ago he came out of his apprenticeship. He had served six years at the business, and £7 premium was paid with him, and such had been the sort of work he had since been occupied upon. Let him work as hard as he could for eighteen hours every day he could not make more than 12s., and out of that sum trimmings cost him 2s., light 6d., and coals 1s. 6d.; so that he had only 8s. for his support.

"Lights, at this season, will cost you 3d. a night," exclaimed a bystander, "if you burn it for ten hours, as you must, expressly for your work."

It was here asked whether this was an extra expense upon the ordinary cost of fire and lighting?

"Yes," resounded from the whole meeting. "And rent, too," said the individual.

"If you were working in a shop, that expense would be saved?" was the next inquiry.

"It would," replied a number of voices; "and we should be saved the expense of irons, boards, and rent."

A WORKMAN at one of the most extensive slop-sellers' said, that some years ago the proprietors of that establishment were in the habit of expressing their readiness to exhibit their book of wages. This book was a deception, inasmuch as each £1 or £2 entered against a name had to be divided between six or even more individuals; so that it could not be correct to ascribe these earnings to one man.

The following statement was then read: —

"Gentlemen—I have worked for the firm of —— about four years. About three weeks ago the foreman sent a sailor's jacket to me, about six o'clock in the evening. it was to be made with slash sleeves, double-breasted, sowed on lappel, and the price was 6d.; and it was wanted at two o'clock the next day. I sent it back again, and said I could not make it by the time. He said I must make it; whereupon I sent it back again, and said I could not make it. Well, then he sent the wife about, from place to place, to see if any one else would make it, but no one else would make it in the time. So then he said he would give me longer time to make it. I undertook it; and when the job was opened, there were no sleeve linings in it. I went in for the sleeve linings, and got them. I sat up all night, and got another man to help me; and when I sent the jacket in, because he said I was behind my time, he fined me 6d., and when I went to receive my wages on the Saturday night 6d. was deducted for the sleeve linings, which I never had. I stood up there one Saturday, and in about three hours I counted 19s. of fines, some 1s., some 2s., and so on. The trimmer took it into his head one day to fine a woman 1s., because he said she was saucy. The husband went to know what was the reason his wife was fined 1s. His answer was, 'I shall fine you another, and then one cannot laugh at the other.' The man, feeling himself badly treated, goes to the head of the firm, and his answer is, 'If you do not like it, you may leave it.' So the man was obliged to put up with the consequences or lose his bread. If I had kept a proper account of all the fines that have been levied on me since I have worked for the firm, it would have amounted to not less than 3l."

The person referred to in this communication here stood up, and said he had asked for the money back, but it was refused, and he was threatened. Having a wife and two children dependent upon him, he was obliged to submit. He had a coat given him last Thursday, to make by half-past three the next day. He sat up to do it, but fell asleep at four, and did not awake till eight on the Friday morning, so that he could not take in the coat till half-past seven at night. The establishment was then closed, but he went to the private door, where he was told the coat would do the next morning. He sent it by his wife the next morning, but when he came to receive his wages on Saturday night, he was fined 6d. out of 8s. for its being late. His fines in four years, he believed, had amounted to £4 15s., and he could hardly tell for what.

A respectable-looking man said that till lately he had been working at the West-end, but that three weeks ago he was sought out by a master sweater, and he got work at one of the slop-establishments. He was paid 4s. for making a paletot, out of which he had to find silk, thread, and basting-cotton. A good man could not make one in less than twenty-four hours. Fourpence per hour was deducted if the garment was sent in late; so that frequently he was obliged to work all night towards the end of the week. Poor men were often obliged to work upon the Sunday. And who did these men work for? Not altogether for the poor; for last week a coat was made where he was serving for Lord ——, and the week before some liveries were ordered by another noble lord, whose name he had forgotten; but he was struck with them as they were only paid 12s. 6d. for. 18s. was the price for making liveries of this description; and as they would only pay 12s. 6d. he struck. Somebody, however, was found to accept it. This was the way in which poor men were ruined. The effect of such a state of things upon morals must be injurious. Numbers of young men in the trade came up from the country to London before their characters were formed. They could find nothing to do at the West-end; they then came down in the City, and were there easily influenced to work upon the Sunday. He knew, indeed, it was a practice with some masters to give out work upon the Saturday night, with directions for it to be brought in on Monday morning [hear, hear]. Under these circumstances he expressed his gratitude for the movement that was being made to improve the condition of the class to which he belonged.

A young man here stepped forward and told a striking tale. He said he had been apprenticed to a tailor in Ipswich; that a premium of £100 had been paid with him; and that, having finished his servitude and being out of work, he resolved to come up to London. In the first year of his apprenticeship he received 8s. a week; in the second 10s., for which he toiled from seven in the morning till ten at night. He had no friend, no home, at Ipswich; and he came to London, where the first person he met was a sweater, who told him he could produce more than 16s. a week.

Well, he toiled from 7 in the morning till 12 at night. The sweater then asked whether he would work upon the Sunday? He objected; and upon the Saturday night, instead of having 2s. or 3s. in his pocket, *he was brought in 6d. in debt.* The sweater he found took coats from —— 3s. 6d., but he paid the workpeople only 2s. 6d., out of which they had to find their own trimmings. When he complained, the sweater told him he must work on Sunday; but he said, "I'll go without my victuals first" [cheers].

"What did you give for your food?" asked a voice in the meeting.

"I took my teas and breakfasts with him," was the reply. "I was charged 4d. for each, 2d. for dinner, and 2d. for supper. I made five coats in the week, which came to 12s. 6d. My victuals cost 1s. a day; lodgings were 2s. 6d.; 1s. 6d. went for fire and candles; 1s. 3d. for trimmings; which makes 12s. 3d. I can't make up the remainder, and I suppose I was cheated out of it. Through my circumstances, I have been obliged to sell my shirt to get lodgings. Yesterday I went to a Frenchman that takes out work in Colchester-street, and he offered me 5s. a week to work from seven in the morning till ten at night. I asked him to give me lodgings besides, but he would not, and I was obliged to walk about. I went to three unions, but none of them would let me in; and I am now without a shirt to my back, because I sold it to get shelter, after I had walked till two o'clock in the morning."

This statement excited great commiseration, and a spontaneous wish arose to make a subscription for the young man upon the spot. Other means, however, were found to relieve his immediate necessities.

Several other statements were afterwards made, all showing the oppressions to which the operative tailors are subjected.

The results of the meeting were as follows: —

The average earnings of those engaged at the slop-trade were 9s. 7¼d., or 8s. clear. The aggregate earnings of 71 hands last week amounted to £34 11s. 1d., or 9s. 4d. each—less than 8s. clear.

The average earnings of the honourable part of the trade were 15s. 5d. per week, clear of all deductions. 77 hands earned last week altogether £57 6s. 10d.

The amount in pawn was £110 5s. by the slop-trade, and £121 1s. 6d. by the members of the honourable trade—in all £231 6s. 6d. by 148 people.

An offer was made to introduce me privately into the workshop of a large show and slop-shop at the East-end of the town, where I might see and interrogate the men at work on the premises; but to this I objected, saying I did not think it fair that I should enter any man's premises with such an object, unknown to him. I was then told that several of the workmen would willingly meet me, and state the price they received for their labour, and the unjust system upon which the establishment was conducted. This statement I said I should be very glad to listen and give publicity to. Accordingly, three of the better class of hands waited upon me, and gave me the following account: —"We work at the slop trade. We mean, by the slop trade, the cheap ready-made trade. The dishonourable part of the tailoring trade consists of two classes, viz., those who are connected with show-shops and slop-shops. The show-shops belong to the cheap 'bespoke trade,' and the slop-shops to the cheap 'ready-made trade.' Many of the large tailoring houses at the East-end of London are both show-shops and slop-shops. By a show-shop we mean one where the different styles of garments are exhibited in the window, ticketed as 'made to measure at a certain price.' By a slop-shop we mean one where the garments themselves are sold ready-made, and not a similar one made to measure at a certain price. In the cheap or ready-made trade a large number of one kind of garments is made up, either for home consumption or for exportation; whereas, in the show or cheap bespoke trade, only one of the same kind or garment is made up at one time. We all three of us work at coat-making. We are paid piece-work. The full price—that is, the highest amount paid for any coat made on the establishment—is 10s. The coat for which this price is given is a full-trimmed frock or dress coat. By 'full-trimmed' we mean lined throughout with silk and with quilted sides. The price for such a coat in the honourable trade is 18s.—that is the very lowest price: the best houses would pay from 21s. to 24s. The time that such coats will take to make is four days, estimating twelve hours' work to the day. They are, however, made in three days, but this is done by working over-hours at home. At dress and frock coat work we can make the most money. At this kind of work—if we could get it—we might earn 15s. a week. But there are other kinds of work which are much worse paid for, and we have to take these with the rest. If we object, we are told we shall have no more to do. The worst kind of work that we have to do consists of drab driving capes; these are made of thick 'box cloth,' or 'Devonshire kersey,' and have 'double-pricked' seams all through (the cloth is too hard to stitch, and consequently the needle has to be passed up and down, or double pricked, as a shoemaker would stitch leather); there are eighteen rows of pricking round the hand —four pockets, with flaps pricked the same as the seams—and the capes are lined entirely with silk, which is quilted all through. The price for making such a description of garment is 9s., and it will take, at least, a week making." "I know I made one," said one of the men, "and I was more than six days over it." "Yes, that you must have been," said another, "and not an hour less. At the best houses at the West-end the price for such a garment would be 36s. We have all worked in the honourable trade, so we know the regular prices from our own personal experience. Taking the bad work with the good work, we might earn 11s. a week upon an average. Sometimes we do earn as much as 15s.; but to do this we are obliged to take part of our work home to our wives and daughters. We are not always fully employed. We are nearly half our time idle. Hence our earnings are, upon an average, throughout the year, not more than 5s. 6d. a week. "Very often I have made only 3s. 4d. in the week," said one. "That's common enough with us all, I can assure you," said another. "Last week my wages was 7s. 6d." declared one. "I earned 6s. 4d.," exclaimed the second. "My wages came to 9s. 2d. The week before I got 6s. 3d." "I made 7s. 9d.;" and "I, 7s. or 8s., I can't exactly remember which." "This is what we term the best part of our winter season. "The reason why we are so long idle is because more hands than are wanted are kept on the premises, so that in case of a press of work coming in our employers can have it done immediately. Under the day-work system no master tailor had more men on the premises than he could keep continually going; but since the change to the piece-work system, masters make a practice of engaging double the quantity of hands that they have any need for, so that an order may be executed 'at the shortest possible notice,' if requisite. A man must not leave the premises when unemployed; if he does he loses his chance of work coming in. I have been there four days together, and not had a stitch of work to do." "Yes; that is common enough." "Aye, and then you're told, if you complain, you can go if you don't like it. I am sure twelve hands would do all they have done at home, and yet they keep forty of us. It's generally remarked, that however strong and healthy a man may be when he goes to work at that shop, in a month's time he'll be a complete shadow, and have almost all his clothes in pawn. By Sunday morning—after the workman has paid what he has run a score for—he has no money at all left, and he has to subsist till the following Saturday upon about a pint of weak tea and four slices of bread and butter per day." "There was a man there who came from Belgium," said one of the workmen; "I don't think he ever earned 5s. a week, and one week I know he got only 1s. 6d.—one half-pair of trousers was all he had to do. He came up to me, and

begged bread by signs, for he could not speak a word of English.
We made a subscription of halfpence for him round the shop, and
his consul sent him back to his own country. There are five
foreigners in our shop, and I can assert positively that in the last
few years a great number of German and Polish Jew tailors have
been brought over to work at the slop trade. I know positively that
hundreds are not engaged at slop work, and every summer brings
a fresh importation." "One of our foremen is a Hungarian Jew,
and he prefers foreign hands to us. We all make for —— ——, the
'poor man's friend,' said they, satirically. We used to have to make
for for him frequently; but now he has shifted to another slop-shop
near London bridge, where the same starvation prices are paid.
We have also made garments for Sir —— ——, Sir —— ——,
Alderman ——, Dr. ——, and Dr. ——. We make for several of
the aristocracy. We cannot say whom, because the tickets frequently
come to us as Lord —— and the Marquess of ——. This could not
be a Jew's trick, because the buttons on the liveries had coronets
upon them. And again, we know the house is patronised largely
by the aristocracy, clergy, and gentry, by the number of court suits
and liveries, surplices, regimentals, and ladies' riding-habits that
we continually have to make up. There are more clergymen among
the customers than any other class, and often we have to work at
home upon the Sunday at their clothes, in order to get a living.
The customers are mostly ashamed of dealing at this house, for
the men who take the clothes to the customers' houses in the cart
have directions to pull up at the corner of the street. We had a
good proof of the dislike of gentlefolks to have it known that they
dealt at that shop for their clothes, for when the trousers buttons
were stamped with the name of the firm, we used to have the
garments returned daily, to have other buttons put on them; and
now the buttons are unstamped. Formerly an operative tailor's wife
never helped him. He worked at the shop—brought his weekly
wages home—from 30s. to 36s. a week; and his wife attended to
her domestic duties, and lived in ease and comfort. This was the
case twenty years ago, but since that time prices have come down
to such an extent, that now a man's entire family, wife and daughters, all have to work, and, with the whole of the family's work,
the weekly income is not one-half what the operative could get
by his own labour some years back. We are all satisfied that there
is scarcely a working tailor whose wife and daughters are not
engaged at some kind of slop; and that five-and-twenty years ago
female labour was unknown in the trade—indeed, it was not
allowed. The decline in the prices of our trade arises, in our

opinion, from our wives and daughters being brought to work, and so to compete with ourselves. There is at our establishment a mode of reducing the price of our labour even lower than we have mentioned. The prices we have stated are those *nominally* paid for making the garments; but it is not an uncommon thing in our shop for a man to make a garment, and receive nothing at all for it. I remember a man once having a waistcoat to do, the price of making which was 2s., and when he gave the job in he was told that he owed the establishment 6d. The manner in which this is brought about is by a system of fines. We are fined, if we are behind time with our job, 6d. the first hour, and 3d. for each hour that we are late." "I have known as much as 7s. 6d. to be deducted off the price of a coat on the score of want of punctuality," one said; "and, indeed, very often the whole money is stopped. It would appear as if our employers themselves strove to make us late with our work, and so have an opportunity of cutting down the price paid for our labour. They frequently put off giving out the trimmings to us till the time at which the coat is due has expired. If to the trimmer we return an answer that is considered 'saucy,' we are fined 6d. or 1s., according to the trimmer's temper." "I was called a thief," another of the three declared; "and because I told the man I would not submit to such language, I was fined 6d. These are the principal of the in-door fines. The out-door fines are still more iniquitous. There are full a dozen more fines for minor offences; indeed, we are fined upon every petty pretext. We never know what we have to take on a Saturday, for the meanest advantages are taken to reduce our wages. If we object to pay these fines, we are told that we may leave; but they know full well that we are afraid to throw ourselves out of work."

I next went to an out-door hand, employed on the superior descriptions of work, and his story was as follows: —

"I work at the out-door work for a large show and slop shop. I do the bespoke work—the best or superior portion of it. I get 10s. for making a sea-otter fur coat, such a one as is advertised at the selling price of 20 guineas. It takes me six days to make one of these. The trimmings are 1s.; the coals and candles are at the very least 1s.; so that at this work — the most expensive on the establishment — I should earn 8s. clear per week. Such a coat at the West-end would be 36s. making. The next description of garment that I make is a peculiar kind of coat, consisting of superfine blue cloth on one side, with silk braid; on the other side it consists of 'Witney' cloth, and is double-stitched at the seams. It has eighteen rows of stitching round the cuffs of the sleeves, and five pockets.

This is made so as to be turned inside out, and admits of being worn with the superfine cloth outside for fine weather, and the 'Witney' outside should the weather be rough. There are very few hands in the trade that can make this kind of garment. I receive 12s. for making each of them. The trimmings would be about 1s. 6d.; the expenses 1s. Hence I should get 9s. 6d. clear, and it would take me seven days to make one of them. I also make dress and frock coats of the best description. The one you saw me working at last week, and which had four pockets, and was faced with black satin through the front, and had the body and back lined throughout with lustre, thickly quilted, and the seams sewn plain and then stitched on each side, so that there were three sewings to each seam, I received 11s. for. Out of the 11s. I had to find trimmings; these came to 9d., and the expenses to 1s., so that 1 got out of this 9s. 3d. clear. It took me six days to make, and in the honourable part of the trade would have been £1 16s. The remainder of my work consists of dress and frocks coats of the best description. For these I get from 8s. to 10s., or, deducting 1s. 6d. for the trimmings and expenses of these — they are mostly made in summer, when the coals and candles are not so expensive — I make from 6s. 6d. to 8s. 6d. in three days. This is the best kind of work I have. I can make at it from 13s. to 17s. per week. Last week my earnings were 8s. clear. I received 19s. from the establishment, but out of that I had to pay 3s. for trimmings and expenses, and 8s. to the party who helped me. The week before I made 9s. clear; I took 21s., and paid 3s. for trimmings and expenses, and 9s. to my fellow-workman. He is here to answer to the truth of this statement." [The "fellow-workman" assured me that he always shared equally in the earnings of my informant; that he did not lodge with him, nor did he have his breakfast or tea on the premises.] "My average clear earnings, I think, are 10s. I am fully employed all the year round, and never lose a day. I am not fined to that extent to which I know some men are, for the reason that I am one of the very best hands, and they would not like me to leave them. But I know the system of fines to be most iniquitous; on an average, I should say each male hand that works for the establishment is docked 1s. 6d. per week. I myself have been fined as much as 2s. on one garment for being behind time with it, because I objected to work on a Sunday." "Last Christmas week," said the man who was working with my informant, "I stood in the cage (that is the name of the place where the work is given in), and saw no less than twenty fined in two hours, and I am sure the whole amount of the fines stopped in that time must have been at least £3. I am quite satisfied, taking one man with another, the prices that are said to be paid for the coats are reduced by the system of fines at least 15 per cent." "Another part of the fraud and deception of the slop system consists in the mode in which the public are made to believe that the men working for such establishments earn more money than they really do. The plan practised is similar to that adopted by the army clothier, who made out that the loopers working on his establishment made per week from 15s. to 17s. each; whereas, on inquiry, it was found that a considerable sum was paid out of that to others who helped to do the looping for those who took it home. When a coat is given to me to make, a ticket is handed to me with the garment, similar to this one which I have obtained from a friend of mine:

448

  Mr. *Smith* 6675 Made by *M*
   Zc = 12s. = *lined lustre quilted double*
      stitched each side seams
44s. No. 6675.
      o'clock *Friday*
Mr. *Smith*

On this you see the price is marked at 12s.," continued my informant, "and supposing that I, with two others, could make three of these garments in the week, the sum of thirty-six shillings would stand in the books of the establishment as the amount earned by me in that space of time. This would be sure to be exhibited to the customers, immediately there was the last outcry as to the starvation price they paid for their work, as a proof that the workpeople engaged in their establishment received the full prices; whereas out of 36s. entered against my name, I should have had to pay 24s. to those who assisted me; besides this, my share of the trimmings and expenses would be 1s. 6d., and probably my share of the fines would be 1s. more; so that the real fact would be, that I should make 9s. 6d. clear, and this it would be almost impossible for me to do if I did not work long over-hours. I am obliged to keep my wife continually at work helping me to make the garments in order to live. I am in a far worse condition now than when I first began the trade. At first I could earn near upon 36s. My wife then attended to her home, but now, though we both work at the trade and longer hours, I cannot make more than one-third what I did then. I am quite satisfied that the low prices paid in my trade do not arise from too many hands; but there is a wholesale importation of cheap labour every year. The German and Polish Jew tailors, Prussians, Austrians, Belgians, and Hungarians are brought to this country every summer like the Italian boys; and besides this, women, who before, owing to the fair and honourable prices paid for our work, were able to attend solely to their family duties, have now, owing to the unjust prices, been drafted into the tailoring business, and it is this cheap foreign and female labour being brought into competition with ours that reduces the wages of the male hands."

The slop system is rapidly extending all over England, more paritcularly in the manufacturing districts. The effect of this is, that the system of indoor work is gradually being changed throughout into the sweating system, and the operative tailors in the provinces must consequently be shortly reduced to the same state of distress as the slop-workers of the metropolis.

My next visit was to an outdoor worker of the inferior description, from whom I received the following account: —

"I work at the inferior work for the slop-trade. This kind of work is never done 'in doors'— that is, on the premises of the master. The inferior work consists of shooting coats, fishing coats. oxonian coats, paletots, reefing jackets, pilot coats, chesterfields. codringtons, bullers, sacks, sailors' jackets, and Spanish cloaks. The last-mentioned garment is the worst paid of all the work I have to do. For making a large Spanish cloak, with a hood to come over the head, and with six holes on each side of the garment, and three banyan plaits at the hips, I get 2s. The cloak has more work in it than an ordinary great-coat; indeed, it is than an ordinary great coat; indeed, it is similar in make to an old-fashioned great coat with a hood to it. It takes two days — working 17 hours each day — or very nearly three ordinary days — to make one of these cloaks. I could earn at this kind of work from 4s. to 4s. 6d., and out of this I should have to pay 7d. for trimmings and about 1s. for lighting and firing. Hence my clear weekly earnings would be from 2s. 6d. to 3s. These garments are given out only at a very slack time of the year, when they know that the men must do them at the employer's own price. About five years ago the price paid for making these garments began to be reduced. They were before that time 2s. 6d., and they have since gradually fallen to 2s. The best-paid work that I do is the shooting coats. The Oxonians are almost as good as they are, but I prefer the shooting coats. These, I think, are the best paid of all the inferior kinds of slop-work. I get 3s. for making one of these. I can make one in two days of twelve hours each; but I am a very quick hand. At this kind of work I could get 9s. per week. I could earn more by working longer time, of course. Out of the 9s. it would cost me 9d. for trimmings, and the expenses of firing and lighting 1s. My clear earnings, therefore, would be 7s. 3d. per week. Taking the good with the bad work that I do, I should say that I make on an average about 5s. or 6s. a week clear. I do make more occasionally, but then I have to work longer time to get it. By working over-hours and Sundays, I manage to make from 8s. to 9s. clear. To get this much, I must begin work at six in the worning, and sit close at it till eleven at night. This statement includes, of course, the necessary loss of time consequent on going backwards and forwards, taking work in, and getting fresh work out, and having to make alterations as well. I work first-handed — that is, I am not employed by any sweater. I originally belonged to the honourable part of the trade. I have made shooting coats for masters at the West-end, and had 14s. for making the very same garment as I now get 3s. for. When working at the honourable trade, my average weekly earnings were about £1, including vacation. Now I don't get half that amount. It is six or seven years ago since I worked for the West-end shops. My wife did no work then. I could maintain her in comfort by the produce of my labour. Now she slaves night and day, as I do: and very often she had less rest than myself, for she has to stop up after I have gone to bed to attend to her domestic duties. The two of us, working these long hours, and the Sundays as well, can get only 15s.— that is to say, the two of us slaving night and day, and all the Sabbath long, can earn only three-quarters as much as I alone could get by working twelve hours each day for six days in the week, and that but seven years ago. I believe mine to be about an average of the condition and earnings of the male hands engaged in the slop-trade. Many are much worse off than I am, but some are better. I attribute the decline in the wages of the operative tailor to the introduction of cheap Irish, foreign, and female labour. Before then we could live and keep our families by our own exertions; now our wives and children must work as well as ourselves to get less money than we alone could earn a few years back. My comforts have not in any way increased with the decrease in the price of provisions. Bread, tea, meat, sugar, are all much cheaper than they were five years ago. Bread, three years since this winter, was 11d. and 11½d. the quartern, now it is 4½d. and 5d.— that is more than half as cheap, and yet I can safely say I am twice as badly off now as I was then; and so I know are all the people in my trade. Our wages have gone down more than provisions; that is to say, we and our wives work more than twice as hard, and we get less food and less comfort by our labour. Fifteen or twenty years ago such a thing as a journeyman tailor having to give security before he could get work was unknown; but now I and such as myself could not get a stitch to do first-handed, if we did not either procure the security of some house-holder, or deposit £5 in the hands of the employer. The reason of this is, the journeymen are so badly paid that the employers know they can barely live on what they get, and consequently they are often driven to pawn the garments given out to them, in order to save themselves and their families from starving. If the journeyman can manage to scrape together £5, he has to leave it in the hands of his employer all the time that he is working for the house. I know one person who gives out the work for a fashionable West-end slop-shop who will not take household security, and requires £5 from each hand. I am informed by one of the parties who worked for this man that he has as many as 150 hands in his employ, and that each of these has placed £5 in his hands, so that altogether the poor people have handed over £750, to increase the capital upon which he trades, and for which he pays no interest whatsoever." [The reader will remember a similar case (mentioned by the poor stay-stitcher in a former letter) of a large wholesale staymaker in the City who had amassed a large fortune by begin-ning to trade upon the 5s. which he demanded to be left in his hands by his workpeople before he gave them employment.] "Two or three years back one of the slop-sellers at the East-end became bankrupt, and the poor people lost all the money that had been deposited as security for work in his hands. The journey-men who get the security of householders are enabled to do so by a system which is now in general practice at the East-end. Several bakers, publicans, chandler's-shop keepers, and coal-shed keepers make a trade of becoming security for those seeking slop-work. They consent to be responsible for the workpeople upon the con-dition of the men dealing at their shops. The workpeople who require such security are generally very good customers, from the fact of their either having large families, all engaged in the same work, or else several females or males working under them, and living at their house. The parties becoming securities thus not only greatly increase their trade, but furnish a second-rate article at a first-rate price. It is useless to complain of the bad quality or high price of the articles supplied by the securities, for the shop-keepers know as well as the workpeople that it is impossible for the hands to leave them without losing their work. I know one baker whose security was refused at the slop-house because he was already responsible for so many, and he begged the publican to be his deputy, so that by this means the workpeople were obliged to deal at both baker's and publican's too. I never heard of a butcher making a trade of becoming security, because the slopwork people cannot afford to consume much meat. The same system is also pursued by lodging-house keepers. They will become responsible if the workmen requiring security will undertake to lodge at their house. Concerning the system of fines adopted at the lower class of slop houses, I know that within the last week a new practice has been introduced of stopping 1d. out of the wages for each garment that is brought in after eleven o'clock on the Saturday. By this means upwards of £1 was collected last Saturday night. This the proprietor of the shop pretends to distribute in charity; but if he does so, the charitable gift passes as his own money, and we have no means of knowing how much he collects and how much he distributes. There is also a fine of 4d. for each louse found on the garments brought in. The fine for vermin at other houses is sometimes as high as 6d., and at others as low as 3d. The poor people are obliged to live in the cheapest and filthiest places, and have, even if they felt inclined, little or no time to 'clean themselves.' If a louse is found on the garments brought in by any of the 'lady sweaters,' who are generally much better dressed than the poor workpeople, it is wrapped up in a piece of clean paper, and presented to the 'lady' in an under tone, so that the other parties present may not be aware of the circumstance. If the vermin be found upon the garments brought in by the poor people, the foremen make no secret of it, and fine them 4d., in the presence of all in the shop. When the wife of a sweater returns home, and tells the hands working under her husband that 4d. has been stopped for a louse found upon the garments taken in, an angry discussion often arises among the workpeople as to whose it was."

My informant tells me that the wives of many sweaters make a practice of being continually on the look-out to entrap young and inexperienced hands from the country. If they see a youth whom they know to be a tailor by the peculiarity of his walk, and he appears to be a stranger in London, they stop him, and inquire if he has come to town for work. If he answers in the affirmative, they tell him that their husband will give him as much as he wants — that if he chooses to come and live and lodge with them he shall be very comfortable, and may earn as much as 16s. a week. The youth is generally inveigled by what he hears, is taken home to the sweater's house, and once in there it is impossible to extricate himself. His coat is soon pledged, and he is forced to remain working with the sweater for the merest pittance, living on the worst food and inhabiting the foulest rooms for months, and perhaps years. My informant assures me that he knows many such cases, and indeed this, he says, has now become so general a practice, that even the old hands in the trade are frequently stopped in the street, and accosted by these women. He himself has had such overtures made to him several times. The system of importing cheap Irish and foreign labour is also very extensively carried on. Letters are sent to Ireland to the friends of the London sweaters, telling them that they are in want of hands, and then a supply is shipped off to the sweater on the promise of good wages. This is the cause, I am assured, of so many Irish hands being at present working at the trade. I hope to be able to bring forward, in my next letter, several cases in proof of this. At present I shall content myself by referring to the speech of the poor shirtless youth who made his appearance, and by citing the following instances: —

I now come to the narrative of a man assuredly a type of a very numerous class — a journeyman tailor, who adhered as long as possible to the "honourable" trade and the rules of the society, but who had to become *a sweater with a family:* — "I am 49, and had been a journeyman tailor for 30 years. My experience of the business in London extends over 25 years. I came to London 25 years ago, and the average of my wages was 36s.; indeed, I've many a week earned £2 and more by my own labour alone. This was the case for eight or nine years. I was very seldom out of work in those days. I was then a married man with a family; but I could and did support and educate my family well and comfortably by my own labour. After the term I have mentioned I felt a difference. Trade fell off gradually, and kept falling, dragging down men's earnings with it, until it's as bad as we find it now. Wages fell more after the change in 1834. A bad job that ever it happened — it was indeed. Wages, or earnings, kept still falling, and, my family growing up, I was compelled to become a sweater, putting my two boys and two girls to work to assist me, as well as my wife, when her health permitted. With all these five hands and my own labour I could not on slop-work, working every day and long hours, earn more than 30s. a week; and I had the best of the work that was given out. A man regularly employed by a slop master cannot earn more than 12s. a week by his own labour, out of which he must find his own sewing-trimmings, candles, &c. Provisions are cheaper than they were, certainly; but wages, I have found, fall faster and sooner than provisions — so cheap tea and sugar's little benefit. I worked for ——, but was only once in their shop in my life. I always sent my wife or one of my children for and with the work. I couldn't spare time to go myself. If I had had only myself I could not have earned more than 10s. at twelve hours' work every day. I have no doubt that the low-priced 'ticketing' shops have brought about this hard state of things, bringing females into the trade, and forcing men to work for almost any wages. If any good soul were to leave me £100 now, or even £500, it would be no use my attempting to do any good with it as a small master. I could not get enough custom. A man could at one time live comfortably under one of them. I have not tasted spirits for seven years come Easter, but with all my endeavours and my family's I cannot save anything. My rent is 3s. 6d. a week for two rooms. If I ever ran off tipping, somebody must want. I left —— because I was employed to make three frock coats, lined through with silk and quilted, for which I received 10s. each (the regular pay would be 21s.), and from the 30s. I earned my employer wanted to deduct 6s. — that is, 2s. on each coat as a fine. I might take less and keep my work, or be paid the 30s. and lose my work. That's the way they gradually lower wages still more. Such masters always take advantage of a slack time. What can men with families do? Men must submit."

From an intelligent man I learned how some employers still further reduced the low wages paid by *fines,* and by *deductions* from the usual charge for garments in the case of men below the average height or bulk, saying that they must be paid for at the same rate as boy's clothing. "If I give way," said the man, "next time, perhaps, a rather bigger man's trowsers would be reckoned as boys', and so it creeps on." On the subject of *fines,* I will relate what was told me by another workman — several representing the same thing to me as very common. His wife had taken up work at ——'s, and when she went home, some part of the stuff was found wanting: It had not been given out by the "trimmer." She went back, but could not get the stuff wanted unless she would pay for it. On her demurring, she was fined 1s., and on the husband's going to expostulate, *he* was fined 1s., that, as he was told, he might not have the laugh against his wife! He complained to the superintendent of the shop who told him he must put up with such things. He had his choice — pay the fines, and keep his work, or to refuse to pay them, and leave it. The "trimmer" pronounced him drunk and abusive, but the man declares he went straight from his work, and was perfectly sober and civil. This same man was fined 1s. for being an hour too late with a jacket, at which he had worked all night, and had not a reasonable time allowed to finish the job. Many men complained of the utter disregard of their convenience shown by some employers or their shopmen; such as getting work in the evening, and being compelled to work all night, without a farthing extra for fire or candle.

The following is the statement of a master in the City, to whom I was referred as a very intelligent man, and one greatly respected: —"I have been in business fifteen years. When I commenced I used to get good prices, but now I am compelled to give as good an article at a lower price — fully twenty per cent. lower — in order to compete with ready-made and cheap clothes shops. I have not in consequence reduced the wages of the men in my employ, so that my profits are considerably reduced, while my exertions, and those of other tradesmen similarly circumstanced, to keep together a 'connection,' which may yield fair prices and a fair remuneration, have to be more strenuous than ever. Year by year I have found the cheap establishments affect my business, and it seems to me that if the system pursued by the show and slop houses be not checked, it will swamp all the honourable trade, which becomes every year smaller. Customers bargain now more than ever as to price, their constant remark being, 'I can get it for so much at ——'s'. When I began business the cheap system had not been started. Slopsellers formerly were those who made inferior clothing, badly cut and badly made, and paid for accordingly. Now, there must be — for these great cheap houses — good work for bad wages. Some years ago a great part of the slopseller's business was to make clothes for the slaves in the West Indies, for East Indian regiments, jackets for sailors, and such like. When I began business the slop trade was a distinct thing from what is understood as the 'regular' trade of the tailor. Tailoring was then kept to itself. There were not half the good hands to be got then that there are now. A really first-rate hand was comparatively scarce. Now I can get any number of first-rate hands, as I give full wages. I could get twenty such hands, if I wanted them, in a few hours. My business, to compete with the slopsellers, requires the most incessant attention, or I am sure it would fall. I cannot now afford to give such a term of credit as formerly. My regular hands earn the same wages as they have earned all along; they perhaps average 25s. to 30s. a week through the year. My trade is looked upon as an exception to the general lowering of price and wretched payment of the workmen round about here. I find the effects of the ready-made trade most at holiday times, Easter and Christmas, when business used to be the best. People at those times now run to the slop-shops. I have worked my business up in my own way, but I am convinced that if I had to begin it now, instead of fifteen years ago, I could not have established myself with a body of respectable and regular customers, at fair prices; not even with more capital at my command, I must have adopted the low-priced system. As businesses 'of the old school' fall off, the customers go to the slop-sellers. Such businesses as mine are becoming fewer; tailors' shops now must be on a very large scale, or they are not to be carried on profitably at all."

A card was put into my hands on my rounds: it ran as follows: —

---

to be raffled
on Monday, the 17TH of December, at the
Angel and Crown, Ship Alley, Wellclose Square
A WAISTCOAT
the property of W. W., who has had a Long fit of Sickness.
Chairman Mr. J. F. — Dep. Mr. P. C.
Tickets 6d. Each   Music Provided.

I lost no time in seeking out the sick man, and found him truly destitute. I was directed to one of the back streets of the Commercial-road; and there, in a small, close, and bare, unfurnished room, stretched on a bed scantily covered, I found the poor sick slopworker. On the floor sat a man cross-legged at work, who had no place to carry on his trade. He had come to sit in the dying man's room, and to use the sleeve-boards and irons that the invalid has no use for.On the narrow wooden mantel-shelf stood a row of empty physic bottles and an old wine glass; beside the man's bed was a small deal table, on which was a mildewed orange, half peeled. The ceiling was browned in patches with the wet that had leaked through from the roof. The wife followed me upstairs. There was no chair in the room, and one was borrowed from below for my accommodation. She told me the house was "dreadful damp; it was never dry, winter or summer; the wet often streamed down the walls." I had seen many squalid, desolate homes, but this was more wretched than all. I asked why the sick man was not taken to the hospital. The man himself could not speak for coughing. The wife told me he could not go to the hospital, his clothes were all in pledge; they had been taken to the pawnshop for the subsistence of the family. "If it hadn't been for that we must all have starved," she said. "This last five weeks he has been confined to his bed, and we have been obliged to make away with all we had. I have pawned all my under-clothing. I have five children; the eldest fourteen, and the youngest two years and a half old. I have pledged almost all their clothes, and if I could have taken anything else off the poor little things, I should have done it to get victuals for them." The man himself now raised his head from below the bed-clothes. His long black hair was thrown off his forehead, and his face, which had once been handsome, was suffused with perspiration. His black unshorn beard made him look paler perhaps than he was. He breathed hard and quickly. He told me he could not go to the hospital because he should lose his work if he did so. "I worked at the out-door work for a large slop-shop. I did the bespoke work" said he. "Look here," cried one of his friends, dragging a coat from off the sick man's bed; "see here; the man has no covering, and so he throws this garment over him as a shelter." [It was a new pilot coat that was to be taken in that evening for the shop.] I expressed my surprise that the bed of the sick man should be covered with the new garment, and was informed that such in the winter time was a common practice among the workpeople. When the weather was very cold, and their blankets had gone to the pawnshop, the slopworkers often went to bed, I was told, with the sleeves of the coat they were making drawn over their arms, or else they would cover themselves with the trowsers or paletots, according to the description of garment they had in hand. The ladies riding habits in particular, I was assured, were used as counterpanes to the poor people's beds, on account of the quantity of cloth in the skirts. "He will get 3s. for making such a coat as this," continued the sick man's friend, still holding up the garment, "and out of that he will have to pay 6d. for trimmings and expenses. It will take him two days to make such a coat, working twelve hours each day. But in the slop trade we hardly understand 12 hours work in a day; our time for labour is mostly 18 hours every day. Doing 12 hours work a day he could make 7s. 6d. a week clear at such work, and out of that he has to keep himself, a wife, and five children, and pay rent. I can earn upon an average," he said, "by my own labour, from 9s. to 10s. a week clear." Here my attention was distracted by a loud voice below stairs. It was one of the servants of the slop-house, come to demand a certain garment that had been given out to the sick man to make, and which he had employed a party to finish for him. It had been pawned when completed to keep the sick man's family from starving, and when the poor fellow was told the cause of the noise below stairs, he trembled like a leaf, and the perspiration again started in large drops to his forehead. "Let me drink," he said. I asked to see the pawn tickets. They were shown me; and I was told by one of the parties present in the room that the firm, having heard of my inquiry into the condition and earnings of the workpeople, were calling in all garments, so as to prevent my seeing the prices marked upon the tickets sent out with the clothes. The same person assured me that a servant of the house had called upon him that morning, and demanded a particular garment that he had to make for them. It was in pawn, he told me, and he had been obliged to pledge the work of another employer, in order to redeem the coat demanded. Indeed, I was assured that such was the distress of the workpeople that there was scarcely one that had not work of their employers in pawn; that one coat was continually substituted for another to prevent inquiries; and that a month's interest was paid on each, though it was generally in pawn but a few days. The workpeople dreaded detection more than anything, because it was sure to be followed by the withdrawal of their security, and this was their ruin. "I came over from Ireland several years back," continued the sick man, in answer to my questions. "I worked from a house of call for about ten years after I came to England, and then I came to this slop work, at which I have been about twelve years. When I was engaged at the honourable trade I could make three times as much as I do now. I was very comfortable then." "We are not so now, God knows," said the wife. "When I fell sick I had 9s. a week from my society; now I have not a farthing from anybody, nor do I know where to get a farthing if I wanted it. Since I have been at the slop work I have neither been able to save anything, nor to keep my children as I wanted to. I couldn't even send them to church of a Sunday for the want of their clothes. I fell ill two years ago, with a pain in my chest and side, and a bad cough. It was working long hours that made me bad. My side is quite raw from blistering. There are many men who are working at this business, who have not been outside the doors and smelt the fresh air for months and months together. In some places the workmen have only one coat to put on between six, and many cannot spare the time. The wife goes to take the work in and get the work out. For two years I have fought against my complaint. I never was to say well in this house. I slept downstairs on the ground-floor, and I think that was the cause of my illness. There are no drains at all to the house, and the stagnant water remains underneath the boards downstairs. In the yard the standing water is like a cesspool. I went on for two years working away, though I was barely able, and at last, five weeks ago, I was dead beat. I couldn't do a stitch more, and was obliged to take to my bed. Since then we have been living on what we pawned. There was nothing else to be done, and, as a last resource, we have got up a raffle. We generally do assist one another, if we can, but we are all so poor we have scarcely a penny for ourselves, any of us. I have come down to my very last now, and if I don't get better in health, what will become of us all I don't know. We can't do without something to eat. My children cry for victuals as it is, and what we shall do in a little while is more than I can say." "Consider," said a fellow-workman of the man to me, "if he goes into the hospital the little employment that he has when he is well will go from him. He is afraid, therefore, to leave here." "As it is, his anxiety of mind makes him worse, for he is fretting all day long," said his wife, "about his children, and whatever will become of them all if he stops as he is much longer, I can't tell."

LETTER XVIII
Tuesday, December 18, 1849

Of the 21,000 journeymen tailors at work in the metropolis there were, in the year 1844, 3,697 employed on the premises of the masters in the "honourable" trade at the West-end of London, and 2,348 working out of doors at the "dishonourable" show and slop trade. Hence there were 6,081 journeymen tailors engaged at the West-end, and about 15,000 employed at the East-end of the metropolis. In the East there are upwards of 80 slop and show shops, many employing from 200 to 300 hands. There were in 1844 only 72 masters in the West who had all the work made on their premises; besides these, there were 270 masters who had only part of their work made in-doors, and 112 who had none at all done at home. Hence the West-end branch of the business consisted principally of 454 masters, of whom less than one-sixth belonged to what is called the "honourable" part of the trade. Since then, I am assured by one who has long made the business his peculiar study, that the 72 honourable masters have declined at least to 60, while the 172 dishonourable ones have been more than doubled. The men employed in-doors have decreased from 3,600 to less than 3,000, and those employed out of doors have increased from 2,300 to more than 4,000. Hence the honourable part of the trade is declining at the rate of 150 men per year; so that in 20 years at least the whole business will have merged in the show and slop shops; and the wages of the men have fallen from 18s. a week — which I find is the average of the honourable part of the trade — to 11s., the average of the slop trade.

The aggregate earnings of the 3,000 men now employed at the honourable part of the trade are £2,700 a week, or £140,000 a year, and the earnings of the 18,000 men working at the show and slop trade £9,900 a week, or £514,800 a year. Hence, as a body, the wages of the metropolitan tailors amount to £655,200 a year. But, according to the rate of decrease before mentioned, in twenty years the honourable part of the trade will have entirely disappeared, and the wages of the whole 21,000 journeymen will have declined to 11s. According to this estimate the workmen generally will, at the expiration of that time, suffer an annual loss of £54,600; that is, they will receive upwards of £50,000 less for their year's work than they do now. By the same calculation I find that they are collectively receiving every year £3,000 less wages than they did the year before.

In the year 1844 there were at the West-end 676 men, women, and children working under "sweaters," and occupying ninety-two small rooms, measuring 8 feet by 10, which upon an average was more than seven persons to each apartment. This number of individuals was composed of 179 men, 85 women, 45 boys, 78 girls, and 256 children — the latter being members of the sweaters' family. I am assured that these numbers have at least been doubled in the last five years, and that the number of boys, girls, and women introduced into the trade by the sweaters since the year 1844 is certainly three times as many as it was then. The number of individuals who made a practice of working on the Sunday, at the time the investigation was made, was 852; this, I am informed, has considerably increased. The better class of artisans denounce the system of Sunday working as the most iniquitous of all the impositions on the honourable part of the trade. They object to it, not only on moral and religious grounds, but economically also. "Every 600 men employed on the Sabbath," they say, "deprive 100 individuals of a week's work; every six men who labour seven days in the week must necessarily throw one other man out of employ for a whole week. The seventh man is deprived of his fair share of work by the overtoiling of the other six." This Sunday working, I am told, is a necessary consequence of the cheap slop trade. The workmen cannot keep their families by their six days' labour; and therefore they not only, under that system, get less wages and do more work, but by their extra labour they throw so many more hands out of employ.

Of the system of "sweating," the report of the operative tailors in 1844 furnishes the following information, which my recent investigations enable me fully to corroborate: —

"Many of the families (consisting of six or seven persons in many cases) are, from their scanty incomes, obliged to live in one room of small dimensions, and when illness attacks any one of its members, whatever be its nature, whether highly contagious or otherwise, no separation from the remainder of the family takes place, but the latter employ themselves as usual in this vitiated atmosphere, exposed frequently to the accumulated influence of contagion, insufficient diet, and constant sedentary work, during sixtxeen out of the twenty-four hours.

"There can be little doubt that woollen clothes remaining for days together in such apartments, and sometimes in contact with the parties labouring under the effects of smallpox, scarlet fever, and other highly contagious diseases, will very likely prove a source from which such contagion may be propagated in the families of those to whom these woollens may be sent. Mr. French, a medical gentleman, states that he has seen a garment (which was a few hours afterwards to be forwarded to a person of rank, serving at the time of his visit as a covering to an individual suffering from small-pox."

On last Friday evening a very numerous meeting was held at the Hanover-square Rooms, in order to arrive at statistical results concerning the earnings of the working tailors of the West-end. As many as 2,000 attended, and the respectable appearance of the operatives formed a striking contrast to those who had been present at the meeting at Shadwell.

MEETING, HANOVER-SQUARE ROOMS, FRIDAY, DECEMBER 14.— The proceedings were commenced by the Metropolitan Correspondent of *The Morning Chronicle,* who explained that the operative tailors had been called together for the purpose of collecting certain information in connection with their trade. The object of the meeting was to obtain an estimate of the earnings of the working classes. There was no other end in view but to ascertain the truth: and the instructions he had received were to search out the fact wheresoever they might lead. In the first place it was desirable to have a history of prices in the trade, and then to follow out the depression and its causes. Besides a history of prices, he wishes to ascertain how many tailors laboured single-handed twenty years ago; whether the change in prices since that period had forced them to employ their wives and families in order to make out a living; and whether prices had been affected by so many extra needlewomen being introduced into the market? With regard to the slop trade, he found, from an inquiry instituted among the operative tailors by their own body, that in the year 1845 there were 72 masters who had all their work done upon their own premises, and that they employed 998 men at the rate of 6s. per day. There were also 270 masters who had only a portion of their work done upon their own premises, and they employed 1,310 men out of doors at scanty and unremunerating prices. Of these 270 there were 112 who had no work done upon their own premises. At that period there were employed within doors altogether 3,697 individuals, and 2,384 out of doors. Now, it was desirable to ascertain how far these numbers had changed since — information which would prove whether or not the slop trade had been gaining ground. If, for example, the number of persons employed in-doors had decreased from 3,600, say, to 2,000, whilst the number employed out of doors had increased from 2,300 to 3,400, the operative tailors might perceive what would be the result in a few years. According to the same authority there were 643 persons employed in sweaters' rooms, occupying 98 small rooms and 33 larger. The total number working upon the Sunday was 389. Now, he should like to know how far these numbers had increased, and to what cause the increase was owing. With reference to another part of the subject — the sufferings and privations endured by the workpeople through the low price paid for their labour — they should contrast their present with their past condition. He wished to discover whether their comforts had increased with the decreased price of provisions. If wages fell faster than provisions, it was very clear the working classes must ultimately lapse into pauperism. If they fell at the same rate, and from the same causes, then no benefit had resulted from the recent change; whereas if the price of labour had no connection with the price of food, then it was evident that if wages had gone down, and provisions had remained at the same price, the working classes must have starved outright. It was for the meeting to state what were the facts; and whilst asking them to make known their experience in connection with this subject, they must understand that he did not himself express any opinion, one way or the other — his only object being to collect the facts from their own lips. He further wished to know how much longer they were obliged to work now, and how many more hands they were obliged to employ, in order to gain the same amount of money and obtain the same comforts as they formerly earned and enjoyed. But the most important aim of the meeting was to discover whether the low prices arose from competition among the masters, or from competition amongst the workpeople. To arrive at this knowledge, it would be necessary, first, to ascertain whether the number of hands among the operative tailors had been stationary; also, whether a certain amount of extraneous labour had not been introduced into the craft; also, provided such extraneous labour had been introduced, would the number of hands have been sufficient to perform the amount of work to be done? Had female labour, Irish labour, and foreign labour been introduced or imported for the sake of cheapness, and so undersold the regular artisan? Had the trade suffered from being overstocked by its own hands, or from the addition of such labour as would not, by the mere increase of population, have been introduced into it? It was for them to bring out the facts. He also wished to know whether, in their opinion, the emigration of the working classes would be sufficient to alter the depression of wages? He desired to consult the operatives themselves upon these important questions. He offered no opinion himself; but he wanted theirs, and the facts on which they founded it.

A WORKING TAILOR then came forward, and said he would take a brief review of the condition of the trade so long as he had known it, and endeavour to point out the progress and causes of its downfall. It had been his misfortune, during a period of twenty-five years, to see, not only a downward motion in the trade as regarded prices, but a very material increase in the amount of labour, and a diminution of the chances of obtaining work. The tailors of the metropolis had never hitherto had the opportunity of making their circumstances clearly known to the public. The public hitherto had never had the means of fairly testing their ignorance or their intelligence; and he complained that, whenever they had expressed their dissatisfaction, they had been set down as ignorant beings, who could not comprehend their position or the benefits which they were said to enjoy. Certainly, within his time, the means of making the working classes happy had increased in the country; but in the proportion of that increase had the tailors, as a class, become miserable. Various causes had conspired to enslave them — for he could describe their condition by no other term. In the year 1825, he recollected the trade discovering an evil just creeping in, which, even then, threatened destruction, if not checked. A desire was then evinced on the part of some masters to get work done off their premises, and they commenced by giving out the light trade, such as waistcoat-making. The trade foresaw this would lead to great evil, and in 1825 they made an attempt to stop it. Every house in London that employed men upon their own premises were told that, unless they would undertake not to give out waistcoats to women, the men would not work for them. The answer given in almost every instance was that they would not; but they did not maintain the honour of their word. They still gave out work to women at home. At that time, having come from the country, he obtained 6s. a day, as certain as he went to work, and he was able to maintain his family in comfort and respectability. But this system was afterwards materially departed from by the men themselves. After they found that there was a great number of women who could be useful in the trade, that the husband, by his wife and daughters becoming waistcoat-makers, could make somewhat more money than he could in the shop, they left the shop. That was a fault upon the part of the men, for he thought they were bound to acknowledge their own faults when they pointed out those of the masters. During this time the "show shops" were progressing; but they were not considered respectable. These shops, it must be understood always, from the first, gave out their work to be done at home, because they discovered they could get it done cheaper, as women were employed, than by having men at work upon their own premises. Then some of the more respectable portions of the trade began to imagine that they might put a trifle into their pockets by commencing the same system. Thus the system was established, and, sooner or later, all must go into the same channel. They had already discovered, by the experience of the East-end, that there was no stopping point but one which was equal to starving them out of existence. Abundant evidence had been given, and indeed they all knew it, of the fact that men earning only half-a-crown a day, by fifteen or sixteen hours' hard work, were reduced even from that. This was a fair expression of what competition would do for the whole class, unless it was guarded by some well-understood principle between the employers and the employed. The Government of the country had really been the means of reducing prices in the tailoring trade to so low a scale that no human being, whatever his industry, could live and be happy in his lot. The Government were really responsible for the first introduction of female labour. He would clearly prove what he had stated. He would refer first to the army clothing. Our soldiers were comfortably clothed, as they had a right to be; but surely the men who made the clothing which was so comfortable, ought to be paid for their labour so as to be able to keep themselves comfortable and their families virtuous. But it was in evidence that the persons working upon army clothing could not, upon an average, earn more than 1s. a day. Another Government department — the Post-office — afforded a considerable amount of employment to tailors; but those who worked upon the Post-office clothing earned at the most only 1s. 6d. a day. The police clothing was another considerable branch of tailoring; this, like the others, ought to be paid for at living prices; but the men at work at it could only earn 1s. 6d. a day, supposing them to work hard all the time fourteen or fifteen hours. The Custom-house clothing gave about the same prices. Now, all these sorts of work were performed by time workers, who, as a natural consequence of the wages they received, were the most miserable of human beings. Husband, wife, and family, all worked at it; they just tried to breathe upon it; to live it never could be called. Yet the same

Government, which paid such wretched wages, called upon these wretched people to be industrious, to be virtuous, and happy. How was it possible, whatever their industry, to be virtuous and happy? The fact was, the men who, at a slack season, had been compelled to fall back upon these kinds of work, became so beggared and broken down by it, notwithstanding the assistance of their wives and families, that they were never able to rise out of it. They were obliged to hang on at it, month after month, till their spirits or their health failed; and the only addition they could possibly expect was the miserable work they received from the slop-shop. And as to the slop-shop, the owners and the sweaters who served them cared not what the sufferings of their workpeople were, so long as they could become rich, and ride in fine carriages through the City and elsewhere. Was this, he asked, a right system? Was it one likely to promote the real strength and prosperity of the country? It was clear that the Government had no idea of what was going on, or they would take some steps in reference to it. It was a delusion on the part of the middle or any other class to suppose it was their interest to reduce the wages of the working man. Recurring to his own trade, he pointed out the evils of the system of middlemen, or sweaters, and said he had evidence that through it first-rate workmen for a house, which had establishments both at the West-end and in the City, had to work 4½ days for 11s. He only hoped they would be able to obtain the countenance of the employers, and induce them to conduct their business upon a different principle. It was clear there was no remedy for the unfortunate condition of the working tailors, save and except in the abolition of home work, and of the sweating system, and in living prices being paid for Government work.

R. E., also a working tailor, said the progress of the miserable system by which his fellow-workmen were being destroyed having been described, he would draw attention to what he conceived to have been its causes, and to what he considered its remedy. During the last twenty months there had been, from time to time, meetings of trade delegates in London. Their own trade was among the number represented. The delegates had gathered a certain amount of information, by which it was shown that there were, at that time, at least 280,000 mechanics in London. It was ascertained further, that of these 280,000 one-third only were fully employed, one-third were partially employed, and one-third were entirely unemployed. These facts were stated to the Government, they were stated to several influential members of both Houses of Parliament; and the invariable reply was that Government was well disposed to do everything that was possible for the benefit of the working classes, if they knew how. Such was the assurance of a very popular nobleman having a seat in the lower house. Now he would point out at least one respect in which Government might benefit the working classes. He held in his hand a pamphlet containing statements of the Admiralty contract prices for navy clothing. The contract system had been mainly instrumental in destroying the living wages of the working man. Now, the Government were the sole originators of the system of contracts and of sweating. Forty years ago there was nothing known of contracts, except Government contracts; and at that period the contractors were confined to making slops for the navy, the army, and the West India slaver. It was never dreamt of then that such a system was to come into operation in the better classes of trade, till ultimately it was destructive of masters as well as men. The Government having been the cause of the contract system, and consequently of the sweating system, he called upon them to abandon it. The sweating system had established the show shops and the ticket system, both of which were countenanced by the Government. Even the Court assisted to keep the system in fashion, and the royal arms and royal warrants were now exhibited common enough by slopsellers. If the royal arms and royal warrants were used, why, the noble lord was asked, should they not be permitted to a house like Stultz's, which paid good wages? Would it not be more worthy of the Court and the Government to appropriate them to such a house, than bestow them as they were bestowed at the present moment? To this the noble lord could only reply that if the facts were made known to her Majesty he was confident that she would not countenance anything of the sort, and that the system would be put an end to. How, then, to bring the facts before her Majesty? He could only see one effectual way, namely, to bring popular opinion to bear upon the Government with all its force. The broad question with regard to Government and other work was, "Shall the labouring man, after the employment of all his industry and skill, exist upon less than slaves' wages, and under worse than slaves' treatment?" Government said, its duty was to do justice. But was it consistent with justice to pay only 2s. 6d. for making navy jackets, which would be paid 10s. for by every "honourable" tradesman? Was it consistent with justice for the Government to pay for Royal Marine clothing (private's coat and epaulets) 1s. 9d.? Was it consistent with justice for the Government to pay for making a pair of trousers (four or five hours' work) only 2½d.? And yet, when a contractor, noted for paying just wages to those he employed, brought this under the consideration of the Admiralty, they declared they had nothing to do with it. Here is their answer: —

"Admiralty, March 19, 1847.

"Sir—Having laid before my Lords Commissioners of the Admiralty your letter of the 8th inst., calling their attention to the extremely low prices paid for making up articles of clothing, provided for her Majesty's naval service, I am commanded by their lordships to acquaint you, that they have no control whatever over the wages paid for making up contract clothing. Their duty is to take care that the articles supplied are of good quality, and well made: the cost of the material and the workmanship are matters which rest with the contractor; and if the public were to pay him a higher price than that demanded, it would not ensure any advantage to the men employed by him, as their wages depend upon the amount of competition for employment amongst themselves.

"I am, sir, your most obedient servant,

"W. Shaw, Esq."   "H. G. WARD.

After this, he repeated, he saw no other means of urging this subject upon the attention of the Court and the Government, but through the force of public opinion. He regarded emigration as, at best, a fallacious remedy. Mr. Bright said, at the late dinner in Manchester, that food was cheaper now than it had been for twelve years, and that wages were higher than they had been for five years. Did anybody in the meeting believe that statement [loud cries of "no"]? Now, he would like to take the sense of the meeting, whether they, as working tailors, were now in a better condition than before, under the present reduced price of provisions?

This question, which was unexpected, was eventually modified into this shape: "Do the working men here assembled feel they are much better off — that their comforts have been greater, and their employment more — since provisions have been cheaper?"

"No, no," was the answer of at least a thousand voices.

Another question was asked in these words: "Provided the laws had not been altered, and the prices of provisions remained as they were, would you have been worse off than you are now?"

"No," replied some; "yes," others.

At the suggestion of a person in the body of the meeting the question was thus put: "Are the working men better paid and better employed now than they were five years ago?"

The meeting instantly replied, "No, no."

Somebody asked why five years were taken, and he wished twenty-five to be substituted. To please this party the question was once more modified in these words: "Are the working men better off now, and better paid, than they were twenty-five years ago?"

A unanimous negative was the immediate answer.

On the recommendation of another party this question was also put: "Are you satisfied, if the laws with regard to provisions had not been altered, you would have been worse off?"

The answer to this was "Yes;" after which, such questions being objected to as involving points not directly connected with the purposes of the meeting, they were discontinued.

—— C., also a working tailor, said he would briefly offer his opinion upon the policy which he thought would for the future guide the trade in the right direction, and also upon the bad policy which had brought it to its present condition. It was manifest that the slop-trade and the sweating system had materially injured the regular and honourable trade. There could be no question that, for the last thirty years, each succeeding year had been worse than its predecessor, and that upon an average wages had, in the same period, been reduced fully one-half. At that period an industrious and efficient workman could calculate upon an average of 30s. per week the year round; now he was a fortunate man, indeed, who could say, "I can calculate certainly upon 15s. the year round." A great majority of the trade, to his certain knowledge, did not average more than 10s. This state of things had been brought about partly by competition among the workmen and partly by competition among the masters; but the workmen had assisted in bringing this result about quite as much as any combination among the masters could have done. It was futile to charge upon the masters of 1849 the faults of the masters of 1825. There could be no doubt that the cause of the sweating system had been the cupidity of the workmen. The greediness of men, not content with their own earnings, led them to abandon the places where they were at work, in order to go home and labour excessive hours. These men employed others, who hung about the houses-of-call or the streets. Under such a system, he put it to the meeting whether it was not likely a class of employers would spring up, ready to catch at the offers to do work which these men made to secure it? The thing, in short, commenced with themselves; their employers availed themselves of it; and the result was, the present depressed state of the trade. The evil had long been apparent, both to masters and men; but a want of unanimity, and perhaps of mutual knowledge, had caused its continuance. He was satisfied it was the interest of masters to keep work in the right channel, and to support a fair amount of remuneration to the working man. But this was a difficult matter. Let the working tailors, then, do the best they could under the circumstances to extricate themselves and the masters from the dilemma — to snatch, as it were, the brand out of the fire. Female labour had also done very much to injure the trade. No other trade employed their wives and families in the same way or to the same extent. As the first step towards bringing back things into a right direction, he believed that the small band of "honourable" men now in union ought to mitigate the rules which prevented out-door workers from coming among them; and, in the next place, that they ought to invite employers — show them, indeed, the benefit of it — to have all their work done upon their premises. If 7,000 or 8,000 of the trade were bound together for these objects, the moral effect would be very great. Under all the circumstances, he could see no better way of effecting the object in view than the practical application of some such idea as he ventured to throw out.

The question was here put, whether the operative tailors present thought that if the system of out-door labour was done away with, the trade generally would be benefited?

The show of hands gave a unanimous answer in the affirmative. The meeting further intimated in the same way their belief that work being done upon the masters' premises was the real practical remedy against sweating.

A WORKING TAILOR from the East-end next rose, and stated that at certain seasons it was a practice among the sweaters to import cheap labour from Ireland, and from different parts of the Continent, so that emigration would be of no practical benefit, because whatever numbers were taken away would soon be replaced by immigration. He mentioned a number of shops, both at the east and west ends, whose work was all taken by sweaters; and several of these shops were under royal and noble patronage. There was one notorious sweater who kept his carriage. He was a Jew, and of course he gave a preference to his own sect. Thus another Jew received it from him second-rate, then it went on to a third — till it came to the unfortunate Christian, at perhaps the eighth rate, and he performed the work at barely living prices; this same Jew required a deposit of £5 in money before he would give out a single garment to be made. He need not describe the misery which this system entailed upon the workmen. It was well known; but it was almost impossible, except for those who had been at the two, to form an idea of the difference between the present meeting and one at the East-end, where all who attended worked for slop-shops and sweaters. The present was a highly respectable assembly, the other presented no other appearance but those of misery and degradation.

A WORKING TAILOR, an Irishman from the county of Kerry, who was introduced by the last speaker, gave rather a humorous account of how he had been "kidnapped" by a sweater's wife into coming to London. He added he was a slave rather than a working man, for he made coats worth from £2 to £3 each for half-a-crown each, and he worked sixteen hours every day. He had not been out for between five and six weeks, because he had no clothes, but being determined to attend the meeting, he had got the loan of the coat he had on. He mentioned the name and address of the party who had "kidnapped" him, and said he knew many of his countrymen now in London who had been brought over under similar pretences to himself — good wages, plenty of diet, full employment; not one of which promises had been kept.

Several other persons testified to the introduction of cheap Irish and foreign labour.

A person in the crowd said there was a system prevailing in some of the shops at the West-end, which was the meanest he had yet heard of. The foremen in those establishments received first-rate wages; still, under the cover of teaching cutting, they got parties from the country who paid them £5, and who were invariably introduced into the shops as working tailors. And if it were a slack season, a regular hand, though a better tailor, and a married man, would be dispensed with before the new hand so introduced.

Other workmen intimated that they could confirm the statement as to the existence of such a practice. The payment of the £5 was called a "penalty" to get work.

Many other statements were made, which occupied the meeting till a late hour. Before the close their opinion, as practical working men, was taken upon the following questions: —

1. Are you of opinion that emigration will serve you, or not? The answer was "no."

2. Do you believe that the surplus needlewomen in the metropolis, taking them at 11,000 odd, whose wages are below subsistence point, are the daughters and wives of working men, and that they are forced into the labour market owing to the working man being unable to live upon the wages he now earns? The answer was "yes."

3. And consequently that the working men's wives and daughters

are obliged to go into the labour market, and compete with their own fathers and husbands?

"Yes, quite true," were the replies.

4. Then the surplus needlewomen of the metropolis may generally be expressed as the wives and daughters of the working man, whom he is unable to maintain?

The answer to this was also in the affirmative; and, like the others, perfectly unanimous.

The proceedings thereupon terminated.

The statistical results of the meeting were as follows: —

Returns of the earnings were obtained from 434 operative tailors. Of these 152 were coat hands, who could earn £298 0s. 9d. by working 1,029 days 8 hours, which is at the rate of 5¾d. per hour. According to the returns of those engaged at the dishonourable part of the trade, the coat hands for the slop-shops could earn only at the rate of 2d. per hour. 97 were trousers hands, and they could earn £14 0s. 9d. in 48 days and 10 hours, being at the rate of 5¾d. per hour. At the slop trade, according to the return of 12 hands, the average rate of earnings was 1¼d. per hour.

The aggregate earnings last week of the 434 hands working at the honourable trade was	£461	12	2½
The amount that they had in pawn was	310	13	6
The average rate of earnings of each of the hands last week was	1	1	3½
And the average rate of weekly earnings throughout the year	0	18	9½

There were 104 hands who earned above £1 a week, 229 who got more than 15s., 79 who made above 10s., and 22 whose earnings exceeded 5s. per week.

Since the above meeting I have devoted my attention to the investigation of the West-end show trade. I have also made further inquiries into the system adopted for the introduction of cheap Irish and foreign labour.

I will first proceed to give the reader a more perfect idea than I have yet been able to do of the principle of sweating. I first sought out a sweater himself, from whom I obtained the following information:—

"I make the best coats, and get 16s. for frock and dress. They take me three days each to do. I have to find my own trimmings, and basting up is included likewise. I use one lamp for my own work; my missus has a candle to herself. The lamp costs me about 1s. 9d. a week, and the extra fire for heating my irons about 1s. per week. The expenses of trimmings for two coats will be about

1s. 6d., which come altogether to 4s. 3d., and this has to be deducted from 32s., leaving 27s. 9d. clear for my own weekly earnings. This is more than the generality of people can make. I make this amount of money weekly upon an average all the year round. I can do thus much by my own single hand. I employ persons to work under me—that is, I get the work, and give it to them to do. I generally have two men working at home with me. I take a third of the coat, and I give them each a third to do. They board and lodge with me altogether—that is, they have their dinners, teas, breakfasts, and beds in my place. I give them at the rate of 15s. a coat—that is, I take 1s. off the price I receive for the trimmings and my trouble. The trimmings come to 9d., and the extra 3d. is the profit for my trouble. They pay me at the rate of 2s. 6d. per week for washing and lodging—the washing would be about 6d. out of the money. They both sleep in one bed. Their breakfasts I charge 4d. each for—if "with a relish" they are 5d. Their teas are 4d., and their dinners are 6d.; altogether I charge them for their food about 8s. 2d., a week, and this, with lodging and washing, comes to from 16s. 6d. to 11s. per week. The three of us working together can make six coats in the week, if fully employed—on an average we make from four to five coats, and never less than four. This would bring us in altogether, for four coats, £3 4s. Out of this, the shares of each of my two men would be £1. The rest I should deduct for expenses. Then their living would be from about 10s. 6d., so that they would get clear 9s. 6d. per week over and above their living. I pay 7s. 6d. a week rent. I have two rooms, and the men sleep in the work room. I get every week for the four of us (that is, for myself, my missus, and the two men—we live all together) about four or five ounces of tea, and this costs me 1s. 5d. I have 1s. worth of coffee, and about 1s. 6d. worth of sugar. The bread is 3s. 6d. per week, and butter 2s. 11d. The meat comes to about 8s., and the vegetables 2s. 4d. The lighting will be 1s. 9d., firing 1s. 6d. This will come to 30s. for the board and lodging of the four of us, or at the rate of 7s. 6d. per head. I should therefore clear out of the living of my men about 3s. a week each, and out of their work about 8d., so that altogether I get 3s. 8d. a week out of each man I employ. This, I believe, is a fair statement. I wish other people dealt with the men as decently as I do. I know there are many who are living entirely upon them. Some employ as many as fourteen men. I myself worked in the house of a man who did this. The chief part of us lived and worked and slept together in two rooms, on the second floor. They charged 2s. 6d. per head for the lodging alone. Twelve of the workmen, I am sure, lodged in the

house, and these paid altogether 30s. a week rent to the sweater.
I should think the sweater paid 8s. a week for the rooms—so that
he gained at least 22s. clear, out of the lodging of these men, and
stood at no rent himself. For the living of the men he charged 5d.
for breakfasts, and the same for teas, and 8d. for dinner, or at the
rate of 10s. 6d. each per head. Taking one with the other, and
considering the manner in which they lived, I am certain that the
cost for keeping each of them could not have been more than 5s.
This would leave 5s. 6d. clear profit on the board of each of the
twelve men, or altogether £3 6s. per week; and this, added to the
£1 2s. profit on the rent, would give £4 8s. for the sweater's gross
profit on the board and lodging of the workmen in his place. But,
besides this, he got 1s. out of each coat made on his premises, and
there were twenty-one coats made there upon an average every
week; so that altogether the sweater's clear gains out of the men
were £5 9s. every week. Each man made about a coat-and-a-half in
the course of the seven days (for they all worked on a Sunday—
they were generally told to 'borrow a day of the Lord'). For this
coat-and-a-half each hand got £1 2s. 6d., and out of it he had to
pay 13s. for board and lodging; so that there was 9s. 6d. clear left.
These are the profits of the sweater, and the earnings of the men
engaged under him, when working for the first-rate houses. But
many of the cheap houses pay as low as 8s. for the making of each
dress and frock coat, and some of them as low as 6s. Hence the
earnings of the men at such work would be from 9s. to 12s. per
week, and the cost of their board and lodging, without dinners—
for these they seldom have—would be from 7s. 6d. to 8s. per week.
Indeed, the men working under sweaters at such prices generally
consider themselves well off if they have a shilling or two in their
pocket for Sunday. The profits of the sweater, however, would be
from £4 to £5 out of twelve men working on his premises. The
usual number of men working under each sweater is about six
individuals: and the average rate of profit about £2 10s., without
the sweater doing any work himself. It is very often the case that
a man working under a sweater is obliged to pawn his own coat
to get any pocket-money that he may require. Over and over again
the sweater makes out that he is in his debt from 1s. to 2s. at the
end of the week, and when the man's coat is in pledge he is compelled to remain imprisoned in the sweater's lodgings for months
together. In some sweating places there is an old coat kept, called
a 'reliever,' and this is borrowed by such men as have none of their
own to go out in. There are very few of the sweaters' men who
have a coat to their backs or a shoe to their feet to come out into

the streets on Sunday. Down about Fulwood's-rents, Holborn, I am sure I would not give 6d. for the clothes that are on a dozen of them; and it is surprising to me, working and living together in such numbers and in such small close rooms, in narrow, close back courts as they do, that they are not all swept off by some pestilence. I myself have seen half-a-dozen men at work in a room that was a little better than a bedstead long. It was as much as one could do to move between the wall and the bedstead when it was down. There were two bedsteads in this room, and they nearly filled the place when they were down. The ceiling was so low that I couldn't stand upright in the room. There was no ventilation in the place. There was no fireplace, and only a small window. When the window was open you could nearly touch the houses at the back, and if the room had not been at the top of the house the men could not have seen at all in the place. The staircase was so narrow, steep, and dark, that it was difficult to grope your way to the top of the house—it was like going up a steeple. This is the usual kind of place in which the sweater's men are lodged. The reason why there are so many Irishmen working for the sweaters is, because they are seduced over to this country by the prospect of high wages and plenty of work. They are brought over by the Cork boats at 10s. a-head, and when they once get here the prices they receive are so small that they are unable to go back. In less than a week after they get here their clothes are all pledged, and they are obliged to continue working under the sweaters."

After this I made the best of my way to one who was working under a sweater, and who was anxious, I was told, to expose the iniquities of the whole system. He said:—

"I work for a sweater. I have been working for such people off and on for this last eight or nine years. I 'belonged to society' before that, and worked for the most honourable masters at this end of the town. I worked in the master's shop, of course. I never did day work, but I had piece work to do. I preferred that. I was a very quick hand, and could make more money that way. At day work I should have got £1 16s. a week, but at piece work I have occasionally made 36s. in four days, but these four days were at the latter end of the week. Upon an average I could get about 38s. a week in the brisk time, which was about two months in the year. I was always employed at that time, unless it was my own fault. During the vacation, or slack, I used often to be for many months and not earn a shilling at all. I used to hang about the houses of call then, waiting for a job, which came in about one day a week throughout the rest of the year, excepting Christmas, when perhaps I should have about three weeks' employment. I had a wife, but no children. Four years come this winter was the last time that I had employment at the honourable part of the trade. But before that I used to work for the sweaters when the regular business was slack. I did this unknown to the society of which I was a member. If it had been known to them, I should have had to pay a certain penalty, or else my name would have been scratched off the books, and I should have no more chance of work at the honourable trade. When working for the honourable trade I was employed about one-third of my time, and I should say I earned about £30 in the year. I was out of work two-thirds of my time. I never saved anything out of my wages when I was fully employed. I generally got into debt in the slack time, and was obliged to work hard to pay it off in the brisk. It was during the vacation, eight years back, that I first went to a sweater. Sweaters were scarcely known 25 years back, and they increased enormously after the change from day work to piece work. I could get no employment at my regular trade, and a sweater came down to the house and proposed to me privately to go and work for him. It was a regular practice then for the sweaters to come to the house and look out for such as had no employment and would work under price. I kept on for four years secretly working for the sweaters during vacation, and after that I got so reduced in circumstances that I could not appear respectable, and so get work amongst the honourable trade. The pay that I received by working for the sweaters was so little that I was forced to part with my clothes. When I first went to work for the sweater I used to get 4s. 6d. for making the third part of a coat. It would take from 11 to 13 hours to make a third. I could have done as many as six thirds, but could not get them to do. The sweater where I worked employed more hands than he had work for, so that he could get any job that was wanted in a hurry done as quickly as possible. I should say upon an average I got two-thirds of a coat to make each week, and earned about 7s. Some weeks, of course, I did more; but some I had only one, and often none at all. The sweater found me in trimmings. His system was the same as others, and I have worked for many since in the last eight years. The sweaters all employ more men than they want, and I am sure that those who work for them do not get more than two-thirds of a coat to make every week, taking one week with another. Another of the reasons for the sweaters keeping more hands than they want is, the men generally have their meals with them. The more men they have with them the more breakfasts and teas they supply, and the more

profit they make. The men usually have to pay 4d., and very often
5d. for their breakfast, and the same for their tea. The tea or
breakfast is mostly a pint of tea or coffee, and three to four slices
of bread and butter. I worked for one sweater who almost starved
the men; the smallest eater there would not have had enough if
he had got three times as much. They had only three thin slices
of bread and butter, not sufficient for a child, and the tea was
both weak and bad. The whole meal could not have stood him in
2d. a head; and what made it worse was, that the men who worked
there couldn't afford to have dinners, so that they were starved
to the bone. The sweater's men generally lodge where they work.
A sweater usually keeps about six men. These occupy two small
garrets; one room is called the kitchen, and the other the workshop; and here the whole of the six men, and the sweater, his wife,
and family, live and sleep. One sweater I worked with had four
children and six men, and they, together with his wife, sister-in-
law, and himself, all lived in two rooms, the largest of which was
about eight feet by ten. We worked in the smallest room and slept
there as well—all six of us. There were two turn-up beds in it, and
we slept three in a bed. There was no chimney, and indeed no
ventilation whatever. I was near losing my life there—the foul air
of so many people working all day in the place and sleeping there
at night was quite suffocating. Almost all the men were consump-
tive, and I myself attended the dispensary for disease of the lungs.
The room in which we all slept was not more than six feet square.
We were all sick and weak, and loth to work. Each of the six of
us paid 2s. 6d. a week for our lodging, or 15s. altogether, and I
am sure such a room as we slept and worked in might be had for
1s. a week; you can get a room with a fireplace for 1s. 6d. The
usual sum that the men working for sweaters pay for their tea,
breakfast, and lodging is 6s. 6d. to 7s. a week, and they seldom
earn more money in the week. Occasionally at the week's end they
are in debt to the sweater. This is seldom for more than 6d., for
the sweater will not give them victuals if he has no work for them
to do. Many who live and work at the sweater's are married men,
and are obliged to keep their wives and children in lodgings by
themselves. Some send them to the workhouse, others to their
friends in the country. Besides the profit of the board and lodging,
the sweater takes 6d. out of the price paid for every garment under
10s.; some take 1s., and I do know of one who takes as much as
2s. This man works for a large show-shop at the West-end. The
usual profit of the sweater, over and above the board and lodging,
is 2s. out of every pound. Those who work for sweaters soon lose

their clothes, and are unable to seek for other work, because they have not a coat to their back to go and seek it in. Last week I worked with another man at a coat for one of her Majesty's Ministers, and my partner never broke his fast while he was making his half of it. The Minister dealt at the cheap West-end show-shop. All the workman had the whole day-and-a-half he was making the coat was a little tea. But sweaters' work is not so bad as Government work, after all. At that we cannot make more than 4s. or 5s. a week altogether—that is, counting the time we are running after it, of course. Government contract work is the worst work of all, and the starved-out and sweated-out tailor's last resource. But still Government does not do the regular trade so much harm as the cheap show and slop shops. These houses have ruined thousands. They have cut down the prices so that men cannot live at the work; and the masters who did and would pay better wages are reducing the workmen's pay every day. They say they must either compete with the large show shops or go into the *Gazette*."

Of the system by which the sweaters are supported, the following information will give the public some little notion:—

"I do the superior out-of-door work for a large show-shop at the West-end," said the party from whom I had the information. "Now I am making the walking and driving capes. There is one that is as heavy as two 10s. coats, and yet I only get 18s. for it. I can't tell how long one of them takes me to make, for it is so tedious a job that I get tired of it, and put it down and commence something else. There is so much stitching in it that a man never sees when he will have finished. It's a week's work for any man. I have made every description of coat in the establishment. The pilot cloth capes, bound all round the bottom with braid, I get 6s. for. They take two days each to make. A Witney coat, double stitched all round, I get 10s. for, and each one takes me three days' hard work. I'm sure no man can do it in less. The 18s. coat that I mentioned before has ten rows of stitching all round; to convince you, just count them yourself. If the capes are made of hard box-cloth we get 12s. for them, and they take every one of them four days to make. You see, the master averages our work at 3s. a day; that is just half the price paid by the houses in the honourable part of the trade, but he considers that with our wives' help each of the men can get as much at the work as they could if working single-handed at the honourable part of the trade. A whole family may certainly make 36s. a week at the West-end show work, but then every woman engaged throws a man out of employ; so that the employer not only gets part of his work done at half price, but he deprives a great number of men of their regular employment. For dress and frock coats the firm pays 10s., 11s., 13s., and 14s. No one working at home can complain of the 14s. coats. He gives 6s. 6d. for making shooting coats; if the linings are creased and stitched an inch apart, he gives 8s. 6d. The last will take three days each to make. He gives 1s. extra for shooting jackets if they are bespoke. For the paletots he pays 8s. if they are oversized. All the stock paletots are given out to a Jew to have made. He has contracted for them at 7s. 6d. This Jew has also contracted for the stock shooting coats at 6s. a-piece. The best work that we have to do are the 14s. coats. At these a man *could* live. The worst work is the driving capes and the paletots. At these a man can barely get a subsistence. At making the box-coats the blood has been coming out of my finger's end, the cloth is so hard. I can make 18s. a week, working twelve hours each day. My expenses out of this are, for trimming, 1s.; coals, 1s.; and candles, 9d.; leaving me 15s. 3d. per week clear. This is to support me and my wife and family. Before I came to the show-shop trade I made about 30s. a week upon an average, or say twice as much as I can do now. I was single then. In 1844 I belonged to the honourable part of the trade. Our house of call supplied the present show-shop with men to work on the premises. The prices then paid were at the rate of 6d. per hour. For the same driving capes that they paid 18s. then, they give only 12s. for now. For the dress and frock coats they gave 15s then, and now they are 14s. The paletots and shooting coats were 12s.; there was no coat made on the premises under that sum. At the end of the season they wanted to reduce the paletots to 9s. The men refused to make them at that price, when other houses were paying as much as 15s. for them. The consequence of this was, the house discharged all the men, and got a Jew middleman from the neighbourhood of Petticoat-lane to agree to do them all at 7s. 6d. a-piece. The Jew employed all the poor people who were at work for the slop warehouses in Houndsditch and its vicinity. This Jew makes on an average 500 paletots a week. The Jew gets 2s. 6d. profit out of each, and having no sewing trimmings allowed to him, he makes the workpeople find them. The saving in trimmings alone to the firm, since the workmen left the premises, must have realised a small fortune to them. Calculating men, women, and children, I have heard it said that the cheap house at the West-end employs 1,000 hands. The trimmings for the work done by these would be about 6d. a week per head; so that the saving to the house since the men worked on the premises has been no less than £1,300 a year, and all this taken out of the pockets of the poor. The Jew who contracts for making the paletots is no tailor at all. A few years ago he sold sponges in the street, and now he rides in his carriage. The Jew's profits are 500 half-crowns, or £60 odd, per week—that is, upwards of £3,000 a year. Women are mostly engaged at the paletot work. When I came to work for the cheap show-shop I had £5 10s. in the savings bank; now I have not a halfpenny in it. All I had saved went little by little to keep me and my family. I have always made a point of putting some money by when I could afford it, but since I have been at this work it has been as much as I could do to *live,* much more to *save.* One of the firm for which I work has been heard publicly to declare that he employed 1,000 hands constantly. Now the earnings of these at the honourable part of the trade would be upon an average, taking the skilful with the unskilful, 15s. a week each, or £39,000 a year. But since they discharged the men from off their premises they have cut down the wages of the workmen one-half—taking one garment with another—*though the selling prices remain the same to the public;* so that they have saved by the reduction of the workmen's wages no less than £19,500 per year. Every other quarter of a year something has been 'docked' off our earnings, until it is almost impossible for men with families to live decently by their labour; and now, for the first time, they pretend to feel for them. They even talk of erecting a school for the children of their workpeople; but where is the use of their erecting schools, when they know as well as we do that, at the wages they pay, the children must be working for their fathers at home? They had much better erect workshops, and employ the men on the premises at fair living wages, and then the men could educate their own children, without being indebted to their 'charity.' "

In my last I merely hinted at the system adopted by wily sweaters to entrap inexperienced country and Irish hands into their service. Since then I devoted considerable attention to the subject, and am now in a position to lay before the public the following facts in connection with this trade:—

The system of inducing men by false pretences on the part of *sweaters,* or more commonly, of *sweaters' wives,* to work for them at wretched wages, I heard described in various terms. Such persons were most frequently called *kidnapped men.* The following narrative, given to me by one of the men concerned, and corroborated by one of his Irish fellow-victims, supplies an instance of the stratagems adopted. The second Irishman had but, as he said to me, "changed his house of bondage"—he had fallen into the hands of another sweater, his coat was in pawn, and he could not, in spite of all his struggles, lay by enough to redeem it. The wife of a sweater (an Irishman long notorious for such practices), herself a native of Kerry, visited her friends in that town, and found out two poor journeymen tailors. One was the son of a poor tailor, the other of a small farmer. She induced these two young men to follow her to London, immediately after her return, and at their own expense. She told them of her husband's success in trade, and of the high wages to be got in London by those who had friends in the trade, and engaged the two for her husband. Their wages were to be 36s. a week *"to begin with."* When the Irishmen reached the sweater's place, near Houndsditch, they found him in a den of a place (I give the man's own words), anything but clean, and anything but sweet, and were at once set to work at trousers making, at 1s. a pair, finding their own trimmings. Instead of 36s. a week, they could not clear more than 5s. by constant labour, and the sweater attributed this to their want of skill— they were not capable of working well enough for a London house. He then offered to teach them if they would bind themselves apprentices to him for a year certain. During the year they were to have board and lodging, and £5 each, paid at intervals as they required it. The poor men having no friends in London, and no acquaintances even whom they might consult, consented to this arrangement, and a sort of document was signed. They then went to work on this new agreement, their board being this:—For breakfast—half a pint of poor cocoa each, with half a pound of dry bread cut into slices, *between the two;* no butter. Dinner was swallowed, a few minutes only being allowed for it, between four and five. It was generally a few potatoes and a bit of salt fish, as lowpriced as could be met with. At seven, each man had half a pint of tea, and the same allowance of bread as for breakfast. No supper. They slept three in a bed, in a garret where there was no ventilation whatever. The two men (apprenticed as I have described) soon found that the sweater was unable to teach them anything in their trade, he not being a superior workman to either of them. At three weeks' end they therefore seized an opportunity to escape. The sweater traced them to where they had got work again, took with him a policeman, and gave them in charge as runaway apprentices. He could not, however, substantiate the charge at the station-house, and the men were set at liberty. Even after that the sweater's wife was always hanging about the corners of the streets, trying to persuade these men to go back again. She promised one that she would give him a handsome daughter she had for his wife, and find the new married pair "a beautiful slop shop" to work for, finding them security and all, and giving them some furniture, if he would only go back. The workman so solicited excused himself on the plea of illness. After this the father of this youth, in Kerry, received an anonymous letter, telling him that his son had run away from his employer, carrying with him a suit of clothes, and that he (the father) should have his son written to, and persuaded to return, and the robbery might be hushed up. This was every word false, and the anonymous letter was forwarded to the son in London, and when shown to the sweater he neither admitted nor denied it was his writing, but changed the conversation.

The third entrapped workman that I saw was a young man from the country, who was accosted in the street by the sweater's wife, put down to work under the same false pretences with the others, faring as they did until he effected his escape. The sweater had then but those three hands—he wanted more if his wife could have entrapped them. He had had six so entrapped or cheated in some similar way. Their hours of work were from seven in the morning to twelve at night.

Of this *street kidnapping system* I give another instance, and in the words of the kidnapped:—"I am now twenty-one, and am a native of Kilfinnan, in the county Limerick, Ireland. My parents died when I was five. A brother, a poor labouring man, brought me up, and had me apprenticed to a tailor. I served seven years. After that, before I ever worked as a journeyman in Ireland, I thought I would come to London to better myself, and I did come, but didn't better myself—worse luck! I 'tramped' from Kilfinnan to Cork, starting with 18s., which I had saved, and with no clothes but the suit I had on. I started because London has such a name among the tailors in Ireland, but they soon find out the difference when they come here. A journeyman tailor in Kilfinnan works for 2s. 6d. a week, his lodging, and two meals a day. In the morning bread and milk, and plenty of it; in the evening potatoes and meat, but meat only twice or thrice a week; fish always on fastdays, and sometimes on other days. I spent in tramping from Kilfinnan to Cork, 38 Irish miles, 6s. I took my passage from the Cove of Cork by a steamer to Bristol, paying 10s. for it. I landed at Bristol with 2s., tramping it up to London. A waggoner once gave me a lift of 18 miles for nothing. I had no help from the trade as I came along. I begged my way, getting bits of bread and cheese at farmers' houses and such places. In five days I reached London, knowing no one but a labourer of the name of Wallace. I found he was dead. That's eighteen months ago. One of Wallace's friends said I should do best at the East-end, but bad's the best I did. I took his advice, and went on that way, and was in Bishopsgate-street, when I met ————, a sweater. He spoke to me, saying, 'Are you a tailor seeking work?' I answered 'Yes, to be sure.' He then said he would give me plenty of good work, if I would go with him. I went with him to Brick-lane, where he lived, and he said I must first go a week on trial. I got nothing but my board for that week's work—working six days, long hours. After that he offered me 3s. 6d. a week, board and lodging—not washing. I had no friends, and thought I had better take it, as I did. For breakfast I had less than a pint of cocoa and four slices of thin bread and butter—bad bread from the 'security' baker's, the worst of bread— only the butter was worse. For dinner—but sometimes only was there dinner, perhaps two days a week, perhaps only one—we had potatoes and salt fish. I couldn't eat salt fish, so he had it regular. Sometimes I got a bite of a bull's cheek. Bad as I lived in Ireland, it was a great deal wholesomer than this—and I had plenty of it too. My master there gave me a bellyfull; here he never did. I slept with another man in a small bed; there were three beds with six men in them in a middle-sized room, the room where the six men worked. My employer, his wife, and I worked downstairs. He boarded and lodged them all—they living as I did. Some of them, working fifteen hours a day, earned 5s. or 6s. a week. I worked and hungered this way for four months, and then we quarrelled, because I wouldn't work all Sunday for nothing; so I left. I'm badly off still."

The continual immigration of foreign labour that I had discovered to be part of the system by which the miserable prices of the slop-trade were maintained, was the next subject to which I directed my inquiries, and I was able to obtain evidence which clearly proves how the honourable part of the trade are undersold by the "sloppers." The party who gave me the following valuable information on this head was a Hungarian Jew sweater. He said:—

"I am a native of Pesth, having left Hungary about eight years ago. By the custom of the country I was compelled to travel three years in foreign parts before I could settle in my native place. I went to Paris after travelling about that time in the different countries of Germany. I stayed in Paris about two years. My father's wish was that I should visit England, and I came to London in June, 1847. I first worked for a West-end show-shop— not directly for them, but through the person who is their 'middle-man,' getting work done at what rates he could for the firm, and obtaining the prices they allowed for making the garments. I once worked four days and a half for him, finding my own trimmings, etc., for 9s. For this my employer would receive 12s. 6d. On each coat of the best quality he got 3s. and 3s. 6d. profit. He then employed 190 hands; he has employed 300; many of those so employed setting their wives, children, and others to work, some employing as many as five hands in this way. The middleman keeps his carriage, and will give fifty guineas for a horse. I became unable to work, from a pain in my back, from long hours at my occupation. The doctor told me not to sit much, and so, as a countryman of mine was doing the same, I employed hands, making the best I could of their labour. I have now four young women (all Irish girls) so employed. Last week one of them received 4s., another 4s. 2d., the other two 5s. each. They find their own board and lodging, but I find them a place to work in—a small room, the rent of which I share with another tailor, who works on his own account. There are not so many Jews come over from Hungary or Germany as from Poland. The law of travelling three years brings over many, but not more than it did. The revolutions have brought numbers this year and last. They are Jew tailors flying from Russian and Prussian-Poland to avoid the conscription. I never knew any of these Jews go back again. There is a constant communication among the Jews, and when their friends in Poland and other places learn they're safe in England, and in work and out of trouble, they come over too, even if they can earn more at home. I worked as a journeyman in Pesth, and got 2s. 6d. a week, my board, washing, and lodging. We lived well, everything being so cheap. The Jews come in the greatest number about Easter. They try to work their way here, most of them. Some save money here, but they never go back; if they leave England, it is to go to America."

To further elucidate the ramifications of the sweating trade, I give the account of a German Jew, who, with his family and an English girl, worked for a middleman, the same man of whom I received an account from the Hungarian Jew. The German Jew spoke little English. I found him surrounded by his family, of whom I give an account from his own lips:—"The revolution made me leave Posen, as it did many others. We thought we should be best here in England. At Posen I and another man earned £2 a week as journeymen tailors. We worked 12 or 13 hours a day, but had an hour for dinner and an hour for pleasure. We all worked out of the shop, finding our own trimmings, and sometimes buttons, for which our employers paid us, in addition to our wages, when the work was taken in. I can't tell what it cost us to come here, as we had help from our countrymen on the way. Since I have been in London (more than a year) I have always worked for ———— [the West-end middleman]. A great many of my countrymen, who came over like myself, worked for him before I did, and a great many do so still. I don't know how many—perhaps thirty other familities. For this paletot you see me making ———— gives 5s. It takes me, hard work too, 26 hours to make it. For the rows of stitching in this quilting we say that the tailor gets paid for only one stitch in three—the others ————'s profit [one row contained 300 stitches]. I suppose he will charge 7s. for his paletot to the show-shop that employs him. I am now 41, and work constantly at this trade; so does my wife, about my own age [now sick], a work girl [a pretty English girl of 17], and my three sons, aged 18, 17, and 12. Among us we may make £2 a week." The English girl [her own account] received 3s. 6d. a week, and her tea morning and evening, to which she supplied her own bread and butter. This man told me that ———— now employed 190 or 200 hands, and he spoke much of his "grand house, horses, and carriage."

I had also found out that there was at the East-end a house of call for women, which had been recently established with a view of facilitating the supply of female labour. The following statement in connection with that subject I took down *verbatim*. All the persons with whom I conversed on the subject attributed great importance to there being no such house of call established, as it would tend materially to strengthen the system under which they were suffering:—"Mr. S——, a trimming-seller," said my informant, "told me that he intended to open a house of call for girls and women at the tailoring, and that if I wanted any, for a fee of 3d. a head to him, I could always obtain them. The women, for having their names put down, paid 3d. each. He has sent me two, and would have sent me a dozen if I had wanted them. I called upon him last week, but he said two gentlemen had been making inquiries, and he was alarmed, as he had no license for registry. What he meant by that I hardly know. He still offered to supply me without a fee, if I was a customer. The system, but for this check, would no doubt have been pursued, and would have increased."

With respect to the system of fines, I subjoin the following account of fines inflicted this year by a slop-shop on one man (cause seldom assigned):—A coat, name B——, No. 8,330, fined 3d.; a jacket, name O——, 7,423, fined 1s.; a jacket, name S——, 7,125, fined 6d.; a jacket, name R——, 8,274, fined 3d.; a coat, name J——, 1,557, fined 1s.; a coat, name T——, 2,047, fined 1s.; a jacket, name L——, 3,870, fined 1s.; a coat, name G——, 3,644, fined 3d.; a jacket, name F——, fined 3d.; 2s. for being abusive to

A——; a coat, name H——, 2,742, fined 1s.; a coat, name C——, 2,882, fined 3d.; a coat, name B——, 3,739, fined 1s.; a jacket, name W——, 3,373, fined 6d.; a coat, name W——, 3,885, fined 6d.; a coat, name R——, 3,819, fined 6d.; a coat, name B. F. B——, 4,286, fined 1s.; a coat, name W——, 4,402, fined 6d.; a coat, name R——, 5,193, fined 6d.; a coat, name L——, fined 6d.

LETTER XIX
Friday, December 21, 1849

The transition from the Artisan to the Labourer is curious in many respects. In passing from the skilled operative of the West-end to the unskilled workman of the Eastern quarter of London, the moral and intellectual change is so great that it seems as if we were in a new land and among another race. The artisans are almost to a man red-hot politicians. They are sufficiently educated and thoughtful to have a sense of their importance in the State. It is true they may entertain exaggerated notions of their natural rank and position in the social scale, but at least they have read and reflected, and argued upon the subject, and their opinions are entitled to consideration. The political character and sentiments of the working classes appear to me to be a distinctive feature of the age, and they are a necessary consequence of the dawning intelligence of the mass. As their minds expand they are naturally led to take a more enlarged view of their calling, and to contemplate their labours in relation to the whole framework of society. They begin to view their class not as a mere isolated body of workmen, but as an integral portion of the nation, contributing their quota to the general welfare. If PROPERTY has its duties as well as its rights, LABOUR, on the other hand, they say, has its rights as well as its duties. The artisans of London seem to be generally well informed upon these subjects. That they express their opinions violently, and often savagely, it is my duty to acknowledge; but that they are the unenlightened and unthinking body of people that they are generally considered by those who never go among them, and who see them only as "the dangerous classes," it is my duty, also, to deny. So far as my experience has gone, I am bound to confess that I have found the skilled labourers of the metropolis the very reverse, both morally and intellectually, of what the popular prejudice imagines them.

The unskilled labourers are a different class of people. As yet they are as unpolitical as footmen. Instead of entertaining violently democratic opinions, they appear to have no political opinions whatever; or, if they do possess any, they rather lean towards the maintenance "of things as they are," than towards the ascendancy of the working people. I have lately been investigating the state of the *coal-whippers,* and these reflections are forced upon me by the marked difference in the character and sentiments of the people from those of the operative tailors. Among the latter class there appeared to be a general bias towards the six points of the Charter; but the former were extremely proud of their having turned out to a man on the 10th of April, 1848, and become special constables for the maintenance of "law and order" on the day of the great Chartist "demonstration." As to which of these classes are the better members of the State, it is not for me to offer an opinion. I merely assert a social fact. The artisans of the metropolis are intelligent and dissatisfied with their political position; the labourers of London appear to be the reverse; and, in passing from one class to the other, the change is so curious and striking, that the phenomenon deserves at least to be recorded in this place.

The labourers, in point of numbers, rank second on the occupation list of the metropolis. The domestic servants, as a body of people, have the first numerical position, being as many as 168,000, while the labourers are less than one-third that number, or 50,000 strong. They, however, are nearly twice as many as the boot and shoe makers, who stand next upon the list, and muster 28,000 individuals among them; and they are *more* than twice as many as the tailors and breeches makers, who are fourth in regard to their number, and count 23,500 persons. After these come the milliners and dressmakers, who are 20,000 in number.

According to the Criminal Returns of the Metropolis (for a copy of which I am indebted to the courtesy of a gentleman who expresses himself most anxious to do all in his power to aid the inquiry), the labourers occupy a most unenviable pre-eminence in police history. One in every twenty-eight labourers, according to these returns, has a predisposition for "simple larceny;" the average for the whole population of London is one in every 266 individuals; so that the labourers may be said to be more than nine times as dishonest as the generality of people resident in the metropolis. In drunkenness they occupy the same prominent position. One in every 22 individuals of the labouring class was charged with being intoxicated in the year 1848; whereas the average number of drunkards in the whole population of London is one in every 113 individuals. Nor are they less pugnaciously inclined; one in every 26 having been charged with a "common assault" of a more or less aggravated form. The labourers of London are therefore nine times as dishonest, five times as drunken, and nine times as savage as the rest of the community. Of the state of their education as a body of people, I have no similar means of judging at present; nor am I in a position to test their improvidence or their poverty in the same conclusive manner. Taking, however, the Government returns of the number of labourers located in the different unions throughout the country at the time of taking the last census, I find that one in every 140 of the class were paupers, while the average for all England and Wales was one in every 159 persons; so that while the Government returns show the labourers generally to be extraordinarily dishonest, drunken, and pugnacious, their vices cannot be ascribed to the poverty of their calling, for, compared with other occupations, their avocation appears to produce fewer paupers than the generality of employments.

Of the moral and prudential qualities of the coal-whippers and coal-porters, as a special portion of the labouring population, the crude, undigested, and essentially unscientific character of all the Government returns will not allow me to judge. Even the census affords us little or no opportunity of estimating the numbers of the class. The only information to be obtained from that document— whose insufficiency is a national disgrace to us, for there the trading and working classes are all jumbled together in the most perplexing confusion, and the occupations classified in a manner that would shame the merest tyro in logic—is the following:—

Of coal and colliery agents and factors there are	16	individuals in London.
Ditto, dealers and merchants	1,541	,,
Ditto, labourers, heavers, and porters	1,700	,,
Ditto, meters	136	,,
Total in the coal trade in London	3,393	,,
Deduct from this the number of merchants from the London Post-office Directory	565	,,
Hence there are in the metropolis	2,828	coal labourers.

But this is far from an accurate result. There are at present in London upwards of 1,900 (say 2,000) registered coal-whippers, and as many more coal "backers" or porters. These altogether would give as many as 4,000 coal labourers. Besides there are 150 meters; so that altogether it may be safely said that the number engaged in the whipping and porterage of coals in London is 4,000 and odd.

The following statistics, carefully collected from official returns, will furnish our readers with some idea of the amazing increase in the importation of coal:—

"About 300 years ago (say about 1550), one or two ships were sufficient for the demand and supply of London. In 1615, about 200 were equal to its demand; in 1705, about 600 ships were engaged in the London coal trade; in 1805, 4,856 cargoes, containing about 1,350,000 tons; in 1820, 5,884 cargoes, containing 1,692,992 tons; in 1830, 7,108 cargoes, containing 2,079,275 tons; in 1840, 9,132 cargoes, containing 2,566899 tons; in 1845, 2,695 ships were employed in carrying 11,987 cargoes, containing 3,403,320 tons; and during the past year (1848), 2,717 ships, making 12,267 voyages, and containing 3,418,340 tons. The increase in the importation during the last ten years—that is to say, from the year 1838 to 1848, when the respective importations were 2,518,085 tons, and 3,418,340 tons—is upwards of 90 per cent. Now, by taking 2,700 vessels as the actual number now employed, and by calculating such vessels to average 300 tons burden per ship, and giving to a vessel of that size a crew of eight men, it will appear that at the present time 21,600 seamen are employed in the carrying department of the London coal trade."

Before visiting the district of Wapping, where the greater part of the coal labour is carried on, I applied to the clerk and registrar of the Coal Exchange for the statistics connected with the body of which he is an officer. Such statistics—as to the extent of their great traffic, the weekly returns of sales, in short, the ramifications of an inquiry embracing maritime, mercantile, mining, and labouring interests—are surely the weekly routine of the business of the registrar's office. I was promised a series of returns by the gentleman in question, but I did not receive and could not obtain them. Another officer, the secretary of the Meters'-office, when applied to, with the sanction of his co-officer, the clerk and registrar, required a written application, which should be attended to! I do not allude to these gentlemen with the slightest inclination unduly to censure them. The truth is, with questions affecting Labour and the Poor they have little sympathy. The labourer, in their eyes, is but a machine; so many labourers are as so much horse-power. To deny or withhold, or delay information required for the purposes of the present inquiry is, however, unavailing. The matter I have given, in fulness and in precision, without any aid from the gentlemen referred to, shows that it was more through courtesy than through necessity that I applied to them in the first instance.

Finding my time therefore only wasted in dancing attendance

upon City coal officials, I made the best of my way down to the Coalwhippers'-office, to glean my information among the men themselves. The following is the result of my inquiries:—

The coal vessels are principally moored in that part of the river called the Pool.

The Pool, rightly so called, extends from Ratcliff-cross, near the Regent's canal, to Execution-dock, and is about a mile long, but the jurisdiction of the coal commissioners reaches from the arsenal at Woolwich to London-bridge. The Pool is divided into the Upper and Lower Pool: it is more commonly called the north and south side, because the colliers are arranged on the Ratcliff and Shadwell side in the Lower Pool, and on the Redriff and Rotherhithe side in the Upper. The Lower Pool consists of seven tiers, which generally contain each from 14 to 20 ships; these are moored stern to stern, and lie from seven to ten abreast. The Upper Pool contains about ten tiers. The four tiers at Mill-hole are equally large with the tiers of the Lower Pool. Those of Church-hole, which are three in number, are somewhat smaller; and those of the fast tiers, which are also three in number, are single, and not double tiers, like the rest. The fleet often consists of from 200 to 300 ships. In the winter it is the largest—many of the colliers in the summer season going foreign voyages. An easterly wind prevents the vessels making their way to London; and, if continuing for any length of time, will throw the whole of the coalwhippers out of work. In the winter the coalwhipper is occupied about five days out of eight, and about three days out of eight in the summer; so that, taking it all the year round, he is only about half of his time employed. As soon as a collier arrives at Gravesend, the captain sends the ship's papers up to the factor at the Coal Exchange, informing him of the quality and quantity of coal in the ship. The captain then falls into some tier near Gravesend, and remains there until he is ordered nearer London by the harbour-master. When the coal is sold, and the ship supplied with the coal meter, the captain receives orders from the harbour-master to come up into the Pool, and take his berth in a particular tier. The captain, when he has moored the ship into the Pool, as directed, applies at "the coalwhippers' office," and "the gang" next in rotation is sent to him.

There are upwards of 200 gangs of coalwhippers. The class—supernumeraries included—numbers about 2,000 individuals. The number of meters is 150; the consequence is, that more than one-fourth of the gangs are unprovided with meters to work with them. Hence there are upwards of fifty gangs (of nine men each) of coalwhippers; or, altogether, 450 men more than there is any real occasion for. The consequence is, that each coalwhipper is necessarily thrown out of employ one-quarter of his time by the excess of hands. The cause of this extra number of hands being kept on the books is, that when there is a glut of vessels in the river, the coal merchants may not be delayed in having their cargoes delivered from want of whippers. When such a glut occurs, the merchant has it in his power to employ a private meter; so that the 450 to 55 men are kept on the year through, merely to meet the particular exigency, and to promote the merchant's convenience. Did any good arise from this system to the public, the evil might be overlooked; but since, owing to the combination of the coal-factors, no more coals can come into the market than are sufficient to meet the demand *without lowering the price*, it is clear that the extra 450 or 500 men are kept on and allowed to deprive their fellow-labourers of one-quarter of their regular work as whippers, without any advantage to the public.

The coalwhippers, previously to the passing of the act of Parliament in 1843, were employed and paid by the publicans in the neighbourhood of the river, from Tower-hill to Limehouse. Under this system none but the most dissolute and intemperate obtained employment—in fact, the more intemperate they were the more readily they found work. The publicans were the relatives of the northern shipowners; they mostly had come to London penniless, and being placed in a tavern by their relatives, soon became shipowners themselves. There were at that time 70 taverns on the north side of the Thames, below bridge, employing coalwhippers, and all of the landlords making fortunes out of the earnings of the people. When a ship came to be "made up"—that is, for the hands to be hired—the men assembled round the bar in crowds, and began calling for drink, and outbidding each other in the extent of their orders, so as to induce the landlord to give them employment. If one called for beer, the next would be sure to give an order for rum; for he who spent most at the public-house had the greatest chance of employment. After being "taken on," their first care was to put up a score at the public-house, so as to please their employer, the publican. In the morning, before going to their work, they would invariably call at the house for a quartern of gin or rum; and they were obliged to take off with them to the ship "a bottle" holding nine pots of beer—and that of the worst description, for it was the invariable practice among the publicans to supply the coalwhippers with the very worst article at the highest prices. When the men returned from their work they went back to the public-house, and there remained drinking the greater part of the night. He must have been a very steady man indeed, I am told, who could manage to return home sober to his wife and family. The consequence of this was, the men used to pass their days and chief part of their nights drinking in the public-house; and I am credibly informed that frequently, on the publican settling with them after clearing the ship, instead of having anything to receive, they were brought in several shillings in debt; this remained as a score for the next ship: in fact, it was only those who were in debt to the publican who were sure of employment on the next occasion. One publican had as many as fifteen ships; another had even more; and there was scarcely one of them without his two or three colliers. The children of the coalwhippers were almost reared in the tap-room and a person who has had great experience in the trade tells me he knew as many as 500 youths who were transported, and as many more who met with an untimely death. At one house there were forty young robust men employed about seventeen years ago, and of these there are only two living at present. My informant tells me that he has frequently seen as many as 100 men at one time fighting pell-mell at King James's-stairs, and the publican standing by to see fair play. The average money spent in drink by each man was about 12s. to each ship. There were about 10,000 ships entered the Pool every year, and nine men were required to clear each ship. This made the annual expenditure of the coalwhippers in drink £54,000, or £27 a year per man. This is considered an extremely low average. The wives and families of the men at this time were in the greatest destitution: the daughters invariably became prostitutes, and the mothers ultimately went to swell the number of paupers at the union. This state of things continued till 1843 when, by the efforts of three of the coalwhippers the Legislature was induced to pass an act forbidding the system, and appointing commissioners for the registration and regulation of coalwhippers in the port of London, and so establishing an office where the men were in future employed and paid. Under this act every man then following the calling of a coalwhipper was to be registered. For this registration 4d. was to be paid; and every man desirous of entering upon the same business had to pay the same sum, and to have his name registered. The employment is open to any labouring man; but every new hand, after registering himself, must work for twenty-one days on half pay before he is considered to be "broken in," and entitled to take rank and receive pay as a regular coalwhipper. All the coalwhippers are arranged in gangs of eight whippers, with a basket-man or foreman. These gangs are numbered from 1 up to 218, which is the highest number at the present time. The basket-men, or foremen, enter their names in a rotation-book kept in the office, and as their names stand in that book so do they take their turn to clear the next ship that is offered. On a ship being offered, a printed form of application kept in the office, is filled up by the captain in which he states the number of tons, the price and the time in which she is to be delivered. If the gang whose turn of work it is refuse the ship at the price offered, then it is offered to all the gangs and if accepted by any other gang, the next in rotation may claim it as their right, before all others. In connection with the office there is a long pave extending from the street to the water side, where the men wait to take their turn. There is also a room called the basket-men's room, where the foremen of the gang remain in attendance. There is likewise a floating pier called a depot, which is used as a receptacle for the tackle with which the colliers are unloaded. This floating pier is fitted up with seats, where the men wait in the summer. The usual price at present for delivering the colliers is 8d. per ton, but in case of a less price being offered, and the gangs all refusing it, then the captain is at liberty to employ any hands he pleases. According to the act, however, the owner or purchaser of the coals is at liberty to employ his own servants, provided they have been in his service fourteen clear days previous, and so have become what the act terms *bona fide* servants. This is very often taken advantage of for the purpose of obtaining labourers at a less price. One lighter-man, who is employed by the gas companies to "lighter" their coals to their various destinations makes a practice of employing parties who calls the *bona fide* servants of the gas company to deliver the coals at 1d. per ton less than the regular price. Besides this, he takes one man's pay to himself, and so stops one-tenth of the whole proceeds, thereby realising, as he boasts, the sum of £300 per annum. Added to this a relative of his keeps a beer-shop, where the *"bona fide* servants" spend the chief part of their earnings, thereby bringing back the system which was the cause of so much misery and destitution to the workpeople. According to the custom of the trade, the rate at which a ship is to be delivered is 49 tons per day, and if the ship cannot be delivered at that rate, owing to the merchants failing to send craft to receive the coals, then the coalwhippers are entitled to receive pay at the rate of 49 tons per day for each day they are kept in the ship over and above the time allowed by the custom of the trade for the delivery of the coals. The merchants, however, if they should have failed to send craft, and so kept the men idle on the first days of the contract, can, by the by-laws of the commissioners, compel the coalwhippers to deliver the ship at the rate of 98 tons per day. This appears to be a gross injustice to the men; for if they can be compelled to make up for the merchant's loss of time at the rate of 98 tons per day, the merchants surely should be made to pay for the loss of time to the men at the same rate. The wrong done by this practice is rendered more apparent by the conduct of the merchants during the brisk and slack period. When there is a slack the merchants are all as anxious to get their vessels delivered as fast as they can, because coals are wanting, and are consequently at a high price; then the men are taxed beyond their power, and are frequently made to deliver from 150 to 200 tons per day, or to do four days' work in one. On the contrary, when there is a glut of ships, and the merchants are not particularly anxious about the delivery of their coals, the men are left to idle away their time upon the decks for the first two or three days of the contract, and then forced to the same extra exertion for the last two or three days in order to make up for the lost time of the merchant and so save him from being put to extra expense by his own neglect. The cause of the injustice of these by-laws may be fairly traced to the fact of there being several coal-merchants among the commissioners, who are entrusted with the formation of by-laws and regulations of the trade. The coal factors are generally ship-owners, and occasionally pit-owners; and when a glut of ships comes they combine together to keep up the prices especially in the winter time, for they keep back the cargoes, and only offer such a number of ships as will not influence the market. Since the passing of the act establishing the coalwhippers office, and thus taking the employment and pay of the men out of the hands of the publicans, so visible has been the improvement in the whole character of the labourers, that they have raised themselves in the respect of all who know them.

Within the last few years they have established a benefit society, and they expended in the year 1847, according to the last account, £646 odd in the relief of the sick and the burial of the dead. They have also established a superannuation fund, out of which they allow 5s. per week to each member who is incapacitated from old age or accident. They are, at the present time, paying such pension to twenty members. At the time of the celebrated Chartist demonstration on the 10th of April the coalwhippers were, I believe, the first class of persons who spontaneously offered their services as special constables.

Further than this, they have established a school with accommodation for 600 scholars, out of their small earnings. On one occasion, as much as £60 was collected among the men for the erection of this institution.

The men are liable to many accidents. Some fall off the plank into the hold of the vessel and are killed; others are injured by large lumps of coal falling on them; and indeed, so frequent are there disasters, that the commissioners have directed that the indivisible fraction which remains, after dividing the earnings of the men into nine equal parts should be applied to the relief of the injured; and although the fund raised by these insignificant means amounts in the course of the year to £30 or £40, the whole is absorbed by the calamities.

Furnished with this information, as to the general character and regulations of the calling, I then proceeded to visit one of the vessels in the river, so that I might see the nature of the labour performed. No one on board the vessel (the ———, of Newcastle) was previously aware of my visit, or its object. I took the first ship which offered. I need not describe the vessel, as my business is with the London labourers in the coal trade. It is necessary, however, in order to show the nature of the labour of coal-whipping, that I should state that the average depth of coal in the hold of a collier, from ceiling to combing, is 16 feet, while there is an additional 7 feet higher to be lifted to the *basket-man's* "boom", which makes the height that the coals have to be raised by the whippers from 23 to 30 feet. The complement of a *gang of coal-whippers* is nine. In the hold are four men, who relieve each other in filling a basket—only one basket being in use—with coal. The labour of these four men is arduous; so exhausting is it in hot weather, that their usual attire is found to be cumbrous, and they have often to work merely in their trousers or drawers. As fast as these four men in the hold fill the basket, which holds 1¼ cwt., four *whippers* draw it up. This is effected in a peculiar, and to a person unused to the contemplation of the process, really an impressive, manner. The four whippers stand on the desk, at the foot of what is called "a way." This way resembles a short rude ladder; it is formed of four broken oars lashed lengthways, from four to five feet in height (giving a step from oar to oar of more than a foot), while the upright spars to which they are attached are called "a derrick." At the top of this derrick is a "gin," which is a revolving wheel, to which the ropes holding the basket "filled" and "whipped" are attached. The process is thus one of manual labour with mechanical aid. The basket having been filled in the hold, the whippers, correctly guessing the time required for the filling—for they never look down into the hold—

skip up the "way," holding the ropes attached to the basket and the gin, and pulling the ropes, at two skips, simultaneously as they ascend. They thus hoist the loaded basket some height out of the hold, and when hoisted so far, jump down, keeping exact time in their jump, from the topmost beam of "the way" on to the deck, so giving the momentum of their bodily weight to the motion communicated to the basket. While the basket is influenced by this motion and momentum, the basket-man, who is stationed on a plank flung across the hold, seizes the basket, runs on with it (the gin revolving) to "the boom," and shoots the contents into "the weighing-machine." The boom is formed of two upright poles, with a cross pole attached by way of step, on to which the basket-man vaults, and rapidly reversing the basket, empties it. This process is very quickly effected, for if the basket-man did not avail himself of the swinging of the basket, the feat would be almost beyond a man's strength, or at least he would soon be exhausted by it.

The "machine" is a large coalscuttle, or wooden box, attached to a scale, connected with $2\frac{1}{2}$ cwt.; when the weight is raised by two deposits in the machine, the coal-meter, who stands the whole time by the machine, which hangs over the side of the ship, discharges it, by pulling a rope connected with it, down a sliding wooden plane into the barge below. The machine holds $2\frac{1}{2}$ cwt., and so the meter registers the weight of coal unladen. This process is not only remarkable for its celerity, but for another characteristic. Sailors, when they have to "pull away" together, generally time their pulling to some rude chant; their "Yo, heave, yo! " is thought not only to regulate, but to mitigate, the weight of their labour. The coalwhippers do their work in perfect silence; they do it, indeed, *like work,* and hard work, too. The basket-man and the meter are equally silent; so that nothing is heard but the friction of the ropes, the discharge of the coal from the basket into the machine, and from the machine into the barge. The usual amount of work done by the whippers in a day (but not as an average— not one day with another) is to unload, or "whip," 98 tons. To whip one ton, 16 basketfuls are required; so that to whip a single ton, these men jump up and down 144 feet; for a day's work of 98 tons they jump up and down 18,088 feet—more in some instances, for in the largest ships the "way" has five steps, and ten men are employed. The coalwhippers, therefore, raise $1\frac{1}{4}$ cwt. very nearly four miles high, or twice as high as a balloon ordinarily mounts in the air; and, in addition to this, the coalwhippers themselves ascend very nearly $1\frac{1}{2}$ miles perpendicularly in the course of the day. On some days they whip upwards of 150 tons—200 have been whipped, when double this labour must be gone through. The 98 tons take about seven hours. The basket-man's work is the most critical, and accidents, from his falling into the hold, are not very infrequent. The complement of men for the unloading of a vessel is, as I have said, nine; four in the hold, four whippers, and the basket-man. The meter forms a tenth, but he acts independently of the others. They seldom work by candlelight, and, whenever possible, avoid working in very bad weather; but the merchant, as I have shown, has great power in regulating their labour for his own convenience. The following statement was given to me by a coalwhipper on board this vessel: —"We should like better wages; but then we have enemies. Now suppose you, sir, are a coal merchant, and this gentleman here freights a ship of the captain—you understand me? The man who freights the ships that way is paid by the captain 9d. a ton for a gang of nine, such as you've seen— nine coalwhippers. But these nine men, you understand me, are paid by the merchant (or buyer) only 8d. a ton, so that by every ton he clears a penny, without any labour or trouble whatsomever. I and my fellows is dissatisfied, but can't help ourselves. This merchant, too, you understand me, finds there's rather an opening in the act of Parliament about whippers. By employing a man as his servant, on his premises, for fourteen days, *he's* entitled to work as a coalwhipper. We call such made whippers *'boneyfides.'* There's lots of them, and plenty more would be made if we was to turn rusty. I've heard, you understand me, of driving a coach through an act of Parliament, but here they drive a whole fleet through it." The coalwhippers all present the same aspect—they are all black. In summer, when the men strip more to their work, perspiration causes the coal dust to adhere to the skin, and blackness is more than ever the rule. All about the ship partakes of the grimness of the prevailing hue. The sails are black; the gilding on the figure-head of the vessel becomes blackened; and the very visitor feels his complexion soon grow sable. The dress of the whippers is of every description; some have fustian jackets, some have sailors' jackets, some loose great coats, some Guernsey frocks. Many of them work in strong shirts, which once were white, with a blue stripe. Loose cotton neckerchiefs are generally worn by the whippers. All have black hair and black whiskers, no matter what the original hue; to the more stubbly beards and moustachios the coal dust adheres freely between the bristles, and may even be seen, now and then, to glitter in the light amidst the hair. The barber, one of these men told me, charged nothing extra for shaving him, although the coal dust must be a formidable thing to the best-tempered razor. In approaching a coal ship in the river, the side has to be gained over barges lying alongside—the coal crackling under the visitor's feet. He must cross them to reach a ladder of very primitive construction, up which the deck is to be reached. It is a jest among the Yorkshire seamen that everything is black in a collier—'specially the soup! When the men are at work in whipping or filling, the only spot of white discernible on their hands is a portion of their nails.

There are no specific hours for the payment of these men; they are entitled to their money as soon as their work is reported to be completed. Nothing can be better than the way in which the whippers are now paid. The basket-man enters the office of the pay-clerk of the coal commission at one door, and hands over an adjoining counter an amount of money he has received from the captain. The pay-clerk ascertains that the amount is correct. He then divides the sum into nine portions, and touching a spring to open a door, he cries out for "gang such a number." The nine men who, with many others, are in attendance in rooms provided for them adjacent to the pay-office, appear immediately, and are paid off. I was present when nine whippers were paid for the discharge of 363½ tons. The following was the work done, and the remuneration received: —

		Day		Tons
Dec.	14	1st		35
,,	15	2nd		56
		(Sunday intervenes)		
,,	17	3rd		84
,,	18	4th		98
,,	19	5th		90½
				363½

These 363½ tons, at 8d. per ton, realised to each man, for five days' work, £1 6s. 4¼d., 10s. of which had been paid to each as subsistence money during the progress of the work. In addition to the sum so paid to each, there was deducted a farthing in every shilling as office fees, to defray the various expenses of the office. From this farthing reduction, moreover, the basket-man is paid 1½d. in the pound as commission for bringing the money from the captain. Out of the sum to be divided on the occasion I specify, there was an indivisible fraction of 1¼d. This, as it cannot be shared among nine men, goes to what is called "The Fraction Fund," which is established for the relief of persons suffering from accidents on

board coal-ships. These indivisible fractions realise between £30 and
£40 yearly.

Connected with the calling of the *whippers*, I may mention the
existence of the *purlmen*. These are men who carry kegs of malt
liquor in boats, and retail it afloat, having a license from the Watermen's Company to do so. In each boat is a small iron grating containing a fire, so that any customer can have the "chill off," should
he require that luxury. The purlman rings a bell to announce his
visit to the men on board. There are several purlmen who keep
rowing all day about the coal fleet; they are not allowed to sell
spirits. In a fog, the glaring of the fire in the purlmen's boats,
discernible on the river, has a curious effect, nothing but the fire
being visible.

I was now desirous of obtaining some information from the
men collectively. Accordingly I entered the basket-men's waiting-
room, where a large number of them were "biding their turn,"
and no sooner had I made my appearance in the hall, and my
object become known to the men, than a rush was made from
without, and the door was obliged to be bolted to prevent the over-
crowding of the room. As it was, the place was crammed so full
that the light was completely blocked by the men piled up on the
seats and lockers, and standing before the windows. The room was
thus rendered so dark that I was obliged to have the gas lighted
in order to see to take my notes. I myself was obliged to mount
the opposite locker to take the statistics of the meeting.

There were 86 present. To show how many had no employment
whatever last week, 45 hands were held up. One had no employment for a fortnight; 24 no work for eight days. The earnings they
represented to be these last week—eight received 20s.; 16 between
15s. and 20s.; 17 between 10s. and 15s.; 10 between 5s. and 10s.;
I received under 5s.; 12 received nothing. The average of employment as to time is this: —None are employed for 30 weeks during
the year; all for 25 weeks or upwards, realising 12s., perhaps, nearly
per week—so many of the men said; but the office returns show
15s. 1½d. as the average for the last nine months. Waterage costs
the whippers an average of 6d. a week the year through: waterage
means the conveyance from the vessels to the shore. Fourteen of
the men had wives or daughters, who work at slop needlework,
the husbands being unable to maintain the family by their own
labour. A coalwhipper stated that there were more of the wives
of the coalwhippers idle, because they couldn't get work, than
were at work. *All* the wives and daughters would have worked if
they could have got it. "Why, your honour," one man said, "we are

better off in this office than under the old system. We were then compulsory drunkards, and often in debt to a publican after clearing the ship." The men employed generally spent from 12s. to 15s. a week. Those unemployed had abundant credit at the publican's. One man said "I work for a publican, who was also a butcher; one week I had to pay 9s. for drink, and 11s. for meat, and he said I hadn't spent sufficient. I was one of his constant men." At the time a ship was cleared, the whipper had often nothing to take home. "Nothing but sorrow," said one. The publican swept all; and some publicans would advance 2s. 6d. towards the next job, to allow a man to live. Many of the whippers now do not drink at all. The average of the drinking among the men, when at hard work, does not exceed three half-pints a day. The grievances that once afflicted the coalwhipper are still felt by the ballast-men. The men all stated the fact as to the 9d. allowed, and the 8d. per ton paid for whipping. They all represented that a lighterman, engaged by the gas companies, was doing them great injury by employing a number of *bonafides,* and taking the best ships away from the regular office, and giving them to the *bonafides* who "whip" the vessel at a lower rate of wages—about 6d. a ton. He is connected with a beer-shop, and the men are expected to buy his beer. If this man gets on with his system (all the men concurred in stating), the bad state of things prevailing under the publicans' management might be brought back. Sixteen years ago each whipper received 11¼d. per ton, prices steady, and the men in union. "If it wasn't for this office," one man said, "not one man who worked sixteen years ago would be alive now." The union was broken up about twelve years ago, and prices fell and fluctuated down as low as 6d., and even 5½d.—sometimes rising and falling 1¼d. a week. The prices continued fluctuating until the present office was established in 1844. The shipowners and merchants agreed at the commencement of the office to give the whippers 9d. a ton, and in three months reduced it to 8d. The publicans, it was stated, formed themselves into a compact body for the purpose of breaking down the present system, and they introduced hundreds of fresh hands to undersell the regular workers. In 1847 wages rose again to 9d., the whippers appealing to the trade, urging the high price of provisions, and their appeal being allowed. This 9d. a ton continued until the 1st June last. At that time the *bonafides* were generally introduced and greatly increased, and getting three times the work the regular men did, they (the regular men) consented again to lower the prices. The *bonafides* are no better off than the regular hands; for, though they have much more work, they have less per ton, and

have to spend more in drink. The coalwhippers represented themselves as benefited by the cheapness of provisions. With dear provisions, they couldn't, at their present earnings, live at all. The
removal of the backing system had greatly benefited the whippers.
On being asked how many had things in pawn, there was a general
laugh, and a cry of "All of us! " It is common to pawn a coat on
Monday and take it out on Saturday night, paying a month's
interest. One man said, "I have now in pawn seven articles, all
wearing apparel, my wife's or my own, from 15s. down to 9d."
Four had in pawn goods to the amount of £5 and upwards, five
to £4, six to £3, thirteen to £2, thirteen to £1; under £1, nineteen;
five had nothing in pawn. When asked if all made a practice of
pawning their coats during the week, there was a general assent.
Some could not redeem them in time to attend church or chapel
on a Sunday. One man said that if all his effects were burnt in his
absence he would lose no wearing apparel. "Our children under
the old system were totally neglected (they said); the public-house
absorbed everything." Under that system as many as 500 of the
children of coalwhippers were transported; now that has entirely
ceased; those charged with crime now were reared under the old
system. "The Legislature never did a better thing than to emanci-
pate us (said the man): they have the blessings and prayers of ourselves, our wives, and children."

After the meeting I was furnished with the following accounts,
of which I have calculated the averages: —

ACCOUNT OF BASKET-MAN
FIRST QUARTER—JANUARY 2, 1849, TO MARCH 28

Employed		50 days	
Delivered	2,570¼ tons		
Amount earned, at 9d. per ton	£10	15	2½
Deduct expenses of office .... 4s. 6d. ⎱			
Ditto waterage .... 8s. 4d. ⎰	0	12	10
	£10	2	4½
Average weekly earnings, about	0	16	6

SECOND QUARTER—APRIL 7 TO JUNE 30

Employed		44 days	
Delivered	2,609 tons		
Amount earned, at 9d. per ton	£10	10	8
Deduct waterage .... 7s. 4d. ⎱			
Office expenses .... 4s. 4d. ⎰	0	11	8
	£9	19	0
Average weekly earnings	0	15	3½

THIRD QUARTER—JULY 4 TO SEPTEMBER 24

Employed		42 days	
Delivered		2,485 tons	
Amount earned, at 8d. per ton		£9 4 4¾	
Deduct waterage .... 7s. 0d. ⎫		0 10 10¼	
Office dues .... 3s. 10¼d. ⎭			

£8 13 6½

Average weekly earnings 0 14 2

FOURTH QUARTER—OCTOBER 4 TO DECEMBER 20

Employed	49 days	
Delivered	2,858½ tons	
Amount earned, at 8d. per ton	£9 16 4¾	
Deduct waterage .... 8s. 2d. ⎫	0 12 3¾	
Office expenses .... 4s. 1¾d. ⎭		

£9 4 1

Average weekly earnings 0 14 1¾

First quarter	£10 2	4½
Second quarter	9 19	0
Third quarter	8 13	6½
Fourth quarter	9 4	1

£37 19 0

Average weekly earnings 0 14 6

The above accounts are rather above than under the average.

I then proceeded to take the statement of some of the different classes of the men. The first was a coalwhipper whom the men had selected as one knowing more about their calling than the generality. He told me as follows: —

"I am about forty, and am a married man with a family of six children. I worked under the old system, and that to my sorrow. If I had been paid in money, according to the work I then did, I could have averaged 30s. a week. Instead of receiving that amount in money I was compelled to spend in drink 15s. to 18s. a week (when work was good), and the publican even then gave me the residue very grudgingly, and often kept me from eleven to twelve on Saturday night before he would pay me. The consequences of this system were that I had a miserable home to go to. I would often have faced Newgate as soon. My health did not suffer, because I didn't drink the liquor I was forced to pay for. I gave most of it away. The liquors were beer, rum, and gin; all prepared the night before, adulterated shamefully for our consumption, as we durstn't refuse it, and durstn't even grumble. The condition of my poor wife and children was then most wretched. Now the thing is materially altered, thank God; my wife and children can go to chapel at certain times, when work is pretty good, and our things are not in pawn. By the strictest economy I can do middling well—very well when compared with what things were. When the new system first came into operation, I felt almost in a new world. I felt myself a free man. I wasn't compelled to drink. My home assumed a better aspect, and keeps it still. Last Monday night I received 19s. 7d. for my work (five days) in the previous week. I shall now (Thursday) have to wait until Monday next before I can get to work at my business. Sometimes I get a job in idle times at the docks or otherwise, and wish I could get more. I may make, one week with another, by odd jobs, 1s. a week. Perhaps for months I can't get a job. All that time I have no choice but to be idle. One week with another, the year through (at 8d. per ton), I may earn 14s. The great evil is the uncertainty of the work. We have all to take our 'rotation.' This uncertainty has this effect upon many of the men—they are compelled to live on credit. One day a man may receive 19s., and be idle for eight days after. Consequently, we go to the dealer where we have credit. The chandler supplies me with bread, to be paid for next pay-day, charging me a halfpenny a loaf more. A man with a wife and family of six children, as I have, will consume sixteen or seventeen quartern loaves a week; consequently he has to pay 8d. a week extra on account of the irregularity or uncertainty. My 'rotation' would come much oftener but for the backing system and the *bona fides*. I also pay the butcher from ½d. to 1d. per lb. extra for credit when my family requires meat—sometimes a bit of mutton, sometimes a bit of beef. I leave that to the wife, who does it with economy. I this way pay the butcher 6d. a week extra. The additional cost to me of the other articles, cheese, butter, soap, etc., which I get on credit, will be 6d. a week. Altogether that will be £3 18s. a year. My rent for a little house, with two nice little rooms, is 3s. per week; so that the extra charge for credit would just pay my rent. Many coalwhippers deal with tally-men for their wearing apparel, and have to pay enormous prices. I have had dealings with a tally-man, and suffered for it, but, for all that, I must make application for a supply of blankets from him for my family this winter. I paid him 45s. for wearing apparel—a shawl for my wife, some dresses for the children, a blanket, and other things. Their intrinsic value was 30s. Many of us, indeed most of us, if not all of us, are always putting things in and out of the pawnshops. I know I have myself paid more than 10s. a year for interest to the pawnbroker. I know some of my fellow-workmen who pay nearly £5 a year. I once put in a coat that cost me £3 12s. I could only get 30s. on it. I was never able to redeem it, and lost it. The articles lost by the coalwhippers, pledged at the pawnshop, are three out of four. There are 2,000 coalwhippers, and I am sure that each has 50s. in pawn, making £5,000 in a year. Interest may be paid on one-half of this amount, £2,500. The other half of the property, at least, is lost. As the pawnbroker only advances one-third of the value, the loss in the forfeiture of the property is £7,500, and in interest £2,500, making a total of £10,000 lost every year, greatly through the uncertainty of labour. A coalwhipper's life is one of debt and struggles—it is a round of relieving, paying, and credit. We very rarely have a halfpenny in the pocket when we meet our credit. If any system could possibly be discovered which would render our work and our earnings more certain, and our payments more frequent, it would benefit us as much as we have been benefited by the establishment of the office." I visited this man's cottage, and found it neat and tidy; his children looked healthy. The walls of the lower room were covered with some cheap prints; a few old books—well worn, as if well used—were to be seen; and everything evinced a man who was struggling bravely to rear a large family well on small means. I took the family at a disadvantage, moreover, as washing was going on.

Hearing that accidents were frequent among the class, I was anxious to see a person who had suffered by the danger of the calling. A man was brought to me, with his hand bound up in his handkerchief. The sleeve of his coat was ripped open, and dangled down beside his injured arm. He walked lame, and on my inquiring whether his leg was hurt, he began pulling up his trousers, and unlacing his boot, to show me that it had not been properly set. He had evidently once been a strong muscular man, but little now remained as evidence of his physical power but the size of his bones. He furnished me with the following statement:—"I was a coalwhipper. I had a wife and two children. Four months ago, coming off my day's work, my foot slipped, and I fell and broke my leg. I was taken to the hospital, and remained there ten weeks. At the time of my accident I had no money at all by me, but was in debt to the amount of 10s. to my landlord. I had a little furniture, and a few clothes of myself and wife. While I was in the hospital I did not receive anything from our benefit society, be-

cause I had not been able to keep up my subscription. My wife
and children lived, while I was in the hospital, by pawning my
things, and going from door to door, to every one she knowed,
to give her a bit. The men who worked in the same gang as myself
made up 4s. 6d. for me; and that, with two loaves of bread that
they had from the relieving-officer, was all they got. While
I was in the hospital the landlord seized for rent the few
things that my wife had not pawned, and turned her and
my two little children into the street—one was a boy three years
old, and the other a baby just turned ten months. My wife went
to her mother, and she kept her and my little ones for three weeks.
till she could do so no longer. My mother, poor old woman, was
most as bad off as we were. My mother only works on the ground.
out in the country, at gardening. She makes about 7s. a week in
the summer, and in the winter she has only 9d. a day to live upon;
but she had at least a shelter for her child, and she willingly shared
that with her daughter and her daughter's children. She pawned
all the clothes she had, to keep them from starving; but at last
everything was gone from the poor old woman, and then I got
my brother to take my family in. My brother worked at garden
work, the same as my mother-in-law did. He made about 15s. a
week in the summer, and about half that in the winter time.
He had a wife and two children of his own, and found it hard
enough to keep them, as times go. But still he took us all in, and
shared what he had with us, rather then let us go to the workhouse. When I was told not to leave the hospital, which I was
forced to do upon my crutches, for my leg was very bad still, my
brother took me in too. He had only one room, but he got in a
bundle of straw for me, and we lived and slept there for seven
weeks. He got credit for more than £1 of bread and tea and sugar
for us; and now he can't pay, and the man threatens to summon
him for it. After I left my brother's I came to live in the neighbourhood of Wapping, for I thought I might manage to do a day's
work at coalwhipping, and I couldn't bear to live upon his little
earnings any longer—he could scarcely keep himself then. At last
I got a ship to deliver, but I was too weak to do the work, and in
pulling at the ropes, my hand got sore, and festered, for want of
nourishment. [He took the handkerchief off, and showed that it
was covered with plaster. It was almost white from deficient circulation.] After this I was obliged to lay up again, and that's the
only job of work I have been able to do for the last four months.
My wife can't do anything; she is a delicate sickly little woman
as well, and has the two little children to mind, and to look after

me likewise. I had one pennyworth of bread this morning. We altogether had half-a-quartern loaf among the four of us, but no tea or coffee. Yesterday we had some bread, and tea, and butter, but wherever my wife got it from I don't know. I was three days, but a short time back, without a taste of food [here he burst out crying]. I had nothing but water that passed my lips. I had merely a little at home, and that my wife and children had. I would rather starve myself than let them do so. Indeed, I've done it over and over again. I never begged. I'd die in the streets first. I never told nobody of my life. The foreman of my gang was the only one besides God that knew of my misery; and his wife came to me and brought me money and brought me food; and himself, too, many a time. ("I had a wife and five children of my own to maintain, and it grieved me to my heart," said the man who sat by, "to see them want, and I unable to do more for them.") If any accident occurs to any of us who are not upon the society, they must be as bad off as I am. If I only had a little nourishment to strengthen me, I could do my work again; but, poor as I am, I can't get food to give me strength enough to do it; and not being totally incapacitated from ever resuming my labour, I cannot get any assistance from the superannuation fund of our men." I told the man that I wished to see him at his own home, and he and the foreman who had brought him to me, and who gave him a most excellent character, led me into a small house in a court near the Shadwell entrance to the London Docks. When I reached the place, I found the room almost bare of furniture. A baby lay sprawling on its back on a few rags beside the handful of fire. A little shoeless boy, with only a light washed-out frock to cover him, ran shyly into a corner of the room as we entered. There was only one chair in the room, and that had been borrowed downstairs. Over the chimney-piece hung to dry a few ragged infants' chemises that had been newly washed. In front of the fire on a stool sat the thinly clad wife; and in the corner of the apartment stood a few old tubs. On a line above these were two tattered men's shirts hanging to dry, and a bed was thrown on some boxes. On a shelf stood a physic bottle that the man had got from the parish doctor; and in the empty cupboard was a slice of bread— all the food, they said, they had in the world, and they knew not where on earth to look for more.

I next wished to see one of the improvident men, and was taken to the lodging of one, who made the following statement:—

"I have been a coalwhipper for twenty years. I worked under the old publicans' system, when the men were compelled to drink.

In those days 18s. didn't keep me in drink. I have now been a tee-totaller for five years. I have the bit of grub now more regular than I had. I earn less than 13s. a week. I have four children and have buried four. My rent is 1s. 6d." "To-night (interrupted the wife), if he won't part with his coat or boots, he must go without his supper." "My wife (the man continued) works at bespoke work—staymaking; but gets very little work, and so earns very little; perhaps 1s. 6d. a week." This family resided in a wretched part of Wapping, called, appropriately enough, "The Ruins." Some houses have been pulled down, and so an open place is formed at the end of a narrow airless alley. The wet stood on the pavement of the alley, and the cottage, in which the whipper I visited lived, seemed, with another, to have escaped when the other houses were pulled down. The man is very tall, and almost touched the ceiling of his room when he stood upright in it. The ceiling was as wet as a newly washed floor. The grate was fireless, the children barefoot, the bedstead (for there was a bedstead) was bedless, and all showed cheerless poverty. The dwelling was in strong contrast with that of the provident whipper whom I have described.

I conclude with the statement of a coal-backer, or coal-porter—a class to which the term "coal-heaver" is usually given by those who are unversed in the mysteries of the calling. The man wore the approved fantail, and well-tarred short smock-frock, black velveteen knee-breeches, dirty white stockings, and lace-up boots.

"I am a coal-backer," he said; "I have been so these 22 years. By a coal-backer, I mean a man who is engaged in carrying coals on his back from ships and craft to the waggons. We get 2¼d. for every fifth part of a ton, or 11¼d. per ton among five men. We carry the coals in sacks of 2 cwt.; the sack usually weighs from 14 lb. to 20 lb., so that our load is mostly 238 lb. We have to carry the load from the hold of the ship over four barges to the waggon. The hold of a ship is from 16 to 20 feet deep. We carry the coals this height up a ladder, and the ship is generally from 60 to 80 feet from the waggon. This distance we have to travel over planks with the sacks on our backs. Each man will ascend this height and travel this distance about 90 times in a day; hence he will lift himself, with 2 cwt. of coals on his back, 1,460 feet, or upwards of a quarter of a mile high, which is three times the height of St. Paul's, in 12 hours. And besides this, he will travel 6,300 feet, or 1¼ mile, carrying the same weight as he goes. The labour is very hard. There are few men who can continue at it." My informant said it was too much for him; he had been obliged to give it up eight months back; he had overstrained himself at it, and been obliged to lay up for many months. "I am forty-five years of age," he continued, "and have as many as eight children. None of these bring me in a 6d. My eldest boy did a little while back, but his master failed, and he lost his situation. My wife made slop shirts at a penny each, and could not do more than three a day. How we have lived through all my illness I cannot say. I occasionally get a little job, such as mending the hats of my fellow-workmen; this would sometimes bring me in about 2s. in the week; and then the parish allowed four quartern loaves of bread and 2s. 6d. a week for myself, wife, and eight children. Since I overstrained myself I have not done more than two days' work altogether. Sometimes my mates would give me an odd seven tons to do for them, for I was not able to manage more. Such accidents as over-straining are very common among the coal-backers. The labour of carrying such a heavy weight from the ship's hold is so excessive, that after a man turns forty he is considered to be past his work, and to be very liable to such accidents. It is usually reckoned that the strongest men cannot last more than twenty years at the business. Many of the heartiest of the men are knocked up through the bursting of blood vessels and other casualties; and even the strongest cannot continue at the labour for three days together. After the second day's work they are obliged to hire some un-employed mate to do the work for them. The coal-backers work in gangs of five men, consisting of two shovelmen and three backers, and are employed to deliver the ship by the wharfinger. Each gang is paid 11¼d. per ton, which is at the rate of 2¼d. per ton for each of the five men. The gang will do from 30 to 40 tons in the course of the day. The length of the day depends upon the amount of work to be done according to the wharfinger's orders. The coal-backers are generally at work at five o'clock in the morning, winter and summer. In the winter time they have to work by the light of large fires in hanging cauldrons, which they call bells. Their day's work seldom ends before seven o'clock in the evening. They are paid every night; and a man after a hard day's work will receive 6s. Strong hearty men, who are able to follow up the work, can earn from 25s. to 30s. per week. But the business is a very fluctuating one. In the summer time there is little or nothing to do. The earnings during the slack season are about one-half of what they are during the brisk. Upon an average their earnings are £1 per week all the year round. The class of coal-backers are supposed to consist of about 1,500 men. They have no provident or benefit society. Between 17 and 18 years ago, each gang used

to have 1s. 0½d. per ton; and about a twelvemonth afterwards it
fell to the present price of 11¼d. per ton. About six weeks back
the merchants made an attempt to take off the odd farthing—
the reason assigned was the cheapness of provisions. They nearly
carried it; but the backers formed a committee among themselves,
and opposed the reduction so strongly, that the idea was abandoned. The backers are paid extra for sifting, at the rate of 2d.
per sack. For this office they usually employ a lad, paying him at
the rate of 10s. per week. Upon this they will usually clear about
from 2s. to 4s. per week. The most injurious part of the backer's
work is carrying from the ship's hold. This is what they object to
most of all, and consider they get the worst paid for. They do a
great injury to the coalwhippers, and the backers say it would be
as great a benefit to themselves as to the coalwhippers if the
system was done away with. By bringing the ships up alongside
the wharf the merchant saves the expense of whipping and lightering, together with the cost of barges, etc. Many of the backers
are paid at the public-house; the wharfinger gives them a note to
receive their daily earnings of the publican, who has the money
from the merchant. Often the backers are kept waiting an hour
at the public-house for their money, and they have credit through
the day for any drink they may choose to call for. While waiting,
they mostly have two or three pots of beer before they are paid,
and the drinking once commenced, many of them return home
drunk, with only half their earnings in their pockets. There is
scarcely a man among the whole class of backers but heartily
wishes the system of payment at the public-house may be entirely
abolished. The coal-backers are mostly an intemperate class of
men. This arises chiefly from the extreme labour and the over-
exertion of the men, the violent perspiration, and the intense thirst
produced thereby. Immediately a pause occurs in their work they
fly to the public-house for beer. One coal-backer made a regular
habit of drinking sixteen half-pints of beer, with a pennyworth
of gin in each, before breakfast every morning. The sum spent
in drink by the "moderate" men varies from 9s. to 12s. a week,
and the immoderate men, on the average, spend 15s. per week.
Hence, assuming the class of coal-backers to be 2,000 in number,
and to spend only 10s. a week in drink each man, the sum that
would be annually expended in malt liquor and spirits by the class
would amount to no less than £52,000. The wives and children of
the coal-backers are generally in great distress. Sometimes no
more than one quarter of the men's earnings are taken home at
night. When I was *moderate* inclined, I used in general to have

a glass of rum the first thing when I came out of a morning, just to keep the cold out—that might be as early as five o'clock in the morning, and about seven o'clock I should want half-a-pint of beer with gin in it, or a pint without. After my work I should be warm, and feel myself dry; then I should continue to work till breakfast time; then I should have another half-pint with gin in it; and so I should keep on through the day, having either some beer or gin every two hours. I reckon that unless a man spent about 1s. 6d. to 2s. in drink, he would not be able to continue his labour through the day. In the evening he is tired with his work, and being kept at the public-house for his pay, he begins drinking there, and soon feels unwilling to move, and he seldom does so until all his wages are gone." My informant tells me that he thinks the class would be much improved if the system of paying the men at the public-house was done away, and the men paid weekly instead of daily. The hard drinking he thinks a necessity of the hard labour. He has heard, he says, of coal-backers being tee-totallers, but none were able to keep the pledge beyond two months. If they drink water and coffee, it will rather increase than quench their thirst. Nothing seems to quench the thirst of a hard-working man so well as ale.

The only difference between the pay of the basket-man and the whipper is the 1½d. in the pound which the former receives for carrying the money from the captain of the ship to the clerk of the pay-office. He has also, for this sum, to keep a correct account of the work done by the men every day, and to find security for his honesty to the amount of £10. To obtain this they usually pay 2s. 6d. a year to the Guarantee Society, and they prefer doing this to seeking the security of some baker or publican in the neighbour-hood, knowing that if they did so they would be expected to become customers of the parties.

Letter XX
Tuesday, December 25, 1849

I continue my inquiry into the state of the Coal Labourers of the Metropolis.

The *coalheavers*, properly so called, are now no longer known in the trade. The class of coalheavers, according to the vulgar acceptation of the word, is divided into *coalwhippers*, or those who whip up or lift the coals rapidly from the hold—and the *coalbackers*, or those who carry them on their backs to the wharf, either from the hold of the ship moored alongside the wharf, or from the lighter into which the coals have been whipped from the collier moored in the middle of the river or "Pool." Formerly the coals were delivered from the holds of the ships by the labourers shovelling them on to a series of stages, raised one above the other, till they ultimately reached the deck. One or two men were on each stage, and *hove* the coals up to the stage immediately above them. The labourers engaged in this process were termed *coalheavers*. But now the coals are delivered at once from the hold, by means of a sudden jerk, which *whips* them on deck. This is the process of *coalwhipping*, and it is performed chiefly in the middle of the river, to fill the "rooms" of the barges that carry the coals from the ship to the wharf. Coals are occasionally delivered *immediately* from the ship on to the wharf, by means of the process of *coal-backing*, as it is called. This consists in the sacks being filled in the hold, and then carried on the men's *backs* up a ladder from the hold, and along planks from the ship to the wharf. By this means, it will be easily understood that the ordinary processes of whipping and lightering are avoided. By the process of coal-whipping the ship is delivered in the middle of the river, or the Pool, as it is called; and the coals are lightered, or carried to the wharf, by means of barges, whence they are transported to the wharf by the process of backing. But when the coals are backed out of the ship itself on to the wharf, the two preliminary processes are done away with. The ship is moored along side, and the coals are delivered *directly* from the ships to the premises of the wharfinger. By this means the wharfingers or coal merchants below bridge are enabled to have their coals delivered at a cheaper price than those above bridge, who must receive the cargoes by means of the barges. I am assured that the colliers, in being moored along side the wharfs, receive considerable damage and strain their timbers severely, from the swell of the steam-boats passing to and fro. Again the process of coal-backing appears to be of so extremely laborious a nature, that the health and indeed the lives of the men are both greatly injured by it. Moreover, the benefit remains solely with the merchant, and not with the consumer, for the price of the coals delivered below bridge is the same as those delivered above. The expense of delivering the ship is always borne by the ship-owner. This is at present 8d. per ton, and was originally intended to be given to the whippers. But the merchant, by the process of backing, has discovered the means of avoiding this process, and so he puts the money, which was originally paid by the ship-owner for whipping the coals, into his own pocket. For the consumer is not a commensurate gainer. Since the merchant below bridge charges the same price to the public for his coals as the merchant above, it is clear that he alone is benefited at the expense of the public, the coal-whippers, and even the coal-backers themselves; for on inquiry among this latter class, I find that *they* object as much as the whippers to the delivery of a ship from the hold—the mounting of the ladder from the hold being of a most laborious and injurious nature. I have been supplied by a gentleman who is intimately acquainted with the expenses of the two processes with the following comparative account: —

EXPENSES OF DELIVERING A SHIP OF 360 TONS BY THE PROCESS OF COALWHIPPING.

For whipping 360 tons, at 8d. per ton £12 0 0
Lighterman's wages for one week engaged in lightering the said 360 tons from ship to wharf 1 10 0
Expenses of backing the said coals from craft to wharf, at 11¼d. per ton 16 17 6

£30 7 6

EXPENSE OF DELIVERING A SHIP OF 360 TONS BY THE PROCESS OF COALBACKING.

For backing a ship of 360 tons directly from the ship to the wharf £16 17 6

By the above account it will be seen that if a collier of 360 tons is delivered in the Pool, the expense is £30 7s. 6d. But if delivered at the wharf-side, the expense is £16 17s. 6d.—the difference between the two processes being £13 10s. Hence, if the consumer were the gainer, the coals should be delivered below bridge 9d. a ton cheaper than they are above bridge. The nine coalwhippers ordinarily engaged in the whipping of the coals would have gained £1 6s. 8d. each man if they had not been "backed" out of the ship. But as the coals delivered by backing below bridge are not cheaper, and the whippers have not received any money, it follows that the £12 which has been paid by the ship-owner to the merchant for the expense of whipping has been pocketed by the merchant, and the expense of lightering, £1 10s., saved by him, making a total profit of £13 10s.—not to mention the cost of wear and tear, and interest of capital sunk in barges. This sum of money is made at the expense of the coal-backers themselves, who are seldom able to continue the labour (so extreme is it) for more than twenty years at the outside, the average duration of the labourers being only twelve years. After this period the men, from having been overstrained by their violent exertion, are unable to pursue any other calling; and yet the merchants, I am sorry to say, have not even "encouraged" them to form either a benefit society, a super-annuation fund, or a school for their children.

Wishing to perfect the inquiry, I thought it better to see one of the seamen engaged in the trade. Accordingly I went off to some of the colliers lying in Mill-hole, and found an intelligent man ready to give me the information I sought. His statement was, that he had been at sea between 26 and 27 years altogether. "Out of that time," he said, "I've had nine or ten years' experience at the coal trade. I've been to the East Indies and West Indies, and served my apprenticeship in a whaler. I have been in the Mediter-ranean, and to several parts of France. I think that, take the general run, the living and treatment of the men in the coal trade is better than in any other going. It's difficult to tell how many ships I've been in, and how many owners I've served under. I have been in the same ship for three or four years, and I have been only one voyage in one ship. You see we are obliged to study our own interest as much as we can. Of course, the masters won't do it for us. Speaking generally of the different ships and different owners I've served under, I think the men are generally well served. I have been in some that have been very badly victualled— the small stores in particular, such as tea, sugar, and coffee, have been very bad. They, in general, nip us very short. There is a regular allowance fixed by act of Parliament, but it's too little for a man to go by. Some owners go strictly by the act, and some give more; but I don't know one that gives under. Indeed, as a general rule, I think the men in the trade have nothing to complain of. The only thing is, the wages are generally small, and the ships are badly manned. In bad weather there is not hands enough to take the sail off her, or else there wouldn't be so many accidents as there are. The average tonnage of a coal-ship is from 60 up to about 250 tons. There are sometimes ships as much as 400 tons, but they come seldom, and when they do they carry but part coal cargo. They only load sufficient coals so that they can come across the bar harbours in the north. If they were loaded altogether with coals they couldn't get over the bar; they would draw too much water. For a ship of about from 100 to 130 tons the usual complement is generally from five to six hands, boys, captain, and men all included together. There might be two men before the mast, a master, a mate, and a boy. This is sadly too little. A ship of this sort shouldn't, to my mind, have less than seven hands. That is the least, to be safe. In rough weather, you see, perhaps the ship is letting water; the master, takes the 'bellum;' one hand in general stops on deck to work the pumps, and three goes aloft. Most likely one of the boys has only been to sea one or two voyages, and if there six hands to such a ship, two of them is sure to be 'green boys,' just fresh from the shore, and of little or no use to us. We haven't help enough to get the sail off the yards in time. There's no one on deck look-out—it may be thick weather, and of course its properly dangerous. About half the accidents at sea occur from the ships being badly manned. The ships generally throughout the coal trade have one hand in six too little. The colliers mostly carry double the registered tonnage: a ship of 250 tons carrying 500 will only have ten hands, when she ought to have twelve or thirteen, and out of the ten that she does have, perhaps four of them is boys. All sailors in the coal trade are paid by the voyage. They vary from £3 10s. up to £4 for able-bodied seamen. The ships from the same port in the north give all alike for a London journey. In the height of summer the wages is from £3 5s. to £3 15s., and in the winter they are £4. Them's the highest wages given this winter. The wages are increased in the winter, because the work's harder and the weather's colder. Some of the ships lay up, and there's a greater demand for those that are in the trade. It's true the seamen of those that are laying up are out of employ; but I can't say why it is the wages don't come down in consequence; all I know is they go up in the winter. This is sadly too little pay—this £4 a journey. Probably in the winter a man may make only two voyages in four months, and if he's got a wife and family his expenses is going on at home all the while. The voyage I consider to last from the time of sailing from the north port to the time of entering the north port again. The average time of coming from the north port to London is from ten to eleven days. Sometimes the passage has been done in six; but I'm speaking of the average. We are generally about twenty-two days at sea, making the voyage from the north and back. The rest of the time we are discharging cargo, or lying idle in the Pool. On making the port of London we have to remain in "the Section" till the cargo is sold. "The Section" is between Woolwich and Gravesend. I have remained there as much as five weeks. I have been there too only one market day—that is three days. It is very seldom this occurs. The average time that we remain in "the Section" is from two to three weeks. The cause of this delay arises from the factors not disposing of the coals, in order to keep up the prices. If a large fleet comes, the factors will not sell immediately, because the prices would go down; so we are kept in "the Section" for their convenience, without no more wages. When the cargo is sold we drop down into the Pool, and there we remain about two days more than we ought, for want of a meter. We are often kept also a day over the day of delivery. This we call "a baulk day." The owners of the ship receive a certain compensation for every one of these baulk days. This is expressed in the charter party, or ship's contract. The whippers and meters too receive a certain sum for these baulk days, the same as if they were working, but the seamen of the colliers are only the parties who receive nothing. The delay arises entirely through the merchant, and he ought to pay us for it. The coal trade is the only trade that pays by the voyage—all others paying by the month—and the seamen feel it as a great grievance, this detention not being paid for. Very often, while I have been laying in Section, because the coal factor would not sell, other seamen that entered the port of London with me have made another voyage and been back again whilst I was stopping idle, and been £3 10s. or £4 the better for it. Four or five years since the voyage was £1 or £2 better paid for. I have had myself as much as £6 the voyage, and been detained much less. Within the last three years our wages have decreased 30 per cent., whilst the demand for coals and for colliers has increased considerably. I never heard of such a thing as supply and demand, but it does seem to me a very queer thing that whilst there's a greater quantity of coals sold, and more colliers employed, we poor seamen should be paid worse.

In all the ships that I have been in I've in general been pretty well fed; but I have been aboard some ships and heard of a great many more where the food is very bad, and the men are very badly used. On the passage, the general rule is to feed the men upon the salt meat. The pork they in general use is Kentucky, Russian, Irish, and, indeed, a mixture of all nations. Any kind of offal goes aboard some ships, but the one I'm on now there's as good meat as ever went aboard; aye, and plenty of it—no stint."

A basket-man, who was present whilst I was taking the above statement, told me that the foreman of the coalwhippers had more chances of judging of the state of the provisions supplied to the colliers than the men had themselves, for the basket-men delivered many different ships, and it was the general rule for them to get their dinner aboard among the sailors. The basket-man here referred to told me he had been a butcher, and was consequently well able to judge of the quality of the meat. "I have no hesitation," said he, "in stating that one-half the meat supplied to the seamen is unfit for human consumption. I speak of the pork in particular. Frequently the men throw it overboard to get it out of the way. Many a time, when I've been dining with the men, I wouldn't touch it. It fairly and regularly stinks as they takes it out of the coppers."

I now come to the class termed *Coal Meters*. These, though belonging to the class of "clerks," rather than labourers, still form so important a link in the chain, that I think it best to give a description of their duty here.

The *coal-meters* weigh the coals on board ship. They are employed by a committee of coal factors and coal merchants—nine factors and nine merchants forming such committee. The committee is elected by the trade. Two go out every year, and consequently two new members are elected annually. They have the entire patronage of the meters' office. No person can be an official coal-meter without being appointed by the coal committee. There were formerly several bye meters chosen by the merchants from among their own men, as they pleased. This practice has been greatly diminished since April last. The office of the coal-meter is to weigh out the ship's cargo, as a middle man between the factor and the merchant. The cargo is consigned by the pit-owner or the ship-owner to the coal-factor. The number of coal-factors is about 25. These men dispose of all the coals that are sold in London. As soon as the ship arrives at Gravesend her papers are transmitted to an office appointed for that purpose, and the factor then proceeds to the Coal-Exchange to sell them. Here the merchants and the factors assemble three times a week. The purchasers are divided into large and small buyers. The large buyers consist of the higher class coal merchants, and they will sometimes buy as many as 3 or 4,000 tons in a day. The small buyers only purchase by multiples of 7—either 14, 21 or 28 tons as they please. The rule of the market is, that the buyers pay one-half of the purchase-money the first market day after the ship is cleared, and for the remainder a bill at six weeks is given. After the ship is sold she is admitted from the Section into the Pool, and a meter is appointed to her from the Coal Meters'-office. This office is maintained by the committee of factors and merchants, and the meters appointed by them are registered there. According as a fresh ship is sold the next meter in rotation is sent down to her. There are in all one hundred and seventy official meters, divided into three classes, called respectively "placemen," "extra men," and "supernumeraries." The placeman has the preference of the work. If there is more than the placeman can do, the extra man takes it, and if both classes are occupied, then the supernumerary steps in. Should the earnings of the latter class not amount to 25s. weekly, that sum is made up to them. Before "breaking bulk," that is, before beginning to work the cargo of the ship, the City dues must, under a penalty, be paid by the factor. These amount to 1s. 1d. per ton. The 1s. goes to the City, and the 1d. to the Government. Formerly the whole of the dues went to the City, but within a short period the odd 1d. has been claimed by Government. The coal dues form one of the principal revenues of the City. The dues are collected by the clerk of the Coal Exchange. All the harbour dues and light dues are paid by the shipowner. After the City dues have been paid, the meter receives his papers, and goes on board to deliver the cargo, and sees that each buyer registered on the paper gets his proper complement. The meter's hours of attendance are from seven to four in winter, and from seven to five in summer. The meter has to wait on board the ship until such time as the purchasers send craft to receive their coals. He then weighs them previously to their delivery into the barge. There are eight weighs to the ton. The rate of payment to the meter is 1½d. per ton, and the merchant is compelled to deliver the cargo at the rate of 49 tons per day, making the meter's wages amount to 6s. 1½d. a day. "If there is a necessity or demand for more coals, we can do double that amount of work. On the shortest day in the year we can do 98 tons." One whom I saw said: "I myself have done 112 tons to-day. That would make my earnings to-day 15s., but as I did nothing on Saturday, of course that reduces them one-half." Upon an average, a place-meter is employed about five days in the week. An extra meter is employed about four days in the week, and a supernumerary about half his time, but *he* has always his 25s. weekly secured to him whether employed or not. Two pounds a week would be a very fair average for the wages of a place-meter since the reduction on the 1st of April. Many declare they do not earn 36s. a week, but many do more. The extra-man gets very nearly the same money as the place-man under the present arrangement. The supernumerary generally makes his 30s. weekly. As the system at present stands, the earnings of the meters generally are not so much as those of superior mechanics. It is an office requiring interest to obtain it; a man must be of known integrity, thousands and thousands of pounds of property pass through his hands, and he is the man appointed to see justice between factor and merchant. Before the act directing all coals to be sold by weight, the meter measured them in a vat holding a quarter of a chaldron. In those days a first class meter could reckon upon an income of from £400 to £500 a year, and the lowest salary was not under £300 per annum. The meter's office was then entirely a City appointment, and none but those of considerable influence could obtain it. This system was altered eighteen years ago, when the meter's office was placed in the hands of a committee of coal factors and coal merchants. Immediately after this time the salaries decreased. The committee first agreed to pay the meters at the rate of 2d. per ton, undertaking that that sum should produce the place-meter an income of £120. One gentleman assured me that he never exceeded £114, but then he was one of the juniors. Under the old system, the meters were paid at a rate that would have been equivalent to 3d. a ton under the present one. In the year 1831, the salary was reduced to 2d., and on the 1st of April in the present year, the payment has again been cut down to 1½d. per ton. Besides this the certificate money, which was 2s. per ship, and generally amounted to 30s. per quarter, was entirely disallowed—making the total last reduction of their wages amount to full 30 per cent. No corresponding reduction has taken place in the price of coals to the consumer. At the same time the price of whipping has been reduced 1d. per ton, so that, within the last year, the combined factors and merchants have lowered the price of delivery 1½d., per ton, and they (the merchants and factors) have been the sole gainers thereby. This has been done, too, while the demand for coals has been increasing every year. Now, according to the returns of the clerk of the Coal Exchange, there were 3,418,340 tons of coals delivered in the port of London in the year 1848, and assuming the amount to have remained the same in the present year, it follows that the factors and merchants have gained no less than £21,364 12s. 6d. per annum, and that out of the earnings of the meters and the whippers.

The *coal-whippers,* described in my last letter, whip the coals by means of a basket and tackle from the hold to the deck of the ship. The *coal-meters* weigh the coals when so whipped from the hold, previously to their being delivered into the barge alongside. The *coal-backer* properly carries the coals in sacks upon his back from the barges, when they have reached the premises of the coal-merchants, on to the wharfs; and I now proceed to speak of the *coal porters:*—

Coal porters are employed in filling the waggons of the merchants at their respective wharfs, and in conveying and delivering the coal at the residence of the customers. Their distinguishing dress is a fantail hat and an outer garment—half smock-frock and half jacket—heavy and black with coal-dust; this garment is often left open at the breast, especially, I am told, on a Monday, when the porter has generally a clean shirt to display. The narrative I give will show how the labour of these men is divided. The men themselves have many terms for the same employment. The man who drives the waggon I heard styled indifferently, the *waggoner, carman,* or *shooter.* The man who accompanies him to aid in the delivery of the coals was described to me as the *trimmer, trouncer,* or *pull-back.* There are also the *scurfs* and the *sifters,* of whom a description will be given presently. The coal porters form a rude class—not, perhaps, from their manners being ruder than those of other classes of labourers whose labour cannot be specified under the description of "skilled" (it is, indeed, but the exertion of animal strength—the work of thew and muscle)—but from their being less educated. I was informed that not one man in six—the manager in a very large house in the coal-trade estimated it at but one in eight—could read or write however imperfectly. As a body they have no fellowship or "union" among themselves, no general sick fund, no organization, no rules for their guidance as an important branch (numerically) of an important traffic; indeed, as it was described to me by one of the class—"no nothing." The coal porters thus present a striking contrast to the *coal-whippers,* who, out of means not exceeding those of the porters, have done so much for the sick among them, and for the instruction of their children. The number of men belonging to the Benefit Society of Coalwhippers is 436; and there are about 200 coalwhippers belonging to another society that was instituted before the new office. There are 200 more in connection with other offices. There were 130 sick men relieved by the Coalwhippers' Society last year. There were 14 deaths out of the 436 members. Each sick man receives 10s. a week, and on death there is a payment of £5 a man and £3 in the case of a wife. The amount of subscription to the fund is 3d. per week under 40 years of age, 4d. to 50, 5d. to 60, and above that 6d. On account of the want of any organization among the coal porters, it is not easy to get at their numbers with accuracy. No apprenticeship is necessary for the coal porter—no instruction even; so long as he can handle a shovel, or lift a sack of coals with tolerable celerity, he is perfect in his calling. The concurrent testimony of the best informed parties gave me the number of the porters (exclusive of those known as *sifters,* or *scurfs,* or *odd men*), as 1,500; that is, 1,500 men employed thus:—In large establishments on "the water-side"—five men are employed as *backers* and *fillers;* two to fill the sacks, and three to carry them on their backs from the barge to the waggon (in smaller establishments there are only two to carry). There are two more then employed to conduct the load of coal to the residence of the purchaser—the *waggoner* (or carman), and the *trimmer* (or trouncer). Of these the waggoner is considered the picked man, for he is expected to be able to write his name. Sometimes he can write nothing else, and more frequently not even so much, carrying his name on the customers' ticket ready written; and he has the care of the horses as driver, and frequently as groom.

At one time, when their earnings were considerable, these coal porters spent large sums in drink. Now their means are limited, and their drunkenness is not in excess. The men, as I have said, are ill-informed. They have all a preconceived notion that beer, sometimes in large quantities (one porter said he limited himself to a pint an hour when at work), is necessary to them "for support." Even if facts were brought conclusively to bear upon the subject to prove that so much beer, or any allowance of beer, was injurious, it would, I think, be difficult to convince the porters, for an ignorant man will not part with a preconceived notion. I heard from one man, more intelligent than his fellows, that a temperance lecturer once went among a body of the coal porters, and talked about "alcohol" and "fermentation," and the like, until he was pronounced either mad or a Frenchman!

The question arises, Why is this ignorance allowed to continue as a reproach to the men, to their employers, and to the community? Of the kindness of masters to men, of the discouragement of drunkenness, of persuasions to the men to care for the education of their children, I had the gratification of hearing frequently. But of any attempt to establish schools for the general instruction of the coal porters' children—of any talk of almshouses for the reception of the worn-out labourer—of any other provision for his old age, which is always premature through hard work—of any movement for the amelioration of this class I did *not* hear. Rude as these porters may be, machines as they may be accounted, they are the means of wealth to their employers, and deserve at least some care and regard on their part.

The way in which the barges are unladen to fill the waggons is the same in the river as in the canals. Two men, standing in the barge, fill the sacks, and three (or two) carry them along planks, if the barge be not moored close ashore, to the waggon, which is placed as near the water as possible. In the canals this work is carried on most regularly, as the water is not influenced by the tide, and the work can go on all day long. I will describe, therefore, what I saw in the City Basin, Regent's Canal. This canal has been opened about twenty years. It commences at the Grand Junction at Paddington, and falls into the Thames above the Limehouse Dock. Its course is circuitous, and in it are two tunnels—one at Islington, three-quarters of a mile long; the other at the Harrow-road, a quarter of a mile long. If a merchant in the Regent's Canal has purchased the cargo of a collier, such cargo is whipped into the barge. For the conducting of this laden barge to the Limehouse Basin of the canal the merchant has to employ licensed lightermen, members of the Watermen's Company, as none else are privileged to work on the river. The canal attained, the barge is taken into charge by two men, who not being regular "watermen," confine their labours to the canal. These men (a steerer and a driver) convey the barge, suppose, to the City Basin, Islington, which, as it is about midway, gives a criterion as to the charge and the time, when other distances are concerned. They go back with an empty barge. Each of these bargemen has 2s. a barge for conveyance to the City Basin. The conveyance of the loaded barge occupies three hours, 64 tons of coal being an average cargo. Two barges a day, in fine weather, can be thus conducted, giving a weekly earning to each man in full work of 24s. This is subject to casualties and deductions, but it is not my intention in this letter to give the condition of these bargemen. I reserve this for a future and more fitting occasion. In frosty weather, when the ice has caused many delays, as much as 6s. a barge, per man, has been paid, and I was told, hard-earned money too. A barge, at such times, has not been got into the City Basin in less than 48 hours. The crowded state of the Canal at the wharfs, at this time of the year, gives it the appearance of a crowded thoroughfare, there being but just room for one vessel to get along.

From the statement with which I was favoured by a house carrying on a very extensive business, it appears that the average earnings of the men in their employ was, the year through, upwards of 28s. I give the payments to twelve men regularly employed as the criterion of their earnings, on the best paid description of coal porter's labour, for four weeks at the busiest time:—

December 22	....	£21	5	5
„ 15	....	21	17	3
„ 8	....	22	10	1
November 17	....	28	8	0

This gives an average of more than £1 19s. per man a week for this period; but the slackness of trade in the summer, when coal is in smaller demand, reduces the average to the amount I have stated. In the two weeks omitted in the above statement, viz., those ending December 1st and November 24th, fourteen men had to be employed on account of the briskness of trade. Their joint earnings were £39 12s. 5d. one week, and £33 6s. 7d. the other. By this firm each *waggoner* is paid £1 a week, and 6s. extra if he "do" 100 tons, that is, 6s. between him and the trimmer. For every ton above 100 carried out by their waggoner and trimmer, 1d. extra is paid, and sometimes 130 are carried out, but only at a busy time; 142 have been carried out, but that only was remembered as the greatest amount at the wharf in question. For each waggon sent out, the waggoner and the trimmer together receive 4d. for "beer money" from their employers. They frequently receive money (if not drink) from the customers, and so the average of 28s. and upwards is made up. I saw two waggoners fully employed, and they fully corroborated this statement. Such payment, however, is not the rule. Many give the waggoner 21s. a week, and employ him in doing whatsoever work may be required. A waggoner, at what he called "poor work," three or four days a week, told me he earned about 13s. on the average.

The *scurfs* are looked upon as, in many respects, the refuse of the trade. They are the men always hanging about the wharfs, waiting for any "odd job." They are generally coal-porters who cannot be trusted with full and regular work, who were described to me as "tonguey or drunken;" anxious to get a job just to supply any pressing need, either for drink or meat, and careless of other consequences. Among them, however, are coal-porters seeking employment, some with good characters. These *scurfs,* with the *sifters,* number, I understand, more than 500, thus altogether making, with the coal-backers and other classes of coal-porters, a body of more than 2,000.

I now come to the following statement made by a gentleman who for more than thirty years has been familiar with all matters connected with the coal-merchants' trade.—"I cannot say," he began, 'that the condition of the coal-porter (not referring to his earnings, but to his moral and intellectual improvement) is much amended now, for he is about the same sort of man that he was thirty years ago. There may be, and I have no doubt is, a greater degree of sobriety, but I fear chiefly on account of the men's earnings being now smaller and their having less means at their command. Thirty-five years ago, before the general peace, labourers were scarce, and the coal-porters then had full and ready employment, earning from £2 to £3 a week. I have heard a coal-porter say that one week he earned £5; indeed, I have heard several say so. After the peace, the supply of labour for the coal trade greatly increased, and the coal porters' earnings fell gradually. The men employed in a good establishment, thirty years ago, judging from the payments in our own establishment as a fair criterion, were in the receipt of nearly £3 a week on the average. At that time coal was delivered by the chaldron. A chaldron was composed of 12 sacks, containing 36 bushels, and weighing about 25 cwt. (a ton and a quarter). For the loading of the waggons a gang of four men, called fillers, was and is employed. They were paid 1s. 4d. per chaldron—that is 4d. per man. This was for measuring the coal, putting it into sacks, and putting the sacks into the waggon. The men in this gang had nothing to do with the conveyance of the coal to the customer: for that purpose two other men were employed, a *waggoner,* and a man known as a *trimmer* or *trouncer,* who accompanied the waggoner, and aided him in carrying the sacks from the waggon to the customer's coal-cellar, and in arranging the coal when delivered so as properly to assort the small with the large, or indeed in making any arrangement with them required by the purchaser. The waggoner and the trimmer were paid 1s. 3d. each per chaldron for delivery; but when the coal had to be carried up or down stairs any distance, their charge was an extra shilling—2s. 3d. Many of the men have at that time, when work was brisk, filled and delivered fifteen chaldrons day by day, provided the distance for delivery was not very far. Drink was sometimes given by the customers to the waggoner and trimmer who had charge of the coal sent to their houses—perhaps generally

given; and I believe it was always asked for, unless it happened
to be given without asking. At that time I did not know one
teetotaller. I do not know one personally among those parties now.
Some took the pledge, but I believe none kept it. In this establishment we discourage drunkenness all that we possibly can. In 1832,
wages having varied from the time of the peace until then, a great
change took place. Previous to that time, a reduction of 4d. per
ton had been made in the payment of the men who filled the
waggon *(the fillers),* but not in that of the waggoner or the
trimmer. The change I allude to was that established by act of
Parliament, providing for the sale of all coal by the merchant
being by weight instead of by measure. This change, it was
believed, would benefit the public by ensuring them the full
quantity for which they bargained. I think it has benefited them.
Coal was, under the former system, measured by the bushel, and
there were frequently objections as to the way in which the bushel
was filled; some dealers were accused of packing the measure,
so as to block it up with large pieces of coal, preventing the full
space being filled with the coal. The then act provided that the
bushel measure should be heaped up with the coal so as to form
a cone, six inches above the rim of the measure. When the new act
came into operation the coal-porters were paid 10d. a ton (among
the gang of four fillers), and the same to the waggoner and trimmer. Before two years this became reduced generally to 9d. The
gang could load 25 tons a day, without extra toil; 40 tons, and
perhaps more, have been loaded by a gang, but such labour continued would exhaust strong men. With extra work there was
always extra drink, for the men fancy that their work requires
beer 'for support.' My opinion is, that a moderate allowance of
good malt liquor, say three pints a day, when work is going on
all day, is of advantage to a coal-porter. In the winter they fancy
it necessary to drink gin to warm them. At one time all the men
drank more than now. I estimate the average earnings of a coal-
porter fully employed now, at £1 a week. There are far more
employed at present than when I first knew the trade, and the
trade itself has been greatly extended by the new wharfs on the
Regent's canal, and up and down the river."

I had heard from so many quarters that "beer" was a necessity
of the coal-labourer's work, that finding the coal-whippers the most
intelligent of the whole class, I thought it best to call the men
together, and to take their opinion generally on the subject.
Accordingly I returned to the basket-men's waiting-room at the
Coalwhippers' Office, and, as before, it was soon crowded. There

were eighty present. Wishing to know whether the coal-backer's statement, given in my last letter, that the drinking of beer was a necessity of hard labour, was a correct one, I put the question to the men there assembled—"Is the drinking of fermented liquors necessary for performing hard work? How many present believe that you can work without beer?" Those who were of opinion that it was necessary for the performance of their labour were requested to hold up their hands, and *four* out of the eighty did so.

A basket-man, who had been working at the business for four years, and for two of those years had been a whipper, and so doing the heaviest labour, said that in the course of the day he had been one of a gang who had delivered as much as 189 tons. For this he had required no drink at all. Cocoa was all he had taken. Three men in the room had likewise done without beer at the heaviest work. One was a coal-whipper, and had abstained for six years. Some difference of opinion seemed to exist as to the number in the trade that worked without beer. Some said 250, others not 150. One man stated that it was impossible to do without malt liquor. "One shilling a day, properly spent in drink, would prolong life full ten years," he said. This was received with applause. Many present declared that they had tried to do without beer, and had injured themselves greatly by the attempt. Out of the eighty present fourteen had tried teetotalism, and had thrown it up after a time, on account of its injuring their health. One man, on the other hand, said he had given the total abstinence principle a fair trial for seven months, and had never found himself in such good health before. Another man stated, that to do a day's work of 98 turns, three pints of beer were requisite. All but three believed this. The three pints were declared to be requisite in winter time, and four pints or two pots were considered to be not too much in a hot summer's day. Before the present office was instituted, each man, they told me, drank half a pint of gin and six pots of beer daily. That was the average; many drank more. Then they could not do their work so well. They were weaker from not having so much food. The money went for drink instead of meat. They were always quarrelling on board a ship. Drunken men could never agree. A portion of beer is good, but too much is worse than none at all. This was the unanimous declaration.

Since this meeting I have been at considerable pains to collect a large amount of evidence in connection with this most important question. The opinion of the most intelligent of the class seems to be, that no kind of fermented drink is necessary for the performance of the hardest labour; but I have sought for and obtained the sentiments of all classes, temperate and intemperate, with the view of fairly discussing the subject. These statements I must reserve till my next letter. At present I shall conclude with the following story of the sufferings of the wife of one of the intemperate class:—

"I have been married 19 or 20 years. I was married at Penton, in Oxfordshire. We came to London fifteen years ago. My husband first worked as a sawyer. For eleven years he was in the coal trade. He was in all sorts of work, and for the last six months he was a *scurf*. What he earned all the time I never knew. He gave me what he liked—sometimes nothing at all. In May last he only gave me 2s. 8d. for the whole month for myself and two children. I buried four children. I can't tell how we lived then. I can't express what I've suffered, all through drink. He gave me twenty years of misery through drink. [This she repeated four or five times.] Some days that May we had neither bit nor sup. The water was too bad to drink cold, and I had to live on water put through a few leaves in the teapot—old leaves. Poor people, you know, sir, helps poor people, and but for the poor neighbours we might have been found dead some day. *He* cared nothing. Many a time I've gone without bread to give it to the children. Was he ever kind to them, do you say, sir? No; they trembled when they heard his step; they were afraid of their very lives, he knocked them about so; drink made him a savage: drink took the father out of him." This was said with a flush, and a rapid tone, in strong contrast with the poor woman's generally subdued demeanour. She resumed: "Twenty miserable years through drink! I've often gone to bring him from the public-house, but he seldom would come. He would abuse me, and would drink more because I'd gone for him. I've often whispered to him that his children were starving, but I dursn't say that aloud when his mates was by. We seldom had a fire. He often beat me. I've 9s. in pawn now. Since we came to London I've lost £20 in the pawn-shop." This man died a fortnight ago, having ruptured a blood-vessel. He lay ill six days. The parish doctor attended him. His comrades "gathered" for his burial, but the widow has still some funeral expenses to pay by instalments. The room they occupied was the same as in the husband's lifetime. There was about the room a cold damp smell, arising from bad ventilation and the chilliness of the weather. Two wretched beds almost filled the place. No article was worth a penny, if a penny had to be realized on it at a sale or a pawnshop. The woman was cleanly clad, but looked sadly pinched, miserable, and feeble. She earns a little as a washerwoman, and did earn it while her husband lived. She bears an excellent character. Her repetition of the words, *"twenty years of misery through drink,"* was very pitiful. I refrained from a prolonged questioning, as it seemed to excite her in her weak state.

In my next letter, I repeat, I purpose going into this question fully.

LETTER XXI
Friday, December 28, 1849

I resume my inquiry whether stimulating drinks are necessary for the performance of severe labour.

It may be recollected that in Letter XIX I published the statement of a coal-backer, who declared that it was an absolute necessity of that kind of labour that the men engaged in backing coals from the hold of a ship should, though earning only £1 per week, spend at least 12s. weekly in beer and spirits to stimulate them for the work. This sum, the man assured me, was a moderate allowance, for 15s. was the amount ordinarily expended by the men in drink every week. Hence it followed, that if this quantity of drink was a *necessity* of the calling, the men pursuing the severest labour of all—doing work that cripples the strongest in from twelve to twenty years— were the worst paid of all labourers, their actual clear gains being only from 5s. to 8s. per week. This struck me as being so terrible a state of things, that I could hardly believe it to be true, though I was assured by several coal-whippers, who were present on the occasion, that the coal-backer who had made the statement had in no way exaggerated his account of the sufferings of his fellow-workmen. I determined, nevertheless, upon inquiring into the question myself, and ascertaining, by the testimony and experience of different classes of individuals engaged in this, the greatest labour, perhaps, performed by any men, whether drink was really a necessity or luxury to the working man.

Accordingly I called a meeting of the coal-whippers, that I might take their opinion on the subject, when I found that out of eighty individuals only four were satisfied that fermented liquors could be dispensed with by the labouring classes. I was, however, still far from satisfied upon the subject, and I determined, as the question is one of the greatest importance to the working men— being more intimately connected with their welfare, physical, intellectual, and moral than any other—to give the subject my most patient and unbiased consideration. I was anxious, without advocating any opinion upon the subject, to collect the sentiments of the coal-labourers themselves; and in order that I might do so as impartially as possible, I resolved upon seeing—first, such men as were convinced that stimulating liquors were necessary to the labouring man in the performance of his work—2d. such men as once thought differently, and, indeed, had once taken the pledge to abstain from the use of all fermented liquors, but had been induced to violate their vow in consequence of injury to their health—and 3d. such men as had taken the pledge and kept it without any serious injury to their constitutions. To carry the subject out with the fulness and impartiality that its importance seemed to me to demand, I further determined to prosecute the inquiry among both classes of coal-labourers—the coal-whippers, and coal-backers as well. The result of these investigations I shall now subjoin. Let me, however, in the first place lay before the reader the following

COMPARATIVE TABLE OF DRUNKENNESS OF THE DIFFERENT TRADES IN LONDON.
ABOVE THE AVERAGE.

Buttonmakers, 1 individual in every	7.2	Printers, 1 individual in every	52.4
Toolmakers	10.1	Hatters and trimmers	53.1
Surveyors	11.8	Carpenters	53.8
Papermakers and stainers	12.1	Ironmongers	56.0
Brass founders	12.4	Dyers	56.7
Goldbeaters	14.5	Sawyers	58.4
Millers	16.6	Turners	59.3
French polishers	17.3	Engineers	59.7
Cutlers	18.2	Butchers	63.7
Corkcutters	19.7	Laundresses	63.8
Musicians	22.0	Painters	66.1
Opticians	22.3	Brokers	67.7
Bricklayers	22.6	Medical men	68.0
Labourers	22.8	Brewers	70.2
General and marine store dealers	23.2	Clerks	73.4
Brushmakers	24.4	Shopkeepers	77.1
Fishmongers	28.2	Shoemakers	78.0
Coach and cabmen	28.7	Coachmakers	78.8
Glovers	29.4	Milliners	81.4
Smiths	29.5	Bakers	82.0
Sweeps	32.2	Pawnbrokers	84.7
Hairdressers	42.3	Gardeners	97.6
Tailors	43.7	Weavers	99.3
Tinkers and tinmen	45.7	Drapers	102.3
Saddlers	49.3	Tobacconists	103.4
Masons	49.6	Jewellers	104.5
Glassmakers, &c.	50.5	Artists	106.3
Curriers	50.6	Publicans	108.0
Average			113.8

Carvers and gilders	125.2	Grocers	226.6
Artificial flowermakers	128.1	Clockmakers	286.0
Bookbinders	148.6	Parish officers	373.0
Greengrocers	157.4	Clergymen	417.0
Watchmakers	204.2	Servants	585.7

The above calculations have been made from the official returns of the Metropolitan Police for 1848. The causes of the different degrees of intemperance here exhibited I leave to others to discover.

After the meeting of coal-whippers, described in my last letter, I requested some of the men who had expressed the various opinions respecting the necessity for drinking some kind of fermented liquor during their work, to meet me, so that I might take down their sentiments on the subject more fully. First of all came two of the most intelligent, who believed malt liquor to be necessary for the performance of their labour. One was a basket-man, or fireman, and the other an "up-and-down" man, or whipper; the first doing the lighter, and the second the heavier kind of work. The basket-man—who, I afterwards discovered, was a good Greek and Latin scholar—said, "If I have anything like a heavy day's work to do, I consider three pints of porter a day necessary. We are not like other labouring men, having an hour to dinner. Often, to save time, we take only ten minutes to our meals. One thing I wish to remark is, that what renders it necessary to have the three pints of beer, in winter, and two pots in summer is the coal-dust arising from the work, which occasions great thirst. In the summer time the basket-man is on the plank all day, and continually exposed to the sun, and in winter to the inclemency of the weather. What with the labour and the heat, the perspiration is excessive. A basket-man with a bad gang of men has no sinecure. In the summer he can wear neither coat nor waistcoat—very few can bear the hat on the head, and they wear nightcaps instead. The work is always done in summer time with only the shirt and trousers on. The basket-man never takes off his shirt like the whippers. The necessity for drink in the summer does not arise so much from the extent of the labour as from the irritation of the coal-dust getting into the throat. There is not so much dust from the coals in the winter as in the summer, the coals being more damp in wet than in fine weather. It is merely the thirst that makes the drink requisite, as far as the basket-man is concerned. Tea would allay the thirst, but there is no opportunity of having this on board ship. If there were an opportunity of having tea at our work, the basket-man might manage to do with it as well as with beer. Water I don't fancy, especially the water of the river—it is very impure; and at the time of the cholera we were prohibited from drinking it. If we could get pure water I do not think it would do as well for us, especially in winter time. In winter time it would be too cold, and too great a contrast to the heat of the blood. It would, in my opinion, produce stagnation in the circulation. We have had instances of men dying suddenly through drinking water when in a state of excitement" (He distinguishes between excitement and perspiration—he calls the basket-man's labour an exciting one, and the whipper's work a heating one). "The men who died suddenly were whippers. I never heard of a basket-man dying from drinking cold water when at his work. I don't think they ever tried the experiment. The whippers have done so through necessity, not through choice. Tea is a beverage that I don't fancy, and I conceive it to be equally expensive, so I prefer porter. When I go off to my work early in the morning I take about a pint of coffee with me in a bottle, and warm it up on board, at the galley fire, for my breakfast; that I find quenches my thirst for the time as well as porter. Porter would be too insipid the first thing in the morning. I never drank coffee through the day while at my work, so I cannot say what the effect would be. I drink porter when at my work, not as giving me greater strength to go through my labour, but merely as a means of quenching my thirst—it being as cheap as any other drink, with the exception of water, and less trouble to procure. Water I consider dangerous at our work; but I can't say that it is so from my own experience. I was in the hospital about seven years ago, and the doctor there asked me how many pints of beer I was in the habit of drinking per day. This was before the office was established. I told him, on the lowest calculation, six or seven—it was the case then under the old system—and he then ordered me two pints of porter a day, as I was very weak, and he said I wanted a stimulus. I am not aware that it is the habit of the publicans to adulterate their porter with salt and water. If such is the case it would without a doubt increase rather than diminish the thirst. I have often found that the beer sold by some of the publicans tends more to create than allay thirst. I am confident, if the working men generally knew that salt and water was invariably mixed with the porter by the publicans, they would no longer hold to the notion that it could quench their thirst; but to convince them of that it would almost be necessary that they should see the publican adulterating the beer with their own eyes. If it really is the case that beer is adulterated with salt and water, it must be both injurious and heating to the labouring man. Some of the men, who are in the habit of drinking porter at their work, very probably attribute the thirst created by the salt and water in the porter, to the thirst created by the coal-dust or the work, and continue drinking it from the force of habit. The habit of drinking is doubtlessly the effect of the old system, when the men were forced to drink by the publicans who paid them. A most miraculous change and one unparalleled in history has been produced by altering the old mode of employing and paying the men. The reformation in the morals and characters of the men is positively wonderful. The sons are no longer thieves, and the daughters are no longer prostitutes. Formerly it was a competition who could drink the most; for he who could do so got the most work. The introduction for a job was invariably—'you know Mr. So-and-so, I'm a good drinking man.' Seeing the benefit that has resulted from the men not drinking so much as formerly, I am of opinion, though I take my beer every day myself, a great good would ensue if the men would drink even less than they do now, and eat more. It would be more conducive to their health and strength. But they have not the same facility of getting food when over their work, as there is for getting beer. You see they can have credit for beer when they can't get a morsel of food on trust. There are no floating butchers or bakers like there are floating publicans or purl-men. If there were, and men could have trust for bread and meat while at their work on the river, I am sure they would eat more and drink less, and be all the better for it. It would be better for themselves and for their families. The great evil of the drink is, that when a man has a little he often wants more, and doesn't know where to stop. When he once passes the rubicon, as I call it, he is lost. If it wasn't for this evil I think a pint or two of porter would make them do their work better than either tea or water. Our labour is peculiar. The air is always full of coal-dust, and every nerve and muscle of the body is strained, and every pore of the body open, so that he requires some drink that will counteract the cold."

The next two that I saw were men who did the heaviest work—that is, "up-and-down" men, or coal-whippers, as they are usually called. They had both of them been teetotallers. One had been so for eight years, and the other one had tried it for three months. One, who stood at least six feet and a-half high, and was habited in a long blue great coat that reached to his heels, and made him look even taller than he was, said, "I was a strict teetotaller for many years, and I wish I could be so now. All that time I was a coal-whipper, at the heaviest work, and I have made one of a gang that have done as many as 180 tons in one day. I drank no fermented liquor the whole of the time. I had only ginger-beer and milk, and that cost me 1s. 6d. It was in the summer time. I didn't 'buff it' on that day; that is, I didn't take my shirt off. I did this work at the Regent's Canal, and there was a little milk shop close on shore, and I used to run there when I was dry. I had about two quarts of milk and five bottles of ginger-beer, or about three quarts of fluid altogether. I found that amount of drink necessary. I perspired very violently—my shirt was wet through, and my flannels wringing wet with the perspiration over the work. The rule among us is that we do 28 tons on deck, and 28 tons filling in the ship's hold. We go on in that way throughout the day, spelling at every 28 tons. The perspiration in the summer time streams down our foreheads so rapidly, that it will often get into our eyes before we have time to wipe it off. This makes the eyes very sore. At night when we get home we cannot bear to sit with a candle. The perspiration is of a very briny nature, for I often taste it as it runs down to my lips. We are often so heated over our work that the perspiration runs into the shoes; and often, from the dust and heat, jumping up and down, and the feet being galled with the small dust, I have had my shoes full of blood. The thirst produced by our work is very excessive. It is completely as if you had a fever upon you. The dust gets into the throat, and very nearly suffocates you. You can scrape the coal-dust off the tongue with the teeth; and do what you will, it is impossible to get the least spittle into the mouth. I have known the coal-dust to be that thick in a ship's hold, that I have been unable to see my mate, though he was only two feet from me. Your legs totter under you. Both before and after I was a teetotaller, I was one of the strongest men in the business. I was able to carry seven hundredweight on my back for fifty yards, and I could lift nine half-hundreds with my right arm. After finishing my day's work I was like a child with weakness. When we have done 14, or 28 tons, we generally stop for a drop of drink, and then I have found that anything that would wet my mouth would revive me. Cold tea, milk, or ginger-beer, were refreshing, but not so much as a pint of porter. Cold water would give a pain in the inside, so that a man would have to lie down and be taken ashore, and perhaps give up work altogether. Many a man has been taken to the hospital merely through drinking cold water over his work. They have complained of a weight and coldness in the chest. They say it has chilled the fat of the heart. I can positively state," continued the man, "that during the whole of eight years I took no fermented drink. My usual drink was cold tea, milk, ginger-beer, or coffee—whichever I could catch. The ginger-beer was more lively than the milk, but I believe I could do more work upon the milk. Tea I found much better than coffee. Cold tea was very refreshing; but if I didn't take it with me in a bottle, it wasn't to be had. I used to take a quart of cold tea with me in a bottle, and make that do for me all day, as well as I could. The ginger-beer was the most expensive, and would cost me 1s., or more than that, if I could get it. The milk would cost me 6d. or 8d. For tea and coffee the expense would be about 2d. the day. But often I have done the whole day's work without any drink, because I would not touch beer, and then I was more fit to be carried home than walk. I have known many men scarcely able to crawl up the ladder out of the hold, they were so fatigued. For myself, being a very strong man, I was never so reduced, thank God. But often when I've got home I've been obliged to drink three pints of milk at a stretch before I could touch a bit of victuals. As near as I can guess, it used to cost me when at work 1s. a day for milk, ginger-beer, and other teetotal drinks. When I was not at work my drink used to cost me little or nothing. For eight years I stuck to the pledge, but I found myself failing in strength and health; I found that I couldn't go through a day's work as clever as I used before I left off drink, and when first I was a teetotaller. I found myself failing in every inch of my carcase, my limbs, my body, and all. Of my own free will I gave it up. I did not do so in a fit of passion, but deliberately, because I was fully satisfied that it was injuring my health. Shortly after I had taken the pledge I found I could have more meat than I used to have before, and I found that I neither got strong nor weak upon it. After about five years my appetite began to fail, and then I found my strength leaving me; so I made up my mind to alter the system. When I returned to beer, I found myself getting better in health and stronger daily. Before I was a teetotaller I used to drink heavy, but after teetotalism I was a temperate man. I am sure it is necessary for a hard-working man that he should drink beer. He can't do his work so well without it as he can with it, in moderation. If he goes beyond his allowance he is better without any. I have taken to drinking beer again within the last twelve months. As long as a man does not go beyond his allowance in beer, his drink will cost him quite as much when he is a teetotaller as it will when he has not taken the pledge. The difference between the teetotal and fermented drinks I find to be this—when I drank milk it didn't make me any livelier; it quenched my thirst, but did not give me any strength. But when I drink a pint or a quart of beer, it does me so much good after a day's labour, that after drinking it I could get up and go to my work again. This feeling would continue for a considerable time. Indeed, I think the beer is much better for a hard-working man, than any unfermented drink. I defy any man in England to contradict me in what I say, and that is, 'A man who takes his reasonable quantity of beer, and a fair share of food, is much better *with* it than *without.*' "

Another man, who had been a teetotaller for three months at one time, and seven years at another, was convinced that it was impossible for a hard-working man to do his work as well without beer as with. He had tried it twice, and he spoke from his own experience, and would say that a little—that is, two pints or three for a very hard day's labour—would never hurt no man. Beyond that a man has no right to go; indeed, anything extra only makes him stupid. Under the old system I used to be obliged to buy rum, and over and over again I've had to pay 15d. for a half a pint of rum in a ginger-beer bottle, and have gone into the street and sold it for 6d., and got a steak with the money. No man can say drink has ruined my constitution, for I've only had two pennyworth of antibilious pills in twenty-five years; and I will say a little beer does a man more good than harm, and too much does a man more harm than good."

The next two "whippers" that I saw were both teetotallers. One had taken the pledge eight months ago and the other four years, and they had both kept it strictly. One had been cellarman at a public-house; and he said, "I neither take spruce, nor any of the cordials. Water is my beverage at dinner." The other had been an inveterate drunkard. The cellarman is now a basket-man, and the other an up-and-down man, or whipper, in the same gang. The basket-man said, "I can say this from my own experience, that it is not necessary for a working man, doing the very hardest labour, to drink fermented liquors. I was an up-and-down man for two years without tasting a drop of beer or spirits. I have helped to whip 189 tons of coal in one day without any, and that in the heat of summer. What I had with me was a bottle of cocoa, and I took with that plenty of steak, potatoes, and bread. If the men was to take more meat, and less beer, they would do much better. It's a delusion to think beer necessary. Often the men who say the beer is necessary will deliver a ship, aye, and not half a dozen half-pints be drank aboard. The injury is done ashore. The former custom of our work—the compulsory system of drinking that we was under—has so embedded the idea of drink in the men, that they think it is actually necessary. It's not the least to be wondered at that there's so many drunkards among them. I don't think we shall ever be able to undo the habit of drinking among the whippers in this generation. As far as I am concerned, since I have been a teetotaller, I have enjoyed a more regular state of health than I used before. Now that I am a basket-man I drink only water with my dinner, and during my work I take nothing. I have got a ship "in hands," going to work on Monday morning. I shall have to run backwards and forwards on a one-and-twenty foot plank, and deliver 300 tons of coals, and I shall do that upon water. That man," pointing to the teetotaller who accompanied him, "will be in it, and he'll have to help to pull the coals twenty foot above the deck, and he'll do it all upon water. When I was a coal-whipper myself I used to drink cocoa. I took it cold with me of a morning and warmed it aboard. They prophesied it would kill me in a week, but I know it's done me every good in life. I have drunk water when I was a working up-and-down, and when I was in the highest perspiration, and never found it injure me. It allays the thirst more than anything. If it didn't allay the thirst, I should want to drink often; but if I take a drink of water from the cask, I find my thirst immediately quenched. Many of the men who drink beer will take a drink of water afterwards, because the beer increases their thirst and heats them; that I believe is principally from the salt-water in it; in fact, it stands to reason that, if beer is half brine, it can't quench thirst. Ah! it's shocking stuff the purlmen make up for them on the river. When I was drinking beer at my employment I used seldom to exceed three pints of beer a day—that is what I took on board. What I had on shore of course was not to help me to do my labour. I know the beer used to inflame my thirst, because I've had to drink water after it over and over again. I never made a habit of drinking—not since the establishment of the office. Previous to that, of course I was compelled to drink. I've got "jolly" now and then; but I never made a habit of it. It used to cost me about 2s. or 2s. 6d. a week on the average for drink at the uttermost, because I couldn't afford more. Since I've taken the pledge I'm sure it hasn't cost me 6d. a week. A teetotaller feels less thirst than any other man. I don't know what natural thirst is, except I've been eating salt provisions. I belong to a total abstinence society, and there are about a dozen coal-whippers, and about the same number of coal-backers, members of it. Some have been total abstainers for twelve years, and are living witnesses that fermented drinks are not necessary for working men. There are about 200 to 250 coal-whippers, I have been given to understand, who are tee-totallers. Those coal-whippers who have been total abstainers for twelve years are not weaker or worse in health for the want of beer. [This statement was denied by a person present; but a gentle-man, who was intimately acquainted with the whole body, men-tioned the names of several men who had been—some ten years, and some upwards of twelve years—strict adherents to the prin-ciple of teetotalism.] "The great quantity of drinking is carried on ashore. I should say the men generally drink twice as much ashore as they do afloat. Those who drink beer are always thirsty. Through drinking over their work, aboard, a thirst is created, which they set to drinking when ashore to allay; and after a hard day's labour a very little overcomes a man. One or two pots of beer, and the man is loth to stir. He is tired, and the drink, in-stead of refreshing him, makes him sleepy and heavy. The next morning after drinking he is thirstier still, and then he goes to work drinking again. The perspiration will start out of him in large drops like peas; you will see it stream down his face and his hands with the coal-dust sticking to them just like as if he had a pair of silk gloves on him. It's a common saying with us about such a man that he's got the gloves on. The drunkards always per-spire the most over their work. The prejudice existing among the men in favour of drink is such that they believe they would die if they went without it. I am quite astonished to see such an im-provement in them as there is; and I *do* think that if the clergymen of the neighbourhood did their duty and exerted themselves, the people would be better still. At one time there was as many as 500 coal-whippers total abstainers, and the men were much better clothed, and the homes and appearance of the whippers were much more decent. What I should do if I drunk I don't know. I got £1 for clearing a ship last week, and I shan't get any more till Monday night, and I have six children and a wife to keep out of that. For this last fortnight I have only made 10s. a week, so I am sure I couldn't even afford 1s. a week for drink without rob-bing my family."

The second teetotaller, who had been an inveterate drunkard in his time, stated as follows:—Like the rest of the coal-whippers, he thought once that he could not do his work without beer. He used to drink as much as he could get. He averaged two pots at his work, and when he came on shore he would have two pots more. He had been a coal-whipper for upwards of twenty years, and for nineteen years and three months of that time he was a hard drinker—"a regular stiff one," said he. "I not only used," he added, "to get drunk myself, but I taught my children to do so. I have got sons as big as myself, coal-backers, and total abstainers. Often I have gone home of a Sunday morning drunk myself, and found two of my sons drunk. They'd be unable to sit at the table. They were about fourteen then, and when they went out with me I used to teach them to take their little drops of neat rum or gin. I have seen the youngest 'mop up' his half-quartern as well as I did. Then I was always thirsty; and when I got up of a morning I used to go stalking round to the first public-house that was open, to see if I could get a pint or a quartern. My mouth was dry and parched as if I had got a burning fever. If I had no work that day, I used to sit in a public-house, and spend all the money I'd got. If I had no money, I would go home and raise it somehow. I would ask the old woman to give me the price of a pint, or perhaps the young on's were at work, and I was pretty safe to meet them coming home. Talk about going out of a Sunday! I was ashamed to be seen out. My clothes were ragged, and my shoes would take the water in at one end and let it out again at the other. I keep my old rags at home to remind me of what I was, I call them the regimentals of the guzzileers. I pawned everything I could get at. For ten or twelve years I used a beer-shop regularly. That was my house of call. Now my home is very happy. All my children are teetotallers. My sons are as big as myself, and they are at work, carrying 1¾ cwt. to 2 cwt. up a Jacob's ladder thirty-three steps high. They do this all day long, and have been doing so for the last seven days. They drink nothing but water or cold tea, and say they find themselves the better able to do their work. Coal-backing is about the hardest labour a man can perform. For myself, too, I find I am quite as able to do my work without intoxicating drinks as I was with them. There's my 'basketman,' said he, pointing to the other teetotaller, "and he can tell you whether what I say is true or not. I have helped to whip 147 tons of coal in the heat of summer. The other men were calling for beer every time they could see or hear a purl-man, but I took nothing. I don't think I perspired so much as they did. When I was in the drinking custom I have known the perspiration run down my legs and arms as if I'd been in a hot bath. Since I've taken the pledge I scarcely perspire at all. I'll work against any man that takes beer, provided I have a good teetotal pill—that is, a good pound of steak with plenty of gravy in it. That's the stuff to work upon. That's what the working man wants—plenty of it, and less beer, and he'd beat a horse any day. I am satisfied that the working man can never be raised above his present position until he can give over drinking. That is the reason why I'm sticking to the pledge, that I may be a living example to my class that they can and may work without beer. It has made my home happy, and I want it to make every other working man's as comfortable. I tried the principle of teetotalism first on board a steamboat. I was stoker, and we burnt twenty-seven cwt. of coals every hour we were at sea—that's very nearly a ton and a half per hour. There, with the heat of the fire, we felt the effects of drinking strong brandy. Brandy was the only fermented drink we were allowed. After a time I tried what other stimulants we could use. The heat in the hold, especially before the fires, was awful. There were nine stokers and four coal trimmers. We found the brandy that we drank in the day made us ill—our heads ached when we got up in the morning; so four of us agreed to try oatmeal and water as our drink, and we found that suited us better than intoxicating liquor. I myself got as fat as a bull upon it. It was recommended to me by a doctor in Falmouth, and we all of us tried it eight or nine voyages. Some time after I left the company I went to strong drink again, and continued at it till the first of May last; and then my children's love of drink got so dreadful that I got to hate myself as being the cause of it. But I couldn't give up the drinking. Two of my mates, however, urged me on to try. On the 1st of May I signed the pledge. I prayed to God on the night I went to give me strength to keep it, and never since have I felt the least inclination to return. When I had left off a fortnight I found myself a great deal better; all the cramps that I had been loaded with when I was drinking left me. Now I am happy and comfortable at home. My wife's about one of the best women in the world. She bore with me in all my troubles, and now she glories in my redemption. My children love me, and we club all our earnings together, and can always on a Sunday manage a joint of sixteen or seventeen pounds. My wife, now that we are teetotallers, need do no work; and in conclusion, I must say, that I have much cause to bless the Lord that ever I signed the teetotal pledge.

"After I leave my work," added the teetotaller, "I find the best thing I can have to refresh me is a good wash of my face and shoulders in cold water. This is twice as enlivening as ever I found beer. Once a fortnight I go over to Goulston-square, Whitechapel, and have a warm bath. This is one of the finest things that ever was invented for the working man. Any persons that use them don't want beer. I invited a coal-whipper man to come with me once. 'How much does it cost?' he asked. I told him 1d. 'Well,' he

said, 'I'd sooner have half a pint of beer. I haven't washed my
body for these 22 years, and don't see why I should begin to have
anything to do with these new-fangled notions at my time of life.'
I will say that a good wash is better for the working man than the
best drink."

The man ultimately made a particular request that his statement
might conclude with a verse that he had chosen from the Temperance Melodies:—

> " And now we love the social cheer
> Of the bright winter eve ;
> We have no cause for sigh or tear—
> We have no cause to grieve.

> " Our wives are clad, our children fed ;
> We boast, where'er we go,
> 'Twas all because we signed the pledge
> A long time ago."

At the close of my interview with these men I received from
them an invitation to visit them at their own houses whenever I
should think fit. It was clearly their desire that I should see the
comforts and domestic arrangements of their homes. Accordingly,
on the morrow, choosing an hour when there could have been no
preparation, I called at the lodgings of the first. I found the whole
family assembled in the back kitchen, that served them for a
parlour. As I entered the room the mother was busy at work,
washing and dressing her children for the day. There stood six
little things—so young that they seemed to be all about the same
height—with their faces shining with the soap and water, and
their cheeks burning red with the friction of the towel. They were
all laughing and playing about the mother, who, with comb and
brush in hand, found it no easy matter to get them to stand still
whilst she made "the parting." First of all, the man asked me to
step upstairs, and see the sleeping-room. I was much struck with
the scrupulous cleanliness of the apartment. The blind was as
white as snow, half rolled up, and fastened with a pin. The floor
was covered with patches of different coloured carpet, showing
that they had been bought from time to time, and telling how difficult it had been to obtain the luxury. In one corner was a cupboard, with the door taken off, the better to show all the tumblers,
teacups, and coloured glass mugs, that, with two decanters well
covered with painted flowers, were kept more for ornament than
use. On the chimney-piece was a row of shells, china shepherdesses
and lambs, and a stuffed pet canary in a glass case for a centre
ornament. Against the wall, surrounded by other pictures, hung

a half-crown water-colour drawing of the wife with a child on her knee, matched on the other side by the husband's likeness, cut out in black paper. Pictures of bright coloured ducks, and a print of Father Moore, the teetotaller, completed the collection.

"You see," said the man, "we manages pretty well; but I can assure you we has a hard time of it to do it at all comfortably. Me and my wife is just as we stands. All our other things are in pawn. If I was to drink, I don't know what I should do. How others manage is to me a mystery. This will show you I speak the truth," he added; and going to a secretary that stood against the wall, he produced a handful of duplicates. There were 17 tickets in all, amounting to £3 0s. 6d., the highest sum borrowed being 10s. "That'll show you! I don't like my poverty to be known, or I should have told you of it before. And yet we manages to sleep clean," and he pulled back the patchwork counterpane and showed me the snow white sheets beneath. "There's not enough clothes to keep us warm, but at least they're clean. We're obliged to give as much as we can to the children. Cleanliness is my wife's hobby, and I let her indulge it. I can assure you last week my wife had to take the gown off her back to get a shilling with it. My little ones seldom have a bit of meat from one Sunday to another, and never a bit of butter."

I then descended into the parlour. The children were all seated on little stools that their father had made for them in his spare moments, and warming themselves round the fire, their little black shoes resting on the white hearth. By their regular features, small mouths, large dark eyes, and fair skins, no one would have taken them for a labouring man's family. In answer to my questions he said, "The eldest of them (a pretty little half clad girl, seated in one corner) is ten, the next seven, that one five, that three, and this (a little thing perched upon a table near the mother) two. I've got all their ages in the Bible upstairs." I remarked a strange look about one of the little girls, "Yes, she always suffered with that eye, and down at the hospital they lately performed an operation on it." An artificial pupil had been made.

The room was closed in from the passage by a rudely-built partition. "That I did myself in my leisure," said the man; "it makes the room snugger." As he saw me looking at the clean rolling-pin and bright tins hung against the wall, he observed, "That's all my wife's doing. She has got them together by sometimes going without dinner herself, and laying out the 2d. or 3d. in things of that sort. That is how she manages. To-day she has got us a sheep's head and a few turnips for our Sunday's dinner," he added, taking off the lid off the boiling saucepan. Over the mantelpiece hung a picture of George IV, surrounded by four other frames. One of them contained merely three locks of hair. The man, laughing, told me, "Two of them are locks of myself and my wife, and the light one in the middle belonged to my wife's brother, who died in India." "That's her doing again," he added.

After this I paid a visit to the other teetotaller at his home, and there saw one of his sons. He had six children altogether, and also supported his wife's mother. If it wasn't for him the poor old thing, who was 75, and a teetotaller too, must have gone to the workhouse. Three of his six children lived at home. The other three were out at service. One of the lads at home was a coal-backer. He was twenty-four years of age, and on an average could earn 17s. 6d. It was four years since he had taken to backing. He said, "I am at work at one of the worst wharfs in London. It is called 'The Slaughterhouse' by the men, because the work is so excessive. The strongest man can only last twelve years at the work there. After that he is overstrained, and of no use. I do the hardest work, and carry the coals up from the hold. The ladder I mount has about 35 steps, and stands very nearly straight on end. Each time I mount, I carry on my back 238 lb. No man can work at this for more than five days in the week. I work three days running, then have a day's rest, and then work two days more. I myself generally do five days' work out of the six. I never drink any beer, and have not for the last eight months. For three years and four months I took beer to get over the work. I used to have a pint at eleven, a pot at dinner, a pint at four o'clock, and double allowance, or a couple of pots, after work. Very often I had more than double allowance. I seldom in a day drank less than that; but I have done more. I have drank five pots in four minutes and a half. So my expenditure for beer was 1s. 4d. a day regularly. Indeed, I used to allow myself three half-crowns to spend in beer a week, Sundays included. When a coal-worker is in full work, he usually spends 2s. a day, or 12s. a week in beer. The trade calls these men temperate. When they spend 15s., the trade think they are intemperate. Before I took the pledge, I scarcely ever went to bed sober after my labour. I was not always drunk; but I was heavy and stupid with beer. Twice within the time I was a coal-backer I have been insensibly drunk. I should say three-fourths of the coal-backers are drunk twice a week. Coal-backing is as heavy a class of labour as any performed. I don't know any that can beat it. I have been eight months doing the work, and can solemnly state I have never tasted a drop of fermented liquor. I have found

I could do my work better and brisker than when I drank. I never feel thirsty over my work now; before I was always dry, and felt as if I could never drink enough to quench it. Now I never drink from the time I go to work till the time I have my dinner; then my usual beverage is either cold coffee or oatmeal and water. From that time I never drink till I take my tea. On this system I find myself quite as strong as I did with the porter. When I drank porter, it used to make me go along with a sack a little bit brisker for half an hour, but after that I was dead and obliged to have some more. There are men at the wharf who drink beer and spirits that can do six days' labour in the week. I can't do this myself; I *have* done as much when I took fermented liquors, but I only did so by whipping myself up with stimulants. I was obliged to drink every hour a pint of beer to force me along. This was only working for the publican, for I had less money at the week's end than when I did less work. Now I can keep longer and more steadily at my work. In a month I would warrant to back more coals than a drunkard. I think the drunkard can do more for a short space of time than a teetotaller. I am satisfied the coal-backers, as a class, would be better off if they left off the drinking, and then masters would not force them to do so much work after dark as they do now. They always pay at public-houses. If that system was abandoned, the men would be greatly benefited by it. Drinking is not a necessity of the labour. All I want when I'm at work is a bit of coal in the mouth. This not only keeps the mouth cool, but as we go up the ladder, we very often scrunch our teeth—the work's so hard. The coal keeps us from biting the tongue—that's one use; the other is, that, by rolling it along in the mouth, it excites the spittle, and so moistens the mouth. This I find a great deal better than a pot of porter."

In order to complete my investigations concerning the necessity of drinking in the coal-whipping trade, I had an interview with some of the more intelligent of the men who had been principally concerned in the passing of the act that rescued the class from the "thraldom of the publican:"

"I consider," said one, "that drink is not a necessity of our labour, but it is a necessity of the system under which we were formerly working. I have done the hardest work that any labouring man can do, and drank no fermented liquor. Nor do I consider fermented liquors to be necessary for the severest labour. This I can say of my own experience, having been a teetotaller for sixteen months. But if the working man don't have the drink, he must have good solid food, superior to what he is in the habit of having.

A pot of coffee and a good beef dumpling will get one over the most severe labour. But if he can't have that he must have the stimulants. A pint of beer he can always have on credit, but he can't the beef dumpling. If there is an excuse for any persons drinking, there is for the coalwhippers, for under the old system they were forced to become habitual drunkards to obtain work."

I also questioned another of the men who had been a prime mover in obtaining the act. He assured me that before the "emancipation" of the men the universal belief of the coalwhippers, encouraged by the publicans, was, that it was impossible for them to work without liquor. In order to do away with that delusion, the three principal agents in procuring the act became teetotallers of their own accord, and remained so—one for 16 months, and another for nine years—in order to prove to their fellow-workmen that drinking over their labour could be dispensed with, and that they might have "cool brains to fight through the work they had undertaken."

Another of the more intelligent men, who had been a teetotaller for three years, told me: "Whilst I was a teetotaller I performed the hardest labour I ever did before or after, with more ease and satisfaction than ever I did under the drinking system. It is quite a delusion to believe that, with proper nutriment, the health declines under habits of total abstinence."

After this I was anxious to continue my investigations among the coal porters, and see whether the more intelligent among them were as firmly convinced as the better class of coal-whippers were, that intoxicating drinks were not necessary for the performance of hard labour. I endeavoured to find one of each class—pursuing the same plan as I had adopted with the coal-whippers, viz., I sought first one who was so firmly convinced of the necessity of drinking fermented liquors during his work that he had never been induced to abandon them—secondly, I endeavoured to obtain the evidence of one who had tried the principle of total abstinence, and had found it fail; and, thirdly, I strove to procure the opinion of those who had been teetotallers for several years, and who could conscientiously state that no stimulant was necessary for the performance of their labour. Subjoined is the result of my investigations:—

Concerning the motives and reasons for the great consumption of beer by the coalporters, I obtained the following statement from one of them:—"I've been all my life at coal portering, off and on, and am now 39. For the last two years or so I've worked regularly as a filler to Mr. ——'s waggons. I couldn't do my work without a good allowance of beer. I can't afford so much now, as my family costs me more, but my regular allowance one time was three pots a day. I have drunk four pots, and always a glass of gin in the morning to keep out the cold air from the water. If I got off then for 7s. a week for drink, I reckon'd it a cheap week. I can't do my work without my beer, and no coal-porter can properly. It's all nonsense talking about ginger beer, or tea, or milk, or that sort of thing—what body is there in any of it? Many a time I might have been choked with coal-dust if I hadn't had my beer to clear my throat with. I can't say that I'm particular thirsty like next morning, after drinking three or four pots of beer to my own work, but I don't get drunk." He frequently, and with some emphasis, repeated the words, "but I don't get drunk." "You see, when you're at such hard work as ours, one's tired soon, and a drop of good beer puts new sap into a man. It oils his joints like. He can lift better, and stir about brisker. I don't care much for beer when I'm quiet at home on a Sunday. It sets me to sleep then. I once tried to go without to please a master, and did work one day with only one half pint. I went home as tired as a dog. I should have been soon good for nothing, if I'd gone on that way—half-pinting in a day! Lord love you, *we* know a drop of good beer. The coal porters is admitted to be as good judges of beer as any men in London; may be the best judges, better than publicans. No salt and water will go down with us. It's no use a publican trying to gammon us with any of his cag-mag stuff. Salt and water for us! Sartainly a drop of 'short' (neat spirit) does one good in a cold morning like this; it's uncommon raw by the waterside, you see. Coal-porter's doesn't often catch cold; beer and gin keeps it out. Perhaps my beer and gin now costs me 5s. a week, and that's a deal out of what I can earn. I dare say I earn 18s. a week. sometimes I may spend 6s. That's a third of my earnings, you say, and so it is; and as it's necessary for my work, isn't it a shame a poor man's pot of beer, and drop of gin, and pipe of tobacco should be so dear? Taxes makes them dear. I can read, sir, and I understand these things. Beer—four pots a day of it—doesn't make me step unsteady. Hard work carries it off, and so one doesn't feel it that way. Beer's made of corn as well as bread, and so it stands to reason it's nourishing. Nothing'll persuade me it isn't. Let a tee-total gentleman try his hand at coal work, and then he'll see if beer has no support in it. Too much is bad, I know; but a man can always tell how much he wants to help him on with his work. If beer didn't agree with me, why of course I wouldn't drink it—but it does. Sartainly, we drops into a beer-shop of a night, and does tipple a little, when work's done; and the old women (our wives) comes for us, and they get a sup to soften them, and so they may get to like it overmuch, as you say, and one's bit of a house may go to rack and manger. I've a good wife myself, though. I know well enough all them things is bad—drunkenness is bad; all I ask for is a proper allowance at work; the rest's no good. I can't tell whether too much or no beer at coal work would be best—perhaps none at all—leastways it would be safer. I shouldn't like to try either. Perhaps coal porters does get old sooner than other trades, and mayn't live so long, but that's their hard work, and it would be worse still without beer. But I don't get drunk."

I conversed with several men on the subject of their beer-drinking, but the foregoing is the only statement I met with where a coal-porter could give any reason for his faith in the virtues of beer, and vague as in some points it may be, the other reasons I had to listen to were still vaguer. "Somehow, we can't do without beer; it puts in the strength that the work takes out." "It's necessary for support." Such was the pith of every argument.

In order fully to carry out this inquiry, I obtained the address of a *coal-backer from the ships,* who worked hard and drank a good deal of beer, and who had the character of being an industrious man. I saw him in his own apartment, his wife being present while he made the following statement:—"I've worked at backing since I was twenty-four, and that's more than twelve years ago. I limit myself now, because times is not so good, to two pots of beer a-day; that is, when I'm all day at work. Some takes more. I reckon that when times was better, I drank fifteen pots a week, for I was in regular work, and middling well off. That's 780 pots, or 195 gallons, a year, you say. Like enough it may be—I never calculated, but it does seem a deal. It can't be done without, and men themselves is the best judges of what suits their work—I mean of how much to take. I'll tell you what it is, sir. Our work's harder than people guess at, and one must rest sometimes. Now, if you sit down to rest without something to refresh you, the rest does you harm instead of good, for your joints seem to stiffen; but a good pull at a pot of beer backs up the rest, and we start light-somer. Our work's very hard. I've worked till my head's ached like to split, and when I've got to bed, I've felt as if I had the weight on my back still, and I've started awake when I fell off to sleep, feeling as if something was crushing my back flat to my chest. I can't say that I ever tried to do without beer altogether. If I was to think of such a thing, my old woman there would think I was out of my head. [The wife assented.] I've often done with a little when work's been slackish. First, you see, we bring the coal up from the ship's hold. There sometimes it's dreadful hot, not a mouthful of air, and the coal-dust sometimes as thick as a fog. You breathe it into you, and your throat's like a flue, so that you must have something to drink. I fancy nothing quenches you like beer. We want a drink that *tastes*. Then there's the coals on your back to be carried up a nasty ladder, or some such contrivance, perhaps 20 feet—and a sack full of coals weighs 2 cwt. and a stone at least; the sack itself's heavy and thick. Isn't that a strain on a man? No horse could stand it long. Then when you get fairly out of the ship you go along planks to the waggon, and must look sharp, 'specially in slippery or wet weather, or you'll topple over, and then there's the hospital or the workhouse for you. Last week we carried along planks 60 feet at least. There's nothing extra allowed for distance, but there ought to be. I've sweat to that degree in summer that I've been tempted to jump into the Thames just to cool myself. The sweat's run into my boots, and I've felt it running down me for hours as I had to trudge along. It makes men bleed at the nose and mouth, this work does. Sometimes we put a bit of coal in our mouths to prevent us biting our tongues. I do sometimes, but its almost as bad as if you did bite your tongue; for when the strain comes heavier and heavier on you, you keep scrunching the coal to bits, and swallow some of it, and you're half choked, and then its no use, you *must* have beer. Some's tried a bit of tobacco in their mouths, but that doesn't answer; it makes you spit, and often spit blood. I know I can't do without beer. I don't think they 'dulterate for us. They may for fine people that just tastes it, and, I've heard has wine and things. But *we* must have it good, and a publican knows who's good customers. Perhaps a bit of good grub might be as good as beer to strengthen you at work, but the straining and sweating makes you thirsty more than hungry, and if poor men must work so hard, and for so little, for rich men, why, poor men will take what they feel will satisfy them, and run the risk of its doing them good or harm, and that's just where it is. I can't work three days running now without feeling it dreadful. I get a mate that's fresher to finish my work. I'd rather earn less at a trade that would give a man a chance of some ease; but all trades is overstocked. You see we have a nicish, tidy room here, and a few middling sticks, so I can't be a drunkard."

I now give the statement of a *coalporter who had been a teetotaller:*—"I have been twenty-two years a coalheaver. When I began that work I earned 50s. a week as backer and filler. I am now earning, one week with another, say 15s. We have no sick

fund among us—no society of any sort—no club—no schools—
no nothing. We had a kind of union among us before the great
strike, more than fourteen years back, but it was just for the strike.
We struck against masters lowering the pay for a ton a man to
2¼d. from 2½d. The strike only lasted two or three weeks, and the
men were forced to give way; they didn't all give way at once,
but came-to gradual. One can't see one's wife and children without
bread. There's very few teetotallers among us, though there's not
many of us now that can be called drunken; they can't get it, sir.
I was a teetotaller myself for two years, till I couldn't keep to it
any longer. We all break. It's a few years back, I forget zactly
when. At that time teetotallers might drink shrub, but *that* never
did me no good; a good cup of tea freshened me more. I used
then to drink ginger-beer, and spruce, and tea and coffee. I've paid
as much as 5s. a week for ginger-beer. When I teetotalled I always
felt thirsty. I used to long for a drink of beer, but somehow man-
aged to get past a public-house until I could stand it no longer.
A clerk of ours broke first, and I followed him. I certainly felt
weaker before I went back to my beer. Now I drink a pint or two
as I find I want it. I can't do without it, so it's no use trying.
I joined because I felt I was getting racketty, and giving my mind
to nothing but drink instead of looking to my house. There may
be a few teetotallers among us, but I think not. I only knew two.
We all break; we can't keep it. One of these broke, and the other
kept it, because if he breaks his wife'll break, and they were both
regular drunkards. A coal-porter's worn out before he's what you
may call well old. There's not very many old men among us. A
man's done up at fifty, and seldom lives long after, if he has to
keep on at coal-portering. I wish we had some sick fund, or something of that kind. If I was laid up now there would be nothing
but the parish for me, my wife, and four children. [Here the poor
man spoke in a broken voice.] The masters often discharge old
hands when they get feeble, and put on boys. We have no coals
allowed for our own firesides. Some masters, if we buys of them,
charges us full price; others, a little cheaper." I saw this man in
the evening, after he had left his work, in his own room. It was a
large and airy garret. His wife, who did not know previously of
my visit, had in her domestic arrangements manifested a desire
common to the better-disposed of the wives of the labourers or the
poor—that of *trying* to make her "bit of place" look comfortable.
She had to tend a baby four months old; two elder children were
ill-clad, but clean; the eldest boy, who is fifteen, is in the summer
employed on a river steam-boat and is then of great help to his

parents. There were two beds in the room, and the bedding was decently arranged so as to form a bundle, while its scantiness or worn condition was thus concealed. The solitary table had a faded green cloth cover, very thread-bare, but still a cover. There were a few cheap prints over the mantel-helf, and the best description I can give is, in a phrase not uncommon among the poor, that the whole was an attempt "to appear decent." The woman spoke well of her husband, who was kind to her, and fond of his home, and never drank on Sundays.

Last of all I obtained an interview with two coal-porters who had been teetotallers for some years.

"I have been a coal-porter ever since I have been able to carry coals," said one. "I began at 16. I have been a backer all the time. I have been a teetotaller eight years, on the 10th of next March. My average earnings where I am now is about 35s. per week. At some wharfs work is very bad, and the men don't average half that. They were paid every night where I worked last, and sometimes I have gone home with 2½d. Take one with the other I should say the coal-porter's earnings average about £1 per week. My present place is about as good a berth as there is along the waterside. There is only one gang of us, and we do as much work as two will do in many wharfs. Before I was a teetotaller I principally drank ale. I judged that the more I gave for my drink the better it was. Upon an average I used to drink from three to four pints of ale per day. I used to drink a good drop of gin, too. The coal-porters are very partial to dog's-nose—that is, half-a-pint of ale with a pennyworth of gin in it, and when they have got the money, they go up to what they term 'the lucky shop' for it. The coal-porters take this every morning through the week, when they can afford it. After my work I used to drink more than when I was at it. I used to sit as long as the house would let me have any. Upon an average, I should say I used to take three or four pints more of an evening; so that altogether I think I may fairly say I drank my four pots of ale regularly every day, and about half-a-pint of dog's-nose. I reckon my drink used to cost me 13s. a week when I was in work. At times I was a drunken noisy gentleman then." Another coal-porter, who has been a teetotaller ten years on the 25th of last August, told me that before he took the pledge he used to drink a great deal after he had done his work, but while he was at work he could not stand it. "I don't think I used to drink above three pints and a half and a pennyworth of gin in the day-time," said this man. "Of an evening I used to stop at the public-house generally till I was drunk, and unfit to work in the morning.

I will vouch for it I used to take about three pots a day after I had done work. My reckoning used to come to about 1s. 8d. a day, or, including Sundays, about 10s. 6d. per week. At that time I could average all the year round about 30s. a week, and I used to drink away 10s. of it regularly; I did indeed, sir, more to my shame." The other coal-porter told me his earnings averaged about the same, but he drank more. "I should say I got rid of nearly one-half of my money. I *did* like the beer then; I thought I could not live without it. It's between twelve and thirteen years since the first coal-porter signed the pledge. His name was John Sturge, and he was looked upon as a madman. I looked upon him myself in that light. The next was Thomas Bailey, and he was my teetotal father. When I first heard of a coal-porter doing without beer I thought it a thing onpossible. I made sure they wouldn't live long. It was part of my education to believe they couldn't. My grandfather brewed home-brewed beer, and he used to say to me, 'Drink, my lad, it'll make thee strong.' The coal-porters say, now if we could get the genuine home-brewed, that would be the stuff to do us good—the publicans' wash is no good. I drank beer then for strength. The stimulation caused by the alcohol, I mistook for my own power." "Richard Hooper—he's been a teetotaller now about twelve years. He was the fourth of the coaleys as signed the pledge, and he first instilled teetotalism on my mind," said the other man. "Where he works now, there's nine out of fifteen men is teetotallers. Seeing that he could do his work much better than when he drinked beer, induced me to become one. He was more regular to his work after he had given it up, than whenever I knowed him before." "The way in which Thomas Bailey put it into my head was this here," continued the other. "He invited me to a meeting. I told him I would come, but he'd never make a teetotaller of me, I knowed. I went with the intention to listen to what they could have to say. It was a little bit curious to know how they could make out that beer was no good for a body. The first man that addressed the meeting was a tailor. I thought it might do very well for him; but then, says I, if you had the weight of 238lbs. of coals on your back, my lad, you couldn't do it without beer or ale. I thought this here because I was taught to believe I couldn't do without it. I cared not what any man said about beer, I believed it was life itself. After the tailor, a coal-porter got up to speak. Then I began to listen more attentively. The man said he once had a happy home and a happy wife—everything the heart could wish for, but through intoxicating drinks he had been robbed of everything. The man pictured the drunkard's home so faithfully that the arrows of conviction stuck fast in my heart, and my conscience said, 'thou art a drunkard, too.' The coal-porter said his home had been made happy through the principle of total abstinence. I was determined to try it from that hour. My home was as miserable as it possibly could be, and I knowed intoxicating drink was the cause on it. I signed the pledge that night, after the coal-porter was done speaking, but was many months before I was thoroughly convinced I was doing right in abstaining altogether. I kept thinking on it after going home of a night, tired and fatigued with my hard work, sometimes scarcely able to get up stairs through being so overwrought, and not being quite satisfied about it, I took every opportunity to hear lectures on the subject. I heard one on the properties of intoxicating drinks, which quite convinced me that I had been labouring under a delusion. The gentleman analysed the beer in my presence, and I saw that in a pint of it there was 14oz. of water—that I had been paying 2d. for—1oz. of alcohol—and 1oz. of what they call nutritious matter, but which is the filthiest stuff man ever set eyes upon. It looked more like cobbler's wax than anything. It was what the lecturer called—the residyum, I think, was the name he gave it. The alcohol is what stimulates a man, and makes him feel as if he could carry two sacks of coals while it lasts, but afterwards comes the depression, that's what the coal-porters calls the 'blues,' and then he feels that he can do no work at all, and he either goes home and puts another man on in his place, or else he goes and works it off with more drink. You see where we coal-porters have been mistaken, is believing alcohol was nutriment, and in fancying that a stimulant was strength. Alcohol is nothing strengthening to the body—indeed, it hardens the food in the stomach, and so hinders digestion; you can see as much any day if you go into the hospitals, and look at the different parts of animals preserved in spirits. The strength that alcohol gives is unnatural and false. It's food only that can give real strength to the frame. I have done more work since I've been a teetotaller in my eight years than I did in ten or twelve years before. I have felt stronger. I don't say that I do my work better; but this I will say, without any fear of successful contradiction, that I do my work with more ease to myself, and with more satisfaction to my employer, since I have given over intoxicating drinks. I scarcely know what thirst is. Before I took the pledge I was always dry; and the mere shadow of the pot-boy was quite sufficient to convince me I wanted something. I certainly haven't felt weaker since I have left off malt liquor. I have eaten more and drank less. I live as well now as any of the publicans do—and who has a better right to do so than the man that works? I have backed as many as sixty tons in a day since I took the pledge, and have done it without any intoxicating drink with perfect ease to myself, and walked five miles to a temperance meeting afterwards. But before I became a teetotaller, after the same amount of work I should scarcely have been able to crawl home. I should have been certain to have lost the next day's work at least; but now I can back that quantity of coals week after week without losing a day. I've got a family of six children under twelve years of age. My wife's a teetotaller, and has suckled four children upon the principle of total abstinence. Teetotalism has made my home quite happy, and what I get goes twice as far. Where I work now four of us out of five are teetotallers. I am quite satisfied that the heaviest work that a man can possibly do may be done without a drop of fermented liquor. I say so from my own experience. All kind of intoxicating drinks is quite a delusion. They are the cause of the working man's wages being lowered. Masters can get the men who drink, at their own price. If it wasn't for the money spent in liquor, we should have funds to fall back upon, and then we could stand out against any reduction that the masters might want to put upon us, and could command a fair day's wage for a fair day's work; but as it is, the men are all beggars, and must take what the master offers them. The backing of coals out of the holds of ships is man-killing work. It's scandalous that men should be allowed to force their fellow-men to do such labour. The calves of a man's leg is as hard as a bit of board after that there straining work. They hardly know how to turn out of bed of a morning after they have been at that for a day. I never worked below bridge, thank God, and hope I never shall. I have not wanted for a day's work since I've been a teetotaller. Men can back out from a ship's hold better without liquor than with it. We teetotallers can do the work better—that is, with more ease to ourselves, than the drinkers can. Many teetotallers have backed coals out of the hold, and I have heard them say over and over again that they did their work with more comfort and ease than they did when they drank intoxicating drink. Coal-backing from the ship's hold is the hardest work that it is possible for a man to do. Going up a ladder sixteen feet high, with 238lbs. weight on a man's back, is sufficient to kill any one; indeed, it does kill the men in a few years—they're soon old men at that work; and I do say that the masters below bridge should be stopped going on as they're doing now. And what for? Why, to put the money they save by it into their own pockets, for the public a'n't no better off—the coals is just as dear there. Then the whippers and the lightermen are all thrown out of work by it; and, what's more, the lives of the backers are shortened many years—we reckon at least ten year." "I wish to say this much," said the other teetotaller; "it's a practice with some of the coal merchants to pay their men in public-houses, and this is a chief cause of a great portion of the wages being spent in drink. I once worked for a master upon Bankside as paid his men at a public-house, and I worked a week there, which yarned me 28s. and some odd half-pence. When I went on Saturday night the publican asked me what I was come for. In reply I said, I'm come to settle. He says, 'You're already settled with'—meaning that I had nothing to take. I had drinked all my lot away, he said, with the exception of 5s. I had borrowed during the week. Then I told him to look back, and he'd find I'd something due to me. He did so, and said there was a halfpenny. I had nothing to take home to my wife and two children. I asked the publican to lend me a few shillings, saying my young uns had nothing to eat. His reply was, 'That's nothing to me—that's your business.' After that I made it my business. While I stood at the bar, in came the three teetotallers that worked along with me, and picked up the 28s. each that was coming to them; and I thought how much better they was off than me. The publican had stopped all my money for drink that I knowed I'd not had; and yet I couldn't help myself, cause he had the paying on me. Then something came over me as I stood there, and I said, from this night, with the help of God, I'll never taste of another drop of intoxicating liquors—that's ten years ago the 25th of last August—and I've kept my pledge ever since, thank God. That publican has been the making of me. The master that discharged me before for getting drunk, when he heard that I was sober, sent for me back again. But before that, the three teetotallers who was working along with me, was discharged by their master to oblige the publican that stopped my money. The publican, you see, had his coals from the wharf. He was a 'brass-plate coal merchant' as well as a publican, and had private customers of his own. He threatened to take his work away from the wharf if the three teetotallers wasn't discharged, and sure enough, the master did discharge them rather than lose so good a customer. Many of the masters now are growing favourable to teetotalism. I can say that I've done more on the principle of total abstinence than ever I done before. I'm better in health. I've no trembling when I goes to my work of a morning, but on the contrary I'm ready to meet it. I'm happier at home. We never has no angry words now," said the man with a shake of the head; and a strong emphasis on the *now*. "My children never runs away from me as they used to before. They come and embrbace me more. My money now goes for eatables and clothes, what I and my children once was deprived on through my intemperate habits, and I bless God and the publican that made me a teetotaller—that I do sincerely—every night as I go to bed. And as for men to hold out that they can't do their work without it, I'm prepared to prove that we have done more work without it than ever we done, or could do, with it."

I have been requested by the coalwhippers to publish the following expression of gratitude on their part towards the Government for the establishment of the Coalwhippers'-office: —

"The change that the Legislature has produced in us, by putting an end to the thraldom of the publican, by the institution of this office, we wish it to be generally known that we and our wives and children are very thankful for."

I shall now conclude with the following estimate of the number of the hands, ships, &c., engaged in the coal trade of London: —

There are about 400 wharfs, I am informed, from Wapping to Chelsea, as well as those on the City Canal. A large wharf will keep about 30 horses, 6 waggons, and 4 carts, and it will employ constantly from 3 to 4 gangs of 5 men; besides these there will be 6 waggoners, 1 cart carman, and about 2 trounsers—in all from 24 to 29 men. A small wharf will employ one gang of 5 men, about 10 horses, 3 waggons, and 1 cart; 3 waggoners, 1 trounser, and 1 cart carman. At the time of the strike, sixteen years ago, there were more than 3,000 coal-porters, I am told, in London. It is supposed that there is upon an average 1 gang and a-half, or about 7 men, employed in each wharf; or, in all, 2,800 coal-porters in constant employment, and about 200 odd men out of work. There are, in the trade, about 4 waggons and 1 cart to each wharf, or 1,600 waggons, and 400 carts, having 5,200 horses; to these there would be about 3 waggoners and 1 cart carman upon an average to each wharf, or 1,600 in all. Each wharf would occupy about 2 trounsers, or 800 in the whole.

Hence the statistics of the coal trade will be as follows: —

Number of		Number of	
Ships	2,177	Coal-factors	25
Seamen	21,600	Coal-merchants	502
Tons of coal entering the		Coal-dealers	295
port of London each		Coal-waggons	1,600
year	3,418,340	Horses for ditto	5,200
Coal-meters	170	Waggoners	1,600
Coal-whippers	2,000	Trimmers	800
Coal-porters	3,000		

Letter XXII
Tuesday, January 1st, 1850

Having finished with the different classes of Coal-labourers in
London—the whippers, backers, pull-backs, trimmers, and waggoners—I purpose now dealing with the Ballast men—including the
ballast-getters, the ballast-lightermen, and the ballast-heavers of
the Metropolis. My reason for passing from the Coal to the Ballast
labourers, is because the latter class of workpeople are suffering
under the same iniquitous and pernicious system of employment as
that from which the coal labourers have recently been "emanci-
pated;" and the transition will serve to show not only the present
condition of the one class of men, but the past state of the other.

After treating of the ballast labourers, I propose inquiring into
the condition and income of the stevedores—or men engaged in
the stowing and unstowing of vessels—and of the lumpers and
riggers—or those engaged in the rigging and unrigging of them.
It is then my intention to pass to the corn labourers—such as the
corn porters, corn runners, and turners—touching incidentally
upon the corn-meters. After this I mean to devote my attention to
the timber labourers engaged at the different timber docks—as,
for instance, the "Commercial," the "Grand Surrey," and the
"East Country" Docks. Then, in due course, I shall come to the
wharf labourers and porters, or men engaged at the different
wharfs of London; thence I shall digress to the bargemen and
lightermen, or men engaged in the transport of the different
cargoes from the ships to their several points of destination, up or
down the river; and finally I shall treat of the watermen, the steam-
boat men, and pier men, or those engaged in the transit of passengers along the Thames. These—with the dock labourers, of
whom I have before treated—will, I believe, exhaust the subject
of the long-shore labourers; and the whole will, I trust, form, when
completed, such a body of facts and information, in connection
with this particular branch of labour, as has never before been
collected. I am happy to say that, with some few exceptions, I
receive from the different official gentlemen not only every
courtesy and consideration, but all the assistance and co-operation

that it lies in their power to afford me. Every class seems to look upon the present inquiry as an important undertaking, and all—save the Clerk of the Coal Exchange and the Deputy-Superintendent of the London Docks—appear to be not only willing but anxious to "lend a hand" towards expediting the result.

Before quitting the subject of the Coal Market, let me endeavour to arrive at an estimate as to the amount of wealth annually brought into the port of London by means of the "colliers," and to set forth as far as possible the proportions in which it is distributed. In my last Letter certain statistics were given, which—notwithstanding the objection of a "Coal Merchant," who, in a letter to this Journal, states that I have reckoned the number of ships at twice the real quantity—have been obtained from such sources, and, I may add, with so much care and caution, as to render them the most accurate information capable of being procured at present on the subject. The statistics of the number of tons of coals brought into the port of London in the year 1848, the number of vessels employed, of the voyages made by those vessels collectively, and of the seamen engaged in the traffic, were furnished by the Clerk of the Coal Exchange at the time of the opening of the new building. Had the "Coal Merchant," therefore, made it his duty to devote the same time and care to the investigation of the truth of my statements as I give to the collection of them, he would not only have avoided committing the very errors he condemns, but would have displayed a more comprehensive knowledge of his business.

In 1848 there were imported into the London coal market 3,418,340 tons of coal. These were sold to the public at an average rate all the year round of 22s. 6d. per ton. Hence the sum expended in the metropolis for coal in that year was £3,845,632 10s.

There are 21,600 seamen engaged in the coal trade, and getting on an average £3 10s. per man per voyage. Each of these men makes between four and five voyages in the course of the year. Hence the average earnings of each man per year will be £15 18s. exclusive of his keep; calculating this at 5s. per week, or £13 per year, we have £28 18s. for the expense of each of the seamen employed. Hence, as there are 21,600 sailors in the trade, the total yearly cost would be £624,240

There are 170 coal-meters, earning, on an average, £2 per week, or £104 per year each man. This would make the total sum paid in the year to the coal-meters 17,680

There are 2,000 coal-whippers, earning 15s. 1½d. each per week, or £39 6s. 6d. per man. Hence the total sum paid in the course of last year to the coal-whippers was	78,650
There are 3,000 coal-porters, earning, on an average, £1 per week, or £52 per year, per man, so that they receive annually	156,000
Hence the total amount paid per year to the working men engaged in bringing and delivering the coals in the London market is	£876,570

The area of all the coal-fields of Great Britain has been roughly estimated at 9,000 square miles. The produce is supposed to be about 32,000,000 tons annually, of which 10,000,000 tons are consumed in the ironworks, 8,500,000 tons are shipped coastwise, 2,500,000 tons are exported to foreign countries, and 11,000,000 tons distributed inland for miscellaneous purposes. Near upon 4,000,000 tons were brought to London by ships and otherwise in the year 1848; and it is computed that about one-eighth part of this, or 500,000 tons, were consumed by the gas works.

The price of coals, as quoted in the London market, is the price up to the time when the coals are whipped from the ships to the merchants' barges. It includes—1st, the value of the coals at the pit's mouth; 2nd, the expense of transit from the pit to the ship; 3rd, the freight of the ship to London; 4th, the Thames dues; and, 5th, the whipping. The difference between the market price and that paid by the consumer is made up of the expense incurred by the coal merchant for barges, wharfs, waggons, horses, wages to coal-porters, etc., together with his profit and risk. In 1836 the expenses incurred by the merchant from the time he bought a ship-load of coals to the deposition of them in the cellars of his customers, amounted, on an average, it was said, to 7s. per ton. These expenses comprise commission, lighterage, porterage, cartage, shootage, metage, market dues, land metage, and other items. At the present time the expenses must be considerably lower, the wages of the labourers and the meters having been lowered full 50 per cent., though the demand for and consumption of coal has increased at nearly the same rate—indeed the law of the Coal-market appears to be, that, in proportion as the demand for articles rises, so do the wages of the men engaged in the supply of it fall.

As the ballast-heavers are under the thraldom of the same

demoralizing and oppressive system as that which the coal-whippers recently suffered under, it may be as well, before entering upon the immediate subject of this letter, to lay before the reader the following concise account of the terms on which the latter were engaged before the Coalwhippers' office was established.

Until within the last few years, the coalwhippers suffered themselves to be duped in an extraordinary way by publicans and petty shopkeepers on shore. The custom was for the captain of a coal ship, when he required a cargo to be whipped, to apply to one of these publicans for a gang; and a gang was thereupon sent from the public-house. There was no professed or pre-arranged deduction from the price paid for the work; the captain paid the publican, and the publican paid the coal-whippers; but the middleman had his profit another way. The coal-whipper was expected to come to the public-house in the morning; to drink while waiting for work; to take drink with him to the ship; to drink again when the day's work was done; and to linger about and in the public-house until almost bedtime before his day's wages were paid. The consequence was, that an enormous ratio of his earnings went every week to the publican. The publicans were wont to rank their dependents into two classes—the "constant men," and the "stragglers;" of whom the former were first served whenever a cargo was to be whipped; in return for this, they were expected to spend almost the whole of their spare time in the public-house, and even to take up their lodgings there.

The captains preferred applying to the publicans rather than engaging the men themselves, because it saved them trouble; and because (as was pretty well understood) the publicans curried favour with them by indirect means. Grocers and small shop-keepers did the same; and the coal-whippers had then to buy bad and dear groceries instead of bad and dear beer and gin. The Legislative tried by various means to protect the coal-whippers, but the publicans contrived means to evade the law. At length, in 1843, an act was passed, which has placed the coal-whippers in a far more advantageous position.

The transition from coal labour to ballast labour is gradual and easy, even if the labourers were not kindred in suffering.

The coal ships, when discharged by the whippers, must get back to the north; and as there are not cargoes enough from London to freight them, they must take in ballast to make the ships heavy enough to sail in safety. This ballast is chiefly gravel or sand, dredged up from the bed of the Thames, in and near Woolwich Reach. The Trinity House takes upon itself this duty.

The captain, when he requires to sail, applies to the Ballast-Office, and the required weight of ballast is sent to the ship in lighters belonging to the Trinity House, the captain paying so much per ton for it. About eighty tons on an average are required for each vessel; and the quantity thus supplied by the Trinity House is about 10,000 tons per week. Some of the ships are ballasted with chalk taken from Purfleet; all ballast taken from higher up the river than that point must be supplied by the Trinity House. When the ship reaches the Tyne, the ballast is of no further use, but it must not be emptied into that river; it has therefore to be deposited on the banks of the river, where huge mounds are now collected, two or three hundred feet high.

New places on the banks of the river have to be discovered for this deposit, as the ballast mounds keep increasing, for it must be recollected that the vessels leave these parts, no matter for what destination, with coal, and may return in ballast. Indeed, a railway has been formed from the vicinity of South Shields to a waste place on the sea-shore, hard by the mouth of the Tyne, where the ballast may be conveyed at small cost, its further accumulation on the river bank being found an incumbrance. "It is hardly something more than a metaphor," it has been said, "to designate this a transfer of the bed of the Thames to the banks of the Tyne." We may add another characteristic. Some of the older ballast mounds are overgrown with herbage, and as the vessels from foreign ports, returning to the coal ports in ballast, have, not infrequently, to take soil on board for ballast, in which roots and seeds are contained—some of which struggle into vegetation—Italian flowers not infrequently attempt to bloom in Durham, Yorkshire, or Northumberland, while of these plants some have survived the climate and have spread around, and thus it is that botanists trace the history of plants which are called indigenous to the ballast hills.

Before treating of the ballast labourers themselves, I shall give a brief history of the ballast laws.

Ships are technically said to be in ballast when they sail without a cargo, having on board only the stores and other articles requisite for the use of the vessel and crew, as well as of any passengers who may be proceeding with her upon the voyage. In favour of vessels thus circumstanced it is usual to dispense with many formalities at the custom-houses of the ports, and to remit the payment of the dues and charges levied upon ships having cargoes on board. A foreign vessel proceeding from a British port may take chalk on board as ballast. Regulations have at various times been made in different ports and countries determining the modes in which ships may be supplied with ballast, and in what manner they may discharge the same; such regulations being necessary to prevent injury to harbours. Charles I published a proclamation in 1636, ordering "that none shall buy any ballast out of the river Thames but a person appointed by him for that purpose," and this appointment was sold for the King's profit. Since then the soil of the river Thames has been vested in the corporation of the Trinity House, and a fine of £10 may be recovered for every ton of ballast taken out of the river without the authority of the corporation. Ships may take on board "land ballast" from any quarries or pits east of Woolwich, by paying 1d. per ton to the Trinity House. For "river ballast" the corporation are authorised by act of Parliament to make other charges. The receipts of the Trinity House from this source were £33,591 in the year 1840, and their expenses were £31,622, leaving a clear profit of £1,969. The ballast of all ships or vessels coming into the Thames must be unladen into a lighter, and if any ballast be thrown into the river, the master of the vessel whence it is thrown is liable to a fine of £20. Some such regulation is usually enforced at every port.

Before proceeding further with my present subject, it is proper that I should express my acknowledgement of the ready courtesy with which the official information necessary for the full elucidation of my subject was supplied to me by the Secretary of the principal Ballast-office, at Trinity House, Tower-hill. I have always observed that when the heads of a department willingly supply information to go before the public, I find in the further course of my investigations that under such departments the claims of the labourers are not only acknowledged but practically allowed. On the other hand, if official gentlemen neglect (which is to refuse) to supply the returns and other information, it is because the inquiry is unpalatable to them, as the public in those departments will find that the fair claims of the labourer are *not* allowed. Were the poor ballast-heavers taken under the protection of the Corporation of the Trinity House (something in the same way that Parliament placed the coal-whippers under the guardianship of a board of commissioners), the good done would be great indeed, and the injury would be none, for it cannot be called an injury to prevent a publican forcing a man to buy and swallow bad drink.

By charter of Queen Elizabeth, in the thirty-sixth year of her reign, "the lastage and ballastage, and office of lastage and ballastage" of all ships, and other vessels betwixt the bridge of the city of London and the main sea, I am informed by the secretary of the

Trinity Company, was granted to the master, wardens, and assistants of the Trinity House of Deptford Strond. This was renewed; and the gravel, sand, and soil of the River Thames granted to the said master, wardens, etc., for the ballasting of ships and vessels, in the fifteenth year of Charles the Second; and again in the seventeenth year of the reign of that Monarch. This last-named charter remains in force, and has been confirmed by acts of Parliament at different times; by which acts, also, various regulations in relation to the conduct of the ballast service, the control of the persons employed therein, and the prices of the ballast supplied, have been established. The act now in force is the sixth and seventh Victoria, cap. 57.

The number of men employed in lighters as ballast-getters, or in barges conveying it from the dredgers, is 245, who are paid by the ton raised.

The number of vessels entered for ballast in the year 1848 was—

Colliers	6,480
British merchant-vessels	2,690
Aliens	1,054
Total vessels	11,224

The total quantity of ballast supplied to shipping, in the year 1848, was 615,619 tons, or thereabouts; such ballast being gravel raised from the bed of the River Thames, and delivered alongside of vessels, either lying in the different docks, or being afloat in the stream between London Bridge and Woolwich.

The number of craft employed in this service is 69, viz:—

	Men.
3 steam dredging-vessels, having 8 men in each	24
43 lighters, having 4 men in each	172
9 lighters, having 5 men in each	45
14 barges, having 2 men in each	28
69	Total 269

The ballast is delivered into the vessels from the lighters and barges by men called ballast-heavers, who are employed by the vessel, and are not in the service of the Trinity House.

I now come to the nature of the ballast labour itself. This is divisible into three classes—the *ballast-getters,* or those who are engaged in raising it from the bed of the Thames; the *ballast-lighters,* or those who are engaged in carrying from the getters to the ships requiring it; and the *ballast-heavers*—or those who are engaged in putting it on board of such ships. The first and second of these classes have, even according to their own account, "nothing to complain of," being employed by gentlemen who, judging by the wanton neglect of the labouring men by their masters, so general in London, certainly exhibit a most *extraordinary* consideration and regard for their workpeople, and the change from the indifference and callousness of the coal-merchants to the kindness of the Corporation of the Trinity-house is most gratifying. The ballast-heavers constitute an entirely different class. They have every one to a man deep and atrocious wrongs to complain of—such as I am sure are unknown, and which, when once made public, must at once demand some remedy.

I must, however, first deal with the ballast-getters. Of these there are two sub-classes, viz., those engaged in obtaining the ballast by steam power, and those who still procure it as of old, by muscular power.

Of *Steam Dredging-engines* employed in the collecting of ballast from the bed of the Thames there are three—the "Hercules," the "Goliath," and the "Sampson." These are now stationed respectively in Barking-Reach, Half-Reach, near Dagenham; and the bottom of Halfway-Reach, off Rainham. Most persons who have proceeded up or down the Thames will have perceived black unshapely masses, with no visible indications that they may be classed with steam-vessels, except a chimney and smoke. These are the dredging-vessels. They are of about 200 tons burden. The engines of the Hercules and the Sampson are of 20-horsepower; those of the Goliath are of 25. When the process of dredging is carried on, the use of the dredging-vessel is obvious to any spectator; but I believe that most persons imagine the object to be merely to deepen the river by removing inequalities in its bed, and so to render its navigation easier by equalising its depth, and in some degree checking the power of cross current. Few are aware that an ulterior object is attained. I visited one of these steam-dredgers, and was very courteously shown over it. The first feeling was an impression of the order, regularity, and trimness that prevailed. In the engineers' department, too, there was an aspect, as well as a feeling, of extreme snugness, the more perceptible, both to the eye and the body, from its contrast with the intense cold on the muddy river outside, then running down in very strong ebb. In the engineers' department there was more than cleanliness— there was a brightness about the brass handles attached to the machinery, and indeed about every portion of the apparatus at all susceptible of brightness, which indicated a constant and systematic attention by well-skilled hands. Each dredger carries eight men—

the master (called "the captain" commonly enough on the river),
two engineers, an engineer's assistant, two legsmen (who attend to
the ladders), and three men for general purposes. They are all
called enginemen. The master of the dredger I visited had the
weather-beaten look of the experienced seaman, and the quiet way
of talking of past voyages which is found generally in men who
have really *served,* whether in the merchant service or royal
navy. He resided on board the dredger, with his wife and family,
the principal cabin being a very comfortable parlour. All the men
live on board, having their turns for visits to the shore from
Saturday morning, noon, or evening (as their business permits),
to Monday morning. Their sleeping-places are admirable for cleanliness. All the dredgers are under the control of the Corporation
of the Trinity House. They are, as it was worded to me, "as strong
as wood and iron can make them." But for secure anchorage these
dredgers would soon go adrift. Colliers beating up or down occasionally run against the dredgers; this happens mostly in light
winds, when the masters of these colliers are afraid to let go their
anchors. The machinery consists of a steam-engine and spur-gear
for divesting the buckets. The application of the steam power I
need not minutely describe, as it does not differ from other ap-
plications where motion has to be communicated. It is connected
with strong iron beams, having cogged and connected wheels,
which, when put into operation, give upward and downward
motion to the buckets. These buckets are placed on *ladders,* as
they are called, one on each side the vessel. These ladders (or
shafts) consist of three heavy beams of wood, firmly bolted
together, and fitted with friction wheels. To each ladder, 29
buckets are attached, each bucket holding 2½ cwt. of gravel. Each
bucket is attached by joints to the next, and a series of holes permits the water drawn up with the deposit to ooze out. When the
bucket touches the bottom of the river, it dips, as it is called.
A rotary motion being communicated, the construction ensures
the buckets being brought up flat on the ladder, until a due height
is attained, when the rotatory (or circular) motion again comes
into play, and the contents of the bucket are emptied into a
lighter, moored alongside, and the empty bucket is driven down
to be refilled. The contents so drawn up are disposed of for ballast,
which is the ulterior purpose I have alluded to. Upon an average,
the buckets revolve once in two minutes. That time, however,
varies, from the nature of the bed of the river. The Goliath and
the Sampson being fitted up with marine engines, drive the fastest.
The three vessels have for the last year worked within a circle of

a mile. The quantity of ballast raised depends upon the demand as well upon the character of the deposit at the bottom of the river. Between 900 and 1,000 tons have been raised in seven hours and a half; sometimes in a like period less than 300 tons have been raised. The dredger I was on board of has taken in a year from 180,000 to 190,000 tons. She was then at work to clear away a shoal of 10 feet. A stratum of mud (two-and-a-half feet) had been raised; then three feet of gravel and a chalk bottom was anticipated. In some places 15 feet have been so cleared away to a chalk bottom. In others 15 feet have been so worked off, and no bottom but gravel reached. The gravel lies in shoals. Sometimes the dredgers come to hard conglomerate gravel, as compact as rock. No fossils have been found. In a few places a clay bottom has been met with. The men in the dredgers are paid according to the number of tons raised, the proceeds being duly apportioned. They work as frequently by night as by day, their work depending upon the time when an order for a supply of ballast is received. Each lighter holds 60 tons of ballast. The dredgers above-bridge are the property of individuals working with the concurrence of the civic Corporation of London. Those below-bridge are, as I have said, under the control of the Corporation of the Trinity House. The Hercules was the first Trinity House dredger worked by steam. Private individuals, however, employed steam sooner than the Trinity House authorities, to draw up materials to mix with lime for building purposes. The first Trinity House steam-dredger was started in 1827.

I had some conversation with a man employed on one of the steam-dredgers. He described the process carried on there as I have given it, estimating the tons of ballast raised as about 4,000 a week. He expressed a sense of his good fortune in having the employment he had; he was well used, and wouldn't like to change. He declined stating his earnings (otherwise than that he had his fair share) until he saw his master; and, of course, I did not press him further on the subject.

The *Ballast-getters* are men employed in raising ballast from the bed of the river by bodily labour. The apparatus by which this is effected consists of a long staff or pole, about thirty-five feet in length. At the end of this is an iron "spoon" or ring, underneath which is a leathern bag, holding about 20 cwt. The ballast is raised on board the working lighters by means of this spoon. The working lighters carry six hands—that is, a staffsman, whose duty it is to attend to the staff; a bagsman, who empties the bag; a chainsman, who hauls at the chain; a heelsman, who lets go the pall of the winch; and two trimmers, who trim the ballast in the lighter as fast as it comes in. Previous to the men getting at work, the staffsman takes hold of the spoon to feel whereabout the ballast-bed lies. When this is found he puts down his "sets," as it is termed—that is to say, he drives the iron-tipped spars that he has with him in the lighter into the ground, so as to steady the craft. This done, the staffsman seizes hold of the middle of the staff, while the bagsman takes the bag and the chainsman the chain which is fastened to the iron ring or spoon. The staff is thus thrown overboard into the water, about midway of the lighter, and the tide carries the spoon down towards the stern. The staffs-man then fastens the staff to the lighter by means of the gaff-string or rope attached to the side of the vessel. At the same time the men go forward to heave at the winch, round the roll of which the chain attached to the spoon itself is wound. All the men, with the exception of the staffsman, then heave away, and so drag the spoon along the bed of the river. When the staffsman feels that the bag is full, he leaves go of the gaff-string, and goes forward to heave with the men as well. Immediately the gaff-string is undone, the top part of the staff falls back on an oar that projects from the after part of the vessel, and the bag is then raised by means of the winch and chain to the level of the gunwale of the craft. Then the bagsman hauls it in, and empties it into the lighter, while the two trimmers spread the ballast discharged. The spoon can only be worked when the tide is nearly down, because the water would be too deep for the sets to keep the craft steady. To hoist the 20 cwt. of ballast in the bag will require the whole force of the six men, and none but the very strongest are of use. The ballast-getters are all very powerful men. They are mostly very tall, big-boned, and muscular. Many of them are upwards of six feet high, and have backs two feet broad. "I lifted seven half-hundred weights with one of my hands," said one whom I saw. He was a man of thirty-nine years of age, and stood half an inch over six feet high, while another was six feet two inches. They were indeed extra-ordinarily fine specimens of the English labourer, making our boasted life-guardsman appear almost weak and effeminate in comparison with them. Before the steam-dredging engines were introduced, I am informed the ballast-getters were even bigger and heavier men than they are now. The ballast-getters seldom or never fish up anything besides ballast. Four or five years back they were lucky enough to haul up a box of silver plate, but they consider a bit of old iron, or a bit of copper, very good luck now. The six men generally raise 60 ton 18 feet high in the course of the tide, which is at the rate of 22,400 lb. each man in three hours. This makes the quantity raised per hour by each man upwards of 7,400 lb. The price paid is 8d. per ton, or £2 for 60 ton. This is shared equally among five of the men, who receive 8s. apiece as their proportion, and out of this they pay 3s. 6d. a tide to the stern-trimmer whom they employ, the Trinity Company allowing only five men, and the ballast-getters engaging the sixth hand themselves. Upon an average, the ballast-getters do about three loads in the week throughout the year; this, deducting the money paid to the sixth man, makes the earnings of each ballast-getter come to about 22s. throughout the year. The staffsman is allowed £20 a year to keep the craft in gear. The ballast-getters usually work above the dredging-engines, mostly about Woolwich; there the cleanest ballast is to be got. The Trinity Company they speak most highly of; indeed the Corporation is universally spoken of as excellent masters. The men say they have nothing to complain of. They get their money every Friday night, and have no call to spend a farthing of their earnings with any man but what they please. They only wish, they add, that the ballast-heavers were as well off. "It would be a good job if they was, poor men," say one and all.

The second class of ballast labourers are the *Ballast-lightermen*. These are men engaged by the Trinity Company to carry the ballast in the company's barges and lighters from the steam dredging-engines to the ships' side. The Corporation has 52 lighters and 14 barges—all 60 ton craft. Each lighter carries four men, and there are two men in each barge, so that altogether 108 lightermen and 28 bargemen are employed in bringing the ballast from the engines. These men are not required to have a license from the Watermen's Company like other lightermen and bargemen on the Thames, and that is one of the reasons for my dealing with them in this place. They form a class of labourers by themselves, and I treat of them here because it appears the fittest place for a statement of their condition and earnings. Besides the lightermen and bargemen engaged in carrying the ballast from the steam dredging-engines, there are others employed on board what are called the "working-lighters." These are vessels in which ballast is got up from the bed of the river by muscular labour. There are ten of these working-lighters, and six men engaged in each, or in all sixty men employed in raising ballast by such means. There are three steam dredging-engines, employing each eight men, or twenty-four in all; so that there are altogether 220 labouring men engaged in the ballast service of the Trinity Company. Each of the carrying lighters has a staffsman or master, and three men. The lighters all carry 60 tons of ballast, and make upon an average between three and four voyages a week, or about seven in the fortnight. There is no place of deposit for the ballast brought up the river from the engines. It is left in the lighters until required. The ballast chiefly consists of gravel; indeed, the ships will mostly refuse anything else. When there is a plentiful supply of ballast they will refuse clay in particular. Clayey ballast is what is termed bad ballast. Upon an average there are thirty loads, or 1,800 tons, of ballast brought up by the lighters every day from the engines. In the course of the year there are between 550,000 and 600,000 tons of ballast supplied by the three steam dredging-machines. "It is about three-and-twenty years since the steam dredging-engine first came out," said the party who gave me the above information. "For the last twenty years, I should think the company have been raising about 500,000 tons of gravel from the bed of the river. Thirty years ago, I thought the ballast would soon be out, but there appears to be little or no difference; and yet the shoals do not fill up again after being once taken away. In Barking-Reach, I am sure there is six feet more water now than there was thirty years ago. There was at that time a large shoal in that part of the river, called Barking-Shelf. It was certainly a mile long and half a mile wide. The vessels would ground upon it long before low water. At some tides it used 'to strip dry,' and at low tide generally there was about six foot of water over it. That part of the river is now the deepest about Barking, and as deep as the best of places in the Thames. When I first came to London we were prevented from getting the ballast from anywhere else than Barking, on account of the great shoals there; but now the great ballast-bed is between four and five miles lower down. The river has been very nearly cleared of shoals, by the dredging-engines, from Limehouse-Reach to the bottom of Half-Reach. The only shoal in the way of the navigation below 'the Pool' is what is called Woolwich-Shelf. There is, indeed, another shoal, but this consists of stiff clay or conglomerate, and the engines cannot work through it. The men on board the carrying lighters are paid 5d. a ton for bringing the ballast from the dredging-engines to the ships. This is equally divided among the four men. The staffs-man, in addition to his fourth share, receives £10 a year for his extra duties, but out of this he has to buy oars for the boat and lighter, locks, 'fenders,' and shovels. Upon an average, the cost of these will be about 30s. a year. Each man's share of the 60 ton load is 6s. 3d., and there are about seven loads brought up by each lighter in the fortnight. Some weeks the men can earn as much as 37s., but at others they cannot get more than 12s. 6d. "I did myself only two load last week," said my informant. "When there is little or no 'vent,' as we call it, for the ballast—that is, but a slight demand for it—we have but little work. Upon an average each lighterman makes from 21s. to 22s. a week. At the time of the strike among the pitmen in the North the lightermen generally only did about two load a week throughout the year, but then the following year we had as much as we could do. The Trinity Company, whom I serve and have served for thirty years, are excellent masters to us, when we're sick or well. The Corporation of the Trinity House allow the married lightermen in their service 10s., and the single men 7s. 6d., a week so long as they are ill. I have known the allowance given to men for two years, and for this we pay nothing to any benefit society or provident fund. If we belong to any such society we have our sick money from them independent of that. The superannuation money is now £6 a year, but I understand," said my informant, "that the Company intend increasing it next Tuesday. Some of the old men were ordered up to the House a little while ago, and were asked what they could live comfortably upon, and one of the gentlemen there promised them that no more of us should go to the workhouse. They do not provide any school for our children. A great many of the lightermen cannot read or write. I never heard any talk of the Company erecting a school either for the instruction of their men or their men's families. All I can say is, that in all my dealings with the Trinity Corporation I have found them very kind and considerate masters. They are always ready to listen to the men, and they have hospitals for the sick in their employ, and midwives for the wives of the labourers, and they bury free of expense most of the men that die in their service. To the widows of their deceased servants they allow £6 a year, and if there be any children, they give 2s. a month to each under fourteen years old. I never knew them to reduce the lightermen's wages; they have rather increased than lowered them. After the introduction of the steam dredging-machines, we were better off than we were before. Previous to that time, the lightermen were 'getters' as well, and then the labour was so hard that the expenses of the men for living were more than they are now."

I now come in due order to the ballast-heavers. Of these I can at present but give a description. The individual instances of oppression that I have sought out, I must reserve for my next letter, when I do most heartily hope that the publication of the iniquity of which these poor fellows are the prey, will be at least instrumental to putting an end to this most vile and wicked plan for the degradation and demoralization of our fellow creatures. The tales I have to tell are such as must rouse every heart not positively indurated by the love of gain. I must, however, be here content, as I said before, by merely describing the system: —

The duty of the *ballast-heaver* is to heave into the holds of the ship the ballast brought along-side the vessel by the Trinity lighters, from the dredging engines. The ships take in ballast either in the Docks or in the Pool. When the ship is "cranky built," and cannot stand steady after a portion of her cargo has been discharged, she usually takes in what is called "shifting" or "stiffening ballast." The ballast is said to stiffen a cranky vessel, because it has the effect of making her firm or steady in the water. The quantity of ballast required by cranky vessels depends upon the build of the ships. Sixty tons of cargo will stiffen the most cranky vessel. I am informed by those who have been all their lives at the business, that they never knew a vessel, however cranky, but what sixty tons weight would stiffen her. Some vessels are so "stiff built" that they can discharge the whole of their cargo without taking in any ballast at all. These are generally flat-bottomed vessels, whereas cranky vessels are built sharp towards the keel. The "colliers" are mostly flat-bottomed vessels, and could in calm weather return to the north without either ballast or cargo in them. This, however, is not allowed by the owners. The generality of ships discharge all their cargo before they take in any ballast. The cranky-built ships form the exception, and they begin taking in ballast when they are about three parts discharged. When a ship requires ballast, the owner, or one of his agents or servants, applies at the Trinity-house for the quantity needed. If the ship belongs to the merchant service, and is lying in any of the docks, the owner has to pay 1s. 7d. per ton to the Trinity Company for the ballast supplied; but if the merchant vessel be lying in the Pool, then the price is 1s. 3d. per ton; and if the vessel be a collier, the price is 1s. per ton. On application being made at the "Ballast-office," the party is supplied with a bill specifying the name and situation of the vessel, the quantity of ballast required for her, and the price that has been paid for it. This bill is then taken to the "Ruler's-office," where it is entered in a book, and the ship supplied with the ballast according to the place that she has on the books. If the weather is rough, a ship has often to remain three or four days without receiving the ballast she wants. The application for ballast is seldom made directly by the captain or shipowner himself. There are parties living in the neighbourhood of Wapping and Ratcliff who undertake for a certain sum per score of tons to have the requisite quantity of ballast put on board the ship. These parties are generally either publicans, grocers, butchers, lodging-house keepers, or watermen, and they have a number of labourers dealing with them whom they employ to heave the ballast on board. The publicans, butchers, grocers, or lodging-house keepers, are the ballast contractors, and they only employ those parties who are customers at their houses. It is the owner or captain of the vessel who contracts with these "truckmen" for the ballasting of the ship at a certain price per score of tons, and the truckmen for that sum undertake not only to obtain the ballast from the Trinity Company, and save the owner or captain all the trouble of so doing, but to have it hove from the Trinity lighters on board the ship. The reason of the publicans, grocers, butchers, or lodging-house keepers undertaking the job, is to increase the custom at their shops, for they make it a rule to employ no heavers but those who purchase their goods from them. The price paid to these truckmen varies considerably. Their principal profit, however, is made out of the labourers they employ. The highest price paid to the contractors for putting the ballast on board "colliers" (exclusive of the cost of the ballast itself), is 10s. per score tons. Many contractors charge less than this; not a few, indeed, undertake to do it for 9s.; and there are one or two who will do it for 8s. the score. But these I am informed are "men who are trying to get the work away from the other contractors." The highest price paid to the contractors for ballasting small merchant vessels is 12s. per score as well. For large vessels the price varies according to their size and the number of heavers consequently required to put the ballast on board. The lowest price paid per score to the contractors for small merchant vessels is 10s. Eight or nine years ago the price for ballasting small merchant vessels was much higher. Then the highest price paid to the contractor was 15s. Since that time the prices, both for merchant vessels and colliers, have been continually falling. This, I am told, arises from the number of contractors increasing, and their continual endeavours to underwork one another. Before the establishment of the Coalwhippers'-office, the contractors for ballast were solely publicans; and they not only undertook to put ballast on board, but to deliver the coals from the ships as well. At this time the publicans engaged in the business made rapid and large fortunes, and soon became shipowners themselves; but after the institution of the Coalwhippers'-office, the business of the publicans who had before been the contractors declined. Since that period the contracts for ballasting ships have been undertaken by butchers and grocers as well as the publicans, and the number of these has increased every year; and according as the number of the contractors has increased so have the prices decreased, for each one is anxious to undersell the other. In order to do this, the contractors have sought everywhere for fresh hands, and the lodging-house keepers in particular have introduced labouring men from the country, who will do the work at a less price than those who have been regularly brought up to the business; and I am credibly informed that whereas nine or ten years ago every ballast-heaver was known to his mates, now the strangers have increased to such an extent, that at least two-thirds of the body are unacquainted with the rest. There is treble the number of hands at the work now, I am told, to what there was but a few years back. The prices paid by the contractors to the ballast-heavers are very little below what the owners pay to them; indeed, some of the publicans pay the heavers the same price as they themselves receive, and make their profit solely out of the beer and spirits supplied to the workmen. The butchers and grocers generally pay the men sixpence, and some a shilling, in the score, less than they themselves get; but, like the publicans, their chief profit is made out of the goods they supply. The lodging-house keepers seldom contract for the work. They are generally foremen employed by the publican, butcher, or grocer contracting; and they make it a rule that the ballast-heavers whom they hire shall lodge at their house, as well as procure their beer, meat, or grocery, as the case may be, from the shop of the contractor by whom they are employed. All the English ships that enter the port of London are supplied with ballast in this manner. The owners always make it a rule to contract with some publican, butcher, grocer, baker, or lodging-house keeper for the ballasting of their vessels, and it is impossible for a ballast-heaver to obtain employment at his calling, but by dealing at the shops of some or other of these parties. According to the Government returns, there were 170 ballast-heavers in the metropolis in 1841, and I am assured that there are more than double that number at present, or nearly four hundred labourers, engaged in the business. There are now twenty-seven publicans who make a regular business of contracting for the supply of ballast. Besides these, there are four butchers, the same number of grocers, and as many lodging-house keepers. Further than this, there is a foreman attached to each of the public-houses, or butchers', or grocers' shops, and these foremen are mostly lodging-house keepers as well. The foremen in general have the engagement of the heavers, and the first hands they employ are those who lodge at their houses; these hands are expected also to deal with the contractor under whose foreman they serve. The heavers generally, therefore, are obliged to lodge at the house of some foreman, and to obtain their meat, beer, and grocery from the different ballast contractors, in order to obtain work; indeed, with the exception of clothing, the heaver is compelled to obtain almost every article he consumes through the medium of some contractor. The greater the number of contractors the heaver deals with, the greater is his chance of work. The rule with each of the contractors is to give credit to the hands they employ, and those who are the most in debt with them have the preference of labour. The butchers and grocers generally charge 1d. per lb. extra for everything they sell to the heavers, and the publicans make it up in adulteration. Each of the publicans, butchers, and grocers who make a rule of contracting for the supply of ballast, has, on average, two gangs of men constantly dealing at his house, and if he has more ships to supply than his regular hands are capable of doing, then he sends the foreman to either of the places of call where the unemployed men wait for hire throughout the day. Each ship requires from four to six heavers to put the ballast on board, and the men generally ship about 50 tons in the course of the day. They often do as much as 100 tons, and sometimes only 20, in the day. The heavers are divided into "constant" and "casualty" men. The constant men are the first gang working out of the public-house or butcher's or grocer's shop. The constant men with the publicans are those that are the best customers. "If they didn't drink," said my informant, "they'd be thought of very little use." These constant men make three times as much as the casualty men; or, in other words, they have three times as much to drink. Generally one-fifth part of what the publican's constant men earn is spent in drink. The casualty men are those who belong to no regular house, but these, if taken on by a publican, are expected to spend the same amount in drink as the constant men. There are no ballast-heavers who are teetotallers—"Indeed, it would be madness," says my informant, "for a man to think of it, for to sign the pledge would be to deprive himself and his family entirely of bread."

To complete the different classes of labourers, I will conclude with the statement of a "casualty man: "—

"I am now about 57 (said my informant, who was six feet high, and looked like a man far older than 57), and have been thirty-five years a *ballast-heaver,* with the exception of seven or eight years, when I had the care of some horses used in coal-waggons. When I first knew the trade, earnings was good. I might clear my £1 a week. On that I brought up four sons and one daughter—all now married. At that time—I mean when I first worked at ballast-heaving—the men were not so much employed by publicans and other tradesmen. A gang of men could get work on their own account a good deal easier than they can get it now through the tradesmen that supply the ballast. As the trade got more and more into the hands of the publicans and such like, it grew worse and worse for such as me. We earned less, and were not anything like to call free men. Instead of my £1, I had to stir myself to make 15s., or as low as 12s. a week. Lately I have been what is called *a Casualty Man*. There's *Constant Men* and *Casualties*. Each publican has a foreman, to look out and get men, and see after them. These foremen—all of them that I know of—keeps lodgers, charging them 2s. 6d. or 3s. a week for a room they could get, but for this tie, for 2s.—aye, that they would. Suppose now, a publican has a ship to supply with ballast; he acquaints his fore-man, and the foreman calls on his lodgers, and sets them to work. These are the Constant Men—they have always the first turn out of the house. If they return from work at four, and there's another job at five, they get it. That's interest, you see, sir. The more such men earn this way, the more they're expected to spend with the publican. It's only bad stuff they have to drink at a full price. It's only when all the constant men are at work, and a job must be done at once, that me, and such as me, can get work. If I hear of a chance of a job. I call on the foreman. If I have the money, why I must drink myself, and treat the foreman with a drop of gin, or what he fancies. If I haven't the money I have the worse chance for a job. Suppose I get a job, and earn 6s., out of 60 tons of ballast. Out of that 6s. I may have 4s., or at most 4s. 6d. to take home with me, after paying for what I must drink at the publican's—what I'm forced to spend. Casualty men have sad trouble to get any work. Those that belong to the houses have all the call. Last week I was on the look-out every day, and couldn't get a single job nor earn a single farthing. Last night I had to get a bite of supper at my son's, and a bite of breakfast this morning as well, and I had to borrow a pair of shoes to come out in. The best week's work I've had this winter was 15s. I had five days in one ship. For that five days' work I was entitled, I fancy, to 20s., or may be 21s., so that the difference between that and 15s. went for drink. I only wanted a pint of beer now and then at my work—two or three a day. The worst of it is, we don't get drink at our work so much as at the public-house we're employed from. If we want to go home, some of the constant men want to have more and more, and so the money goes. Other weeks I've carried home 10s., 8s., 5s., and many a week nothing—living as I could. It would be a deal better for poor men like me, if tradesmen had nothing to do with ballast work. If the men that did the work were paid by the gentleman what wants the ballast, there might be a living for a poor man. As it is it's a very bad, hateful system, and makes people badly off. There's tidy and clean doings in a workhouse, but a ballast man may sit in a taproom, wet and cold and hungry (I've felt it many a time), and be forced to drink bad stuff, waiting to be paid. It always happens, unless they're about shutting up, that we have to wait. We have no sick fund or benefit societies. I declare to you that if anything happened to me—if I was sick, I have nothing to call my own, but what I've on—and not all that, as I've told you—and there's nothing but the parish to look to. [Here the man somewhat shuddered.] I pay 2s. a week rent. Then there's the *basket-men* at the docks—all the docks. They're as bad to a poor man as the publican, or worse. The way they do is this. They're not in any trade, and they make it their business to go on board ships, foreign ships, Americans generally. In better times, 20 or 25 years ago, there used to be 1s., and as high as 1s. 6d. paid for a ton, from such ships, to a gang of six ballast-men. I've earned 6s., 7s., and 8s., a day myself then. We heaved the ballast out of the lighters with our shovels on to a stage, and from that it was heaved into the hold. Two men worked in the lighter, two on the stage, and two in the hold of the vessel. The basket-men manage to fill the hold now by heaving the ballast up from the lighter in baskets, by means of a windlass. The basket-man contracts with the captain, and then puts us poor men at the lowest rate he can get; he picks them up anywhere, anything in the shape of men. For every half-crown he pays these men he'll get 9s. for himself and more. An American liner may require 300 tons of ballast, and may-be a captain will give a basket-man 8d. a ton, that would be £10. The basket-man employs six men, and he makes another. He never works himself—never, not a blow; but he goes swaggering about the ship when his men are at work, and he's on the look out in the streets at other times. For the £10 he'll get for the 300 tons he'll pay his men each 2s. 6d. for 60 tons, that's £3 15s., and so there's £6 5s. profit for him. Isn't that a shame, when so many poor men have to go without dinner or breakfast? There's five basket-men to my knowledge. They are making money, all out of poor men that can't help themselves. The poor suffers for all."

Letter XXIII
Friday, January 4th, 1850

In the present Letter it is my intention to set forth as fully as possible the nature of the system by which the Ballast-heaver is either forced by the fear of losing all chance of future employment, or induced by the hope of obtaining the preference of work from the publican, his employer, to spend at least one-half of his earnings every week in intoxicating drinks.

Let me, however, before proceeding directly to the subject of my present communication, again lay before the reader the conclusions which I lately drew from the Metropolitan Police Returns for 1848, concerning the intemperance of the labouring classes of London. It is essential that I should first prove the face, and show its necessary consequences. This done, the public will be more ready to perceive the cause, and to understand that until this and similar social evils are removed, it is worse than idle to talk of "the elevation of the masses," and most unjust (to use the mildest term) to condemn the working men for sins into which they are positively forced. To preach about the virtues of teetotalism to the poor, and yet to allow a system to continue that compels them to be drunk before they can get *work*—not to say bread— is surely a mockery. If we would really have the industrious classes sober and temperate men, we must look first, it seems, to their *employers*. We have already seen that the intemperance of the coal-labourer is the fault of the employer rather than the man, but we have only to go among the ballast-labourers to find the demoralization of the working man arising not from any mere passive indifference, but from something like a positive conspiracy on the part of the master.

According to the Criminal Returns for the Metropolis, there were 9,197 males and 7,264 females, making altogether a total of 16,461 individuals, charged with drunkenness in the year 1848. This makes one in every 110 individuals in London a drunkard— a proportion which, large as it seems, is still less than one-half what it was some ten or fifteen years back. For the sake of comparison I subjoin a table taken from the Government Report on Drunkenness: —

Return of the Number of Charges of Drunkenness which have been entered upon the Books of the Metropolitan Police in the Years 1831, 1832, and 1833 ; with the Number of Officers employed in, and the Locality of, each Division ; also the Amount of Population in each, according to the Parliamentary Returns of 1831.

Locality of each Division.	Number of Officers employed in each Division.	Computed Population in each Division according to the Parliamentary Returns.	Number of Charges of Drunkenness each Year, in the Years 1831, 1832, and 1833.									Public-houses and Beer-shops in each Division.		
			1831.			1832.			1833.			Public-houses.	Beer-shops.	Total.
			Males.	Females.	Total.	Males.	Females.	Total.	Males.	Females.	Total.			
(A) Whitehall.........	120	6,238	406	230	636	384	243	627	371	228	599	32	5	37
(B) Westminster......	168	53,147	1,596	800	2,396	2,396	831	2,660	1,864	1,193	3,057	186	58	244
(C) St. James.........	188	105,862	2,290	1,127	3,417	2,119	1,055	3,174	2,208	1,256	3,464	302	20	322
(D) St. Marylebone.	166	122,206	1,375	727	2,102	1,300	650	1,950	1,019	605	1,624	148	54	202
(E) Holborn..........	168	75,241	1,785	1,079	2,864	1,241	897	2,138	879	618	1,497	249	19	368
(F) Covent-garden..	168	41,010	2,238	1,555	3,793	2,165	1,617	3,782	1,665	1,388	3,053	309	23	332
(G) Finsbury.........	236	115,266	2,141	1,423	3,564	2,192	1,440	3,632	1,916	1,270	3,186	368	100	468
(H) Whitechapel.....	191	119,042	1,253	812	2,065	1,631	1,268	2,899	1,803	1,295	3,098	359	102	461
(K) Stepney..........	296	143,137	899	574	1,473	1,387	732	2,119	1,125	762	1,887	437	131	568
(L) Lambeth.........	191	101,561	1,732	1,271	3,003	1,581	1,234	2,815	1,291	944	2,235	183	70	153
(M) Southwark.......	189	107,537	1,655	1,050	2,705	1,470	982	2,452	1,284	843	2,127	321	66	387
(N) Islington........	269	140,407	850	373	1,223	1,165	573	1,738	826	409	1,235	267	144	311
(P) Camberwell......	243	77,825	256	87	343	201	75	276	203	80	283	138	96	234
(R) Greenwich.......	212	58,778	363	137	500	513	240	753	418	210	628	283	51	334
(S) Hampstead.......	223	112,136	573	301	874	613	326	939	697	319	1,016	138	74	212
(T) Kensington......	184	70,296	124	24	148	303	109	412	464	137	601	220	93	313
(V) Wandsworth....	186	62,039	212	35	247	210	60	270	235	55	290	133	76	209
Totals............	3,398	1,511,728	19,743	11,605	31,353	20,304	12,332	32,636	18,268	11,612	29,880	4,073	1,182	5,255

Now, comparing these returns with those of the year before last, we find that the decrease of intemperance in the metropolis has been most extraordinary. In the year 1831, one in every 48 individuals was drunk; in 1832 the number increased to one in 46—whereas in 1833 it decreased to one in 50, and in 1848 the average had again fallen to one individual in every 110. This decrease of intemperance was attended with a similar decrease in the number of metropolitan beer-shops. In 1833 there were 1,182 and in 1848 only 779 beer-shops in London. Whether this decrease preceded or succeeded—and so was the cause or the consequence—of the increased sobriety of the people, it is difficult to say. The number of public-houses in London, however, during the same period had increased from 4,073 to 4,235. Upon the cause and effect of this I leave others to speculate.

Of the total of 16,461 persons, male and female, who were charged with being intoxicated in the year 1848, no less than one individual in every seven belonged to the labouring class; and, excluding the females from the number, we shall find that, of the males, every fourth individual taken up for drunkenness was a labouring man. Taking the whole population of London, temperate and intemperate, only one in every 110 is a drunkard, but with the labouring classes the average is as high as one in every 22. Of course, where the habit of drinking is excessive, we may expect to find also excessive pugnacity. That it is the tendency of all intoxicating liquors to increase the irritability of the individual is well known. We might infer, therefore, *à priori,* that the greater number of "common assaults" would be committed by the greatest drunkards. In 1848 there were 7,780 individuals assaulted in London, and nearly one-fourth of these, or 1,882, were attacked by labouring men—one in every 26 of the entire body of labourers having been charged with this offence. The "simple larceny" of which the labouring classes appear, by the same returns, to be more guilty than any other body of individuals, is also explained by their inordinate intemperance. When a man's bodily energy is destroyed by drink, labour is so irksome to him, that he would rather peril his liberty than work. What wonder, then, that as many as one in every twenty-eight labourers should be charged with theft—whereas of the rest of the population there are only one in every 266 individuals. Thus, of the labouring classes, one in every 22 is charged with being drunk; one in every 26 with committing an assault; and one in every 28 with being guilty of simple larceny. For the truth of this connection between drink, pugnacity, and theft, I would refer to the statement of one of the most intelligent and experienced of the coal-whippers—one, indeed, to whose unceasing and heroic exertions that class principally owe their redemption: —"The children of the coal-whippers," he told me, "were under the old system, *almost reared* in the taproom. He himself had known *as many as 500 youths who were transported*" and this be it remembered out of a class numbering only 2,000 men).

Such, then, are the proved consequences of an inordinate use of intoxicating liquors. It becomes, therefore, the duty of every one who is anxious for the well-being of the people, to diminish the occasions for drinking, wherever possible. To permit the continuance of certain systems of employment and payment, which are well known both to tempt and compel the men to indulge in intoxicating liquors, is at once to breed the very crimes that it is the office of Government to suppress. The custom pursued by the coal merchants, of paying the labourers in their employ in public-houses, as I lately exposed, appeared bad enough. The "backer," jaded and depressed with his excessive work through the day, was entrapped into the public-house in the evening, under the pretence of receiving his wages. Once inside, he was kept waiting there hour after hour by the publican (who, of course, was out of silver, and had to send some distance for it). Beer is called for by the men in the meantime. Under the influence of the stimulant, the fatigue and the depression begin to leave the labourers, the burden that is still on their backs (it will be remembered that such is the description of the men themselves) is shaken off, and their muscles no longer ache and are stiff, but relax while their flagging spirits gradually revive under the potent charm of the liquor. What wonder, then, that the poor creatures, finding so easy and—when the habit is once formed—so pleasant a cure for their ills, should be led to follow up one draught with another, and another. This system appeared to me to be vicious enough, and to display a callousness on the part of the employers that quite startled me. But the system under which the Ballast labourers are now suffering is an infamy hardly to be credited as flourishing in these days. I have, therefore, been at considerable pains to obtain such a mass of evidence upon the subject as shall make all earnest men look upon the continuance of such a system as a national dishonour.

Let me, before proceeding to cite cases of individual injustice as I had them from the men themselves, first describe more minutely than I have yet done the labour of the ballast-heavers.

In order to assure myself of the intensity of the labour of ballast-heaving, of which I heard statements on all sides, I visited a gang of men at work, ballasting a collier in the Pool. My engagements prevented my doing this until about six in the evening. There was a very dense fog on the river, and all along its banks; so thick was it, indeed, that the water which washed the steps where I took a boat could not be distinguished, even with the help of the adjacent lights. I soon, however, attained the ballast-lighter I sought. The ballast-heavers had established themselves alongside a collier to be filled with 43 tons of ballast, just before I reached them, so that I observed all their operations. Their first step was to tie pieces of old sail, or anything of that kind, round their shoes, ankles, and half up their legs, to prevent the gravel falling into their shoes, and so rendering their tread painful. This was rapidly done, and the men set to work with the quiet earnestness of those who are working for the morrow's meal, and who knew that they must work hard. Two men stood in the gravel (the ballast) in the lighter; the other two stood on " an stage," as it is called, which is but a boarding placed on the partition beams of the lighter. The men on this stage, cold as the night was, threw off their jackets, and worked in their shirts, their labour being not merely hard, but rapid. As one man struck his shovel into the ballast thrown upon the stage, the other hove his shovelful through a small port-hole in the vessel's side, so that the work went on as continuously and as quickly as the circumstances could possibly admit. Rarely was a word spoken, and nothing was heard but an occasional gurgle of the water, and the plunging of the shovel into the gravel on the stage by one heaver, followed instantaneously by the rattling of the stones in the hold, shot from the shovel of the other. In the hold, the ballast is arranged by the ship's company. The throwing of the ballast through the port-hole was done with a nice precision. A tarpaulin was fixed to prevent any of the ballast that might not be flung through the port-hole being wasted by falling into the river, and all that struck merely the bounds of the port-hole fell back into the lighter; but this was the merest trifle. The men pitched the stuff through most dexterously. The port-hole might be six feet above the stage from which they hove the ballast; the men in the lighter have an average heave of six feet on to the stage. The two men on the stage and the two on the lighter fill and discharge their shovels twelve times in a minute; that is, one shovelful is shot by each man in every alternate five seconds; so that every one of the four men engaged at the work flings the heights of 36 feet every minute, or 2,160 feet an hour, and in that time, according to the concurrent computation of the heavers, the four men may easly fling in ten tons, or 5,600lb. a man. The men work with the help of large lanterns, being employed mostly by night.

I shall now state the sentiments of the men *generally,* and then *individually,* upon the subject of their grievances: —

To be certain as to the earnings of the men, to see their state, and to hear from a large number of them their own opinions of the hardships they suffered and the sums they earned, I met two bodies of the ballast-heavers, assembled without pre-arrangement. At one station fifty were present, at the other thirty. The men were chiefly clad in coarse, strong jackets, some of them merely waist-coats, with strong blue flannel sleeves, and coarse trousers, thick with accumulated grease from long wear. They had, notwithstanding their privations, generally a hardy look. There is nothing squalid in their appearance, as in that of men who have to support life on similar earnings with indoor employment. Their manners were quiet, and far from coarse. At the first meeting fifty were present. One man said, "Well, I think I'm the oldest man present, and I don't get above 5s. a week, but that's because I'm an old man and can't work with the young ones." Upon an average the common men earned 10s. a week the year through, taking home 5s. I inquired, "Are you all compelled to spend a great part of all that you earn in drink with the publican?" The answer was, and simul-taneously, "All of us—all—all." Of the remainder of their earnings, after the drink deductions, the men were all satisfied they spent so much that many only took 2s. 6d. a week home to their wives and families on an average. Last week two earned 20s., the publican taking 10s. from each. Three earned 15s.—one of these took 1s. 6d. home, another 3s., both working for publicans; the third, who worked for a grocer, took home 13s.—the other 2s. being spent in tea and sugar, he being a single man. Three earned 10s.—one, working for a publican carried home 6s., the difference going in compulsory drink; another 4s., and another 5s. Six did one load of ballast, receiving 7s. 6d. each for it; one took home 4s. 11d., another 6s. 6d. (a private job); another, who did a load for 5s. 3d., took home 2s. 3d.; the other two took home 5s. each. One man earned 3s., and took it all home, having worked at a private job for a foreigner. Fifteen earned nothing in the course of the last week. For the last fortnight, nine had earned nothing. There were none present but what had earned something in the last three weeks. "The fortnight before Christmas," said one, "I didn't earn 5s. all that fortnight." "Nor I, nor I," said several others. On being asked, "Are you *compelled* to spend half your earnings in drink?" there was a general cry of "More than that, sir; more than that."

I asked if men were forced to become drunkards under this system; there was a general cry of "We are—and blackguards too." Seventeen were married men; of them, three had no children, three had one child, four had two children, two had three, three had four, one had five, one had six. The men all said that to get away from the publican would be "a new life to them—all to their benefit—no force to waste money in drink—and the only thing that would do them good." Many threw away the drink they had to take from the publicans, it was so bad; they drank Thames water rather. They were all satisfied that they earned 10s. a week the year through, spending of that sum, what they *must* spend and what they were induced to spend, from 5s. to 7s. 6d. a week." "Another thing," they said, "If you get a job, the publican will advance 1s., now and then may be, but they hate to give money; there's trust for as much grog as we like." All hailed with delight any possible chance of their being freed from the publican. One man said he was compelled oft enough to pawn something of his own or his wife's to go and spend something at the public-house, or he would have no chance of a job. All declare "such a system never was known to have been carried on for years." Many said, "We shall be discharged if they hear we have told you the truth." They stated that the ballast-heavers numbered between 300 and 400—there were sixty craft, each requiring four heavers, and many men were idle when all the craft were at work. Thirty were present when I counted the second meeting. A man said there might be three times that number looking for work then, and as many at work, belonging to that station alone. In 1841, the census returns showed that there were 170 ballast-heavers; the men assembled declared that their numbers had nearer trebled than doubled since then. Within the last two or three years many new hands had got to work on account of the distress in Ireland. The men agreed with the others I saw that they earned, one week with another, 10s., taking home but 5s. at the outside, and often 2s. 6d. In answer to my questions they said—The winter time is the best season; the trade is very slack in summer. Many agricultural labourers work among the heavers in winter when they cannot be employed on the land. Earnings in winter are pretty well double what they are in summer. Of this body all said they were sober men before they came to ballast-heaving, and would like to be able to be sober men again (a general assent). Three of the men had taken the pledge before becoming ballast-heavers, and were obliged to break it to get work. They have to drink five pots of beer, they declared, where, if they were free men, they would drink one. When asked if the present system made them drunkards, they answered with one voice, "all; every ballast-heaver in it." Twenty were married men. All their wives and children suffered (this was affirmed generally with a loud murmur), and often had nothing to eat or drink, while their husbands had but the drink. It was computed (with general concurrence) that 150 ballast-heavers paid foremen for lodgings, not half of them ever seeing the bed they paid for. About twelve years ago they could earn twice and three times as much as they can now, but prices were higher (12s. per score for what is now 3s.), and the men were far less numerous. The following is a precise statement of the sums to which each ballast-heaver present was entitled, followed by the amount that he carried home last week, after payment of his compulsory drinkings, and of what he might be induced to drink at the house of his employer while waiting to be paid: —

Earned.		Took home.		Earned.		Took home.
£ s. d.		£ s. d.		£ s. d.		£ s. d.
0 12 0	....	0 7 0		0 12 6	....	0 3 6
0 7 0	....	0 3 6		1 0 0	....	0 9 0
0 15 0	....	0 9 0		0 12 0	....	0 4 0
0 12 0	....	0 6 0		0 15 0	....	0 9 0
0 13 0	....	0 4 0		0 15 0	....	0 8 6
0 11 0	....	0 5 0		0 12 0	....	0 3 6
0 16 0	....	0 6 0		0 9 0	....	0 5 0
0 15 0	....	0 5 0		1 0 0	....	0 4 6
Nothing	....	—		1 0 0	....	0 10 0
Nothing	....	—		0 10 0	....	0 3 0
Nothing	....	—		0 10 0	....	0 5 0
Nothing	....	—		0 12 0	....	0 2 6
0 5 0	....	0 2 6		0 8 0	....	0 3 6
0 8 0	....	0 5 0		0 14 0	....	0 9 0
0 9 6	....	0 5 0				
1 0 0	....	0 10 0		16 13 0		7 0 0

This statement shows, out of 11s. 1½d. earnings, a receipt of less than 5s. a week.

According to the returns of the Trinity House, there were 615,619 tons of ballast put on board 11,234 ships in the year 1848. The ballast-heavers are paid at the rate of 6d. per ton for shovelling the ballast out of the Trinity Company's lighters into the holds of the vessels. Hence, the total earnings of the ballast-heavers in that year were £15,390 9s. 6d. And calculating two-thirds (the men say they always get rid of half and often three-fourths of their earnings in drink) of this sum to have been spent in liquor, it follows that as much as £10,260 6s. 4d. went to the publican, and £5,130 3s. 2d. to the labouring men. According to this estimate of their gross earnings, if we calculate the body of the ballast-heavers as number-ing 350 men, the average wages of the class are about 16s. 6d. per week each man; or, if we reckon the class at 400, then the average wages of each person would be about 14s. 6d. per week. From all I can learn this appears to be about the truth—the earnings of the men being about 15s. a week, and their real income about 5s.

The men shall now speak for themselves.

The first that I saw were two of the better class of foremen, who volunteered to give me an account of the system.

"I am a foreman, or ganger, of the ballast-heavers," said one. "I work under a man who is a publican and butcher; and I also work under another who is only a butcher. I moreover work under a grocer. I engage the different gangs of men for the parties under whom I work. I also pay the men. The publican, butcher, or grocer, as the case may be, agrees to give me 9s. a score tons. The fore-men often give the men the same money as they themselves receive, barring a pot of beer, or perhaps a quartern of gin, that they may have out of the job. Some foremen take much more." Another foreman who was present while I was taking the statement of this man, here observed that "many foremen claim tow row, or a 'fifth-handed' proportion—that is, they will have 10s. when the working men have only 5s. There is a great deal of imposition on the working classes here, I can assure you. The general thing, when we go to a job out of a public-house, is, that the publican expects the men to drink to the amount of 4s. out of every £1, and 6s. out of every 30s. that's coming to them—that is, one-fifth part of the men's money must be spent in liquor. The drink is certainly not the best—indeed, if there is any inferior stuff, they have it. It's an obligation on them that they drink. If they refuse to drink, they won't get employed—and that's the plain truth of it. Oh, it's long wanted looking to; and I'm glad at last to find some one inquiring into it. If they went to get the regular beer from the fair public-houses they would have to pay 3d. a pot for it; and at the contracting publicans they must give 4d. a pot, and have short measure, and the worst of stuff too. Every six pots of beer they give to the men is only five pots fair measure; and the rum they charge them 2d. a half-pint more for than the regular public-houses would, and far worse rum into the bargain. Besides the profit on their drink some publicans charge 6d. per score tons as well. Out of the money coming to the men after the publican has been paid his score, many foremen claim one-fifth part over and above their regular share; or, in other words, the foreman takes two shares and the men only one each. When the men have been paid, the publican paying them expects them to spend a further sum in drink, looking black at a man who goes away without calling for his pint or his pot, and not caring if they drink away the whole of their earnings. There's a good many would be glad if the men sat in their houses and spent their last farthing, and then had to go home penniless to their wives and families." "I am a 'ganger' to a butcher as well as to a publican," said one of the foremen. "His practice is just the same as the publican's. He receives 10s. per score tons and pays me for the men 9s. The men and myself are all expected to spend about one half of our earnings with the butcher in meat. He charges 6½d. per lb., and at other houses, with ready money, I am sure the men might get it for 4d. as good. His meat is at least one-third dearer than other butchers'. I am also ganger to a grocer. and he gets about the same profit out of the men he employs— that is to say, the articles he supplies the men with are at least one-third dearer than at other shops. If anything, he makes more out of the men than the butcher, for if any man goes a score— which he always encourages—he stops the whole out of the man's earnings, and often leaves him without a penny after the job is done. When the publican, grocer, butcher, or lodging-house keeper has a contract for ballast, he directs the foreman working under him to get together the gang that regularly work from his house. This gang are men who always deal at the shop, and the contractor would dismiss me if I was to engage any other men than those who were his regular customers. Many a time a publican has told me that some man was a good hard drinker, and directed me to engage him whenever I could. If a man sticks up a score, he also tells me to put him on first of all. The grocer and the butcher do the same. This system is the cause, I know, of much distress and misery among the men. The publicans make the men drunkards by forcing them to drink. I know many wives and children who starve half their time through it. They haven't a bit of shoe or clothing, and all through the publican compelling the men to spend their earnings in drink. After the gang is paid, at least three out of the four get drunk, and often the whole four. Many a time I have seen the whole of the men reeling home without a penny to bless themselves, and the wife and children have to suffer for all this. They are ill-treated and half starved. This I can safely say, from my own knowledge."

I then took, for the sake of avoiding repetition, the statements of two ballast-heavers together—*constant men,* working under different publicans. The account they gave me of the way in which the publican contracted to ballast a ship was the same as I have given elsewhere. "I have been twenty years a ballast-heaver," said one, "and all that time I have worked for a publican; and poor work it is, for I hardly can live, and haven't a coat to my back, saving your presence. Twenty years ago the publican had the same number of hands, but had more work for them, and I might then earn 20s. a week; but I couldn't fetch that home from the publican. If I did, I need look for no more work from him. He expected me to spend one-half of my earnings with him; and when I left his house drunk, I might spent the other half. If I'd got it sober I'd have taken it every farthing home to my wife. You may depend on it I've drunk gallons of drink against my will. I've drunk stuff that was poison to me. I turned teetotaller six years back, and the publican my employer *sacked* me when he found it out, saying, 'He'd be d—d if he'd have such men as me—he didn't make his living by teetotallers.' " "Yes," added the other man, "and so *my* publican told me; for I turned teetotaller seven year ago, and took the pledge from Father Mathew, in the Commercial-road. The publican told me—that if Father Mathew chose to interfere with me, why Father Mathew might get employment for me, for he— that's the publican—wouldn't. So I was forced to break my pledge to live—me and my youngsters—I had six then, and I've buried two since." "Work," resumed the man who first gave me the state- ment, "keeps getting worse. Last week I carried 8s. home, and if I'd got paid by the captain of a ship for the amount of work I did, and on the same terms as he paid the publican, I should have taken home 16s. The publican that employs us gives us only 8s. a score, and receives 10s. from the captain, so that he does a profit there as well as on the money that I am forced to spend in drink (to keep my work). All the publicans don't do this; some give what they get from the captain, but there's very few of them do so, and some publicans take two-thirds, and that's the truth." [The second man assented.] "One week with another I've taken home this winter from 12s. to 13s., and but for this shameful and starva- tion system, having to work for a publican's profit, and to drink his drink, I'd take home my 20s. every week. It makes a man feel like a slave; indeed, I'm not much better. We should be in Heaven if we got away from the publican, or the butcher either; it's com- pulsion one's life through. Sometimes the beer is so bad that we have to chuck it away, but whatever it is, and whatever we do with it, it must be paid for; and the highest price is charged—of course it is. The man that drinks most, and puts up a score (runs in debt) has the first turn for work." "And that's the case with me," said the second man, "and I know a couple of hundred men as badly off as we are, and under these publicans' control. Some of the publicans have as many as sixty single men lodging in their houses, paying half a crown a week; aye! and men that *don't* lodge with them, when the house is full, must pay the half-crown all the same to get a turn of work, as well as paying for the places where they *do* lodge." The first man continued, "The gin and rum is the worst that can be supplied, but we must drink it or waste it. We often spill it on the ballast, it's that bad" ["often, often," was the response of the other man]. "And that's not the worst. When we get a job of putting sixty tons of ballast on board we are forced to take six pots of beer with us to our work, but only four pots are supplied, and we must pay for six. We are robbed on every side. I cannot describe how bad it is; a man would hardly believe it; but all will tell you the same—all the men like us." [So indeed the poor fellows did afterwards.] "When we call to be paid we are kept for hours, without fire, in a cold tap-room, forced to drink cold stuff, without being let have a strike of fire to take the chill off it." The other man then made a further statement. "I've been forced to put my sticks in pawn—what I had left, for I was better off once, though I was always a ballast-heaver, and have worked for the same publican fourteen years. I have £3 in pawn now. I blame this present system for being so badly off—sorrow a thing else! Now, just look at this. A single man, a lodger, will go into a publican's and call for 1s. worth of rum, and the publican will call me a scaly fellow if I don't do the same; that will be when I'd rather be without his rum if I got it for nothing." One publican (the men gave me this account concurrently, and it was fully confirmed by a host of others) married the niece of a waterman employed to pull the harbour-master about the river. He kept a public-house, and carried on the system of lodgers for ballast-heaving, making a great deal of money out of them; by this means he got so much work at his command that the rest of the publicans complained to the harbour-master, and the man was forced to give up his public-house. When he had to give it up he made it over to his niece's husband, and that man allowed him 1s. for every ship he brought him to ballast. I've known him—that's the publican that succeeded the man I've been telling you of—have forty ships in a day—one week with another he's had 100 ships, that's £5, and he has them still. It's the same now. We've both worked for him. His wife's uncle (the harbour-master's waterman) says to the captains, and he goes on board to see them, after the harbour master's visit to them, 'Go to ——, get your ballast of him, and I'll give you the best berth in the river.' ".

I next obtained an interview with a young man who was the victim of a double extortion. He stated as follows: —

"I work under a publican, and lodge in his house. I have done so for five years. I pay 2s. a week, there being ten of us in two rooms. We're all single men. These two rooms contain four beds, three in the larger room, and one in the other. We sleep two in a bed, and should have to sleep three in some, only two of the men don't occupy the lodgings they pay for. The bigger room may be 16 feet by 10, the smaller a quarter of that size. You cannot turn in it—the bed can't be brought out of the room unless it's taken to pieces. We must cook in the tap-room, which is a room for the purpose—it contains forms and an old table, with a large grate. We are found frying-pans, and gridirons, and pans, and fire, and candle; but we must find our own knives and forks. The room is shamefully dirty—I mean the tap (cooking) room. It looks as if it hadn't been washed for years. It's never been washed to my knowledge. The bed-rooms are very little better. The bedding is very bad—a flock bed, with a pair of blankets, a quilt, and a sort of a sheet, clean once a fortnight. There's very bad ventilation, and very unpleasant smells. It's a horrid den altogether. None of us would stop there if we could help it—but we *can't* help it; for if we leave we get no work, and if he (the publican) knew I'd told you this, I should be discharged directly. We have peaceable, quiet sort of men in the house—bad a place as it is. We are all obliged to send our washing out of the house, paying 3d. a shirt. We are forced to find locks for our rooms to keep our bits of things from being stolen, as the place is open, and there's common stairs, and anybody may walk into the rooms. One man *was* robbed; my clothes was in the box with his, the box was broken open, but the clothes was left; and a few halfpence, put away in the box, were taken. There's lots of bugs. We can only sleep after hard work, and we must drink when we're at work. I've poured my beer into the river many a time, it was so bad—it tasted as if it was poisonous. Men have been sick after it—I have, at different times. We have drank water in preference; if it's good country water, out of the ship's stores, it's a treat; but we have drank Thames water rather than the bad beer. We're all forced to drink. To show how we're treated I'll tell you this: I owe so much, and so much a week's stopped to pay it, but it never gets less. I am always charged the same. There it is, the same figures are on the slate, keep paying, paying off as you will. They won't rub it off; or, if they do rub it off, it's there again next time. Last week a man was discharged for grumbling because he objected to pay eighteenpence twice over. He has'nt had a day's work since."

Then came one who was the *employé* of a publican and a grocer. He said: —

"I work under a publican and a grocer. I'm any man's man. I stand with my fingers in my mouth at Ratcliff-cross, watching, and have done it the last nine years. Half of us is afraid to come and speak to you. When I volunteered, the big-whiskered and fat-faced men (the foremen) were looking at me and threatening me, for coming to you. No matter, I care for nobody. Worse nor I am I can't be. No more I can't. I go to one publican to work 60 tons, and for that I get 4s.; but 6s. is my rights. The remainder 2s. is left—I'm *forced* to leave it—for me to drink out on Sunday night. If I was in a fair house the publican would pay me 7s. 6d.; as it is, I get 4s., and 2s. must be drunk. It's the rule at that house—he's in opposition, and works low. If I was at liberty it wasn't to his house I'd go for a drink. The hardest drinking man gets the first work, and when a man's half drunk he doesn't care what stuff he puts into his belly. Before we go to a job, the four of us are expected to drink half-a-pint of rum or gin: the publicans expect it. If I was a teetotaller I must pay my whack, and the other men may drink it, for the score against the ship is divided among the men equal. Suppose two foremen meet and have a drop of brandy or rum together about a ship's ballast, that's charged to us poor fellows; its stuck up to our score, but we mustn't say nothing, tho' we know we never had a sup of it, but if we say a word it's all up —no more work. Once on a time I worked for a publican close by, and when I came to the house I had nothing to drink. My oldest mate whispered to me on our way from the London Dock, and told me to speak my mind, for he knew there was a false score against the ship, and the others was afraid to say a word. Well, I *did* speak when I got into the house, and the foreman was there, and he asked me what business I had to speak more nor another. There was 6s. charged to the score for drink that we never touched nor ever saw—not a sup of it. He—that's the foreman—told me I shouldn't go to finish the ship. I said I would in spite of him. I told the missus I expected she wouldn't give no more drink but what we had to drink ourselves, or would get when we came home; and she said she wouldn't, and that's two years ago, but I haven't had a job for them parties since. Suppose I get to the public-house for my money at six in the evening, I'm forced to wait until eleven— until I'm drunk very often—drunk from vexation—stopped when I'm hungry, after five or six hours' hard work on the river, and not let take the money home to my wife and family, nor let have anything to eat, for I'm waiting for that money to get a bit of grub; but when I'm half drunk the hunger goes off, just for a time. I must go and drink in a morning if my children go without breakfast, and starve all day till I come home at night. I can get nothing from my employers but *drink*. If I ask them for 1s., I can't get it. I've finished my load of ballast without breaking my fast but on the beer we're forced to take with us. I've found grocers better to work under than publicans—more honesty in them. They charged a middling fair price, but they'll have *tow-row* out of it—that's dry money—so much a score. They'll stop 6d. a score for giving us the job. I can get as good sugar as I have from them at 4d., for 3½d.—but then the difference between the grocer and publican is, that the wife and family can have a bit of something to eat under the grocer, but not under the publican. All goes in drink with the publican, for we can't carry drink home. When I go home drunk from the publican's, I tumble on the floor, perhaps, and say, 'Is there anything to eat for me?' and my old woman says 'Where's the money?—give me that, and I'll give you something to eat.' Then a man gets mad with vexation, and the wife and children runs away from him—they're glad to get away with their lives, they're knocked about so. It makes a man mad with vexation, to see a child hungry; it kills me, but whatever the foreman gives me, I *must* take. I dare never say no. If I get nothing—if all is gone in drink—I must go from him with a blithe face, to my starving children, or I need never go back again for another job."

I next saw two men who stated that they were oppressed by the publican and the foreman also. The first said—"I work under a publican, and have to pay the foreman one-fifth of my earnings; I only have fourpence out of every shilling I earn, and I must be a sober man indeed to get that. Both the publican and the foreman get eightpence out of a shilling, and make their money out of my sweat. Nine years ago I was left, to my sorrow, with nine motherless children, and I am the slave of the publican. He is my destruction, and such are my sufferings that I don't care what I do if I can destroy the system. I shall die happy if I can see an end to it. I would go to bed supperless to-night, and so should my children, if I could stop it. After I have a had a job of work, many's the time I have not had a penny to take home to my children; it has all gone betwixt the foreman and the publican, and what is more, if I had brought anything home I should have stood a worse chance of work the next day. If I had gone away with sixpence in my pocket, the work that would have come to me would have gone to those who had spent all in the house. I can solemnly say that the men are made regular drunkards by the publicans. I am nine-and-twenty years dealing with this oppression, and I wish from my heart I could see an end to it, for the sake of my children, and my fellow-creatures' children as well. But I suffer quite as much from the foreman as I do from the publican. I am obliged to treat him before I can get a job of work. The man who gives him the most drink, he will employ the first. Besides this, the foreman has two fifth parts of the money paid for the job—he has twice as much as the men if he does any of the work—and if he does none of the work, he takes one-fifth of the whole money—besides this, the men do three times the foreman's labour. If I could get the fair value of my sweat, I could lay by to-morrow, and keep my family respectably. In the room of that, now my family want bread often—worse luck, for it hurts my feelings. I have been idle all to-day; for hearing of this, I came to make my statement, for it was the pride of my heart to do all that I could to put an end to the oppression. The publicans have had the best of me, and when the system is done away with I shan't be much the better for it. I have been nine-and-twenty years at it, and it has ruined me both body and soul; but I say what I do for the benefit of others, and those who come after me."

The other man said that he worked under a publican, and a grocer as well, and lodged with a foreman. "I pay 2s. a week for my lodgings," he said; "there are two beds in the room, and two men in each. The room where we all sleep is not more than seven feet long by five feet wide, and barely seven feet high. There is no chimney in it. It is a garret, with nothing in it but the two beds. There hadn't need to be much more, for it wouldn't hold even a chair besides. There's hardly room, in fact, for the door to open. I find it very close sleeping there at night time, with no ventilation; but I can't help myself. I stay there for the job of work. I *must* stay. I shouldn't get a day's work if I didn't. The lodgings are so bad, I'd leave them to-morrow if I could. I know I pay twice as much as I could get them for elsewhere. That's one way in which I, for one, am robbed. Besides this, I am obliged to treat the foreman; I am obliged to give him two glasses of rum, as well as lodging at his house, in order to get employment. I have also to drink at the public-house; one-fifth of my money is kept, first and foremost, by the publican. That goes for the compulsory drink—for the swash which he sends us on board, and that we think the Thames water is sweet and wholesome to it. It is expressly adulterated for our drink. If we speak a word against it we should be left to walk the streets, for a week and more forward. Even if we were known to meet a friend, and have a pint or a pot in another public-house, we should be called to an account for it by the publican we worked under, and he would tell us to go and get work where we spent our money—and God knows very little money we would have, coming out of his house after our hard sweat. After the compulsory drink, and the publican has settled with us, and stopped his fifth part of our hard-earned money for the swash —'tis nothing else! —that he has given us to drink, then I should be thought no man at all if I didn't have two pots of beer or half-a-pint of gin—so that I would count myself very lucky indeed if I had a couple of shillings to take home, and out of that I should have to spend two-thirds of it to get another job. I am a married man, and my wife and three children are in Ireland. I can't have them over, for it is as much as I can do to support myself. I came over here, thinking to get work, and to send them money to bring them over after me, but since I have been here I have been working at the ballast-work, and have not been able to keep myself. I don't complain of what is paid for the work; the price is fair enough, but we don't get a quarter of what we earn, and the Irish ballast-heavers suffer more here than in their own country. When I came over here I had a good suit of clothes to my back, and now I'm all in rags and tatters, and yet I have been working harder and earning more money than I did in all my life. We are robbed of all we get by the foremen and publicans. I was eight years a teetotaller before I went to ballast work, and now I am forced to be a drunkard, to my sorrow, to get a job of work. My wife and children have a bit of land in Ireland to keep them, and they are badly enough off, God knows. I can neither help them nor send money to bring them over to me, nor can I get over to them myself. The grocers whom we work under rob us in the same manner. I have worked under one. He supplied bread, butter, tea, sugar, coffee, candles, tobacco, cheese, &c. It is a larger kind of chandler's shop. He charges us 5½d. for the same bread as I can buy for 4½d. at other shops. The tea, sugar, and other articles he supplies us with are at the same rate; they are either worse or dearer than at other shops. They generally manage to get a fifth part of our earnings wherever we go—but the grocers are best of all, for they don't ruin our health, as what they give us don't make us sick. I work for these two houses because the foreman that I lodge with has work out of both houses, and we are obliged to deal at the houses that he works under; if we didn't we shouldn't get the job; so that if we are not robbed by the publican we are by the grocer. They *will* have it out of the poor, hard-working men, and the foreman must have his gain out of us as well. I only wish to God it was done away with, for it is downright oppression to us all, and if I never have another stroke of work, I will strive all I can to have it done away with for the sake of my fellow-men."

After these two came one who said—"I have been three years a ballast-heaver. Just before that, I came to this country. When I came I got to be a lodger with a foreman to a publican. I paid him 2s. 6d. a week. My family—a wife and two children—came over when I had got work as a ballast-heaver. I couldn't take them to the lodgings I then had—they were all for single men; so I had to take another place, and there I went to live with my family; but to keep my work I had to pay the foreman of the publican—him that lets these lodgings to the ballast-heavers—2s. 6d. a week, all the same as if I'd been living there. That I had: and I had to do it for two years. Yes, indeed. I didn't earn enough to pay for two lodgings; so, two or three months back, I refused to pay the 2s. 6d. a week for a place I hadn't set my foot in for two years; and so I lost my work under that foreman and his publican. If me and my children was starving for want of a bite of bread, neither of them would give me a farthing. There's plenty as bad as them too, and plenty used like me, and it's a murdering shame to tax poor men's labour for nothing." This man reiterated the constant story of being compelled to drink against his will, hating the stuff supplied to him, being kept for hours waiting before he was paid, and being forced to get drunk whether he would or no. The man also informed me that he now works under a butcher, who pays 8s. a score to the hands he employs, he (the butcher) receiving from the captain 10s. "Suppose," he said, "I have a sixty ton job. I'd be entitled to 7s. 6d. without beer or such like, but under this butcher I get only 5s. 3d., and out of that 5s. 3d.—that's all I get in hard money—I'm expected to spend 4s., or thereabouts, in meat, such as he chooses to give. I have no choice. He gives what he likes, and charges me 6½d. a pound for what I could buy at 4d. in a regular way. Very inferior stuff he keeps. Working under a butcher we must all live on this poor meat. We can't afford bread or vegetables to it." This same butcher, I was afterwards informed, had been twice fined for using false weights to customers such as the man whose statement I have given; he even used wooden weights, made to look like lead.

The following is an instance of the injustice done to the men by those who contract to *"whip,"* rather than *heave* the ballast on board: —

"I now work," said the man whom I was referred to as an exponent of the wrong, "for Mr. ——, a publican, who contracts to supply ships with ballast by the lump. He'll contract to supply a ship with all the ballast she wants, by the lump; that is, so much money for all she wants, instead of so much by the ton. Or he may contract with a ship at 2s. 6d. a ton. We—that is, a gang of 8 men—may put two loads, or 120 tons, on board in the course of a day. For those 120 tons he will receive 120 half-crowns; that's £15. For putting in those 120 tons, we—that is, the 8 ballast heavers employed—receive 2s. 6d. a day of 12 or 14 hours; that is eight half-crowns or 20s., with 3s. 6d. a day for a basket-man, in addition to the eight; so leaving the publican a profit of £13 16s. 6d." I could hardly believe in the existence of such a system—yielding a mere pittance to the labourer, and such an enormous profit to the contractor; and I inquired further into the matter. I found the statement fully corroborated by several persons present; but that was not all I learned. When the men, by incessant exertion, get in 120 tons in a day, as they often do, nothing is charged them for the beer they have had, 4 or 5 pints a day each; but if only 60 tons be got in, as sometimes happens, through the weather and other circumstances, then the men employed on the half-crown a day must pay for their own beer, and pay their private scores; for, unless they have private scores, for treating a friend, or the like, "there's no chance of a job," said my informant—"not a bit of it." He continued, "Very bad drink it is—the worst; it make's me as sick as a dog. There's two brothers there, what they call 'blood-hounds.' They're called so because they hunt up the poor men to get them to work, and to see that they spend their money at their employer's public-house when work's done. If you don't spend something, no bread to cut next morning—not a bit of it—and no chance of another job there. He employs us ballast-heavers, when we're not at the ballast, in backing coals into the steamers." I have given the statement of a ballast-heaver as to the system pursued by those whom he called *basket-men.* The employer here alluded to is one of that class, the difference being, that the ballast-heavers shovel the ballast out of the lighter on to the stage, and from the stage through a port-hole into the hold. Four men are thus employed—two in the lighter and two on the stage. With a large ship five men are employed, and two stages. When the basket-man, or the man contracting by the lump, is employed, this process is observed: —There are two men in the lighter, alongside the vessel to be ballasted, whose business it is to fill five baskets employed. There are five men at the winch on board ship, employed in heaving up the baskets, and a basket-man to turn them over and empty out their contents.

To ascertain that there was no provident fund, no provision whatever for sickness, I investigated the case of a man who, in consequence of illness, occasioned by his trade, was afflicted with a pulmonary complaint. This man was formerly one of the wine-cellarmen in the London Docks; he was then made a "permanent man" at the St. Katharine Dock, and was dismissed for having taken a lighted pipe in while at his work; and for the last fourteen years and upwards he has been a ballast-heaver. I now give his wife's statement: —"My husband has been ill for three months, and has been six weeks in Guy's Hospital, and I'm afraid he'll never get out again, for he kept up as long as he could, for the sake of the children. We have five at home, one of whom (twelve years old) I hope to get to sea, having two older sons at sea, and being the mother of twelve children altogether. I will tell you what led to my poor husband's illness; he was a kind husband to me. I consider it was his hard work that made him ill, and his not getting his rights—not his money, when entitled to it. After doing a heavy day's work he had to go and sit in a cold tap-room, drinking bad beer; but it wasn't beer—muck I call it; and he had to wait to be paid, aye, and might have to wait till the day after, and then come home cold, and have to go to bed without a bit of victuals. His illness is owing to that. No horse could stand it long. Ballast-men are worse than slaves in the West Indies. When at work, he earned what the others did. He only drank what he couldn't help—the worst of stuff. No drink, no work. Six weeks ago he went to the hospital, I conveying him. When I returned home, I found three strange men had turned my four children into the street, doing it in a brutal way. I rushed into the house, and one said, 'Who are you?' I seized the fellow who said this by the handkerchief, and put him out. One of them said 'Be off, you old Irish hag; you have no business here—we have possession.' When I saw the children in the street, passion made me strong, and so I put him out. The collector of the rent, who employed the broker, is a publican, for whom my husband worked as a ballast-heaver until he was unable to work from illness. I was given into custody for an assault, and taken before Mr. Yardley. He considered the assault proved, and, as an honest woman, I couldn't deny it, and so I had fourteen days with bread and water. The children were placed in the workhouse, where they were well treated. I was very glad they were so taken care of. As soon as I got out I went to see about my children—that was the first thing I did. I couldn't rest till I did that. I brought them home with me, though it was only to bread and water, but I was with them. I only owed about 15s. rent, and had been four years in the house at the time the publican put the broker in. We paid 6s. 6d. a week. It was no use asking such a man as that for any mercy. He was in the habit of employing ballast-heavers for many years, and if that doesn't harden a man's heart, nothing will. In general, these ballast publicans are cruel and greedy. At present I go out washing, or charing, or doing anything I can to maintain my children; but work's very slack. I've had a day-and-a-half this fortnight, earning 2s. 6d.— that's all for a fortnight. The parish allows me four loaves of bread a week. The children, all boys, just get what keeps a little life in them. They have no bed at night, and are starved almost to death, poor things! I blame the system under which my husband had to work—his money going in drink—for leaving me destitute to the world. On Christmas-day we lived on a bit of workhouse bread, nothing else—and had no fire to eat it by. But for the money gone in drink, we might have had a decent home, and wouldn't so soon have come to this killing poverty. I have been tenderly reared, and never thought I should have come to this. May God grant the system may be done away with, for poor people's sake."

I now give the statement of two women, the wives of ballast-heavers, that I may further show how the wives and families of these men are affected by the present system. "I have been eleven years married," said one, "and have had five children, four being now living." The other woman had been married 23 years, but has no children living. "We are very badly off," said the woman with a family, "my husband drinking hard. When I first knew him, when we were sweethearts, in a country part of Ireland—he was a farm labourer, and I was a cottier's daughter—he was a sober and well-behaved man. Two years after, we were married, and he was a sober man those two years still. We came to London to better ourselves—worse luck! The first work he got was ballast-heaving. Then he was obligated to drink, or he couldn't get work; and so, poor man, he got fond of it. This winter oft enough he brings me and the children home 2s. or 1s. 6d. after a job, and on that we may live for two or three days. We're half starved in course. The children have nothing to eat. It's enough to tear any poor woman's heart to pieces. What's gone into the publican's till would get the children bread and bedding and bits of clothes. Nothing but his being employed at ballast-heaving made him a drunkard, for he *is* a drunkard now. He often comes home and ill-uses me, but he doesn't ill-use the children. He beats me with his fists; he strikes me in the face—he has kicked me. When he was a sober man, he was a kind, good husband; and when he's sober now—poor man! —he's a kind, good husband still. If he was a sober man again, with his work, I'd be happy and comfortable to what I am now. Almost all his money goes in drink." "We can't get shoes to our feet" said the second woman. "When my husband is sober, and begins to think (continued the first) he wishes he could get rid of such a system of drinking—he really does wish it, for he loves his family, but when he goes out to work he forgets all that. It's just the drink that does it. I would like him to have a fair allowance at his work—he requires it; but beyond that it's all waste and sin; but he's forced to waste it and to run into sin, and so we all have to suffer. We are often without fire. Much in the pawn-shop, do you say, sir? Indeed I haven't much out." "We," interposed the older woman, "haven't a stitch but what's in pawn, except what wouldn't be taken. We have 50s. worth in pawn altogether—all for meat and fire." "I can't, I daren't (the younger woman said) expect anything better while the present system of work continues. My husband's a slave, and we suffer for it." The elder woman made a similar statement. After his score is paid, her husband has brought her 4s., 3s., 2s., 1s., and nothing—coming home drunk with nothing at all. Both women stated that the drink made their husbands sick and ill, and for sickness there was no provision whatever. They could have taken me to numbers of women situated and used as they were. Their rooms are four bare walls, with a few pieces of furniture and bedding such as no one would give a penny for. The young woman was perfectly modest in manner, speech, and look, and spoke of what her husband was, and still might be, with much feeling. She came to me with a half-clad and half-famished child in her arms.

Tuesday, January 8th, 1850

Before dealing with the Lumpers, or those who discharge the timber and other ships—in contradiction to the Stevedores, or those who stow the cargoes of vessels—I will give the following report of a meeting held yesterday afternoon among the Ballast-heavers' wives. It is the wife and children who are the real sufferers from the intemperance of the working man; and being anxious to give the public some idea of the amount of misery entailed upon these poor creatures by the compulsory and induced drunkenness of the husbands, I requested as many as could leave their homes to meet me at the British and Foreign School, in Shakespeare-walk, Shadwell. The meeting consisted of the wives of ballast-heavers and coal-whippers. The wives of the coal-whippers had come there to contrast their present state with their past, with the view of showing the misery which they had endured when their husbands were under the same thraldom to the publican as the ballast-heavers are now, and the comparative happiness which they have experienced since they have been freed from it. They had attended unsolicited, in the hope, by making their statements public, of getting for the ballast-heavers the same freedom from the control of the publican which the coal-whippers had obtained.

The meeting consisted of the wives of ballast-heavers and coal-whippers. Thirty-one were present. Of the thirty-one, nine were the wives of coal-whippers; the remainder, twenty-two, the wives of ballast-heavers. Many others, who had expressed a desire to attend, were prevented by family cares and arrangements; but small as the meeting was comparatively, it afforded a very fair representation of the circumstances and characters of their husbands. For instance, those who were coalwhippers' wives appeared comfortable and "well-to-do." They wore warm gowns, had on winter bonnets, and clean, tidy caps underneath; the ballast-heavers' wives, on the contrary, were mostly ragged, dejected, and anxious-looking.

An endeavour was made to ascertain, in the first instance, how many children each person had. This was done by questioning them separately; and from the answers it appeared that all had families. Eight had one child each, the rest varied from two to eight, and one woman stated that she had twelve children, all of whom were living, but that only four now resided with her and her husband. Five had infants in their arms; and several had children sick, either at home or in some hospital.

In the next place, the ballast-heavers' wives were asked whether their husbands worked under publicans. "All of them," was the reply, "work under publicans;" and, said one, "worse luck for us" —a sentiment that was very warmly concurred in by all the rest.

This fact having been specifically ascertained from each woman, the Metropolitan Correspondent of *The Morning Chronicle* proceeded to inquire from them separately how much their husbands earned, and how much of their earnings was spent at the publicans' houses through which they obtained work, or where they were paid.

"My husband," said the first woman, "works under a publican, and I know that he earns now 12s. or 13s. a week, but he brings home to me only half-a-crown, and sometimes not that much. He spends all the rest at the public-house, where he gets his jobs; and often comes home drunk."

"My husband," exclaimed the second, "will sometimes get from 24s. to 28s. a week, but I never see anything the likes o'that money from him. He spends it at the publican's. And when he has earned 24s., he will sometimes bring home only 2s. or 2s. 6d. We are badly off, you may be sure, when the money goes in this way. But my husband cannot help spending it, for he is obliged to get his jobs at the public-house."

"Last week," interposed another, "we had not one penny coming into our house; and the week before—which was Christmas week— my husband got two jobs, which would come, he told me, to 8s. or 9s., if he had brought it all home; but he only brought me 1s. This was all the money I had to keep me and my five children for the whole week; and I'm sure I don't know how we got through. This is all owing to the public-house; and when we go to fetch our husbands at eleven or twelve at night, they shut us out and say they are not there, though we know very well they are inside in a back place. My husband has been kept in that back place many a time till two or three in the morning—then he has been turned out, and come home to his family drunk, without sixpence in his pocket, though the same day he has received 8s. or 9s. at the same public-house."

"They go to the public-house," added another woman, "to get

jobs, and to curry favour they spend their money there, because if they did not spend their money they would get never a job. The men who drink the greatest quantity of money will get the most jobs. This leaves their families and their wives miserable, and I am sure me and my poor family are miserable through it."

"My man," said another, "earned 11s. last week. He brought home 5s. out of it, and that at two o'clock on the Sunday morning, when he was quite drunk. He had spent all the remainder at the publican's who paid him. I have two children, and this 5s. was all we had to keep us the week round, and pay rent besides."

"But this," interposed a quiet elderly woman, "is the beginning of the tenth week, in all of which my husband has had only four jobs. Those four jobs for the ten weeks just make it 1s. 3½d. a week, that I have received from him, and we stand in 2s. 6d. a week rent. I am sure I don't know how we get along. But our publicans are very civil, for my husband works for two. They lay down the money for him when he comes to be paid; still, if he does not drink a good part of it away, we know very well he will get no more work."

"It is very little," said a female, with an infant in her arms, "that my husband earns; and of what little he does earn he does not fetch much to me. He got one job last week, heaving 45 tons, and he fetched me home 1s. 6d. for it. I was then in lodgings at 1s. 6d. a week, but I could not afford them, and now we are in lodgings at 9d. This week he has no work yet. In Christmas week my man told me he earned 25s., and I believe he did, but he only fetched home between 8s. and 9s. on Saturday. I had myself and child and husband to keep out of that. My husband works for a publican, and it was at his house he spent the money. One day last week this publican said to him, when he asked for a job, 'I cannot give you a job, for there is nothing against you upon the slate but 1s.;' and so he got none there. He works for another public-house, and he went there; but the publican would not give him a job unless he spent all he earned. My infant is six weeks old to-day, and this woman by me (appealing to the female next to her) knows well it is the truth that I tell—that for two nights in last week my child and myself were obliged to go to bed breadless. We had nothing neither of those days. It was the same one night in the week before Christmas, though my husband received that same night 8s.; but all was spent at the public-house. On Christmas night we could not get any supper. We had no money, and I took the gown off my back and pawned it for 2s., to provide something for us to eat. I have nothing else to say but this—that whatever my husband earns I get little or nothing of it, for it goes to the public-house where he gets his jobs."

Another ballast-heaver's wife, also with an infant in her arms, said—"We have seven children. This in my arms is the seventh. My husband has frequently earned from 10s. to 15s. a week during the last year; but sometimes he has been idle for a week or a fortnight together. I reckon he brings home, as nearly as he can, all that he earns, but of course he has a score with the publican. The publican has the best part of all he earns; and whatever he earns, I believe the publican gets, one week with another, full 10s. a week out of it. We have to live the best way we can out of what little that remains. Very often we have been without food a whole day, and have not had much chance of any the next day, unless we pledged everything that we had to get it."

"Some weeks," said a middle-aged woman, "my husband gets 25s., but then he may have no work the week after. He brings home all he gets; but out of the 25s. at least 5s. goes to the publican for whom he works, and he is obliged to take beer to have the work. My husband is very good, however. Sometimes, if he takes it into his head, he will spend the whole of his earnings at his master's house; but sometimes he will spend none. One week with another, I dare say he brings home clear 10s.; but one week with another the public-house gets as much out of him—that is, 10s. a week. He would bring all his money home, if it were not for the publican, where he gets his jobs, and where he is paid."

"I do not know what my husband gets," said the next. "He never tells me where he goes; and for that reason I do not know how much he earns; but I do know, and I have known it a good while, that he is obliged to spend at the public-house where the jobs are given one-fifth of what is due to him. He often comes home drunk; and sometimes when he is in that way he ill-treats me. He never ill-treats me except he is drunk. I believe he brings home all he can; for if he did not, we should all starve. We have eight children and ourselves; so that we have had hard times of it often. My husband works for any place where he can get work; but it is mostly under the publicans."

"I know what my husband can do for his family pretty well," added another. "He brings home for them 7s. a week, one week with another; but for this he does £1's worth of work, and he is compelled to spend the rest where he gets the work. If he did not he would not get another job. One publican where he went to to-day for a job told him, 'I shall give you no more work.' My husband asked why? 'Because,' he said, 'you went the other day to an office-man' (meaning that he had supplied information to this journal). My husband said he had, for he had a family to keep. 'Well,' said the publican, 'you shall have no more work from me for doing that;' and he has had no work to-day through it. I really think that my man earns, one week with another, £1, for he works hard when he has it to do, and I am sure he would bring it all home if he had not to spend it for the score. He must pay the score and a shilling besides. This makes it so that if he earns 6s., we will say, he fetches home only 2s. 6d., and no more. May be, that sometimes it will reach 3s., but then the next day he will come to me for a shilling back again, to treat the ganger, so that the foreman may give him another job."

An infirm woman, approaching fifty years of age, who spoke in a tone of sorrowful resignation, said—"We have had very little money coming in of late. My husband has been very bad for ten weeks back. He throws up blood. I suppose he has strained himself too much. All the money I have had for six weeks to keep us both has been 8s. If he was earning money he would bring it to me."

Another Woman: "Not without the publican's allowance, I am sure."

The First Woman: "No; the publican's allowance would be taken off; but the publicans. you see, must have a little. I do not know how much it is, but they must have something if they give us their jobs. I do not know how much my husband earns, for he never told me."

This woman was here asked if her husband ever came home drunk?

"Yes," she replied, "many a time he comes home drunk; but he must have the drink to get the jobs."

"My husband," proceeded the next, "earns 3s. 6d., and sometimes 4s. a day, but he never brings anything like that home to his family. He cannot, because he pays so much to the publican; and out of what he does bring I have often to give him 1s. to seek out another job. He comes home drunk very often; when he is drunk he is very violent; but when he is sober there is not a quieter husband anywhere."

"My husband," said a woman who was miserably dressed, "does not tell me what he earns; but when he is in work he brings me, in general, 10s. or 12s. the week. He works for a publican, and I know very well that more than he gives me he gives to the publican. Still, when he has it he gives it me. Indeed, he must; for we have six children, which makes eight of us altogether. He comes home drunk three times a week. According as he has a job he must have drink. He cannot get jobs without getting drunk upon them, so it's of no use thinking any more about it."

"My man is a very good husband," was the observation of the next female. "He gets one job, and sometimes two in a week, but he is obliged to spend half of what he earns in the public-house where the work is given. Sometimes I have from him 3s., sometimes 5s., sometimes 7s. a week; several times it has been 10s., but some weeks he does not get any work at all. I should say we have 6s. a week coming in the year round. That is very little with our family, but we are obliged to be content with it."

"Last week," said another, "I had just 5s. 6d., and the week before, which was Christmas week, I had 7s. 8d. from my husband. He generally tells me what he gets; and I know, from what he told me, that in both weeks he earned more than double what he gave me. All the rest he was obliged to spend. He feeds the publicans as well as other folks out of his wages. By 'other folks' I mean his family."

A number of other women having made statements confirmatory of the above—

"Do you think," the meeting was asked, "your husbands would be sober as well as industrious men if they could be got away from the public-house system of employment and payment of wages?"

"God Almighty bless you," exclaimed one woman, "they would love us and their families all the better for it! We should all be much the better for it!"

"And so say all of us," was the next and perfectly unanimous exclamation.

"If we could see that day," said one who had spoken before, "their families would have little in the world to complain of."

Another added, "The night-houses ought to be closed. That would be one good thing."

"They have been many a bitter cup to me," said one who, from her dress, appeared to be in mourning.

Some inquiries were then made as to whether these poor women were ill-treated by their husbands when they came home in a state of intoxication. There was a good deal of hesitation before any answers could be obtained. At last one woman said her husband certainly did beat her, "of course—but then," she added, "he did not know what he was doing." "I," said another, "should not know what it was to have an angry word with my husband if he were always sober. He is a quiet man—very, when the drink is out

of him; but we have many words together when he is tipsy, and
——" she stopped without completing the sentence.

Several others gave similar testimony; and many declared that
it was the public-house system which led their husbands to drink.

One woman here said that the foremen of gangs, as well as the
publican, helped to reduce the ballast-heavers' earnings; for they
gave work to men who took lodgings from them, though they did
not occupy them, and through such persons men with families
had no chance. In fact, the taking of the lodgings was, it was said,
just a way of giving the foreman so much money for work, because
in many cases the men did not live at the lodgings at all.

This was confirmed by another woman, who spoke with great
warmth upon the subject. She said that married men, who could
not afford to spend with the publican and lodge with the foreman
in the manner pointed out, would be sure to have no work. Other
men went straight from one job to another, while her own husband,
and other women's husbands, had been three and four weeks without lifting a shovelful of ballast. She considered this very hard on
men who had families.

A question was here asked, whether any women were present
whose husbands, in order to obtain work, were obliged to pay for
lodgings which they did not use?

One immediately rose and said—"They do it regular at a publican's in Wapping; and I know that the men who have paid for
them have had six jobs together, when my husband has had none
for weeks together." "There are now," added another, "fourteen
at that very place who never lodge there though they are paying
for lodgings."

They were next asked, who had suffered from want, owing to
their husband's drinking their earnings, as described, at the public-
houses in question?

"Starvation has been my lot," said one; "and mine," added
another. "My children," said a third, "have often gone to bed at
night without breaking their fast the whole length of the day."
And mine, said one, "have many a time gone without a bit or a
sup of anything all the day, through their father working for the
publican " "I cannot," exclaimed the next, "afford my children a
ha'porth of milk a day. My husband does not seem to work for
them." "Many a time," said one, who appeared to be very much
moved, "have I put my four children to bed, when the only meal
they have had the whole day has been 1lb. of bread, but it's of
no use opening my mouth." "I," said the last, "have been in
London 27 years, and during that time, I can safely say that I have

never taken myself a second glass of spirits or anything else; but in that time I have suffered the martyrdom of 40 years—all through my husband and the public-house. I have two children who bring me in, one 2s. 6d. and the other 6s. 6d. a week, which is all we have, for my husband gets nearly nothing. If he could bring his earnings home, instead of spending them at the public-house, we should be very comfortable."

These questions led to one concerning the late-hour system at the public-houses frequented by ballast-heavers. "I often go for my husband," said one, "at one or two o'clock in the morning, after I know he has been paid, but they have kept him in a back apartment away from me till I have threatened to smash the windows if they did not let him out. I threatened to smash the windows because my children were wanting the money for bread that he was spending there. If our husbands were inclined to come home sober there is little chance, for they have cards and bagatelle to keep them till they become heady, and when they are become heady, there is nothing left for their families—then the publicans kick our poor men out and lock the doors."

This statement was confirmed; and after several other persons had described their sufferings,

The coalwhippers' wives were asked whether or not their condition and that of their families had been improved since the system of carrying on the trade had been altered by the Legislature.

The answer was a most decided affirmative. Their husbands, they said, used to spend all, or very nearly all, their earnings, with the publicans; but now, when they got a good ship they brought home the greatest part of their earnings, which was sufficient to make their families comfortable. Their husbands had become quite different men. They used to ill-treat them when they were paid at the public-house—very much so, because of the drink; but now they were very much altered, because they had become sober men from what they were. None were now distressed to provide for their families, and if there were plenty of work, they would be quite happy. The improvement, one woman said, must have been very great, otherwise there would not have been so many institutions and benefit societies, pension societies, and schools for their children.

This declaration was very warmly applauded by the ballast-heavers' wives. They declared that similar measures would produce similar benefits in their case, and that they hoped the day might soon come when they should be secure in the enjoyment of them.

So terminated the proceedings.

This meeting took place at three in the afternoon, and at seven another was held in the same rooms, at which upwards of 1,500 labouring men were present. The report of the latter meeting will be given in this Journal tomorrow.

The *"Lumpers"* are, if possible, in a more degraded state than the ballast-heavers. They are not, it is true, under the same amount of oppression from the publican; but still they are so besotted with the drink which they are tempted to obtain from the publicans who employ them, as to look upon the man who tricks them out of their earnings rather as a friend than an enemy. The lumpers make, during six months in the year, as much as 24s., and during the other six months they have nothing to do. Of the 24s. that they earn in their busy time, 20s., it will be seen, is spent in the public-house. One master lumper, who is a publican, employs as many as 100 men. This information I have, not only from the men themselves, but from the managers of the Commercial Docks, where the greater number of lumpers are engaged. The 100 men in the publican's employ, as will be seen from the evidence of the wives, spend upon an average £1 a week in the house, taking generally but 4s. home to their wives and families—so that no less a sum than £100 a week is squandered in the publican- contractor's house by the working men in drink. There is not only a pay-night, but two "draw-nights" are appointed in each week, as a means of inveigling the men to their master's tap-room; and indeed the same system, which gives the greatest drunkard the best chance of work, prevails among the lumpers as among the ballast-heavers. The effect of this is, that the lumpers are the most drunken, debased, and poverty-striken of all the classes of labouring men that I have yet seen—for, earning more than the ballast-heavers, they of course have more to spend in the public-house. I made a point of looking more minutely into the state of these men on the Sunday, for I have found that on that day it is easy to tell the habits of men by their external appearance. The greater part that I saw were either intoxicated, or else reeking of liquor, as early as eleven o'clock on the Sunday morning. One foreman was decently dressed, it was true; but then he was sent to me, I was credibly informed, by the master publican, who had heard of my previous investigations, to give me a false impression as to the state of the labourers. The rest of the men that I saw were unwashed and unshaven, even up to five and six in the afternoon of that day. Their clothes were the same tattered and greasy garments that I had seen them in, the day before—indeed the wives of the lumpers appeared to be alone alive to the degradation of their husbands. At one house that

I visited late on the Sunday evening, I found two of the children in one corner of the small close room, on the bare boards, covered with a piece of old carpet, and four more boys and girls stowed away at the top and bottom of the one bed in which the rest of the family slept. Dirty wet clothes were hanging to dry on lines across the room—and the face of the wife, who was alone, in all her squalid misery, was black and gashed with cuts and bruises.

Not a step I took but I was dogged by some foreman or other, in the hopes of putting me on a wrong scent. I had arranged with the men on Saturday morning to have a meeting with them on that night after their labour; but on going to the appointed place I found not one labouring man there, and I learnt the next day that the publican had purposely deferred paying them till a late hour, so that they might have no chance of meeting me.

On Monday morning, while at the office of the superintendent of the Commercial Docks Company, one of the lumpers staggered drunk into the room, intent upon making some insolent demand or other.

That this drunkenness with all its attendant vices is not the fault of the lumpers, but the necessary consequence of the system under which they are employed, no man who has seen the marked difference between the coal-whippers and that class of labourers who will "work out of the public-house," can for a moment doubt. The sins of the labouring man, so far as I have seen, are, in this instance, most indisputably the sins of his immediate employer. If he is drunken, it is his master who makes him so; if he is poor— his house bare—his wife ragged—his children half clothed, half fed, and wholly uneducated, it is mainly because his master tricks him out of his earnings at the public-house.

Let me now give a description of the Lumpers' labour, and then of their earnings.

The timber trade is divided, by the custom of the trade, into two classes, called *timber* and *deals*. By "timber" is meant what is brought in uncut logs; this is American red pine, yellow pine, elm, ash, oak, and birch. The teak trade is more recent, and seems to be an exception to the classification I have mentioned; it is generally described as *teak;* mahogany and dye woods again are not styled timber. The "deals" are all sawn ready for the carpenter's or joiner's use. At the Custom-house, the distinctions are "hewn" and "sawn" woods; that is, timber and deals. On timber there is now a duty of 1s. per load (a load being 50 cubic feet), and on deals of 2s. The deals are sawn in Canada, where immense steam-mills have been erected for the purpose. The advantage to the trader in having this process effected in Canada rather than in England seems to be this: the deals brought over (prepared as I have described), of different lengths, varying from six feet to 20, while three inches is a usual thickness, are ready for the workman's purpose, and no refuse matter forms a part of them. Were the pine brought in logs, the bark and the unevenness of the tree would add to the freight for what was only valueless. Timber and deals require about the same time for their discharge. The largest vessels in this trade that enter the port of London are to be found in the West India South Dock, formerly the City Canal. On one occasion in this dock a vessel of 800 tons, containing 24,000 deals and ends, was discharged in twenty-six working hours, forty-five men being employed. I am informed that twenty men would discharge a ship of 600 tons, of timber and deals, in seven days; forty men will do it in four days. In order to become acquainted with the system of *Lumping* I went on board a vessel in the river, where a gang of twenty men were at work. She was a vessel of 600 tons, from Quebec. She lay alongside the Flora, a Norwegian vessel, the first timber ship that had reached the port of London since the change in the navigation-laws had come into operation. The Flora's cargo was 900 pieces of timber, which would be discharged by her crew, as the lumpers are only employed in British vessels. The vessel that I visited, and which lay next to the Flora, had her hold and the between-decks (which might be 38 yards in length) packed closely with deals. She held between 17,000 and 18,000 deals. She was being lightened in the river before going into dock. Twenty men were at work; two barges were moored alongside close to two port-holes in the stern of the ship. There were three men in each barge, who received and packed the deals into the barge as they were thrust out of the port-holes. The larger deals were carried along by two men as soon as a sufficient clearance had been made to enable them to run along—at first bent half double. The two men who carried the deals ran along in a sort of jog-trot motion, keeping time, so that the motion relieved the pressure of the weight. The men all said, "It's easier to run than to walk with the deals." The shorter deals (ends) were carried one by each man, who trotted on in the same measured step. Each man, or each two men employed, delivered his or their "deal" to one especial man in the barge, so that a constant communication from the ship to the barge was kept up, and the work went on without hitch or stoppage. This same vessel, on a former occasion, was discharged in thirty-six hours, which shows (as there were between 17,000 and 18,000 carryings and deliverings of the deals)

how rapidly the work is conducted. The "timber" is all dragged
from the hold or the between-decks of the ship by machines. The
lumpers "bouse" it from its place in the ship by means of winches,
tackles, and "dogs"—which latter are iron links to lay hold of the
log. Three of these winches and tackles are stationed at equal
distances on each side of a large ship, and thus, with the aid of
crowbars, the several pieces of timber are dragged along the hold,
and then dropped gently into the water (either in the docks or the
river), and floated in rafts to its destination. All "timber" is floated,
as a rule. Sometimes, when the ship is discharged in dock, timber
or deals are let down a slide on to a platform, and so carried to
the pile or the waggon. Contractors are employed by the shipowners in the West India Dock, as they will do some ships cheaper
by £10 than the company could afford to do it. The shipowners
bear the expense of discharging the ship.

The following statement of one of the working men was given
most unwillingly; indeed it was only by a series of cross-questionings
that any approximation to the truth could be extracted from him.
He was evidently in fear of losing his work, and the tavern to
which I had gone to take his statement was filled with foremen
watching and intimidating him. He said:—

"I am a *working lumper,* or labourer at discharging timber and
deal ships. I have been sixteen years at the work. I should think
that there are more than two hundred men in Deptford who are
constantly engaged at the work. There are a great many more
working lumpers living at Limehouse, Poplar, and Blackwall. These
do the work principally of the West India Docks; and when the
work is slack there, and brisk at the Commercial, East Country,
or Grand Surrey Canal Docks, the men cross the water and get
a job on the Surrey side of the river. In the summer a great many
Irish labourers seek for work as lumpers. They come over from
Ireland in the Cork boats. I should say there are altogether upwards of 500 regular working lumpers, but in the summer there
are at least 200 more, owing to the number of Irish who come to
England to look for work at that time of year. The wages of the
regular lumpers are not less when the Irishmen come over in the
summer, nor do the men get a less quantity of work to do. There
are more timber and deal ships arriving at that season, so more
hands are required to discharge them. The ships begin to arrive
in July, and they continue coming in till January; after that time
they lay up till March, when they sail for the foreign ports.
Between January and July the regular working lumpers have little
or nothing to do. During that time there are scarcely any timber

or deal ships coming in, and the working lumpers then try to fall
in with anything they can—either ballasting a ship, or carrying a
few deals to load a timber-carriage, or doing a little 'tide-work.'
Between July and January the work is very brisk. We are generally
employed every day for those six months. Sometimes we lose a day
(after lightening a ship in the river) while the vessel is going into
dock. We call it lightening a ship when she is laden too heavy and
draws too much water to enter the docks. In such a case we
generally begin discharging the timber or deals in the river, either
off Deptford or Blackwall, according as the ship may be for the
docks on the Middlesex or Surrey side. In the river we discharge
the deals into lighters, whereas, when the ship is in dock, we
generally discharge along a stage on to the shore. Timber we put
overboard in both cases, and leave it for the raftsmen to put
together into rafts and float into the timber-ponds of the different
docks. The deals we merely land. It is our duty to put them ashore,
and nothing more. After that the deal porters take them and sort
and pile them. They sort the white from the yellow deals, and
each kind into different lengths, and then arrange them in piles all
along the side of the dock. Our usual time of working is from six
to six in the summertime, and from daylight to dark in the winter.
We always work under a foreman. There are two foremen lumpers
to almost every ship that we discharge, and they engage the men,
who work in gangs under them. Each gang consists of from four
to twelve men, according as the size of the ship is large, or she is
wanted to be discharged quickly. I have known as many as thirty
lumpers engaged in discharging one ship; she was 1,000 tons, and
wanted to be got out quick, so that she might make another voyage before the winter set in abroad. The foreman and men are
employed by the master lumper. Some of the master lumpers are
publicans; some others keep chandlers' shops; and others do nothing else, that I know of. The master pays the working men 3s. 6d.
a day, and the foreman 1s. extra. We are settled with every Saturday night. We have two draw-nights in each week—that is, the
master advances either a part or the whole of our earnings if we
please, on Tuesday and Thursday nights. I work under a publican.
My master has only gone into the public line very recently. I don't
think he's been at it for more than eighteen months. He has been
a master lumper, I should say, for these ten or twelve years past.
I worked under him before he had a public-house. Then he paid
every Tuesday, Thursday, and Saturday nights, at the same house
as he is now the proprietor of. The master lumpers always pay
the men they employ at the public-house, whether they are publi-

cans or not. My master employs, I should say, in the spring season, from 80 to 100 hands regularly, and most of these meet at his house every Tuesday and Thursday night, and all on Saturday night, either to be settled with in full, or have a part of their wages advanced. We are usually paid at seven in the evening. I *have* been paid as late as three o'clock on a Sunday morning, but that was some years ago, and I was all that time in the public-house. We go straight to the public-house after we have done our work. At this time of the year we knock off work at dark—that is, at five [I am informed at the Commercial Docks that the usual hour is *four*] o'clock, and we remain at our master's until pay time—that is seven o'clock. This we do for three nights in the week certain, and after our work on other nights we mostly meet at our master's public-house. The men generally draw on a Tuesday from 2s. to 4s., and on a Thursday night the same sum is advanced to them. The men are not *forced* to spend anything in the house. Each man has a little beer while the master is getting ready to pay him on the draw-nights, and he generally remains in the house some time after he has received his money, according as he thinks proper. On a draw-night, in the brisk season, many out of the 100 he employs will stop drinking till ten o'clock. Some go away home immediately after they have drawn their money. At least half stop for some time—that is till nine o'clock. Some sit there and spend all they draw. All the beer that the lumpers have on board ship, while at their work, is supplied by the master. He supplies any quantity that is wanted. The reason why he keeps the public-house is to have the right of supplying the beer to the men. He wouldn't, of course, like to see us take beer from any other public-house than his. If we did, he would give us the 'sack.' Every master lumper works out of a public-house, and the men *must* have their beer from the house that he works out of, and if they don't, why they aint wanted. We generally take about two pots per man a day with us from the house when we go to our work of a morning. On a Saturday night we mostly stop longer than on the draw-nights. Upon an average the working lumpers, I should say, spend about 2s. a day in the season in the public-house. [It will be seen hereafter, that the lumpers' wives whom I saw declare that the men spend, generally, 20s. out of the 24s.] After a hard week's work I think they have generally about 8s. or 9s. out of the £1 4s. that they earn in the busiest time of the year. I myself have taken home as little as 5s. [According to this statement, assuming that there are 100 hands—many say there are more—regularly at work out of this public-house in the spring season, and spending each, upon an average, from 12s. to 20s., or say 16s. a week, this will give 1,600s., or £80 a week, squandered in beer.] I should say, taking all the year round, the men make 10s. 6d. a week. For at least four months in the year there is no work at all, and for two months more it is very slack. I am a married man with one child. When I am in full work I take home 5s. a week at the least. My wife and child has to suffer for it all.''

The next I saw was one who had volunteered to speak out, so that, by comparing the following statement with the foregoing, we may be able to come to some notion of the truth. The man's statement was as follows:—

"I have worked as a *journeyman lumper* seventeen years. When I first began that work I was paid 3s. 6d. a day, being employed two days and a half or three days in a week the year through. The young hands are generally knocked about and sent from one ship to another, humbugged about, and obliged to wait and wait, never getting anything for the time they have to wait. In a timber ship this is the way the work is carried on to lump her (unload her). Well, say a ship is 1,000 tons burthen; suppose her cargo is timber and with a deck load of yellow wood pine, the heaviest cargo that comes to London on deck. I'll tell you the truth if I lose my work. I don't care a fig. I can't be worse. That man you just seen hasn't told you the whole truth. He's afeard. He works out of a public-house, and daren't speak. The ships come up, and eight or nine master lumpers go aboard, and the captain may say, 'The cheapest man's to have her. One man will say, 'I've done this ship before;' and he'll get the ship because he knows how to tip some proper party, and he tips five bob or half a sovereign. Suppose this man gets the ship; he's a master man, and he goes to a foreman, and he says, 'Get me a gang together,' and the foreman gets a gang together, and he must get a good set if the work's to be done quick. The master lumper has all the pull; the foreman doesn't get much—only his shilling a day extra. Oft enough he gets the best hands at first, and when a quantity that may be wanted is got off he puts on cheaper hands—new Irish Grecians, some people calls them, or others. Any new hands is the same. I never show these men how to work. They ruin our trade, and are ruining it more and more; they'll work for nothing. Each man gets 3s., the master paying the waterage. In August, September, and October, work is the best. Then we get 4s. and a pint of beer. They give us 4s. 2d., but we must pay the twopence for a pint of beer—that lies in a man's option it's said: but if a man doesn't do so he's thought scaly. If we don't have our beer, we're done. The master lumpers who are not publicans pay at public-houses, and have sometimes to borrow the money of the publicans to pay the men, before they get their money from the shipowner. I shall lose my work, maybe, and have to go to the Mount—that is, you see, a place between the Commercial Dock and the Dog and Duck, where we walk looking out for a job— because I speak this way to you. If jobs don't come, there's the workhouse. Lots come from Ireland, and go to work, knowing nothing about it. But they'll work for anything, and so get on. [This he repeated frequently.] I am a married man with a family, but don't say how many, or I should be more a marked man. I wish I could write as slick as you. I'd do only head work then, and work no more. I have spent 25s. a week in drink. I ought to have as good a suit as you, when I get work as a foreman, which I do sometimes. Last week I got 20s., and took home 3s. I'm afraid to speak, I should lose my work. [This he said over and over again.] I must spend my money in drink some way, or I can't get on in any work; there's stoppages and bothers. I was told I couldn't get paid last Saturday night, for fear I should have anything to do with telling you or anybody the truth. I didn't get all my money until Sunday, and it was all gone on Sunday night. You understand; if a man gives offence, next morning he's told 'You're not wanted, there's a hand short of what we expected to want—you understand.' In less than three years a publican that contracts may make his fortune. Where these men sell a pint to a neighbour they sell three pots to a lumper. It's compulsion, as you may say—and it's no compulsion. A contractor, on a tidy job, will get his £4 profit—sometimes £10 or £15 on a good job; and he keeps moving on that way; no matter how our kids starves. Aye, and more than that, I've known contractors have £50 for a ship, and has done it for £16. I went on board the ————, for Mr. ————. He wanted to employ me as foreman, at 4s. a day, but he wanted me to pay waterage, and I refused. I have had 6s. a day as foreman. An average lumper will get 4s. a day when he is at work. I was threatened to be flung out of the windows if I came to any meeting with you. When I'm out of work, the old woman has to keep me. She works at gowns, or anything. How she lives God only knows! "

The following is the statement of one who appeared to me to be both a truthful and a just man. His wife was a superior woman, and being present at his home—where the information was obtained—she acted as a check upon him, even if he had been disposed to lean either to master or workman. The man's house was comfortably furnished, evidently owing to the greater prudence of his wife, for I have found it is a rule that when the wife is cleanly and thrifty, the husband is always a higher class man:—

"I have been a lumper nine years. Prices are not so good now as when I first knew the business. We got 4s. 6d. a day then; that is, the old hands did. In a year after it fell to 4s. Work was slack, and so employers could get men to work at their own prices. Three or four years back prices fell to 3s. 6d. a day." My informant then repeated what I had formerly heard, attributing this further decrease to the great influx of Irish labourers, owing to the distress in Ireland, and their willingness to work for any wages whatever, which enables employers to get the old hands on easier terms. "The lumpers," my informant continued, "are employed principally in timber and deal ships, but will undertake any work to which their employer chooses to set them. The corn-ships are all discharged by the fellowship porters; excepting the vessels in the South-west India Dock (formerly the City Canal), where the servants of the company are employed; but they must then have one of the regularly appointed meters. There is far too much drinking among us. One man I know had 14s. to receive for wages the other week, but he went on 'on tick' at the public-house, had nothing to take on Saturday night, and was 5s. in debt. It is a great disadvantage in our business that work is so uncertain. Last Christmas twelvemonth, all that I earned the week before Christmas was 6d. I have now 15s. in pawn, and as we have no club nor anything of that kind, if I was to be sick there's only the parish. In a slack time I have sold Christmas carols or anything."

I will now give the statement of one of the foremen who was sent to me intoxicated by the publican-contractor, to persuade me that the system under which the working men are employed and paid is a beneficial and a just one to the labourer. The inconsistencies in the statement the reader will easily detect. He said:—

"I am the foreman of a gang of lumpers. The gangs vary in number according to the size of the vessel to be laden. They vary from eight to 26. When the gang exceeds 10 men, two foremen are employed, as the work is carried on on both sides of the ship at the same time. I work under a publican, who contracts with the shipowner to do the work of unlading the vessel *by the lump;* that is, so much for the entire job, without any reference to weight or measurement. I engage the men employed, anybody I please— and they are paid by the contractor. At this time of the year, when work cannot be carried on longer than from half-past seven in the morning until towards five in the evening, each man is paid 3s. 6d. for his day's work: he is paid that sum in money. He is not re-

quired to spend any of that money; nor would any man have a
worse chance of work who didn't spend anything in drink at the
house of the contractor. He hasn't been a publican long— about a
year. We take a pot of beer a man, or twelve pots for every ten
men—more usually from the house of the contractor. I consider
that we are not obliged to do this. It is very seldom that any gang
of men has a full week's work. I calculate that they are not employed above three days in the week, take the average of the year;
that gives an average earning of 10s. 6d. per week. For the next
three months there will be hardly anything doing in the timber-
ships, on account of the ice in the St. Lawrence and the Baltic.
During this slack time the men go off to any job. They may pick
up a little tide-work; that is, to assist in taking a ship from a wet
dock into a dry one, or any arrangement of that kind. We have
no sick fund among us—no benefit club, no society of any kind.
When a man's fairly beat out, his fellow workmen may subscribe
a trifle for him. Drunkenness is too common among us, but I don't
know that the system of working under publicans has much to do
with it. My employer would as soon see his men take their money
home. Many of the men are in great distress; their families are
hard put to it; they are the people that have to suffer for it. The
foreman, by agreement with his employer, has so much a day
over what the men have, but no per centage, and nothing to do
with the paying of the lumpers. I dare say from 700 to 1,000 men
are employed as lumpers in timber ships, when work is good;
lumpers work only in timber ships. There are a far greater number
of men in the trade than there used to be, on account of the number of labouring men that have come over from Ireland lately.
These Irishmen, when they first go to lumping, are very awkward
about it, and don't soon get handy. Before they came in such lots,
wages were better. They have been 4s. 6d. a day to men that knew
their work. For the last three years and more wages have been no
higher than 3s. 6d. a day. Of course the Irishmen, when first set
to work, weren't worth so much as the old hands, but they were
employed, and so wages fell down to their level. There is only one
publican among the contractors for lumping. There are four principal contractors, and several small ones. I don't know the exact
number. They all pay the men and the foremen alike. My employer
will not allow any lumper to run up drink scores at his house to
be worked out afterwards. There are too many men in the lumping
business. There is no system of giving a gang of men their turn.
We employ those we consider best to do the work."

I next saw two lumpers' wives. The husband of one had been fourteen years, and the other ten years, at the business. They both worked under a master who is a publican. One said, "My husband is such a strange man that he never tells me what he does get." The husband of the other, who is a foreman, according to the wife's statement, occasionally gets 5s. and sometimes 4s. 6d. a day. The first woman said, "It is a very bad principle for a man to have work out of a public-house; it makes a man spend a shilling where otherwise he would not." The wife of the one whose husband was a foreman said, "I have had many a bitter bruise for the last fifteen years, and all through the drink. Sometimes he stops till after twelve or one o'clock. I have not had anything to eat today—not a taste of anything, or even a bit of fire. On draw-nights he usually comes home about ten o'clock, and I call that a very good hour for a lumper, for draw-nights are very bad nights; the men then generally spend at the public-house three parts of what they earn. On pay-night the men generally stop till the public-house is closed, and then some of them doesn't bring a penny home, but comes home in debt. When the men are in work they may go trust for anything they want. Those that drink the hardest get the most work; they are the most looked upon. If the men was to bring all they earn home—aye, or even one-third of it—it would make the family very comfortable, as there would be a few more blankets and sheets on the bed—yes, and good shoes to their wives' and children's feet. Mine are two odd ones," added the woman, thrusting out her feet; "our dog stole this one, and brought it in in his mouth. The men, when they are in full work, earn 24s. per week, and they bring home upon an average 4s. out of that sum. Ah, that's about it, and there is a fourth part of them don't do that— the rest goes for what the publicans please to stick up to them." "I know if mine brought home more than he does," said the other, "I and the children would have some flannel petticoats. I have got one thin one, but a puff of wind would blow that away. They won't take it in pawn, or it would have gone long ago." The second woman added, "I have not got anything that would get me a penny, else it would have been in pawn to fetch me over today. When my husband beats me it is when I am in bed; but when I am not in bed I can fly from him. I know of one woman who is in the union now. Her husband always made his 24s. a week in the spring, but he brought only a shilling or two home to her at the week's end. He was almost always drunk, and then he would knock her down and jump upon her, and leave her for dead. When he was sober he was a good quiet sort of a man. He worked out of a public-house, and that is only a part of what the women have to suffer through their husbands being entrapped by the publican into his house. The woman I speak of has gone into the union to get away from the man's ill-treatment, and to have something nourishing to keep her, for it was very little she got at home, poor thing! She is suffering in the union now. She is very bad indeed." "I have not seen my husband," said the other one, "since last Thursday evening. He has gone away, and has not left me a farthing piece. I have taken my aprons on and pawned them for 9d., and that is all gone now. I had out of the 9d. I got 14lbs. of coal—that is 2d.—and a ¾d. candle, and a farthing bundle of wood; that is 3d. altogether. Then I had a three-ha'porth of bread and half a quartern of butter, and a ha'porth of tea, and a ha'porth of sugar, and a quarter of a pound of bacon 1½d., beside a ha'porth of onions, and a pennyworth of potatoes—that's all; and I think I laid my money out very well; and that has been all I have had since last Thursday, and now it's Sunday. Today I have had nothing at all. I don't know where my husband is gone, for the publican won't let me know. If I go and ask at the public-house they only laugh at me. Indeed, whenever a wife goes after her husband at the public-house to fetch him home, she is sent miles out of the way for a lark, so as to keep him there drinking. On the Saturday night the publican keeps the men there till the house is closed, and many of them stays there drinking far into the Sunday morning in spite of the law. Take the generality of the lumpers' wives, they are very badly off indeed." One of the women produced a bundle of pawn-tickets of things belonging to herself and her landlord. She told me that she had been obliged to make away with the blankets, sheets, and fire-irons of the lodgings that she occupied in order to live. She had kept the door shut all day (she said), for fear the landlord should come in, and missing the property, send her to Maidstone gaol.

To show the temptations that beset the poor, I give the statement of a woman known to all her neighbours as a very thrifty housewife, and an active, industrious woman. Her children's, her own, and her husband's clothing, scant and old as it was, all showed great care-taking; her home was very tidy. A few years back, a little after Christmas, she and her husband (now a lumper, but then pursuing a different calling) had been out all day, penniless, and returned to their room a little before dusk, without having earned a farthing. The wife was then suckling her first child, which was two months old. She felt very faint, and the only thing in the house on which she thought it possible to raise a penny was a glass tumbler—"that very tumbler," she continued, "which you see on the table. Everything but that had gone to the pawn-shop. Well, it cost 5½d., and I went to ——— and tried to sell it for 2d. I couldn't sell it at all, as the dealer had too many of such things. I then went to a neighbour and said, 'Mrs. B———, for God's sake lend me 2d. on this glass, for we're starving.' 'Mrs. ———,' said she, 'I'm sure you should have 3d., but I haven't 3d., nor a halfpenny.' Well, when I'd gone back it was dark, and my husband had gone to bed, such as it was—for we had neither blankets nor sheets left to cover us—as the best way to forget he was hungry and cold. We hadn't a bit of fire nor candle, but there was a bit of light came from the lamp in the street through the window. I sat down by the fire, that wasn't in, to suckle my child—poor little Bill! he's a fine lad now—and I found I had hardly any milk; and what would become of the child? All at once a thought came into my head, and I said to myself, 'Yes, I'll cut my own throat, and then little Bill's'—and I determined I would. Then I said to myself, 'No, I won't; for if I can cut my own throat, I know I can't cut the child's; so it'll be little use, I'll go to the waterworks, and jump in with him in my arms. I got up to do it, and then another thought came on me, and I laid down the child on that chair, and I shook my husband and said, 'You villain, I'll cut your throat, I will,' and he jumped up and seized hold of me, and then I felt how bad I'd been; but one's passion must have some vent, so I seized that very kettle you see there by the spout—the gas rather lighted it—and I smashed it on the floor; it was the first thing that came to hand—and broke a hole in it that cost me 2½d. to get mended. After that I felt calmed a bit, and began to see how wicked I'd been, and I fell down on my knees and cried like a child, for I was thankful to God I'd been preserved. Then I went to bed and prayed never to feel the like again." This statement was made with perfect simplicity; it came out incidentally, and the poor woman had no reason to believe that it would be printed.

LETTER XXV
Friday, January 11, 1850

Before proceeding to the subject-matter of the present letter, let me cite the following table, which I have been at considerable trouble in obtaining, as the only means of arriving at a correct estimate as to the collective earnings of the "Journeymen Lumpers," or men generally engaged in discharging the cargoes of the British timber and deal ships. The information has, in the three principal instances, been derived directly from the books of the Dock Companies, through the courtesy and consideration of the superintendents and directors, to whom I am greatly indebted:—

NUMBER OF SHIPS, WOOD LADEN, DISCHARGED AT THE DIFFERENT DOCKS, 1849.

	By the Dock Company.		By Lumpers.		By Crews.		Total.	
	Ships.	Tonnage.	Ships.	Tonnage.	Ships.	Tonnage.	Ships.	Tonnage.
West India Docks	36	22,556	60	24,347	24	6,796	129	33,699
Commercial Docks	2	1,186	154	63,213	259	75,096	415	139,495
Grand Surrey Canal	—	—	153	45,900	59	16,000	212	62,900
East Country Docks	—	—	11	3,409	64	19,001	75	22,500
Regent's Canal	—	—	2	600	—	—	2	600
Total	36	23,742	339	137,469	406	117,983	833	279,194

By the above returns it will be seen that in the course of last year 389 timber and deal ships, of 137,469 tons burthen collectively, were discharged by lumpers. This, at 9d. per ton—which is the price generally given by the dock companies—would give

£5,155 1s. 9d., as the gross amount paid to the contractors. The master lumper derives little or no profit out of this sum directly. This will be evident from the subjoined statement. A gentleman at the West India Docks, who has been all his life connected with the timber trade, informs me that twenty men will discharge a wood-laden ship in seven days. Now—

Twenty men at 3s. 6d. per day for seven days comes to £24 10 0
And 600 tons at 9d. per ton to 22 10 0

So that the master lumper by this account would lose by}
the job at the very least ....∫ £2 0 0

This statement is fully borne out by the fact, that the master lumpers will often agree to discharge a ship for £10 less than the Company could possibly afford to do it with their own men. The question then arises, how is it that the master lumper is enabled to do this and live? This is easily answered. He is generally either a publican himself, or connected with one, and the journeymen in his employ spend at his public-house, according to the account of the wives, five-sixths of their wages in drink, or £1 out of every 24s. they earn. Say, however, that only four-fifths of the gross earnings are thus consumed, then four thousand and odd out of the £5,155 will go to the publican, and one thousand and odd pounds to the men.

I am now obliged to leave the long-shore labourers for a while, in order that certain returns, which are necessary for the perfect elucidation of the subject, may be completed in the interim. I purpose, therefore, in the meantime, devoting myself to the investigation of the condition of the classes frequenting the Houses of Refuge for the Destitute Poor. I do this, at present, not because the subject comes next in the order of my inquiry, but because these places of shelter for the houseless are only open at certain periods of the year, and at this season a large proportion of the country labourers who are out of employ flock to London, either to seek for work in the wintertime, or to avail themselves of the food and lodging afforded by these charitable institutions. Others again, who are professional vagrants, "tramping" through the country, and sleeping at the different unions on their road, come to town as regularly as noblemen every winter, and make their appearance annually in these quarters. Moreover, it is at this season of the year that the sufferings and privations of the really poor and destitute are rendered ten-fold more severe than at any other period, and it is at the Houses of Refuge that the great mass

284

of London—or rather English and Irish—poverty and misery is to be met with. To give the reader an idea of the motley assemblage to be found in places, I subjoin the following table (taken from the forthcoming report by which it will be seen that almost every quarter of the globe contributes its quota of wretchedness. The congregation at the Refuges for the Destitute is indeed a sort of ragged congress of nations—a convocation of squalor and misery—a synopsis of destitution, degradation, and suffering, to be seen perhaps nowhere else: —

PLACES TO WHICH THE INDIVIDUALS SHELTERED BY THE HOUSELESS POOR SOCIETY DURING THE WINTER 1848-9 APPEARED TO BELONG: —

Africa	12	Lincolnshire	85
America	78	London	343
Bedfordshire	55	Middlesex	214
Berkshire	267	Norfolk	163
Buckinghamshire	88	Northamptonshire	67
Cambridgeshire	88	Northumberland	72
Cheshire	40	Nottinghamshire	68
Cornwall	32	Oxfordshire	100
Cumberland	12	Poland	4
Derbyshire	48	Portugal	5
Denmark	6	Russia	7
Devonshire	209	Rutlandshire	24
Dorsetshire	46	Scotland	230
Durham	54	Shropshire	42
East Indies	19	Somersetshire	246
Essex	392	Spain	10
France	14	St. Helena	8
Germany	53	Staffordshire	129
Gibraltar	3	Suffolk	133
Gloucestershire	163	Surrey	204
Guernsey	32	Sussex	147
Hampshire	414	Wales	122
Herefordshire	45	Warwickshire	160
Hertfordshire	181	West Indies	25
Huntingdonshire	25	Westmoreland	6
Ireland	8,068	Wiltshire	87
Italy	7	Worcestershire	36
Jersey	15	Yorkshire	126
Kent	523	Unknown	29
Lancashire	811	Born at sea	5
Leicestershire	75		

Nor are the returns of the bodily ailments of the wretched inmates of these abodes less instructive as to their miserable modes of life—their continual exposure to the weather—and their want of proper nutriment. The subjoined medical report of the diseases and bodily afflictions to which these poor creatures are liable, tells a tale of

suffering which to persons with even the smallest amount of patho-
logical knowledge, must need no comment. The catarrh and in-
fluenza, the rheumatism, bronchitis, ague, asthma, lumbago—all
speak of many long nights' exposure to the wet and cold; whereas
the abscesses—ulcers—the diarrhœa, and the excessive debility
from starvation, tell—in a manner that precludes all doubt—of the
want of proper sustenance and extreme privation of these, the
very poorest of all the poor: —

MEDICAL REPORT FOR 1848-49

Of the persons who applied at the Central Asylum, there were afflicted
with:—

Catarrh and influenza	149	Atrophy	3
Incipient fever	52	Dropsy	3
Rheumatism	50	Incised wounds	3
Diarrhœa	60	*Diseased Joints*	4
Cholera	2	Erysipelas	3
Bronchitis	13	Rupture	3
Abscesses	15	Cramps and pains in bowels ...	2
Ulcers	11	Spitting of blood	4
Affections of the head	12	*Lumbago*	1
Ague	13	Rheumatic ophthalmia	2
Excessive debility from starva-		Strumous disease	2
tion	17	Sprains	1
Inflammation of Lungs	2	Fractures	4
Asthma	10	Pregnant	30
Epilepsy	4		

The return of the different callings of the individuals seeking for
the shelter of the Refuges are equally curious and worthy of study.
These, however, I shall reserve for my next letter, as by comparing
the returns for each year since the opening of the institutions—
now thirty years ago—we shall be enabled to arrive at almost an
historical account of the distress of the different trades since the
year 1820. These tables I am now preparing from the valuable
yearly Reports of the Society—one of the most deserving among
all our charitable institutions—and one which, especially at this
bitter season, calls for the support of all those who would give
a meal and a bed to such as are too poor to have either.

I will now proceed to a description of the Refuge itself.

The only refuge for the houseless now open, which is really a
home for the homeless, is that in Playhouse-yard, Cripplegate.
The doors open into a narrow by-street, and the neighbourhood
needs no other announcement that the establishment is open for
the reception of the houseless, than the assembly of a crowd of
ragged shivering people, certain to be seen on the night of open-

ing, as if they knew by instinct where they might be housed under a warm and comfortable roof. The crowd gathers in Playhouse-yard, and many among them look sad and weary enough. Many of the women carry infants at the breast, and have children by their sides holding by their gowns. The cries of these, and the wrangling of the hungry crowds for their places, is indeed disheartening to hear. The only sounds of merriment come from the boys—the "errand boys," as they call themselves—whom even starvation cannot make sorrowful for two hours together. The little struggle that there usually is among the applicants is not for a rush when the doors are opened, but for what they call the "front rank." They are made to stand clear of the footpath, and when five o'clock— the hour of admission—comes, an officer of the Refuge steps out, and quietly, by a motion of his hand or a touch on the shoulder, sends in about 150 men and boys, and about 50 women and girls. He knows the great majority of those who have tickets which entitle them to one or two nights further lodging (the tickets are generally for three nights), and these are commonly in the foremost rank. The number thus admitted show themselves more or less at home. Some are quiet and abashed, but some proceed briskly, and in a business-like way, to the first process—to wash themselves. This is done in two large vessels, in what may be called the hall or vestibule of the building. A man keeps pumping fresh water into the vessels as fast as that used is drained off, and soap and clean towels are supplied when thought necessary—the clean towels, which are long and attached to rollers, soon becoming, in truth, exceedingly dirty. I noticed some little contention—whether to show an anxiety to conform to the rules of the Refuge, or to hurry through a disagreeable but inevitable task, or really for the comfort of ablution, I will not pretend to determine—but there was some little contention for the first turn among the young men at the washing. To look down upon them from the main staircase, as I did, was to survey a very motley scene. There they were—the shirtless, the shoeless, the coatless, the unshaven, the uncouth, aye and the decent and respectable. There were men from every part of the United Kingdom, with a coloured man or two, a few seamen, navigators, agricultural labourers, and artisans. There were no foreigners on the nights that I was there, and in the returns of those admitted there will not be found one Jew. It is possible that Jews may be entered under the heads of "Germans" or "Poles"—I mean foreign Jews—but on my visits I did not see so much as any near approach to the Hebrew physiognomy. To attempt to give an account of anything like a prevailing garb among these men is impossible, unless I described it as—rags. As they were washing, or waiting for a wash, there was some stir, and a loud buzz of talk, in which "the brogue" strongly predominated. There was some little fun, too, as there must be where a crowd of many youths is assembled. One in a ragged coarse striped shirt, exclaimed, as he shoved along, "By your leave, gentlemen," with a significant emphasis on his "gentlemen." Another man said to his neighbour, "The bread's fine, Joe, but the sleep—isn't *that* plummy?" Some few, I say, seemed merry enough, but that is easily accounted for. Their present object was attained, and your real professional vagabond is happy when it *is* attained—for a forgetfulness of the past, or an indifference to it, and a recklessness as to the future, are the primary elements of a vagrant's enjoyment. Those who had tickets were of course subjected to no further examination, unless by the surgeon subsequently; but all the new admissions—and the officers kept admitting fresh batches as they were instructed—were not passed before a rigid examination, when a ticket for three nights was given to each fresh applicant. On the right hand, as you enter the building, is the office. The assistant-superintendent sits before a large ledger, in which he enters every name and description. His questions to every fresh candidate are: —"Your name? how old are you? what trade? how do you live? (if no trade), where did you sleep last night? to what parish do you belong?" In order to answer these questions, each applicant for admission stands before the door of the office, a portion of the upper division of the door being thrown open. Whilst I was present, there was among a portion of the male applicants but little hesitation in answering the inquiries glibly and promptly. Others answered reluctantly. The answers of some of the boys, especially the Irish boys, were curious: "Where did you sleep last night?" "Well, then, sir, I slept walking about the streets all night, and very cowld it was, sir." Another lad was asked, after he had stated his name and age, how he lived, "I beg, or do anything," he answered. "What's your parish?" "Ireland." (Several pronounced their parish to be the County Corruk.) "Have you a father here?" "He died before we left Ireland." "How did you get here, then?" "I came with my mother." "Well, and where's she?" "She died after we came to England." So the child had the streets for a stepmother.

Some of the women were as glib and systematic in their answers as the men and boys. Others were much abashed. Among the glib-tongued women there seemed no shamefacedness. There was, moreover, an absence of all the characteristics which are considered part of modesty and refinement. For instance, some of the women were good-looking; and when asked how old they were, they answered at once, and, judging by their appearance, never understated their years. Many I should have pronounced younger than they stated. Vanity, even with silliness and prettiness, does not seem to exist in their utter destitution. Some of the women admitted here, however, have acquitted themselves well when provided (through charitable institutions) with situations. The absence of shame which I have remarked upon is the more notable because these women were questioned by men, with other men standing by.

These processes observed (and the women have a place for their ablutions after the same fashion as the men), the applicants admitted enter their several wards. The women's ward is at the top of the building. It supplies accommodation, or berths, for 95 women in an apartment thirty-five yards in length and six in width. At one corner of this long chamber a few steps lead down into what is called "the nursery," which has 30 berths. Most of these berths may be described as double; being large enough to accommodate a mother and her children. The children when I saw them were gambolling about in some of the berths, as merry as children elsewhere, or, perhaps, merrier, for they were experiencing the unwanted luxuries of warmth and food. The matron can supply these women and their children with gruel at her discretion, and it appeared to be freely given. Some who had children seemed the best of all there in point of physiognomy. They had not, generally, the stolid, stupid, indifferent, or shameless look of many of the other women; it was as though the motherly feeling had somewhat humanized them. Some of the better sort of women spoke so low as to be hardly audible. Among them were, indeed, many very decent looking females.

The men's wards are the Chapel Ward (for the better sort of persons), containing 90 berths, one line being ranged two berths deep; the Lower Ward, containing 120 berths; the Boys' Ward, containing 60 berths; and the Straw Loft, 40. There is a walk alongside the berths in each ward. What is called the Boys' Ward is not confined to boys; it used to be so, but they were found so noisy that they could no longer be allowed a separate apartment. They are now scattered through the several wards with the men— the officers arranging them, and varying the arrangements as they consider best. Before there can be any retirement to rest, each man, woman, and child must be examined by a surgeon. Whilst I was present a young assistant conducted the investigation in a careful, yet kindly and gentlemanly manner—indeed, I was much struck with the sympathy and gentleness he displayed; and it was evident, from the respect of the people, that kindness and consideration are the very qualities to impress and control the class he has to deal with. All afflicted with cutaneous disorders (and there were but five men so afflicted) were lodged apart from the others. Bronchitis and rheumatism are the prevalent disorders, occasioned by their exposure to the weather, and their frequent insufficiency of food. Ninety per cent. of them I was told by Mr. Gay, the intelligent surgeon of the establishment, might have coughs at some periods, but of that they thought nothing. Women advanced in pregnancy, and men with any serious (especially any infectious) ailment, are not permitted to sleep in the Refuge; but the institution, if they have been admitted, finds them lodgings elsewhere.

Each person admitted receives in the evening half a pound of the best bread. Every child has the same allowance. If a woman be admitted with four children, she receives 2½lbs. of bread—a half-pound for every one, no matter if one be at the breast, as is not unfrequently the case. The same quantity of bread is given in the morning, with water *ad libitum,* evening and morning. In the night that I was present, 430 were admitted, and consequently (including the evening and morning allowances) 430lbs. of bread were disposed of. On Sundays, when divine service is celebrated by a clergyman of the Church of England, three half-pounds of bread and 3 oz. of cheese are distributed to each inmate, children and babies included. I witnessed a number of young men eating the bread administered to them. They took it with a keen appetite; nothing was heard among them but the champing of the teeth, as they chewed large mouthfuls of the food.

The berths, both in the men's and women's wards, are on the ground, and divided one from another only by a wooden partition about a foot high; a similar partition is at the head and feet; so that in all the wards it looks as if there were a series of coffins arranged in long catacombs. This burial-like aspect is the more apparent when the inmates are all asleep, as they were, with the rarest exceptions, when I walked round at ten o'clock at night. Each sleeper has for covering a large basil (dressed sheepskin), such as cobblers use for aprons. As they lie in long rows, in the most profound repose, with these dark brown wrappers about them, they present the uniform look and arrangement of a long line of mummies. Each bed in the coffin or trough-like divisions is made of waterproof cloth, stuffed with hay, made so as to be easily cleaned. It is soft and pleasant to the touch. Formerly the beds were plain straw, but the present plan has been in use for seven years. In this Refuge only three men have died since it was established, thirty years ago. One fell dead at the sink-stone while washing himself; the other two were found dead in their berths during the prevalence of the cholera.

Every part of the building was most scrupulously clean. On the first night of the opening, the matron selects, from the women who have sought an asylum there, three, who are engaged for the season to do the household work. This is done during the day when the inmates are absent. All must leave by eight in the morning, the doors being open for their departure at five, in case any wish to quit early—as some do for the chance of a job at Coventgarden, Farringdon, or any of the early markets. The three women helpers receive 7s. a week each, the half of that sum being paid them in money every Saturday, and the other half being retained and given to each of them, in a round sum on her departure at the closing of the Refuge. The premises in which this accommodation to the houseless is now supplied were formerly a hat manufactory on a large scale; but the lath and plaster of the ceilings, and the partitions, have been removed, so that what was a suite of apartments on one floor now forms a long ward. The rafters of the ceilings are minutely whitewashed, as are the upright beams used in the construction of the several rooms before the place was converted to its present charitable end. These now are in the nature of pillars, and add to the catacomb-like aspect that I have spoken of. In different parts of each ward are very large grates, in which bright fires are kept glowing and crackling; and as these are lighted some time before the hour of opening, the place has a warm and cosy feel, very grateful to those who have encountered the cold air all the day, and perhaps all the night before.

In order to arrive at a correct estimate as to the really poor and homeless availing themselves of the establishment—and to afford nightly shelter to whom the Refuge was originally instituted by its benevolent founder, Mr. Hick, the City mace-bearer—I consulted with the Superintendent as to the class of persons he found most generally seeking shelter there. These were—among the men—mostly labourers out of work—agricultural, railway, and dock—distressed artisans, chiefly carpenters and painters—seamen, either cast away or without their registry tickets—broken-down tradesmen—clerks, shopmen, and errand-boys, who either through illness or misfortune had been deprived of their situations—and, above all, Irish immigrants, who had been starved out of their own country.

These he considered the really deserving portion of the inmates for whom the institution was designed. Among the females, the better and largest class of poor were needlewomen, servants, charwomen, gardenwomen, sellers of laces in the street, and occasionally a beggar-woman. Under his guidance I selected such as appeared the most meritorious among the classes he had enumerated, and now subjoin the statements of a portion of the number, reserving the rest for my next communication.

The first of the homeless that I saw was a railway navigator. He was a fine, stout-built fellow, with a fresh-coloured, open countenance and flaxen hair—indeed, altogether a splendid specimen of the Saxon labourer. He was habited in a short blue smock-frock, yellow in parts with clay, and he wore the heavy high lace-up boots so characteristic of the tribe. These were burst, and almost soleless with long wear.

The poor fellow told the old story of the labourer compelled to squander his earnings at the public-house of his master: —

"I have been a navvy for about eighteen years. The first work that I done was on the Manchester and Liverpool. I was a lad then. I used to grease the railway waggons, and got about 1s. 6d. a day. Then we had a tommy-shop, and we had to go there to get our bit of victuals, and they used to charge us an extra price. The next place I had after that was on the London and Brummagem. There I went as horse driver, and had 2s. 6d. a day. Things was dear then, and at the tommy-shop they was much dearer, for there was tommy-shops on every line then, and indeed every contractor and every sub-contractor had his shop, that he forced his men to deal at, or else he wouldn't have them in his employ. At the tommy-shop we was charged half as much again as we should have had to pay elsewhere; and it's the same now wherever these tommy-shops is. What the contractors you see can't make out of the Company they fleeces out of the men. Well, sir, I worked on that line through all the different contracts till it was finished; sometimes I was digging, sometimes shovelling. I was mostly at work at open cuttings. All this time I was getting from 2s. 6d. to 3s. and 3s. 6d. a day; that was the top price, and if I'd had the ready money to lay out myself I could have done pretty well, and maybe have put a penny or two by against a rainy day. But the tommy-shop and the lodging-house took it all out of us. You see the tommy-shop found us in beer, and they would let us drink away all our earnings there if we pleased, and when pay time came we should have nothing to take. If we didn't drink and eat at the tommy-shop, we should have no work. Of an evening we went to the tommy-shop after the drink, and they'd keep drawing beer for us there so long as we'd have anything coming to us next pay day (we were paid every fortnight, and sometimes every month), and when we had drunk away all that would be coming to us, why they'd turn us out. The contractor who keeps these tommy-shops is generally a gentleman, a man of great property, who takes some four, five, or seven lengths to do. Well, with such goings on, in course there wasn't no chance in the world for us to save a half-penny. We had a sick fund among ourselves, but our masters never cared nothing about us further than what they could get out of us at their tommy-shops. They was never satisfied if a man didn't spend all his money with them; if we had a penny to take at the month's end they didn't like it, and now the half of us has to walk about and starve, or beg, or go to the union. After I left the Brummagem line I went on to the Great Western. I went to work at Maidenhead. There it was on the same system and on the same rules—the poor man being fleeced and made drunk by his master. Sometimes the contractor would let the work out to some sub-contractor, and he, after the men had worked for a month, would run away, and we should never see the colour of his money. After the Great Western I went into Lancashire, on the Manchester and Oldham branch. I started there to work at nights, and there I worked a month for the contractors, when they went bankrupt, and we never received a farthing but what we had got out of the tommy-shop. Well, I came away from there and got on to the London and Brighton, and I worked all up and down there, the tommy-shop and imposition was wherever we went. Well, from there I went on to the London and Dover. It was month's payments on that. There, too, I worked for a month, when the sub-contractor runned away with all the men's moneys—£900, sir, it were calculated. After that another party took it, and it was the same all up and down—the tommy-shop, and beer as much as we liked on credit. Then I went on to the London and Cambridge, and there it was the same story over and over again. Just about this time railway work began to get slack. Before that there was plenty of work for all railroad men. Hands was very scarce, and masters would give us a quart of beer to go to work; but when all the main lines were done, railway work got very slack, and then farmer's work was slack too, and you see that made things worse for the navvies, for all came to look for employment on the railroads. This is about seven years ago. After that some more fresh lines started throughout Lancashire and Yorkshire, and trade being bad in them parts all the weavers applied for work on the railways, so the regular navvies had a hard time of it then. But we managed to get on somehow—kept lingering on—till about three years agone, when trade got a little bit better. That was about the time when things was very dear, and our wages was rose to 3s. 6d. a day—they'd been only 2s. 6d. and 3s. before that; and we did much better when our pay was increased, because we had the ready money then, and there was no tommy-shops that summer, for the company wouldn't have them on that line. At the end of that year the work was all stopped on account of the Chartist rising, and then there was hundreds of men walking about begging their bread from door to door, with nothing to do. After this—that's two years ago the back-end of this year—I went to work on the London and York. Here we had only 2s. 9d. a day, and we had only four days' work in the week to do bedsides; and then there was a tommy-shop, where we were forced to get our victuals and drink—so you see we were very bad off then. I stopped on this line (for work was very scarce, and I thought myself lucky to have any) till last spring. Then all the work on it stopped, and I dare say 2,000 men were thrown out of employ in one day. They were all starving—the heap of them— or next door to it. I went away from there, over to the Brummagem and Beechley branch line. But there I found things almost as bad as what I left before. Big, strong, able-bodied men were working for 1s. 8d. a day, and from that to 2s.—that was the top price—for wages had come down, you see, about one-half, and little or no work to do at that price; and tommy-shop and beer, sir, as before, out of the little we did get. The great cause of our wages being cut down was through the work being so slack in the country—everybody was flocking to them parts for employment, and the contractors, seeing a quantity of men walking backwards and forwards, dropped the wages; if one man wouldn't work at the price, there was hundreds ready to do it. Besides, provisions was very cheap, and the contractors knew we could live on less, and do their work quite as well. Whenever provisions goes down, our wages does too; but when they goes up, the contractors is very slow in rising them. You see, when they find so many men walking about without work, the masters have got the chance of the poor man. Three year agone this last winter—I think it was '46—provisions was high and wages was good, and in the summer of the very same year food got cheap again, and our wages dropped from 3s. 6d. to 3s. and 2s. 9d. The fall in our wages took place immediately the food got cheaper. The contractors said, as we could live for less we must do the work for less. I left the Brummagem and Beechley line about two months the Christmas before last, and then I came to Copenhagen-fields, on the London and York—the London end, sir—and there I was till last March, when we were all paid off, about sixty on us; and I went back to Barnet, and there I worked till the last seven weeks, and had 2s. 9d. a day for what, four years ago, I had 3s. 6d. for, and I could only have three or four days' work in the week then. Whilst I was there I hurted my leg, and was laid up a month. I lived all that time on charity—on what the chaps would come and give me. One would give a shilling, another sixpence, another a shilling, just as they could spare it; and poorly they could do that, God knows! I couldn't declare on to the sick fund, because I hadn't no bones broke. Well, when I come to look for work—and that's three weeks agone, when I could get about again—the work was all stopped, and I couldn't get none to do. Then I come to London, and I've looked all about for a job, and I can't find nothing to do. I went to a lodging-house in the Borough, and I sold all my things —shovel and grafting tool and all—to have a meal of food. When all my things was gone I didn't know where to go. One of my mates told me of this Refuge, and I have been here two nights. All I have had to eat since then is the bread night and morning they gives us here. This will be the last night I shall have to stop here, and after that I don't know what I shall do. There's no railway work—that is, there's none to speak of, seeing the thousands of men that's walking about with nothing to do, and not knowing where to lay their heads. If I could get any interest I should like to go away as an emigrant. I shouldn't like to be sent out of my native country as a rogue and a vagabone; but I'm tired of stopping here, and if I can't get away, why I must go home and go to the parish, and its hard for a young man that's willing and able like me to work, and be forced to want because he can't get it. I know there is thousands—thousands, sir, like I am—I know there is, in the very same condition as I am at this moment, yes I know there is." This he said with great feeling and emphasis. "We are all starving. We are all willing to work, but it ain't to be had. This country is getting very bad for labour; it's so overrun with Irish that the Englishman hasn't a chance in his own land to live. Ever since I was nine years old I've got my own living, but now I'm dead beat, though I'm only twenty-eight next August."

The next man to whom I spoke was tall and hale-looking, except that his features were pinched, and his eyes had a dull lack-lustre look, common to men suffering from cold and hunger. His dress

was a coarse jacket, fustian trousers, and coarse, hard-worn shoes.
He spoke without any very provincial accent: —

"I am now 48, and have been a farm labourer all my life. I am
a single man. When I was a boy of 12, I was put to dig, or see
after the birds, or break clods, or anything, on a farm, at Croland,
in Lincolnshire. I had very little school before that, and can neither
read nor write. I was then living with my parents, poor people,
who worked on the land whenever they could get a day's work.
We had to live very hard, but at hay and harvest times we had
meat, and lived better. I had 3s. a week as a boy. When I grew
up to fourteen I left home. I thought my father didn't use me
well; perhaps it was my own fault. I might have been a bad boy;
but he was severe when he did begin with me, though he was
generally quiet. When his passion was up there was no bearing it.
Anyhow, I started into the world at fourteen to do the best I
could for myself, to make my fortune if I could. Since then I have
had work in all sort of counties (Midland counties principally).
When a boy I got employment readily enough at bird-scaring, or
hay-making, but I soon grew up and took a man's place very early,
and I could then do any kind of farmer's work except ploughing
or seeding. They have men on purpose for that. Farm work was
far better in my younger days than it is now. For a week, when
hired by the day, I never get more than 15s., regular work. For
taken work [by the job], I have made as much as 42s. in a week;
that is, in reaping and mowing, when I could drop on such jobs
in a difficult season, when the weather was uncertain. I talk of
good times. The last good job I had was three years ago, come
next summer. Now I should be glad to get 9s. a week constant
work—anything but what I'm doing now. As I went about from
place to place, working for farmers, I generally lodged at the
shepherds' houses, or at some labourer's. I never was in a lodging-
house when I was in work—only, when money runs low, one must
have shelter. At some lodging-houses I've had a good feather bed;
others of them are bad enough—the best, I think, are in Norfolk.
I have saved a bit of money several times—indeed, year after year,
until the last three or four years; but what I saved in the summer,
went in the winter. The most that ever I had at once was £10,
one summer, a good many years ago, and that went in the winter.
In some summers I could save nothing. It's how the season comes.
I never cared for drink. I've done middling till these last two
seasons. My health was good, to be sure; but when a man's in
health his appetite is good also; and when I'm at regular work I
don't eat half so much as when I am knocking about idle and

get hold of a meal. I often have to make up for three or four days then. The last job I had was six weeks before Christmas, at Boston, in Lincolnshire. I couldn't make 1s. 6d. a day on account of the weather. I had 13s., however, to start with, and I went on the road, not standing for a straight road, but going where I heard there was a chance of a job, up or down anywhere, here or there, but there was always the same answer, 'Nobody wanted—no work for their own constant men.' I was so beat out as soon as my money was done, and it lasted ten days, that I parted with my things one by one. First my waistcoat, then my stockings (three pair of them), then three shirts. I got 2s. 4d. for three shirts, and 6d. a pair for my stockings. My clothes were done, and I parted with my pocket-knife for 2d., and with my 'bacco-box for 1½d. After I left Boston I got into Leicestershire, and was at Cambridge, and Wisbeach, and Lynn, and Norwich, and I heard of a job among brickmakers at Low Easthrop, in Suffolk, but it was no go. The weather was against it too. It was when the snow set in. And then I thought I would come to London, as God in his goodness might send me something to do. I never meant anything slinking. I'm only happy when I'm at work, but here I am destitute. Some days as I walked up I had nothing to eat. At others I got half-pennies or pennies from men like myself that I saw at work. I've given shillings away that way myself at times. Sometimes I had to take to the road, but I'm a very poor beggar. When I got to London I was a stranger, and lodged here the first night—that's a week ago. A policeman sent me here. I've tried every day to get work—labouring work for builders, or about manure carts, or anything like that, as there's no farming in London, but got none; so but for this place I had starved. When this place is closed I must tramp into the country. There are very many farm labourers now going from farm to farm and town to town to seek work—more than ever I saw before. I don't know that the regular farm work-men come so much to London. As I travelled up from Suffolk 'I lay rough' often enough. I got into stables or any places. Such places as this save many a man's life. It's saved mine, for I might have been found dead in the street, as I didn't know where to go.'' This man appeared to be a very decent character.

The large number of Irish found among the inmates of these establishments is one of the peculiar features of the Refuges. By the returns above given, it will be seen that they constitute more than one-half of the total applicants. Such being the fact, I selected two from among the more decent, as types of the better class of immigrants, and subjoin their narratives: —

One of these men had a half-shrewd, half-stolid look, and was clad in very dirty fustian. His beard was some days old, and he looked ill-fed and wretched. His children, for he had two boys with him, ten and twelve years old, were shoeless—their white skins being a contrast to their dirty dress, as the former appeared through the holes in their jackets. They looked on with a sort of vacant wonder, motionless, and without a word. The father said, "I've been knocking about in England these four years, from place to place. I'm telling you the truth, sir [this he often repeated]. I came here to betther myself, to knock out something betther, but I wish to God I'd been buried before I buried my wife and children. I do indeed, sir. I was a labourer in Ireland, working in farms and gardens for anybody. My wages warn't much—only 3s. a week and my datal house (that is a house rent-free), and two meals of victuals a day, sometime 'taties and milk for meals, and sometimes 'taties and fish, and sometimes—aye, often—'taties and nothing. My wife and me, and four children, came from Cork—it was in the county Cork I lived—to Wales. I don't know the name of the part—they've such queer names there—sure, then, they have, sir. It cost me half-a-crown apiece for the six of us. I raised the money partly by digging up a garden I had, and selling what stuff there was; and the rest was made up by the farmers in the neighbourhood, giving their 3d. or 6d. apiece to me, so that I might lave. I wasn't on the poor-law rate—but I soon might. When I got to Wales I had only 6d. lift. I went to the workhouse for a night's lodging, to be sure—what else? I started next day for London with my wife and children, begging as we came, and going from workhouse to workhouse, and very badly we got along. It finished a fortnight to get to London. When we got to London (that's about four years agone) we got work at peas picking, my wife and me, in the gardens about. That is for the summer—in the winter we sold oranges in the streets while she lived; and we had nothing from the parishes. I can't complain of the living till this time, sir. It was better than I knew in Ireland. I don't know what we got, she managed all. Last autumn we went into the hop county, to Ellis's farm. I don't know the town nearest; and there my wife and two children died of the cholera at the farm. The three of them weren't a week ill. The parish kept them and buried them. Since that I've been worse off than ever, and will always be worse off than ever, because I've lost a good wife. Since her death I jobbed about in the country, living very bare, me and the children, until the frost came, and then we came to London. I was knocking about for a fortnight, and begged a little; but sorrow a much I got by that. How did I know of this place? Musha, all the neighbours know about it." The younger man, who was tall and gaunt, more intelligent than the other, and less squalid in his appearance, said: —"I have been in England two years last August. I came to better my living. I tilled a portion of land in Ireland. It was £30 a year rent, and forty acres. That was in the county Cork, parish of Kilmeen. I rented the land of a middleman, and he was very severe. My family and I couldn't live under him. I had a wife and three children. We all came to England, from Cork to Bristol. I kept a little substance back to pay my way to England. The voyage cost 25s. From Bristol I went to Cardiff, as I got no work at Bristol. At Cardiff I worked on the railway, at 2s. 6d. a day. I did well for a couple of months; I would like to continue at that, or at 1s. a day here, better than Ireland these times. I worked in Cardiff town with a bricklayer, after I'd done on the railway, at 12s. a week. I next year had a twelve-month's work, on and off, with a farmer near Bristol, at 10s. a week. I was still plenty comfortable. I made for London at the hay-harvest. I had a little money to start with, but I got no hay-work, only a trifle of work at the docks. In corn-harvest, near Brighton, I worked for six weeks, making 10s. an acre for cutting wheat by piece-work, and 7s. for oats, and 2s. for any day's work. I made £4 altogether. I got back to London with 40s. I could get no work at all, but five days' work at a stoneyard at 1s. a day. I sold a few things in the streets—oranges and apples—so did my wife. It helped to keep us. All was gone at last, so I got in here with one child (a fine boy)—my wife's got three with her. She's in a lodging in Gray's-inn-lane. She's starving, I'm afraid; but she wished me to come here with the child, as I could do nothing at night-time. I don't know how many came over about the time I did. The gentry give poor men money, or did give it to them, to send them over here to free the land from its expenses."

To complete the picture of this Irish destitution, I add the following: —

One wretched creature had come to the Refuge with her four children. She herself was habited in a large blue cloth cloak, her toes were through the end of her shoes, and her gown clung tight to her limbs, telling that she was utterly destitute of under-clothing. In her arms she carried an infant, round which were wound some old woollen rags. As the little thing sucked at its mother's breast it breathed so hard that it needed no words to tell one of its long exposure to the cold. Though the mother was half-clad, still there was the little bit of clean net inside the old rusty straw bonnet. The children were respectively eleven, six, and three years old. The eldest (a good-looking grey-eyed girl who stood with her forefinger in her mouth, half simple) was covered with a tattered plaid shawl. This, at her mother's bidding, she drew from her shoulder with an ostentation of poverty, to show that what had before appeared a gown beneath, was nothing more than a bombasin petticoat. On her feet were a pair of women's old fashionable shoes, tied on with string. These had been given in charity to her by a servant, a week back. The next child, a boy, laughed as I looked at him, and seemed, though only six years old, to have been made prematurely "knowing" by his early street education. He put out his foot as he saw my eye glance downward to his shoes, to show me that he had one boot and one shoe on. He was clad in all kinds of rags, and held in his hand a faded velvet cap. The youngest boy was almost a dwarf. He was three years old, but so stunted that he seemed scarce half that age: —

"I come from the county of Corruk—the worst and the poorest part of it—yes, indeed, sir, it is," said the woman, "and the gentlemen know that I do. When I had it to do, I manufactured at flax and wool. I knit and sewed, to be sure I did—but God Almighty was plazed to deprive me of it. It was there I was married. My husband was a miner. Distress and want, and hunger and poverty, nothing else drove us to this counthry. It was the will of God— glory be to his holy and blessed name—to fail the taties. To be sure I couldn't dig one out of the ground not fit to ate. We lived on taties and milk and fish and iggs. We used to have hins thin. And the mining failed too, and the captains came over here—yes to be sure, for here they lived, sir. Yes, sir, indeed, and I could tell you that I used to be eight days—yes, that I used, before I could get one ha'porth to ate—barrin the wather I boiled and drank to keep the life in mysilf and childer. It was Doctor O'Donovan that paid for our passage. When he see all the hunger, and distress, and want— yes, indeed, sir, that I went through— he gave a letther to the stame packet office, and then they brought me and my three childer over. It was here that this baby was borrun. My husband was here before me, he was about seven or eight months. He hadn't sent me any money, for he couldn't a pinny. He wrote home to see if I lived, for he didn't think I lived; and then I showed the letther to Doctor O'Donovan. My husband niver got a day's work since he came over; indeed, he couldn't give the childer their breakfast the next morning after they came. I came to London-bridge, and met my husband there. Well, indeed, that is nearly three years agone. Oh, then I had nothing to do since but what little we done at the harvest. It was tin weeks before Christmas that I came over, and I don't know what month it was, for I don't read or write, you know. Oh. then, indeed, we had to live by bigging from thin up to harvest time. I had to big for him sooner than let him die with the hunger. He didn't do any work, but he'd be glad of a sixpence he'd earn. He'd rather have it that way than if he bigged tin pound—it would be more plisure. Never a day's work could he get; and many beside him. Oh, Lord, there *is* many, sir. He never does anything but at the harvest-time, and thin he works at raping the corrun. I know nothing else that he does; and I bind the shaves afther him. Why, indeed, we get work thin for about a fortnight or three weeks—it don't howld a month. Oh no, sir, no; how could my children do anything—but as fast as we'd earn it to ate it. I declare I don't know how much we'd make a week then. They got only 3s. an acre last year for it. I declare I don't know what we made; but whatever we had, we hadn't 2s. laving it. Oh, indeed, I had to big all the rist of my time. My husband doesn't big I'll tell you the thruth——the thruth is the bist. When he has e'er a pinny he tries to sell a handful of oranges; and, indeed, he had to lave off silling, for he couldn't buy half a hundred of 'em for to sill back. He done pritty well when the limons were in sason, he did, sir; but there's so many silling oranges he can't sell one of them. Now he does nothing, for he has nothing to reach half a hundred of limons with, and that isn't much. When I gits a pinny to pay for the lodgings, then we lodges and sleeps together; but when I can't, I must go about this way with my childer. When I go out bigging he remains at home in the lodging-house; he has nothing else to do, sir. I always go out with my childer; sure I couldn't look at 'em die with hunger. Where's the use of laving them with the husband, what has he to give them? Indeed if I had left them last night with him he couldn't have give them as much as they'd put in their mouth onced. Indeed I take them out in the cowld to big with me to get a bit of victuals for 'em sure. God knows I can't hilp it—he knows I can't—glory be to his holy name. Indeed I have a part of the brid I got here last night to carry to my poor husband, for I know he wanted it. Oh, if I'm to go to the gallows I'm telling you the thruth. Oh, to be sure, yes, sir, there's many a one would give a bit to the childer when they wouldn't to me—sure the world knows that—and may be the childer will get ha'pence, and that will pay my lodging or buy a loaf of brid for 'em. Oh, sir, to be sure you know I'd get more with all my little childer out than I would with one, and that's the rason indeed. Wes, indeed, that's why I take them out. Oh, then, that's what you want to know. Why, there's some people wouldn't believe I'd have so many. May be some days I wouldn't get a pinny, and may be I'd get a shilling. I met a gentleman the other day that gave me a shilling together. I'd all my childer out with me thin. The sister carries the little fellow on her back, no more would he stop afther me nayther. Only twice I've left him at home. On thin, indeed, he do cry with the cowld, and often again with the hunger, and some of the people says to me it's myself that makes him cry, but then indeed it ain't. May be I've no home to give my husband, may be it's at some union he slept last night. My husband niver goes bigging—he didn't, sir, I won't tell a lie—he didn't, indeed, but he sinds me out in the cowld and in the wit, and in the hate too, but then he can't hilp it. He's the best man that iver put a hat on his hid, and the kindest." She persisted in asseverating this, being apparently totally incapable of perceiving the inhumanity of her husband's conduct. "He don't force me, he don't indeed, but he sits idle at home while I go out. Ah, if you knew what I suffers! Oh yes he'd rather work, if I'd got a guinea in gould for him tonight; and yesterday morning he prayed to God Almighty to put something in his way to give him a day's work. I was in prisin onced for bigging. My children was taken away from me and sint to some union. I don't know the name of it. That was the time my husband was silling the limon. He niver came to spake for me when I was going to prisin, and he doesn't know whether I'm in prisin tonight. Ah, I beg your honour's pardon, he would care, but he can't hilp me. I thought I'd ind my life in the prisin, for I wouldn't be allowed to spake a word. The poor man, my husband, can't hilp it. He was niver counted lazy in his counthry; but God Almighty plazed to deprive him of his work, and what can he do?"

The next was a rather tall and well-spoken woman of 58:—"When I was young," she said, "I used to go out to day's works, or charing, and sometimes as a laundress. I went charing until five years ago, sometimes doing middling, often very badly, when I burst a bloodvessel in lifting a weight—a pail of water to fill a copper. I fell down all at once, and bled at the ears and nose. I was taken to St. Bartholomew's, and was there four months. When I came out I took to sell things in the street. I could do nothing else. I have no friends in London—none in the world. Sometimes I picked up a living by selling laces and iron-holders and memorandum-books in the City. I made the memorandum-books myself—penny books; the pincushions I made myself.

I never had anything from my parish, or rather my husband's—that's Bristol. He was a bricklayer, but I chared when he was out of work. He died 18 years ago. I was known by ladies and others in the City, who would sometimes give me a sixpence for a lace. I was working two months back—it was the general thanksgiving day—when I was working at a fishmonger's in Gresham-street, and fell down the cellar stairs and broke my arm. I was again three weeks in Bartholomew's. I have been destitute ever since. I have made away with everything. A little quilt is all I have left, and that would have gone last night if I hadn't got in here."

The poor woman whom I next accosted was a widow (her husband having died on the 1st of June last). She had altogether what I may call a faded look; even her widow's cap was limp and flat, and her look was miserably subdued. She said—"My husband was a journeyman shoemaker. Sometimes he would earn 20s. a week; but we were badly off, for he drank. But he did not ill-use me—not much. During his last illness we raised £5, on a raffle for a silk-handkerchief among the shoemakers, and 10s. from the Mendicity Society, and a few shillings from the clergyman of the parish. The trade buried him. I didn't get 1s. as his widow—only £5 to bury him; but there was arrears of rent to pay, and about a month after his death I hadn't a farthing, and I took the cholera, and was eight days in St. Bartholomew's, the parish officers sending me there in a cab. I lived in furnished lodgings before that, and had nothing to call my own, when I had pawned my black for my husband. When I got out I helped a neighbour at shoe-binding. One time I have earned 15s. a week at shoe-binding for ————, Regent-street. Now I could only earn 5s., with full work. I have seldom earned 3s. of late weeks. I had to leave my neighbour, because I felt that I was a burthen and was imposing upon her. I then had shelter with a young woman I once lodged with, but I couldn't stay there any longer. She was poor, and had nothing for me to do. So, on Saturday last, I had no work, no money, no friends, and I thought I would try and get in here, as another poor woman had done. Here I've had a shelter."

A pretty, pleasant-spoken young woman, very tidy in her poor attire, which was an old cloak wrapped close round her, to cover her scanty dress, gave me the following statement very modestly: — "I am 22; my mother died six years ago; my father I never knew, for I'm an unlawful child. My mother had a small income from my father, and kept me at school. I can't even guess who my father was. I am an only child. I was taken from school to wait upon my mother; very kind indeed she was to me, but she died in three weeks after I came from school. She'd been in a consumption for six years; she fretted sadly about me. She never told me I was an unlawful child. My aunt, my mother's sister, told me one day afterwards. My mother always said my father lived in the country. I loved my mother, so I seldom spoke of my father, for she would say, 'I don't wish to hear about him.' There was nothing for me at my mother's death, so I put myself to learn fancy-box making, for grocers and pastry-cooks, for their sweetmeats, and for scents. My aunt assisted me. She is now poor, and a widow. I could never earn more than 3s. or 4s. a week at box-making, the pay is so bad. I lived this way for four or five years, lodging with my aunt, and giving her all I earned, and she kept me for it. I then went to learn the mackintosh-coat making. I went into lodgings, my aunt being unable to help me any longer, as at my uncle's death she could only keep a room for herself and children. She makes pill-boxes. I could earn at the mackintoshes only 4s. a week and my tea, when in full work, and oft enough when work was bad I earned only 2s. 6d. It was 8d. a day and my tea. I parted with a good box of clothes to keep myself; first one bit of dress went and another. I was exposed to many a temptation, but I have kept my character, I am thankful to say. On Monday night, I was in the streets all night—I hardly know in what part, I was so miserable—having no place to put my head in, and frightened to death almost. I couldn't pay my lodgings, and so lost them—I was locked out. I went to the station-house and asked to sit there just for a shelter, but the policemen said it was no place for me as I was not guilty of any offence; they could do nothing for me; they were all very civil. I walked the streets all that cold night. I feel the cold of that night in my limbs still. I thought it never would be over. I wasn't exposed to any insults. I had to walk about all Tuesday, without a bite either Monday or Tuesday. On Tuesday evening I got admitted into this place, and was very thankful. Next day I tried for work, but got none. I had a cup of tea from my aunt to live on that day." This girl wished to get into the parish, in order to be sent out as an emigrant, or anything of that kind; but her illegitimacy was a bar, as no settlement could be proved.

It was not difficult to see, by the looks of the poor woman whom I next addressed, the distress and privation she had endured. Her eyes were full of tears, and there was a plaintiveness in her voice that was most touching. She was clad in rusty black, and had a black straw bonnet with a few old crape flowers in it; but still in all her poverty there was a neatness in her appearance that told she was unused to such abject misery as had now come upon her. Hers was indeed a wretched story—the victim of her husband's ill-treatment and neglect: —"I have been working at needlework ever since the end of August. My husband is living; but he has deserted me, and I don't know where he is at present. He had been a gentleman's servant—but he could attend to a garden; and of late years he had done so. I have been married nine years next April. I never did live happily with him. He drank a very great deal; and when tipsy, he used to beat me sorely. He had been out of work for a long time before he got his last situation, and there he had 18s. a week. He lost his place before that through drink. Oh, sir, perhaps he'd give me all his money at the end of the week, within about 3s.; but then he'd have more than half of it back again—not every week alike, of course; but that was mostly the case—and in particular for the last year and a half, for since then he had been worse. While he was with me I have gone out for a day's charing occasionally, but then I found I was no for'arder at the week's end, so I didn't strive so much as I might have done, for if I earned 2s., he'd be sure to have it from me. I was a servant, before he married me, in a respectable tradesman's family. I lived three years and a half at my master's house out of town, and that was where I fell in with my husband. He was a shopman then. I lived with him for more than eight years, and always acted a wife's part to him. I never drank myself, and was never untrue to him; but he has been too untrue to me, and I have had to suffer for it. I bore all his unkindness until August last, when he treated me so badly—I cannot mention to you how—but he deceived me and injured me in the worst possible manner. I have one child— a boy, seven years old last September; but the boy is with him, and I don't know where. I have striven to find him out, but cannot. When I found out how he had deceived me, we had words, and he then swore he wouldn't come home any more to me, and he has kept to his oath, for I haven't set eyes on him since. My boy was down at a friend's house at Cambridge, and they gave him up to the father without my knowledge. When he went away I had no money in the house. Nothing but a few things—tables and chairs, and a bed—in a room. I kept them as long as I could, but at last they went to find me in food. After he had gone I got a bit of needlework. I worked at the dressmaking and several different kinds of work since he has left me. Then I used to earn about 5s. a week; sometimes not so much. I *have* made only 2s. But lately—that is within the last six weeks—I have earned scarcely nothing. About October last I was obliged to sell my things to pay off my rent and get me something to eat. After that I went to lodge with a person, and there I stopped till very lately, when I had scarce nothing, and couldn't afford to pay my rent. Then I was turned out of there, and I went and made shift with a friend by lying down on the boards beside her children. I lay down with my clothes on. I had nothing to cover me, and no bed under me. They was very poor people. At last my friend said her husband didn't like to have people about in the room where they slept; and, besides, I was so poor I was obliged to beg a bit of what they had, and they was so poor they couldn't afford to spare it to me. They were very good and kind to me so long as they could hold out anyhow, but at last I was obliged to leave and walk about the streets. This I did for two whole nights—last Sunday and Monday nights. It was bitter cold, and freezing sharp. I did go and sit on the stairs of a lodging-house on Monday night, till I was that cold I could scarcely move a limb. On Tuesday night I slept in the Borough. A lady in the street gave me 3d. I asked her if she could give me a ticket to go anywhere. I told her I was in the deepest distress, and she gave me all the halfpence she had, and I thought I would go and have a night's lodging with the money. All these three days and nights I had only a piece of bread to keep down my hunger. Yesterday I was walking about these parts, and I see a lot of people standing about here, and I asked if there was anything being given away. They told me it was the Refuge, or else I shouldn't have known there was such a place. Had I been aware of it I shouldn't have been out in the streets all night as I was on Sunday and Monday. When I leave here—and they'll only keep me for three nights—I don't know what I shall do, for I have so parted with my things that I ain't respectable enough to go after needlework, and they do look at you so. My clothes are all gone to live upon. If I could make myself look a little decent I might perhaps get some work. I wish I could get into service again. I wish I'd never left it indeed, but then I want things. If I can't get my things I must try in such as I have got on, and if I can't get work I shall be obliged to see if the parish will do anything for me, but I'm afraid they won't. I am 33 years old, and very miserable indeed."

Since the opening of the Refuges for the Houseless, in 1820, as many as 189,223 homeless individuals have received "nightly shelter" there—being an average of upwards of 6,000 a year. Some of these have remained three and four nights in the same establishment; so that, altogether, no less than 1,141,558 nights' lodgings have been afforded to the very poor, and 2,778,153 lbs., or nearly 25,000 cwt., of bread distributed among them.

Letter XXVI
Tuesday, January 15, 1850

There is a world of wisdom to be learnt at the Asylums for the Houseless Poor. Those who wish to be taught in this, the severest school of all, should pay a visit to Playhouse-yard, and see the homeless crowds gathered about the Asylum, waiting for the first opening of the doors, with their bare feet—blue and ulcerous with the cold—resting for hours on the ice and snow in the streets, and the bleak stinging wind blowing through their rags. To hear the cries of the hungry, shivering children, and the wrangling of the greedy men, scrambling for a bed and a pound of dry bread, is a thing to haunt one for life. There are four hundred and odd creatures utterly destitute—mothers with infants at their breasts—fathers with boys holding by their side—the friendless—the penniless—the shirtless—shoeless—breadless—homeless; in a word, the very poorest of this the very richest city of the world.

The Asylum for the Houseless is the confluence of the many tides of poverty that at this period of the year flow towards the metropolis. It should be remembered, that there are certain callings which yield a subsistence to those who pursue them, only at particular seasons. Brickmakers, agricultural labourers, garden women, and many such vocations, are labours that admit of being performed only in the summer, when, indeed, the labourer has the fewest wants to satisfy. The privations of such classes, then, come at a period when even the elements conspire to make their destitution more terrible. Hence, restless with want, they wander in hordes across the land, making in vain hope for London, as the great emporium of wealth—the market of the world. But London is as overstocked with hands as every other nook and corner of the country. And then the poor creatures, far away from home and friends, find at last to their cost, that the very privations they were flying from pursue them here with a ten-fold severity. I do not pretend to say that all found within the walls of these asylums are such as I have described—many I know trade upon the sympathy of those who would ease the sufferings of the destitute labourers, and they make their appearance in the metropolis at this especial season. Winter is the beggars' harvest. That there are hundreds of professional vagabonds drawn to London at such a time I am well aware. But with them come the unemployed workmen. We must not therefore confound one with the other, nor let our indignation at the vagabond who will not work check our commiseration for the labourer or artisan who cannot get work to do.

The following table, which has been made up with considerable care and no little trouble from the records and reports of the Asylum for the Houseless Poor, shows the different callings of the parties who have frequented these places of nightly shelter for the last seventeen years. The number of individuals of a particular calling who appear annually at these asylums has been compared with the number of individuals belonging to such calling usually located in London, and the result shows us how many of each are utterly destitute. The average for all London, it will be seen, is one in every 219 individuals. In my next Letter I hope to be able to show the counties which contribute most largely to this yearly convention of poverty.

AN AVERAGE DRAWN FROM THE RETURNS FOR 17 YEARS OF THE OCCUPATIONS OF THE PERSONS ADMITTED INTO THE ASYLUMS FOR THE HOUSELESS POOR.

Factory employment	1 in every	3	individuals.
Hawkers	,,	4	,,
Labourer, agricultural	,,	12	,,
Seamen	,,	12	,,
Charwomen and washerwomen	,,	13	,,
Labourers, general	,,	17	,,
Wadding-makers	,,	35	,,
Smiths and ironfounders	,,	36	,,
Weavers	,,	38	,,
Brickmakers	,,	39	,,
Ropemakers	,,	41	,,
Braziers	,,	55	,,
Paper-makers and stainers	,,	58	,,
Skin-dressers	,,	58	,,
Basketmakers	,,	62	,,
Bricklayers, plasterers, and slaters	,,	62	,,
Gardeners	,,	67	,,
File-cutters	,,	70	,,
Sawyers	,,	73	,,
Turners	,,	74	,,
Wire-workers	,,	75	,,
Cutlers	,,	77	,,
Harness-makers and saddlers	,,	80	,,
Stone-masons	,,	88	,,

Dyers	1 in every	94	individuals.
Chimney-sweeps	,,	97	,,
Errand-boys	,,	99	,,
Porters	,,	99	,,
Painters, plumbers, and glaziers	,,	119	,,
Cabinet-makers and upholsterers	,,	128	,,
Shoemakers	,,	130	,,
Printers and compositors	,,	142	,,
Brushmakers	,,	145	,,
Carpenters, joiners, and wheelwrights ...	,,	150	,,
Bakers	,,	167	,,
Brassfounders	,,	177	,,
Tailors	,,	177	,,
Combmakers	,,	178	,,
Coopers	,,	178	,,
Surveyors	,,	198	,,
Fellmongers	,,	203	,,
Glascutters	,,	229	,,
Bedstead-makers	,,	235	,,
Average (for all London)	,,	219	,,
Butchers	,,	248	,,
Bookbinders	,,	255	,,
Mendicants	,,	256	,,
Engineers	,,	265	,,
Miners	,,	267	,,
Lacemakers	,,	273	,,
Poulterers	,,	273	,,
Furriers	,,	274	,,
Straw-bonnet-makers	,,	277	,,
Trimming and button makers	,,	277	,,
Ostlers and grooms	,,	286	,,
Drovers	,,	297	,,
Hairdressers	,,	329	,,
Pipemakers	,,	340	,,
Clerks and shopmen	,,	346	,,
Hatters	,,	350	,,
Tinmen	,,	354	,,
Tallow-chandlers	,,	364	,,
Servants	,,	377	,,
Corkcutters	,,	380	,,
Jewellers and watchmakers	,,	411	,,
Umbrella-makers	,,	415	,,
Sailmakers	,,	455	,,
Carvers and gilders	,,	500	,,
Gunsmiths	,,	554	,,
Trunkmakers	,,	569	,,
Chairmakers	,,	586	,,
Fishmongers	,,	643	,,
Tanners	,,	643	,,
Musicians	,,	730	,,
Leather-dressers and curriers	,,	802	,,
Coachmakers	,,	989	,,

Engravers	1 in every 1,133	individuals.
Shipwrights	,, 1,358	,,
Artists	,, 1,374	,,
Drapers	,, 2,047	,,
Milliners and dressmakers	,, 10,390	,,

In my last letter I dealt principally with the houseless labourers. In the present one I purpose dealing with the artisans and trades-men who are in a similar state of destitution. In my next I shall pass from these to the vagrants, and thence to the beggars of London.

A homeless painter gave me the following statement. His appearance presented nothing remarkable—it was merely that of the poor artisan; there was nothing dirty or squalid about him. "I was brought up a painter," he said, "and am now 27. I served my apprenticeship in Yorkshire, and stayed two years after my term was out with the same master. I then worked in Liverpool, earning but little, through illness, and working on and off as my health permitted. I got married in Liverpool, and went with my wife to Londonderry, in Ireland, of which place she was a native. There she died of the cholera (in 1847). I was very ill with diarrhœa myself. We lived with her friends, but I got work, though wages are very low there. I never earned more than 2s. 6d. a day there. I have earned 5s. 6d. a day in Liverpool, but in Londonderry provisions are very cheap—the best meat at 4d. per pound. It was an advantage to me being an Englishman. English workmen seem to be preferred in Ireland, as far as I can tell, and I have worked in Belfast and Coleraine, and a short time in Dublin, as well as in Londonderry. I came back to Liverpool early in 1848 and got work, but was again greatly distressed through sickness. I then had to travel the country again, getting a little employment at Hemel Hempstead and St. Alban's, and other places about, for I aimed at London, and at last I got to London. That was in November, 1848. When in the country I was forced to part with my clothes—I had a beautiful suit of black among them. I very seldom got even a trifle from the painters in the country towns; sometimes 2d. or 3d. from a master. In London I could get no work, and my shirts and flannel shirts went to keep me. I stayed about a month, and having nothing left was obliged to start for the country. I got a job at Luton, and in a few other places. Wages are very low. I was always a temperate man. Many a time I have never tasted drink for a week together—and this when I had money in my pocket, for I had £30 when I got married. I have, too, the character of being a good workman. I returned to London again three weeks back, but could find no work. I had again to part with any odd things I had. The last I parted with was my stopping-knife and diamond, for I can work as a glazier and plumber; country painters often can—I mean those apprenticed in the country. I have no clothes but what I have on. For the last ten days I declare solemnly I have had nothing but what I picked up in the streets. I picked up crusts that I saw in the streets, put out on the steps by the mistresses of the houses for the poor like myself. I got so weak and ill that I had to go to King's College Hospital, and they gave me medicine which did me good. I often had to walk the streets all night. I was so perished I could hardly move my limbs. I never asked charity—I can't; but I could have eaten anything. I longed for the fried fish I saw; yes, I was ravenous for that and such like, though I couldn't have touched it when I had money and was middling well off. Things are so different in the country, that I couldn't fancy such meat. I was brought to that pitch I had the greatest mind to steal something to get into prison, where at any rate, I said to myself, I shall have some food and shelter. I didn't—I thought better of it. I hoped something might turn up next day; besides it might have got into the papers, and my friends might have seen it, and I should have felt I disgraced them, or that they would think so, because they couldn't know my temptations and my sufferings. When out all night, I used to get shelter, if I could, about Hungerford Market, among the straw. The cold made me almost dead with sleep; and when obliged to move, I couldn't walk at first—I could only crawl along. One night I had a penny given me—all I had gotten in five bitter nights in the streets. For that penny I got half a pint of coffee. It made me sick, my stomach was so weak. On Tuesday I asked a policeman if he couldn't recommend me to some workhouse, and he told me to come here, and I was admitted, and was very thankful to get under shelter."

The next was a carpenter, a tall, fine-built man, with a pleasing expression of countenance. He was dressed in a flannel jacket and fustian trousers, with the peculiar little side pocket for his foot-rule, that told you of his calling. He was about forty years of age, and had the appearance, even in his destitution, of the more respectable mechanic. It is astonishing to mark the difference between the poor artisan and the labourer. The one seems alive to his poverty, and to feel it more acutely than the other. The labourer is more accustomed to "rough it," as it is called; but the artisan, earning better wages and used to better ways, appears among the Houseless Poor as a really pitiable character. Carpenters are among the classes of mechanics in which there appears to be the greatest amount of destitution, and I selected this man as a fair average specimen of the body. He said—"I have been out of work nearly three months. I have had some little work in the meantime—an odd job or two at intervals, but nothing regular. When I am in full work on day work I can make 5s. a day in London, but the masters very generally wishes the men to take piece work, and that is the cause of men's work being cut down as it is, because men is obliged to take the work as they offers. I could get about 30s. a week when I had good employment. I have no one but myself to keep out of my earnings. I have saved something when I was on day work, but then it went again directly I got to piece work. This is generally the case with the carpenters. The last job I had was at Cobham, in Surrey, doing joiner's work, and business with my master got slack, and I was discharged. Then I made my way to London, and have been about from place to place since then endeavouring to get work from every one that I knew or could get recommended to. But I have not met with any success. Well, sir, I have been obliged to part with all I had—even to my tools, though they're not left for much. My tools are pawned for 12s., and my clothes are all gone. The last I had to part with was my rule and chalk-line, and them I left for a night's lodging. I have no other clothes but what you see me in at present. There are a vast many carpenters out of work, and like me. It is now three weeks since the last of my things went, and after that I have been about the streets, and gone into bakers' shops and asked for a crust. Sometimes I have got a penny out of the tap-room of a public-house. It's now more than a fortnight since I quitted my lodgings. I have been in the Asylum eight nights. Before that, I was out in the streets for five nights together. They were very cold nights—oh yes, *very* [the man shivered at the recollection]. I walked up one street and down another. I sometimes got under a doorway, but it was impossible to stand still long, it was so cruel cold. The sleet was coming down one night, and freezed on my clothes as it fell. The cold made me stiff more than sleepy. It was next day that I felt tired, and then if I come to sit down at a fireside I should drop asleep in a minute. I tried when I was dead beat to get into St. Giles's union, but they would not admit me. Then the police sent me up to another union—I forget the name—but they refused me. I tried at Lambeth, and there I was refused. I don't think I went a day without some small bit of bread. I begged for it. But when I walked from St. Alban's to London I was two days without a bit to put in my mouth. I never stole, not a particle, from any person, in all my trials. I was brought up honest, and, thank God, I have kept so all my life. I would work willingly, and am quite capable—yes, and I would do my work with all my heart, but it's not to be got at." This the poor fellow said with deep emotion; and, indeed, his whole statement appeared in every way worthy of credit. I heard afterwards that he had offered to "put up the stairs of two houses" at some man's own terms rather than remain unemployed. He had told the master that his tools were in pawn, and promised, if they were taken out of pledge for him, to work for his bare food. He was a native of Somerset, and his father and mother were both dead.

I then took the statement of a seaman, but one who, from destitution, had lost all the distinguishing characteristics of a sailor's dress of the better description. He wore a jacket such as seamen sometimes work in, too little for him, and very thin and worn; a waistcoat, once black; a cotton shirt, and a pair of canvas trousers. He had an intelligent look enough, and spoke in a straight-forward manner. He stated: —"I am now thirty-five, and have been a seaman all my life. I first went to sea as a cabin-boy at Portsmouth. I was left an orphan at fourteen months, and don't know that I have a single relation but myself. I don't know what my father was. I was brought up at the Portsea workhouse. I was taught to read and write. I went to sea in 1827. I have continued a seaman ever since—sometimes doing pretty well. The largest sum I ever had in my possession was £38, when I was in the Portuguese service, under Admiral Sartorius, in the Donna Maria frigate. He hadn't his flag aboard, but he commanded the fleet, such as it was; but don't call it a fleet, say a squadron. Captain Henry was my last captain there; and after him I served under Admiral Napier—he was admiral out there with his flag on the Real, until Don Miguel's ships were taken. The frigate I was in (the Donna Maria) took the Princessa Real—she was a 44-gun ship, and ours was a 36. It was a stiffish thing while it lasted—was the fight; but we boarded and carried the Princessa. I never got all my prize-money. I stopped in Lisbon some time after the fight; and then, as I couidn't meet with a passage to England, I took ser-vice on board the Donegal, 74 guns, Captain Fanshawe. I liked Lisbon pretty well: they're not a very tidy people—treacherous, too, but not all of them. I picked up a very little Portuguese. Most of my £38 went in Lisbon. The Donegal brought Don Carlos over, and we were paid off in Plymouth; that was in 1834. Since then I have been in the merchant service. I like that best. My last voyage was in the Richard Cobden, a barque of 380 tons belonging to

Dundee, but she sailed from Gloucester for Archangel, and back from Archangel to Dundee with a cargo of hemp and codilla. We were paid off in Dundee, and I received £4 8s. on the 13th of October (he showed me his discharge from the Richard Cobden, and his register ticket). I went to Glasgow and got a vessel there— an American, the Union—and before that I stayed at a lodging-house in Dundee that sailors frequent. There was a shipmate of mine there, a carpenter, and I left my things in his charge, and I went on board the Union at Glasgow, and stayed working on board eighteen days; she was short of men. The agreement between my old shipmate and me was that he should send my things when I required them. My clothes were worth to me more than £5. The ship was to sail on Friday, the 15th of November—sailors don't mind getting under weigh on a Friday now—and I got 10s. from the skipper to take me to Dundee on Thursday, the 14th; but when I got to Dundee for my clothes I found that the carpenter had left a fortnight before, taking all my things with him. I couldn't learn anything as to where he had gone. One man told me he thought he'd gone to Derry, where some said he had a wife. The skipper paid me for what days I had been employed, and offered to let me work a passage to New York, but not on wages; because I had no clothes he couldn't take. I tried every ship in the Broomielaw, but couldn't get a job, nor a passage to London, so me and two other seamen set off to walk to London. I started with 3s. One seaman left us at Carlisle. We didn't live on the way—we starved. It took us a month to get to London. We slept sometimes at the unions; some wouldn't admit us. I was very lame at last. We reached London a month ago. I got three days' work as a rigger, at 2s. 6d. a day, and a week's shelter in the Sailor's Asylum. I had five days' work also on stevedore's work in the Margaret West, gone to Batavia. That brought me 12s., those five days' work. Since that I've done nothing, and was so beat out that I had to pass two days and nights in the streets. One of those days I had a bit of bread and meat from an old mate. I had far rather be out in a gale of wind at sea, or face the worst storm, than be out two such nights again in such weather and with an empty belly. My mate and I kept on trying to get a ship, but my old jacket was all against me. They look at a man's clothes now. I passed these two nights walking about Tower-hill and to London-bridge and back, half dead, and half asleep, with cold and hunger. I thought of doing something to get locked up, but I then thought that would be no use, and a disgrace to a man, so I determined to bear it like a man, and try and get a ship. The man who left us at Carlisle did no better than me, for he's here too, beat out like me, and he told me of this Asylum. The other man got a ship. I'm not a drinking man, though I may have had a spree or two, but that's all over. I could soon get a ship, if I had some decent clothes. I bought these trousers out of what I earned in London. I spun out my money as fine as a man could."

The poor man who gave me the following narrative was a coloured man with the regular negro physiognomy, but with nothing of the light-hearted look they sometimes present. His only attire was a sadly-soiled shirt of coarse striped cotton, an old handkerchief round his neck, old canvas trousers, and shoes. "I am 20," he said, in good English, "and was born in New York. My father was a very dark negro, but my mother was white. I was sent to school and can read a little, but can't write. My father was coachman to a gentleman. My mother spoke Dutch chiefly; she taught it to my father; she could speak English, and always did to me. I worked in a gentleman's house in New York, cleaning knives and going errands. I was always well treated in New York, and by all sort of people. Some of the 'rough uns' in the streets would shout after me as I was going to church on a Sunday night. At church I couldn't sit with the white people. I didn't think that any hardship. I saved seven dollars by the time I was sixteen, and then I went to sea as a cabin-boy on board the Elizabeth, a brigantine. My first voyage was to St. John's, New Brunswick, with a cargo of corn and provisions. My second voyage was to Boston. After that I was raised to be cook. I had a notion I could cook well. I had cooked on shore before, in a gentleman's house, where I was shown cooking. Pretty many of the cooks in New York are coloured people—the men more than the women. The women are chiefly chambermaids. There was a vacancy, I was still in the Elizabeth, when the cook ran away; he was in a bother with the captain about wasting tea and sugar. We went some more voyages, and I then got engaged as cook on board a new British ship, just off the stocks, at St. John's, New Brunswick—the Jessica. About four months ago I came in her to Liverpool, where we were all paid off. We were only engaged for the run. I received £5. I paid £2 10s. to my boarding mistress for two months' board. It was 5s. and extras a week. I laid out the rest in clothes. I had a job in Liverpool in loading hay. I was told I had a better chance for a ship in London. I tramped it all the way, selling some of my clothes to start me. I had 6s. to start with, and got to London with hardly any clothes and no money. That's two months back, or nearly so. I couldn't find a ship. I never begged, but I stood on the highways, and some persons gave me twopences and pennies. I was often out all night, perishing. Sometimes I slept under the butchers' stalls in Whitechapel. I felt the cold very bitter, as I was used to a hot climate chiefly. Sometimes I couldn't feel my feet. A policeman told me to come here, and I was admitted. I want to get a ship. I have a good character as a cook; my dishes were always relished; my peas-soup was capital, and so was my dough and pudding. I often wished for them when I was starving. [He showed his white teeth, smiling as he spoke.] Often under the Whitechapel stalls I was so frozen up I could hardly stir in the morning. I was out all the night before Christmas, that it snowed. That was my worst night, I think, and it was my first. I couldn't walk, and hardly stand, when the morning came. I have no home to go to."

The next was a brickmaker, a man scarce thirty—a stout, big-boned man, but a little pale, evidently from cold and exhaustion. His dress was a short smock frock—yellow with dry clay—and fustian trousers of the same colour, from the same cause. His statement was as follows: —

"I have been out of work now about seven weeks. Last work I done was on the middle level drainage, in Cambridgeshire. Brick-making generally begins (if the weather's fine) about February, or the beginning of March, and it ends about September, and some-times the latter end of November. If the weather's frosty, they can't keep on so long. I was at work up to about the middle of November last, making bricks at Northfleet, in Kent. I was with the same party for three years before. After that, brickmaking was done for the season, and I was discharged with 'five stools' of us beside; each stool would require six people to work it, so that altogether thirty hands were thrown out of work. After that, I went to look for work among the 'slop' brickmakers. They makes bricks slop-way right through the winter, for they're dried by flues. I am by rights a sand-stock brickmaker. Howsomever I couldn't get a job at brickmaking slop-way, so I went down on the middle level, and there I got a job at river cutting, but the wet weather came, and the water was so strong upon us that we got drownded out. That's the last job I've had. At brickmaking I had 3s. 10d. a thousand, this last summer. I *have* had my 4s. 6d. for the very same work. Two years ago I had that. Six of us could make about 65 thousand in a week, if it was fine. On an average, we should make, I dare say, each of us about £1 a week, not more, because if it was a showery day, we couldn't do nothing at all. We used to join one among another in the yard to keep our own sick. We mostly made the money up to 14s. a week when any mate was bad. I *did* save a few shillings, but it was soon gone when I was out of work. Not many of the brickmakers save. They work from 17 to 18 hours every day when its fine, and that requires a good bit to eat and drink. The brickmakers most of them drink hard. After I got out of work last November, I went away to Peterborough to look for employment. I thought I might get a job on the London and York Railway, but I couldn't find none. From there I tramped it to Grimsby—perhaps, I said, I may get a job at the docks; but I could get nothing to do there, so I came away to Grantham, and from there back to Peterborough again, and after that to Northampton; and then I made my way to London. All this time I had laid either in barns at night-time, or slept in the casual wards of the unions—that is, where they would have me. Often I didn't get nothing to eat for two and three days together, and often I have had to beg a bit to keep body and soul together. I had no other means of living since November last but begging. When I came to town, I applied at a large builder's office for work. I heard he had something to do at the Isle of Dogs, but it was the old story—they were full, and had plenty of hands till the days get out longer. Then I made away to Portsmouth. I knew a man there who had some work, but when I got there he had none to give me at the present time. From there I went along the coast, begging my way still, to Hastings, in hope of getting work at the railway, but all to no good. They had none, too, till the days got longer. After that I came round to London again, and I have been here a fortnight come next Monday. I have done no work. I have wandered about the streets any way. I went to the London Docks to see for a job, and there I met with a man as I knowed, and he paid for my lodging for one or two nights. I walked the streets for two whole nights before I came here. It was bitter cold, freezing sharp, indeed, and I had nothing to eat all the time. I didn't know there was such a place as this till a policeman told me. A gentleman gave me 6d., and that's all I've had since I've been in this town. I have been for the last three nights at the Asylum. I don't suppose they'll take my ticket away here till after tomorrow night, and then I thought of making my way down home till my work starts again. I have sought for work all over the country, and can't get any. All the brickmakers are in the same state as myself. They none of them save, and must either starve or beg in the winter. Most times we can get a job in the cold weather, but this year, I don't know what it is, but I can't get a job at all. Former years, I got railway work to do, but now there's nothing doing, and we're all starving. When I get down home, I shall be obliged to go into the union, and that's hard for a young man like me, able to work, and willing, but it ain't to be had—it ain't to be had."

Then came a tailor, a young man only 21 years old, habited in a black frock-coat, with a plaid shawl twisted round his neck. His eyes were full and expressive, and he had a look of intelligence superior to any that I had yet seen. He told a story which my inquiries into the slop trade taught me was "ower true."

"I have been knocking about for near upon six weeks," he replied, in answer to my inquiries. "I was working at the slop-trade at the West-end. I am a native of Scotland. I was living with a sweater. I used to board and lodge with him entirely. At the week's end I was almost always in debt with him—at least he made it out so. I had very often to work all night, but let me slave as hard as I might I never could get out of debt with the sweater. There were often as many as six of us there, and we slept two together in each bed. The work had been slack for some time, and he gave me employment till I worked myself out of his debt, and then he turned me into the streets. I had a few clothes remaining, and these soon were sold to get me food and lodging. I lived on my other coat and shirts for a week or two, and at last all was gone, and I was left entirely destitute. Then I had to pace the streets all day and night. The two nights before I came here I never tasted food nor lay down to rest. I had been in a fourpenny lodging before then, but I couldn't raise even that, and I knew it was no good going there without the money. You must pay before you go to bed at those places. Several times I got into a doorway to shelter from the wind and cold, and twice I was roused by the policeman, for I was so tired that I fell asleep standing against a shop near the Bank. What with hunger and cold, I was in a half-stupid state. I didn't know what to do. I was far from home and my mother. I have not liked to let *her* know how badly I was off. [The poor lad's eyes flooded with tears at the recollection of his parent.] I thought I had better steal something, and then at least I should have a roof over my head. Then I thought I'd make away with myself. I can't say how—it was a sort of desperation—and I was so stupid with cold and want that I can hardly remember what I thought. All I wanted was to be allowed to sit down on some doorstep, and die; but the police did not allow this. In the day-time I went up and lay about the parks most part of the day, but I couldn't sleep then; I hardly know why, but I'd been so long without food, that I couldn't rest. I have purposely kept from writing to my mother. It would break her heart to know my sufferings. She has been a widow this ten year past. She keeps a lodginghouse in Leith, and has two children to support. I have been away eight months from her. I came to London from a desire to see the place, and thinking I could better my situation. In Edinburgh I had made my £1 a week regularly, often more, and seldom less. When I came to London a woman met me in the street, and asked if I wasn't a tailor. On my replying in the affirmative, she told me if I would come and work for her husband I should have good wages, and live with her and her husband, and they would make me quite comfortable. I didn't know she was the wife of a sweater at that time. It was a thing I had never heard of in Edinburgh. After that time I kept getting worse and worse off, working day and night and all Sunday, and still always being in debt to them that I worked for. Indeed I wish I had never left home. If I could get back I'd go in a moment. I have worked early and late, in the hope of accumulating money enough to take me home again, but I could not even get out of debt, much more save, work as hard as I would." I asked if he would allow me to see some letters of his mother's, as vouchers for the truth of his story, and he produced a small packet, from which, with his permission, I copied the following: —

"My dear Son—I have this moment received your letter. I was happy to hear from you, and trust you are well. Think of that God who has carried you in safety over the mighty deep. We are all much as you left us. I hope you will soon write.—Ever believe me,

"Your affectionate mother,

"_____ _____."

This was the first letter written after his absence from home. Since then his mother, who is aged and rheumatic (his letters vouched for this), had been unable to write a line. His brother, a lad of sixteen, says, in one of the letters: —

"I am getting on with my Greek, Hebrew, Latin, and French, only I am terribly ill off for want of books. My mother was saying that you would be bringing me a first rate present from London. I think the most appropriate present you can bring me will be a Greek and English, or a Hebrew and English Lexicon—or some Hebrew, Greek, or Latin book."

A letter from his sister, a girl of eighteen, ran as follows: —

"My dear Brother—I take this opportunity of writing you, as you wrote that you would like to have a letter from me. I am very sorry you have been ill, but I hope you are keeping better. I trust also that affliction will be the means of leading you more closely to the only true source of happiness. Oh, my dear brother, you are still young, and God has told us, in his word, that those who seek him early shall find him. My dear brother, we get many a sad and solemn warning to prepare to meet our God; and oh! my dear brother, what is a man profited if he shall gain the whole world, and lose his own soul?"

The last letter was dated the 5th of December last, and from his brother: —

"We received your kind letter," it ran, "this instant, and we hasten to answer it. It has given my mother and me great relief to hear from you, as my mother and I were very miserable about you, thinking you were ill. We trust you will take care of yourself, and not get any more cold. We hope you will be able to write on receipt of this, and let us know how you are, and when we may expect you home, as we have daily expected you since the month of October."

These letters were shown to me at *my* request, and not produced by the young man himself, so that it was evident they were kept by the youth with no view of being used by him as a means of inducing charity; indeed, the whole manner of the young man was such as entirely precluded suspicion. On my asking whether he had any other credentials as to character, he showed me a letter from a Scotch minister, stating that "he had been under his charge, and that from his conduct, he had been led to form a favourable opinion of his talents and moral character; and that he believed him to be a deserving, industrious young man."

Of the class of distressed tradesmen seeking shelter at this asylum, the two following may be taken as fair types. One was a bankrupt linen-draper, and appeared in a most destitute state. When he spoke of his children his eyes flooded with tears: —

"I have been in business in the linen-drapery line—that's five years ago. I had about £600 worth of stock at first starting, and used to take about £65 every week. My establishment was in a country village in Essex. I went on medium well for the first two or three years, but the alteration of the poor-laws, and the reduction of the agricultural labourers' wages, destroyed my business. My customers were almost all among the working classes. I had dealings with a few farmers, of whom I took butter, and cheese, and eggs, in exchange for my goods. When the poor-laws were altered, the outdoor relief was stopped, and the paupers compelled to go inside the house. Before that, a good part of the money given to the poor used to be expended at my shop. The overseers used to have tickets for flannels, blankets, and shirtings, and other goods; with these they used to send the paupers to my house. I used to take full £8 or £10 a week in this manner; so that when the poor-laws were altered, and the previous system discontinued, I suffered materially. Besides, the wages of the agricultural labourers being lowered, left them less money to lay out with me. On a market day they were my chief customers. I would trust them one week under the other, and give them credit for 7s. or 10s., if they wanted it. After their wages came down, they hadn't the means of laying out a sixpence with me; and where I had been taking £65 a week, my receipts dwindled to £30. I had been in the habit of keeping two shopmen before, but after the reduction I was obliged to come down to one. Then the competition of the large houses in other towns was more than I could stand against. Having a larger capital, they could buy cheaper and afford to take a less profit, and so of course they could sell much cheaper than I could. Then to try and keep pace with my neighbours I endeavoured to extend my capital by means of accommodation bills, but the interest I had to pay on these was so large, and my profits so little, that it soon became impossible for me to meet the claims upon me. I was made a bankrupt. My debts at the time were £300. This is about six years ago. After that I took a public-house. Some property was left me. I came into about £1,000; part of this went to my creditors, and I superseded my bankruptcy. With the rest I determined upon starting in the publican line. I kept at this for about ten months, but I could do nothing with it. There was no custom to the house. I had been deceived into taking it. By the time I got out of it all my money was gone. After that I got a job as a referee at the time of the railway mania, and when that was over I got appointed as a policeman on the Eastern Union line. There I remained two years and upwards, but then they began reducing their establishment, both in men and in wages. I was among the men who were turned off. Since that time, which is now two years this Christmas, I have had no constant employment. Occasionally I have got a little law-writing to do; sometimes I have got a job as under waiter at a tavern. After I left the waiter's place I got to be very badly off. I had a decent suit of clothes to my back up to that time, but then I became so reduced I was obliged to go and live in a low lodging-house in Whitechapel. I was enabled to get along somehow; I knew many friends, and they gave me a little money now and then. But at last I had exhausted these. I could get nothing to do of any kind. I have been to Shoreditch station to try to pick up a few pence at carrying parcels, but there were so many there that I could not get a crust that way. I was obliged to pawn garment after garment to pay for my food and lodging, and when they were all gone I was wholly destitute. I couldn't raise even two pence for a night's lodging, so I came here and asked for a ticket. My wife is dead. I have three children; but I would rather you would not say anything about them if you please, because I have told all the truth, and if the gentleman was to see my statement it might hurt his feelings." I assured the man that his name would not be printed, and he then consented to his children being mentioned. "The age of my eldest child is fourteen, and my youngest nine. They do not know of the destitution of their father. They are staying with one of my relations, who has supported them since my failure. I wouldn't have them know of my state on any account. None of my family are aware of my misery. My eldest child is a girl, and it would break her heart to know where I am, and see the state of distress I am in. My boy, I think, would never get over it. He is eleven years old. I have tried to get work at carrying placard boards about, but I can't. My clothes are now too bad for me to do anything else. I write a good hand, and would do anything, I don't care what, to earn a few pence. I can get a good character from every place I have been in."

The other tradesman's story was as follows: —

"I am now 33, and am acquainted with the grocery trade, both as master and assistant. I served a five years' apprenticeship in a town in Berkshire. The very late hours and the constant confinement made me feel my apprenticeship a state of slavery. The other apprentices used to say they felt it so likewise. During my apprenticeship I consider that I never learnt my trade properly. I knew as much at the year's end as at the five years' end. My father gave my master £50 premium; the same premium, or more, was paid with the others. One, the son of a gentleman at ————, paid as much as £80. My master made an excellent thing of his apprentices. Nearly all the grocers in the part of Berkshire I'm acquainted with do the same. My master was a severe man to us in respect of keeping us in the house, and making us attend the Methodist chapel twice, and sometimes thrice, every Sunday. We had prayers night and morning. I attribute my misfortunes to this apprenticeship, because there was a great discrepancy between profession and practice in the house, so there could be no respect in the young men for their employer, and they grew careless. He carried on his **business in a way to** inspire anything else than respect. On the cheesemongery side we were always blamed if we didn't keep the

scale well wetted, so as to make it heavier on one side than the
other—I mean the side of the scale where the butter was put—
that was filled, or partly filled with water, under pretence of preventing the butter sticking, and so the customer was wronged half
an ounce in every purchase. With regard to the bacon, which, on
account of competition, we had to sell cheap—at no profit sometimes—he used to say to us, 'You must make the ounces pay;'
that is, we were expected to add two or more ounces, calculating
on what the customer would put up with, to every six odd ounces
in the weight of a piece. For instance, if a hock of bacon weighed
6 lb. 7 oz., at 4½d. per lb., we were to charge 2s. 3d. for the 6 lbs.,
and (if possible) adding two ounces to the seven which was the
actual weight, charge each ounce a halfpenny, so getting 2s. 7½d.
instead of 2s. 5d. This is a common practice in all the cheap shops
I'm acquainted with. With his sugars and teas inferior sorts were
mixed. In grinding pepper a quantity of rice was used, it all being
ground together. Mustard was adulterated by the manufacturers,
if the price given showed that the adulterated stuff was wanted.
The lowest-priced coffee was always half chicory, the second quality
one-third chicory; the best was 1 lb. of chicory to 3 lb. of coffee,
or one-fourth. We had it either in chicory-nibs, which is the root
of the endive cultivated in Yorkshire, Prussia, etc.; or else as
spurious chicory powdered, 2d. or 3d. per lb. cheaper, the principal ingredient being parsnips and carrots, cut in small pieces,
and roasted like chicory. A quart of water is the allowance to
every 28 lbs. of tobacco. We had to keep pulling it so as to keep
it loose, for if left to lie long it would mould and get a very unpleasant smell. In weighing sugar, some was always spilt loose on
the scale opposite the weight, which remains in the scale, so that
every pound or so is a quarter of an ounce short. This is the practice only in 'cutting' shops. Often enough, after we have been
doing all these rogueries we were called in to prayers. In my next
situation, with an honourable tradesman in Yorkshire, I found I
had to learn my business over again, so as to carry it on fairly.
In two or three years I went into business in the town where I was
apprenticed; but I had been subjected to such close confinement,
and so many unnecessary restrictions, without any opportunity of
improving by reading, that when I was my own master, and in possession of money, and on the first taste of freedom, I squandered
my money foolishly and extravagantly, and that brought me into
difficulties. I was £150 deficient to meet my liabilities, and my
friends advanced that sum, I undertaking to be more attentive to
business. After that, a man started as a grocer in the same street,

in the 'cutting' line, and I had to compete with him, and he sold his sugar a halfpenny a pound less than it cost, and I was obliged to do the same; the preparing of the sugar for the market day is a country grocer's week's work, and all at a loss. That's the ruin of many a grocer. My profits dwindled year by year, though I stuck very close to business, and in 18 months I gave it up. By that time other 'cutting' shops were opened—none have done any good. I was about £100 bad, which my friends arranged to pay by instalments. After that I hawked tea. I did no good in that. The system is to leave it at the working men's houses, giving a week's credit, the customers often taking more. Nothing can be honestly made in that trade. The Scotchmen in the trade are the only men that can do any good in it. They charge 6s. for what's 4s. in a good shop. About nine months ago my wife—I had been married seven years—was obliged to go and live with her sister, a dressmaker, as I was too poor to keep her or myself either. I then came to London to try for employment of any kind. I answered advertisements, and there were always forty or fifty young men after the same situation. I never got one, except for a short time at Brentford. I had also a few days' work at bill delivery—that is, grocer's circulars. I was at last so reduced that I couldn't pay for my lodgings. Nobody can describe the misery I felt as I have walked the streets all night, falling asleep as I went along, and then roused myself up half frozen, my limbs aching, and my whole body trembling. Sometimes, if I could find a penny, I might sit up in a coffee-shop in Russell-street, Covent-garden, till five in the morning, when I had to roam the streets all day long. Two days I was without food, and determined to commit some felony to save me from starvation, when, to my great joy—for God knows what it saved me from, as I was utterly careless what my fate would be— I was told of this Refuge by a poor man who had been there, who found me walking about the Piazzas in Covent-garden as a place of shelter. I applied, and was admitted. I don't know how I can get a place without clothes. I have one child with my wife, and she supports him and herself, very indifferently, by dressmaking."

A soldier's wife, speaking with a strong Scotch accent, made the following statement. She had altogether a decent appearance, but her features—and there were the remains of prettiness in her look—were sadly pinched. Her manners were quiet, and her voice low and agreeable. She looked like one who had "seen better days"—as the poor of the better sort not unfrequently say in their destitution, clinging to the recollection of past comforts. She wore a very clean checked cotton shawl and a straw bonnet tolerably entire. The remainder of her dress was covered by her shawl, which was folded closely about her, over a dark cotton gown: —"I was born twenty miles from Inverness (she said), and have been a servant since I was eleven. I always lived in good places—the best of places. I never was in inferior places. I have lived as cook, housemaid, or servant of all work, in Inverness, Elgin, and Tain, always maintaining a good character—I thank God for that. In all my distress, I've done nothing wrong; but I didn't know what distress was when in service. I continued in service until I married; but I was not able to save much money, because I had to do all I could for my mother, who was a very poor widow, for I lost my father when I was two years old. Wages are very low in Scotland to what they are in England. In the year 1847 I lived in the service of the barrack-master of Fort George, twelve miles below Inverness. There I became acquainted with my present husband, a soldier; and I was married to him in March, 1847, in the chapel at Fort George. I continued two months in service after my marriage—my mistress wouldn't let me away; she was very kind to me; so was my master: they all were. I have a written character from my mistress." This, at my request, she produced. "Two months after, the regiment left Fort George for Leith, and there I lived with my husband in barracks. It is not so bad for married persons in the artillery as in the line (we were in the artillery) in barracks. In our barrack rooms no single men were allowed to sleep where the married people were accommodated. But there were three or four married families in one room. I lived two years in barracks with my husband, in different barracks. I was very comfortable. I didn't know what it was to want anything I ought to have. My husband was a kind sober man. [This she said very feelingly.] His regiment was ordered abroad, to Nova Scotia. I had no family. Only six soldiers' wives are allowed to go out with each company, and there were 17 married men in the company to which my husband belonged. It's determined by lot. An officer holds the tickets in his cap, and the men draw them. None of the wives are present. It would be too hard a thing for them to see. My husband drew a blank." She continued: "It was a sad scene when they embarked at Woolwich, last March. All the wives were there, all crying and sobbing, you may depend upon that; and the children too, and some of the men; but I couldn't look much at them, and I don't like to see men cry. My husband was sadly distressed. I hoped to get out there and join him, not knowing the passage was so long and so expensive. I had a little money then, but that's gone, and I'm brought to misery. It would have cost me £6 at that time to get out, and I couldn't manage that. So I stayed in London, getting a day's work at washing where I could, making a very poor living of it; and I was at last forced to part with all my good clothes after my money went; and my husband—God bless him! — always gave me his money to do what I thought best with it. I used to earn a little in barracks with my needle, too. I was taken ill with the cholera at the latter end of August. Dear, dear, what I suffered! and when I was getting better I had a second attack, and that was the way my bit of money all went. I was then quite destitute; but I care nothing for that, and would care nothing for anything, if I could get out to my husband. I should be happy then. I should never be so happy since I was born before. It's now a month since I was entirely out of halfpence. I can't beg—it would disgrace me and my husband, and.I'd die in the streets first. Last Saturday I hadn't a farthing. I hadn't a thing to part with. I had a bed by the night, at 3d. a night, not at a regular lodging-house; but the mistress wouldn't trust me no longer, as I owed her 2s. 6d., and for that she holds clothes worth far more than that. I heard of this Asylum, and got admitted, or I must have spent the night in the street, there was nothing else for me; but, thank God, I've been spared that. On Christmas-day I had a letter from my husband." This she produced. It contained the following passage: "I am glad this letter only costs you a penny, as your purse must be getting very low; but there is a good time coming, and i trust in god it will not be long, my deir wife i hope you will have got a good place before this raches you. I am dowing all in power to help you. i trust in god in three months more, if you Help me, between us we'll make it out." She concluded: —"I wouldn't like him to know how badly I am off. He knows I would do nothing wrong. He wouldn't suspect me—he never would. He knows me too well. I have no clothes but what are detained for 2s. 6d., and what I have on. I have on just this shawl and an old cotton gown, but it's not broke, and my underclothing. All my wish is to get out to my husband. I care for nothing else in this world."

Next comes the tale of a young girl who worked at velvet embossing. She was comely, and modestly spoken. By her attire it would have been difficult to have told that she was so utterly destitute as I afterwards discovered. She was scrupulously clean and neat in her dress; indeed it was evident, even from her appearance, that she belonged to a better class than the ordinary inmates of the Asylum. As she sat alone in the long unoccupied wards she sighed heavily, and her eyes were fixed continually on the ground. Her voice was very sorrowful. Her narrative was as follows: —

"I have been out of work for a very long while—for full three months now, and all the summer I was only on and off. I mostly had my work given out to me. It was in pieces of 100 yards—and sometimes less, and I was paid so much for the dozen yards. I generally had 3½d., and sometimes 1½d., according to what it was; 3½d. was the highest price that I had. I could, if I rose at five in the morning and sat up till twelve, earn between 1s. 3d. and 1s. a day. I had to cut the velvet after it had been embossed. I could—of a diamond pattern—do five dozen yards in a day, and of a leaf pattern I could only do three dozen and a half. I couldn't get enough of it to do even at these prices. Sometimes I was two days in the week without work, and sometimes I had work for only one day in the week. They wanted, too, to reduce the 1½d. diamond work to 1d. the dozen yards, and so they would have done, only the work got so slack that we had to leave it altogether. That is now seven weeks ago. Before that I did get a little to do, though it was very little, and since then I have called almost every week at the warehouse, but they have put me off, telling me to come in a fortnight or a week's time. I never kept acquaintance with any of the other young women working at the warehouse, but I dare say about 25 were thrown out of work at the same time as I was. Sometimes I made 6s. a week, and sometimes only 3s., and for the last fortnight I got 1s. 6d. a week, and out of that I had my own candles to find, and 1s. 6d. a week to pay for my lodgings. After I lost my work I made away with what little clothes I had, and now I have got nothing but what I stand upright in." [The tears were pouring down the cheeks of the poor girl; she was many minutes afterwards before she could answer my questions, from sobbing.] "I can't help crying," she said, "when I think how destitute I am. Oh yes, indeed [she cried through her sobs] I have been a good girl in all my trials. I might have been better off if I had chosen to take to that life. I need not have been here if I had chosen to part with my character. I don't know what my father was. I believe he was a clerk in one of the foreign confectionery houses. He deserted my mother two months before I was born. I don't know whether he is dead or not, for I never set eyes on him. If he is alive he is very well off. I know this from my aunt, who was told by one of his fellow-clerks that he had married a woman of property and gone abroad. He was disappointed with my mother. He expected to have a good bit of money with her; but after she married him her father wouldn't notice her. My mother died when I was a week old, so I do not recollect either of my parents. When my aunt, who was his own sister, wrote to him about myself, my brother, and sister, he sent word back that the children might go to the workhouse. But my aunt took pity on us, and brought us all up. She had a little property of her own. She gave us a decent education, as far as lay in her power. My brother she put to sea. My father's brother was a captain, and he took my brother with him. The first voyage he went (he was fourteen) a part of the rigging fell on him and the first mate, and they were both killed on the spot. My sister went as lady's maid to Lady ————, and went abroad with her, now eighteen months ago, and I have never heard of her since. The aunt who brought me up is dead now. She was carried off two years and three months ago. If she had lived I should never have wanted a friend. I remained with her up to the time of her death, and was very happy before that time. After that I found it very hard for a poor lone girl like me to get an honest living. I have been struggling on ever since, parting with my clothes, and often going for two days without food. I lived upon the remainder of my clothes, for some little time after I was thrown entirely out of work; but at last I got a fortnight in debt at my lodgings, and they made me leave—that's a week and three days ago now. Then I had nowhere but the streets to lay my head. I walked about for three days and nights without rest. I went into a chapel; I went there to sit down and pray, but I was too tired to offer up any prayers, for I fell asleep. I had been two nights and three days in the streets before this, and all I had during that time was a penny loaf, and that I was obliged to beg for. On the day that I was walking about it thawed in the morning and froze very hard at night. My shoes were bad, and let in water, and as the night came on my stockings froze to my feet. Even now I am suffering from the cold of those nights. It is as much as I can do to bend my limbs at present. I have been in the Asylum a week, and tonight is my last night here. I have nowhere to go, and what will become of me the Lord God only knows. [Again she burst out crying most piteously.] My things are not fit to go into any respectable workroom, and they won't take me into a lodging either, without I have got clothes. I would rather make away with myself than lose my character. [As she raised her hand to wipe away her tears I saw that her arms were bare, and on her moving the old black mantle that covered her shoulders I observed that her gown was so ragged that the body was almost gone from it, and it had no sleeves.] "I shouldn't have kept this," she said, "if I could have made away with it." She said that she had no friend in the world to help her, and that she would like much to emigrate.

I afterwards inquired at the house at which this poor creature had lodged as to whether she had always conducted herself with propriety while living there. To be candid, I could hardly believe that any person could turn a young friendless girl into the streets because she owed two weeks' rent, though the girl appeared too simple and truthfui to fabricate such a statement. On inquiry I found her story true from the beginning to the end. The landlady, an Irishwoman, acknowledged that the girl was in her debt but 3s., that she had lodged with her for several months, and always paid her regularly when she had money; but she couldn't afford, she said, to keep people for nothing—the girl had been a good well-behaved modest girl with her.

SUBJECT INDEX

Other Publications by Caliban Books

WHEN I WAS A CHILD
Charles Shaw

An autobiography set in the Potteries during the 1830s and 1840s. Published originally in 1903 under the anonym "An Old Potter", the book was used extensively and without acknowledgement by Arnold Bennett for his novel *Clayhanger*. Shaw gives both an account of his own childhood experiences and a description of contemporary social life, including education, child and adult work life, strikes and the emergence of unions, workhouse conditions, the Plug riots of 1842, leisure, politics and religion.

258 pages, 7¼" x 4¾". A facsimile of the 1903 edition
Hardback   £10.00   *ISBN 0 904573 04 4*

A MEMOIR OF ROBERT BLINCOE
John Brown

First published in 1832, this book immediately became famous on account of its grim and harrowing account of factory life at the beginning of the nineteenth century. Robert Blincoe was an orphan from St. Pancras's workhouse, and was sent as an apprentice to cotton factories in Nottinghamshire and Derbyshire. John Brown's memoir gives a full and detailed account of Blincoe's experience of factory life.

vi + 100 pages, 8½" x 5¼". A newly typeset edition based on the 1832 original
Hardback   £7.50   *ISBN 0 904573 05 2*

THE BETTESWORTH BOOK
George Sturt

George Sturt, author of *The Wheelwright Shop* and *Change in the Village*, wrote this biographical account of Frederick Bettesworth (Frederick Grover), at the beginning of this century. The book consists of recorded conversations with Bettesworth during the time he worked for Sturt as a gardener, and gives detailed descriptions of the working and social life of an agricultural labourer, with accounts of his childhood, education, family life, religion and politics.

325 pages, 7¼" x 4¾". A facsimile of the 1902 edition
Hardback   £10.00   *ISBN 0 904573 0 95*

HOM 15

WILLIAM SMITH, POTTER AND FARMER: 1790–1858

George Sturt

George Sturt's biography of his grandfather, William Smith, rivals *The Wheelwright Shop* in creating a vivid and detailed picture of country life during the nineteenth century. In the first part of the book, Sturt gives an autobiographical account of his grandfather's farm, and in later sections develops a full-length biography based on the recollections of his uncle and aunt. The life of a Hampshire farmer and potter is covered in all its aspects: economic, social, educational, religious and political, the latter including an account of the Swing riots of the 1840s. Being set in the era of the industrial and agricultural revolutions, the book provides details of the economic activities of a small trading potter/farmer during a period of great transition.

230 pages, 7¼" x 4¾". Nine black-and-white photographic illustrations. Facsimile reprint of 1920 edition
Hardback   £10.00   *ISBN 0 904573 08 7*

THE COSTUME OF YORKSHIRE

George Walker

This book was first published in 1814, with a second but limited edition brought out in 1885, since which time it has been out of print. Although virtually unknown in its own right because of its unavailability, the book has become famous through the use of its colour plates in a number of works on economic and social history. It contains forty colour illustrations, each depicting an aspect of Yorkshire life in 1814, accompanied by a page or more of explanatory text.

List of colour plates: 1. The Horse Dealer; 2. Cloth Makers; 3. The Collier; 4. The Dog Breaker: 5. The Cloth Dresser; 6. Lowkers; 7. Stone Breakers on the Road; 8. Fishermen; 9. Woman Making Oat Cakes; 10. The Ruddle Pit; 11. The Fool Plough; 12. Nor and Spell; 13. The Cranberry Girl; 14. Rape Threshing; 15. The East Riding or Wolds Waggon; 16. The Milk Boy; 17. Sea Bathing; 18. Whalebone Scrapers; 19. Farmers; 20. Moor Guide; 21. The Preemer Boy; 22. Thirty-Third Regiment; 23. Teasel Field; 24. Line Swinglers; 25. Grenadier, or the First West York Militia; 26. Riding the Stang; 27. Peat Cart; 28. The Cloth Hall; 29. Woman Spinning; 30. Bishop Blaize; 31. Wensley Dale Knitters; 32. Hawking; 33. North York Militia; 34. Alum Works; 35. East York Militia; 36. Midsummer Eve; 37. Leech Finders; 38. Factory Children; 39. Sheffield Cutler; and 40. Jockies.

100 pages, 8¼" x 5¾". Forty-one four-colour illustrations. Facsimile reprint of 1814 edition
Hardback   £15.00   *ISBN 0 904573 06 0*

PROGRESS IN PUDSEY

Joseph Lawson

First published in 1887, Lawson's book gives a comprehensive socio-logical account of an early nineteenth century textile community and how it changed over time. The author, who was born and raised in the town, discusses every aspect of economic and social life, including furniture, lighting, dress, food, marriage customs, religious and magical beliefs, sport and leisure pastimes, the structure of the textile industry and its technology. Changes in the period between the 1820s and the 1880s are covered in detail.

154 pages, 8¼" x 5¾". Newly typeset edition of 1886 original
Hardback   £10.00   *ISBN 0 904573 07 9*

MEMOIRS OF A SURREY LABOURER

George Sturt

This is a sequel to *The Bettesworth Book*, and covers the period from 1896 to 1905, the year of Frederick Grover (Bettesworth)'s death. The book is not only a moving account of Grover's life as it came to an end, but is also a rich source of information on the economic and social life of an agricultural labourer at the end of the nineteenth century. Sturt's life of Grover is both a biography of a rural labourer written through his own words and language, and a study of the countryside before its mechanization and suburbanization in the twentieth century.

318 pages, 7¼" x 4¾". A facsimile of the 1907 edition
Hardback   £10.00   *ISBN 0 904573 10 9*

LUCY BETTESWORTH

George Sturt

The last of a series of three biographical studies written by Sturt on Frederick Grover and his wife Lucy. The book gives additional details of the lives of the Grovers, as well as presenting a number of essays on the changes in the countryside at the end of the ninetenth and beginning of the twentieth century. It was greatly admired by F. R. Leavis and Denys Thompson, and should be of interest to both students of the history of culture and the general reader.

280 pages, 7¼" x 4¾". Facsimile reprint of 1913 edition
Hardback   £10.00   *ISBN 0 904573 11 7*

A FARMER'S LIFE:

With a Memoir of the Farmer's Sister

George Sturt

This biography of Sturt's uncle and aunt was first published in 1922 as a limited edition, and is a sequel to Sturt's biography of his grandfather, William Smith. Sturt's uncle, John Smith, took over his father's farm, and the book is based on conversations and direct observations of his farming experience. As well as a biography, it provides a context for Sturt to develop his writing on the English countryside, and covers a wide range of topics and personalities relating to the Hampshire/Surrey area.

208 pages, 7¼" x 4¾", six black-and-white illustrations. Facsimile reprint of 1922 edition

Hardback   £10.00   ISBN 0 904573 15 X

MANCHESTER FOURTEEN MILES

Margaret Penn

With an introduction by Professor John Burnett

First published in 1947, this autobiography rivals *Larkrise to Candleford* in evoking village life at the end of the nineteenth century. Margaret Penn was brought up in Hollins Green, then a village fourteen miles from Manchester, and the book describes her childhood in a rural community. Born illegitimate, she was adopted by a labourer and his wife, and raised as a member of their family. The book covers all aspects of life in the community, and is invaluable for the student of the history of the family, education, politics, religion and working class culture. Additionally, the author manages to recreate for the reader a vivid sense of the frustrations, as well as the warmth, of a rural working-class community, before its disappearance in the twentieth century.

Approx. 270 pages, 7¼" x 4¾". A facsimile reprint of the 1947 edition

Hardback   £10.00   ISBN 0 904573 16 8

Forthcoming Publications

MEMORIES OF A LABOUR LEADER

John Wilson

The autobiography of John Wilson, first published in 1910, and now reprinted as a facsimile edition. Born in 1837, he spent his childhood travelling with his father, who worked as a railway navvy and labourer. Wilson started work in a Durham coalfield at the age of fifteen and the book gives an account of his working experience in detail, as well as describing the economic and social conditions of Durham mining communities in the nineteenth century. He spent a number of years in the United States as a coal-miner, and describes the political and social attitudes he found there. He returned to England, and after being converted to Primitive Methodism, became active in the organisation of the Durham miners' union. He was eventually elected as the first member of parliament representing the newly-enfranchised mining community, and his autobiography gives an account of both his personal development, and the transformation of the economic and social milieux in which he lived.

Approx. 320 pages, 7¼" x 4¾". A facsimile reprint of the 1910 edition
Hardback £12.00 *ISBN 0 904573 17 6*

LOW COMPANY: Describing the
Evolution of a Burglar

Mark Benney

Greatly admired by H. G. Wells and others when first published in 1936, *Low Company* describes with wit and verve, the making of a burglar before the Second World War. Born in Soho in 1910, Mark Benney gives in this autobiography an account of his experience of unrespectable working class life, and how it contributed to his development as a thief. Detail is given of Soho club life, industrial schools, borstals and prison experience, as well as the criminal sub-culture which flourished between the wars. Publication of the book led to the abandonment of his career as burglar, and after working in journalism, Benney engaged in research on working-class politics, and eventually became a professor of social science in one of the leading American universities.

Approx. 350 pages, 7¼" x 4¾". A facsimile reprint of the 1936 edition
Hardback £10.00 *ISBN 0 904573 18 4*

THE MORNING CHRONICLE SURVEY OF LABOUR AND THE POOR: THE METROPOLITAN DISTRICTS

Six Volumes

Henry Mayhew

In the years 1849 and 1850, Henry Mayhew was the metropolitan correspondent of the *Morning Chronicle* in its national survey of labour and the poor. In all, Mayhew wrote nearly a million words, and then went on to publish a further study of the London poor, in the *London Labour and the London Poor* series. Only about a third of his *Morning Chronicle* material was included in this publication, and although recent further selections of the original survey have been published, these constitute less than one-fifth of the total. Nearly half of Mayhew's survey has never been published to date.

Mayhew has become famous for pioneering the method of recording the history of ordinary people through their own words, and can be justly regarded as the originator of oral history. The present series of six volumes constitutes his complete *Morning Chronicle* survey, published in the sequence that it was originally written. It starts with a letter on cholera in the Jacob's Island area, and ends with the food markets of London. A large proportion of the previously unpublished material is in the form of interviews for which Mayhew is famous, and the publication of the complete survey will make available for the first time the whole of Mayhew's pioneering work. Each volume will be indexed by subject and name, and it is intended that the series will represent the definitive scholarly publication of Mayhew's classical study. It is introduced by Dr Peter Razzell, who was co-editor to the earlier edited version of the national *Morning Chronicle* survey.

Six volumes, approx. 270 pages (8¼" x 5¾") per volume

Hardback   £20.00 per vol.   ISBN for the set of six vols. 0 904573 19 2

Vol. 1: 0 904573 20 6   Vol. 2: 0 904573 21 4   Vol. 3: 0 904573 22 2

Vol. 4: 0 904573 23 0   Vol. 5: 0 904573 24 9   Vol. 6: 0 904573 25 7
